Artificial Intelligence (selected and recent titles)

Patrick Henry Winston, founding editor
J. Michael Brady, Daniel G. Bobrow, and Randall Davis,
current editors

Artificial Intelligence: An MIT Perspective, Volumes I and II, edited by Patrick Henry Winston and Richard Henry Brown, 1979

Robot Motion: Planning and Control, edited by Michael Brady, John M. Hollerbach, Timothy Johnson, Tom Lozanorez, and Matthew T. Mason, 1982

The Acquisition of Syntactic Knowledge, Robert C. Berwick, 1985

The Connection Machine, W. Daniel Hillis, 1985

Reasoning about Change: Time and Causation from the Standpoint of Artificial Intelligence, Yoav Shoham, 1988

Solid Shape, Jan J. Koenderink, 1990

Object Recognition by Computer: The Role of Geometric Constraints, W. Eric L. Grimson, 1990

Representing and Reasoning with Probabilistic Knowledge: A Logical Approach to Probabilities, Fahiem Bacchus, 1990

Do the Right Thing: Studies in Limited Rationality, Stuart Russell and Eric Wefald, 1991

Three-Dimensional Computer Vision: A Geometric Viewpoint, Olivier Faugeras, 1993

Contemplating Minds: A Forum for Artificial Intelligence, edited by William J. Clancey, Stephen W. Smoliar, and Mark J. Stefik, 1994

Rules of Encounter: Designing Conventions for Automated Negotiation among Computers, Jeffrey S. Rosenschein and Gilad Zlotkin, 1994

Qualitative Reasoning: Modeling and Simulation with Incomplete Knowledge, Benjamin Kuipers, 1994

Computational Theories of Interaction and Agency, edited by Philip E. Agre and Stanley J. Rosenschein, 1996

The Art of Causal Conjecture, Glenn Shafer, 1996

Nonmonotonic Reasoning, Grigoris Antoniou, 1997

Nonmonotonic Reasoning

Nonmonotonic Reasoning

Grigoris Antoniou

with contributions by Mary-Anne Williams

The MIT Press
Cambridge, Massachusetts
London, England

This book was set in LaTeX by the author and was printed and bound in the United States of America.

Library of Congress Cataloging-in-Publication Data

Antoniou, G. (Grigoris)
  Nonmonotonic reasoning / Grigoris Antoniou.
   p. cm.-(Artificial Intelligence)
  Includes bibliographical references and index.
  ISBN 0-262-01157-3 (hb: alk. paper)
  1. Nonmonotonic reasoning. I. Title. II. Series: Artificial Intelligence (Cambridge, Mass.)
Q339.2.A58   1996
511.3-dc20   96-15528
                                                 CIP

To Popi and Giorgos, my parents, to whom I owe everything

Contents

Series Foreword   xiii

I   **PRELUDE**   1

1   **Introduction**   3

   1.1   What this book is about   3
   1.2   Style, aims and intended audience   5
   1.3   Book overview   7
   1.4   How to use this book   9
   1.5   Acknowledgments   9

2   **Predicate Logic***   11

   2.1   The syntax of predicate logic   11
     2.1.1 The language of predicate logic   11
     2.1.2 Substitutions   13
   2.2   The semantics of predicate logic   14
     2.2.1 Interpretations and validity   14
     2.2.2 Normal forms   15
     2.2.3 Herbrand algebras   16
   2.3   Proof theory   16
     2.3.1 Sequent calculi   16
     2.3.2 Resolution   17

II   **DEFAULT LOGIC**   19

3   **Default Reasoning**   21

   3.1   The notion of a default   21
   3.2   The syntax of Default Logic   25
   3.3   Informal discussion of the semantics   26

4   **Operational Semantics of Default Logic**   31

   4.1   The definition of extensions   31
   4.2   Some examples   35

4.3   A prototype Prolog implementation   38

4.4   An alternative characterization of extensions   39

4.5   Some properties of Default Logic   43

5   Normal Default Theories   49

5.1   Normal defaults   49

5.2   Some theoretical properties   50

5.3   A proof theory for normal default theories   53

5.4   Limitations of normal default theories   56

6   Semi-normal Default Theories   59

6.1   Ordered, semi-normal default theories*   59

6.2   Proof of the existence of extensions*   62

6.3   Translation into semi–normal form   68

7   Alternative Approaches   71

7.1   Properties of Default Logic   72
      7.1.1 Existence of extensions   72
      7.1.2 Joint consistency of justifications   73
      7.1.3 Cumulativity and Lemmas   74

7.2   Justified Default Logic   75

7.3   Constrained Default Logic   78

7.4   Interconnections and examples   83

7.5   Computability and complexity considerations   87

8   Priorities Among Defaults   91

8.1   PDL: Prioritized Default Logic   92

8.2   PRDL: Reasoning about priorities   94

8.3   An example from legal reasoning   98

8.4   An alternative characterization of extensions*   99

8.5   Properties of PRDL*   100

References for Part II   105

III CLASSICAL APPROACHES TO NONMONOTONIC REASONING   107

9 Autoepistemic Logic   109

9.1 The language of autoepistemic logic   110

9.2 The semantics of autoepistemic formulae   112

9.3 Expansions of autoepistemic theories   114

9.4 Stable sets and their properties   115

10 Computing Expansions of AE-Theories   121

10.1 Motivation and description of the method   121

10.2 Some examples   124

10.3 Correctness proofs*   126

10.4 A prototype implementation in Prolog   129

11 Embedding Default Logic into AE-Logic   131

11.1 Expressing default theories as AE-theories   132

11.2 Minimal expansions   133

11.3 Moderately grounded expansions*   134

11.4 Strongly grounded expansions*   136

11.5 Proofs*   137

12 Circumscription   143

12.1 Predicate circumscription   144

12.2 Minimal models   149

12.3 Consistency and expressive power   152

12.4 Variable circumscription   154

12.5 Prioritized circumscription   157

References for Part III   161

**IV ABSTRACT AND DYNAMIC APPROACHES TO
     NONMONOTONIC REASONING**   163

13 Nonmonotonic Inference Relations   165

    13.1 The notion of an inference relation   165
    13.2 Basic properties: pure conditions   166
    13.3 Basic properties: interaction with logical connectives 168
    13.4 Inference relations in default logic   172
    13.5 Preferential models   175
    13.6 Further properties of inference relations   178

14 Belief Revision   183

    14.1 Introduction   184
    14.2 Expansion   186
    14.3 Contraction   187
    14.4 Revision   189
    14.5 Interrelationships   190
    14.6 Epistemic entrenchment orderings   191
    14.7 Odds and ends*   195

15 Implementing Belief Revision   197

    15.1 Finite partial entrenchment rankings   198
    15.2 A computational model   201
    15.3 A procedural algorithm for adjustment*   204
    15.4 Connections with theory change   208

16 Interconnections*   213

    16.1 Translations between revision and
          nonmonotonic inference   214
    16.2 Nonmonotonic reasoning using entrenchment   216
    16.3 Changing nonmonotonic inference relations   219
    16.4 Example   221

References for Part IV   226

**V NONMONOTONIC REASONING AND LOGIC
   PROGRAMMING**   227

17 The System *Theorist*   229

   17.1 Basic concepts   229

   17.2 Relationship to Default Logic   231

   17.3 Names and constraints   232

   17.4 The programming language of *Theorist*   237

   17.5 Explanation versus prediction   239

18 Stable Model Semantics of Logic Programs   243

   18.1 Basic concepts of logic programming   243

   18.2 Stable models of logic programs   245

   18.3 An alternative characterization   248

   18.4 Logic programs with classical negation   250

19 Well-Founded Semantics   255

   19.1 Motivation   255

   19.2 Partial models   256

   19.3 Definition of the well–founded model   258

   19.4 Some pragmatic guidelines   261

References for Part V   267

VI FINALE   269

**20 Future Directions of Nonmonotonic Reasoning Re-
    search**   271

   20.1 Theory versus practice   271

   20.2 Dynamics of nonmonotonic reasoning   273

   20.3 Pragmatics of nonmonotonic reasoning   273

Bibliography 277

Index 283

Series Foreword

Artificial intelligence is the study of intelligence using the ideas and methods of computation. Unfortunately, a definition of intelligence seems impossible at the moment because intelligence appears to be an amalgam of so many information-processing and information-representation abilities.

Of course psychology, philosophy, linguistics, and related disciplines offer various perspectives and methodologies for studying intelligence. For the most part, however, the theories proposed in these fields are too incomplete and too vaguely stated to be realized in computational terms. Something more is needed, even though valuable ideas, relationships, and constraints can be gleaned from traditional studies of what are, after all, impressive existence proofs that intelligence is in fact possible.

Artificial intelligence offers a new perspective and a new methodology. Its central goal is to make computers intelligent, both to make them more useful and to understand the principles that make intelligence possible. That intelligent computers will be extremely useful is obvious. The more profound point is that artificial intelligence aims to understand intelligence using the ideas and methods of computation, thus offering a radically new and different basis for theory formation. Most of the people doing work in artificial intelligence believe that these theories will apply to any intelligent information processor, whether biological or solid state.

There are side effects that deserve attention, too. Any program that will successfully model even a small part of intelligence will be inherently massive and complex. Consequently, artificial intelligence continually confronts the limits of computer-science technology. The problems encountered have been hard enough and interesting enough to seduce artificial intelligence people into working on them with enthusiasm. It is natural, then, that there has been a steady flow of ideas from artificial intelligence to computer science, and the flow shows no sign of abating.

The purpose of this series in artificial intelligence is to provide people in many areas, both professionals and students, with timely, detailed information about what is happening on the frontiers in research centers all over the world.

J. Michael Brady
Daniel G. Bobrow
Randall Davis

Part I

Prelude

Chapter 1

Introduction

1.1 What this book is about

Humans are constantly faced with the necessity of making decisions. Some may affect everyday situations (such as 'How am I going to work?'), others may be of a long term nature ('What should I study?'). In the ideal case, we would have all the relevant information about the problem at hand, and then would apply logical reasoning to draw a conclusion.

Unfortunately, this is not usually the case. Instead we must decide based on *incomplete information* only. For example, one would need to know, among other things, the job market situation in three or five years in order to make the right choice of what to study. In this case, the information is simply not available. Alternatively, a quick decision may be needed, and there may not be enough time to collect all the relevant information. So, if one is faced with a burning car with a child trapped inside, it is highly improbable that he is going to start collecting all the relevant facts (What type of car is it? Where is the tank located? Let's phone the car company and ask. Now that I know, has the fire reached the tank? – by now probably yes) before acting. Rather the reaction will be determined by some patterns of behaviour that are closely related to one's character. Such patterns might be:

- *Typically, in case a child is in danger, I will try to save it even if this is risky.*

- *If my life could be endangered by helping, then typically I call the emergency.*

- *If somebody else is there who can help, then typically I don't do anything else but stand by and watch what happens*[1].

To give other examples of decision making based on incomplete information,

---

[1] A scandalous prevailing rule of these days.

imagine a doctor in an emergency case. She has to begin immediately with the treatment even without knowing the exact cause of the symptoms; in this case she has to make some assumptions about the most plausible or most dangerous possible causes. Obviously it would be completely inappropriate to await all the necessary test results before making a diagnosis and beginning with the correct treatment – probably by then the patient would be dead[2].

Another area where incomplete information prevails is law. A fundamental legal principle of Western societies is that somebody is assumed innocent unless their guilt has been proven.

When our decisions are based on conjectures due to the incompleteness of the information at hand, they may turn out to be wrong. Consider the following piece of text:

Smith entered the office of his boss. He was nervous.

I claim that most people have a rather clear idea who the word 'he' refers to (Smith). Let's continue with the text.

After all, he didn't want to lose his best employee.

Now most people (including the reader?) would have to revise their assumption. After all, 'he' referred to the boss. The previous assumption was based on the default rule that typically employees are nervous when confronted with their boss. But in the presence of the additional information, the assumption turned out to be wrong. The previous conclusion has to be withdrawn; this phenomenon is called *nonmonotonicity*.

In fact, even complete information may not be sufficient to make a decision that will be correct forever. This would be true in a static environment, but not in a changing world. In other words, *changing information* may be an alternative cause why we may have to revise a previously drawn conclusion.

Note that up to now I[3] have been talking about humans. The examples and arguments above carry over to intelligent information systems in a natural way. After all, these systems are supposed to exhibit human–like behaviour.

---

[2]An additional difficulty may be that sometimes all the tests don't single out a cause, perhaps because something cannot be tested for.

[3]I will refer to myself in singular only in this and the last chapter, whilst in all other chapters I will be using the word 'we' instead. This should not be interpreted in the sense of *pluralis majestatis*, of course. Rather, the word 'we' includes the reader in our common walk through the material of this book.

Nonmonotonic reasoning provides formal methods that enable an intelligent system to operate adequately when faced with incomplete and changing information. In particular, it provides rigorous mechanisms for taking back conclusions that turned out to be wrong and for deriving new, alternative conclusions instead. The important issue is that these mechanisms are based on clear principles rather than nebulous 'heuristics'. Therefore, reasoning with incomplete and changing information is subject to rigorous analysis as classical reasoning, with all the associated advantages (such as transparency, detection of errors, confidence in the system, and simplified maintenance).

Is nonmonotonic reasoning useful for practical purposes? This question has yet to be answered definitively. What we can do, though, is list some fields of potential application which appear to be promising:

- *Legal reasoning.* Most legal regulations are rules with exceptions, and defaults as they will be introduced in Part II are a natural representation of such kind of information. For example, according to German law, criminal foreigners are expelled. However, in case the foreigner is a political refugee expulsion is not allowed.

- *Diagnosis* of telecommunication problems, insurance fraud, and medical diagnosis. In all cases, 'rules of thumb' can guide the system to the most plausible causes of the problem.

- *Natural language understanding.* Natural language is ambiguous, therefore it is open to competing interpretations. The system may choose a working hypothesis to make progress, but if it becomes apparent that the choice was wrong, it will have to adopt an alternative hypothesis. Nonmonotonic reasoning provides mechanisms that support these operations.

- *Intelligent tutoring systems and intelligent interfaces.* In these areas, the intelligent system works based on a model of the human who is interacting with it. The model is based on plausible assumptions, and again is subject to change when found to be inappropriate (for example if the user 'improves' over time).

1.2   Style, aims and intended audience

Given the broad applicational scope of nonmonotonic reasoning, as outlined above, it is a major failure of the field that it has its current image: it is supposed to be too difficult to understand, not relevant to practical problems, mainly of theoretical interest. What are the reasons for this image?

Firstly, research has concentrated for far too long on theoretical issues only, and neglected aspects of implementation and application. This has started to change now. This book does not contribute much in this direction; in fact, a book on implementations and applications would be a good companion to this textbook.

The other reason for the image is that we have not tried to explain the concepts to people outside the field. For a mathematically trained person, a fixed–point definition is not only clear but also elegant; for most users they are simply a mystery. Try to explain what a default rule is and everybody will understand because everybody has come across them; try to explain that an extension is a solution of the equation $\Lambda_T(E) = E$, and most people will flee in panic.

This book seeks to demonstrate that nonmonotonic reasoning is simple! Not so the development of new methods, but rather the task of understanding and using existing methods. For the main logics that are discussed in this book, first I describe the motivations and then I give operational interpretations that should make it a simple, mechanized task to apply the concepts to concrete examples[4]. Additionally I have included prototype programs that can be used to run small examples, even if the efficiency is insufficient for realistic knowledge bases. The programs may help the reader overcome fears they may have of the subject, and to start 'playing' with the methods.

I believe that learning by doing is the best way of learning, and the readers will gain the most out of the book if they try to solve the exercises and check that my discussion of the examples is correct according to the formal definitions; that is to say, once I have introduced an operational method and have illustrated it by some examples, I leave it as a recurrent exercise for the reader to verify that subsequent examples are treated correctly.

So, the good news for those who 'hate' formality is that I have tried to present the motivations, to discuss examples, and to provide easy–to–use tools. The bad news is that I have included proofs. In fact, most results are rigorously proven. I did so simply because I like a *principled way* of doing things. Imagine a textbook without proofs, just stressing ideas, intuitions and methods. A reader would indeed be able to apply the material covered (even though blind faith in the author would be required). But what if a modification, however slight, is necessary?

In such cases the reader of an alternative book without proofs would be faced with the unpleasant choice between two undesirable solutions: either use their intuition

---

[4]Mechanized for a human, not necessarily for a computer in the sense of effective computability.

and hope that the modification is correct and does not have unexpected side effects, or admit that actually they do not know much about the topic and turn to another text. It is my firm belief that if no formal background is provided, the knowledge obtained will be superficial and therefore useless. What I have tried to do with this textbook is find a balance between intuition on the one side and formal rigour on the other. Was I successful? This is up to you to decide, dear reader!

This book primarily addresses students with some basic knowledge of logic, who want to learn about nonmonotonic reasoning and belief revision. It addresses both those who are interested in foundational aspects of knowledge representation, and those who are interested in building operational systems and applications on the basis of sound theory.

Even though this is a textbook, the material covered reaches into current research in the areas of default logic and belief revision. In this sense, it may be of some interest to researchers as well.

References to historically important sources and to current work can be found at the end of Parts II–V in case the reader is interested in studying some topics more thoroughly. Furthermore I included all sources that I have used while preparing this book[5]. By no means is the reference list supposed to contain all important works in the area.

1.3 Book overview

When a textbook author discusses the intended work with colleagues, a peculiar thing happens: everybody expects the author to write the book they would like to write themselves but never find the time to do so. Regardless of how voluminous the book may be, there are always going to be questions as to why material X was included, material Y was omitted, and Z was not discussed in more depth. For my part I can offer the reader the choice of any combination of the following explanations why I have included the material found in the textbook:

- Because I find it interesting.
- Because I am working on this topic.
- Because I think that the reader should have heard something about it.
- Because I think I have something to say about it.
- Because I think it is promising for practical applications.

---

[5]I have avoided including references in the running text.

So, Default Logic has been chosen for all the reasons above, Circumscription for the third reason only. And obviously, I have left out topics because they are not yet mature to find their way into a textbook, because I find them uninteresting or simply because I do not know enough about them. In the following I give a brief overview of the book.

Part I consists of this chapter and Chapter 2 which presents the basic concepts of predicate logic that are needed in subsequent chapters. It should be noted that although the book is self–contained, some familiarity with predicate logic is essential to fully understand and absorb the material.

Part II is devoted to Default Logic, the nonmonotonic reasoning approach that is given the most in–depth treatment in this textbook. Chapters 3 and 4 introduce the basic notions of Default Logic, develop the concept of an extension, and present an operational method to compute extensions. Chapters 5 and 6 deal with restricted classes of Default Logic which have some nice properties. On the other hand, Chapters 7 and 8 discuss modifications and enhancements of Default Logic which make it more suitable for specific application areas.

Part III deals with the two other main classical approaches to nonmonotonic reasoning, Autoepistemic Logic and Circumscription. These take directions quite different from Default Logic, therefore it is instructive for the reader to study them. Chapters 9 and 10 introduce Autoepistemic Logic and give an operational interpretation of its concepts. Chapter 11 investigates the relationship between Autoepistemic and Default Logic, while Chapter 12 is devoted to Circumscription.

Part IV takes an abstract look at nonmonotonicity. Chapter 13 investigates properties of nonmonotonic inference relations, abstracting from concrete approaches (like those discussed up to that chapter). Chapter 14 introduces Belief Revision, which provides operations for modeling change. Chapter 15 provides a computational model for revision by discussing change of finite theory bases and iterated revision, and gives an operational program. Chapter 16 shows that the concepts of nonmonotonicity and change are closely related. Chapters 14–16 were written by Mary–Anne Williams.

Part V looks at nonmonotonic reasoning from a logic programming perspective. Chapter 17 presents *Theorist*, a pioneer default reasoning system which was implemented in Prolog. Chapters 18 and 19 discuss two nonmonotonic semantics of negation in logic programming, the stable model and the well–founded semantics respectively.

Finally, *Part VI* consists of Chapter 20 which contains some thoughts of mine about the field's future.

1.4   How to use this book

It is really difficult to recommend ways of working through the book, especially because readers have different backgrounds, interests and aims. One thing that may be helpful is that I have used a star to mark proofs, sections or whole chapters that may be skipped on first reading. They are mostly of a technical nature and do not contribute strongly to the understanding of the main lines of the discussion. As a matter of fact, I have starred most of the proofs, leaving out those that are illustrative of specific ideas and support a better understanding of the concepts.

A natural way of working through the book is to proceed from Chapter 3 to Chapter 20, referring to Chapter 2 for predicate logic definitions and notation whenever necessary. Many readers, though, may wish to deviate or make a selection. I can just give some hints. The approach that is discussed first and in the broadest way is Default Logic. I recommend that you start with it and go through Chapters 3, 4, 5 and 17. These chapters include much of the intuition and a (hopefully) clear, operational way of dealing with concrete examples. I recommend that you work through the examples and exercises, and invent your own small knowledge bases.

Having finished with these core chapters, several directions can be taken. If you are interested in logic programming, Chapters 18 and 19 are a good choice. More on Default Logic can be found in Chapters 6–8. Chapters 14 and 15 on Belief Revision form another central block. The same applies to Chapters 9 and 10 on Autoepistemic Logic.

1.5   Acknowledgments

I have a theory about why books tend to include acknowledgments. If the book turns out to be a success, then nobody cares about who supported the author. But if something goes seriously wrong then it is good to have people to share the blame.

In this sense, my first and strongest thanks go to Mary-Anne Williams. Mary-Anne's chapters on belief revision (14–16) are the smaller part of her contribution towards the success of this book. She reviewed the manuscript and found millions of mistakes, she was always available for discussions, and helped me survive the difficult year 1995.

One of the most fruitful and pleasurable aspects of my coming to Australia was that I joined the Knowledge Systems Group at Sydney University and met Norman Foo. He supported me in every possible way, used parts of the book in his courses and gave me valuable feedback. I benefited greatly from Norman's deep understanding of knowledge representation, artificial intelligence, and logic.

Back in Germany, my thanks go to Elmar Langetepe and Volker Sperschneider, with whom I was lucky to work and to whom parts of the material goes back. Also to Wolfram Menzel for teaching me logic, and to Joerg Siekmann for 'infecting' me with enthusiasm about the quest to achieve artificial intelligence.

My thanks go also to David Billington, Allen Courtney, Yannis Dimopoulos, Daniel Lehmann, Sebastian Melmoth, Tyrone O'Neill, Joe Thurban, and Graham Wrightson for proofreading parts of the text. And to Corey Venour and Oliver Jack for helping me out with Latex.

Finally, to avoid any misunderstandings from people who do not know me, the beginning of this section was just one of my silly jokes. The truth is that all the people mentioned above (and some anonymous reviewers) helped me in improving the text. All remaining errors and weaknesses are entirely my fault – after all, I am the author!

Brisbane, November 1996.

Chapter 2

Predicate Logic*

Predicate logic is a monotonic, classical logic which provides the logical foundation for all approaches that will be discussed in this book. In a sense, any nonmonotonic reasoning method goes beyond classical logic by supporting more conclusions, so it is necessary to start with the basic knowledge. This chapter is *not* supposed to introduce classical logic to someone who knows nothing about it – in fact, the task of teaching predicate logic would require another textbook. Instead this chapter in intended to refresh the knowledge of predicate logic, and to help the reader get accustomed to our notation (unfortunately, essentially every author has their own favorite notation).

The discussion does not claim to be complete; it just covers those aspects that are used in subsequent chapters of this book. Of course, no proofs are given; they can be found in standard logic textbooks.

2.1 The syntax of predicate logic

2.1.1 The language of predicate logic

The following special characters are used to build predicate logic formulae: $\neg$ (negation), $\vee$ (disjunction), $\wedge$ (conjunction), $\rightarrow$ (implication), $\leftrightarrow$ (equivalence), $\forall$ (universal quantifier), and $\exists$ (existential quantifier). Further special symbols are the opening and closing bracket, and a countable set of *variables* $\{V_0, V_1, \ldots\}$. Finally, we use a special sort symbol s.

Besides these characters we may use a set of application–dependent symbols to model a specific domain; this set is called a *signature*. Formally, a signature Σ is a set of strings of the form $f : s^n \rightarrow s$ or $p : s^n$ where n is a natural number.

- If $f : s^n \rightarrow s \in \Sigma$, then f is called a *function symbol* of *arity n*. Sometimes we say that f is a function symbol in Σ.

- If $p : s^n \in \Sigma$, then p is called a *predicate symbol* of *arity n*. Sometimes we say that p is a predicate symbol in Σ.

- A function symbol of arity 0 is called a *constant*.

- A predicate symbol of arity 0 is called an *atom*.

- We require that no two members of Σ have the same leftmost symbol.

From now on we consider a fixed signature Σ. *Terms* are defined as follows:

- Every variable or constant is a term.

- If f is a function symbol of arity n and $t_1, \ldots, t_n$ are terms, then $f(t_1, \ldots, t_n)$ is a term, too.

- There is no other way of building a term.

A term is called *ground* iff it does not contain any variables. We define *formulae* in the following way:

- If p is a predicate symbol of arity n and $t_1, \ldots, t_n$ are terms, then $p(t_1, \ldots, t_n)$ is a formula, called an *atomic formula*; if all terms $t_1, \ldots, t_n$ are ground then $p(t_1, \ldots, t_n)$ is a *ground atomic formula*.

- If φ and ψ are formulae and X a variable, then the following are formulae, too: $\neg\varphi, (\varphi \vee \psi), (\varphi \wedge \psi), (\varphi \rightarrow \psi), (\varphi \leftrightarrow \psi), \forall X\varphi, \exists X\varphi$. Sometimes we write $(\varphi \rightarrow \psi)$ as $(\psi \leftarrow \varphi)$.

- There is no other way of building formulae.

The use of parentheses ensures that the syntax of formulae is unique. In cases there is no confusion, especially in examples, we may omit some parentheses. A term t' is a *subterm* of a term t if t' is a substring of t.

- For an occurrence of $\forall X\varphi$ or $\exists X\varphi$ within a formula ψ, we call φ the *scope* of the quantification $\forall X$ or $\exists X$ respectively.

- An occurrence of a variable X in a formula ψ is called *bound* iff it is included in the scope of a quantification $\forall X$ or $\exists X$; otherwise it is called *free*.

- The variables for which there exists at least one free occurrence in a formula ψ are the *free variables* of ψ.

- A formula is *closed* if it has no free variables, otherwise it is *open*; closed formulae are often called *sentences*. For every open formula ψ we define $\forall(\psi)$, the *universal closure* of ψ, to be the formula $\forall X_1 \ldots \forall X_n \psi$, where $X_1, \ldots, X_n$ are all the free variables of ψ (given in some fixed ordering to make the syntactical definition of the universal closure unique). The *existential closure* $\exists(\psi)$ is defined in a similar way.

A *literal* is either an atomic formula (*positive literal*) or its negation (*negative literal*). The negation of a literal L is denoted by $\sim L$ and is defined as follows: If L is an atomic formula $p(t_1, \ldots, t_n)$, then $\sim L$ is $\neg p(t_1, \ldots, t_n)$. If L is $\neg p(t_1, \ldots, t_n)$ then $\sim L$ is $p(t_1, \ldots, t_n)$.

If the signature contains only atoms (which in this case are also called *propositions*) and there are no variables, then we are talking of *propositional logic*.

2.1.2 Substitutions

A *substitution* σ is a finite set $\{X_1/t_1, \ldots, X_n/t_n\}$ such that $X_1, \ldots, X_n$ are different variables, and t_i is a term different from X_i, for all $i = 1, \ldots, n$. If all terms t_j are ground, then σ is a *ground substitution*.

The result of applying σ to a term t, denoted by $t\sigma$, is obtained from t by simultaneously replacing all occurrences of X_i in t by t_i[1]. The result of applying σ to a formula φ, denoted by $\varphi\sigma$, is obtained by simultaneously replacing all free occurrences of X_i in φ by t_i. $\varphi\sigma$ is a *ground instance* of φ if $\varphi\sigma$ contains no free variables.

$\varphi\sigma$ is *admissible* if none of the variables of any t_i becomes bound after σ has been applied to φ. If this property is violated then some undesirable semantic anomalies may occur.

Given terms $t_1, \ldots, t_n$ and a formula φ with free variables $X_1, \ldots, X_n$, we often write $\varphi(t_1, \ldots, t_n)$ instead of $\varphi\{X_1/t_1, \ldots, X_n/t_n\}$.

The composition of two substitutions $\sigma = \{X_1/t_1, \ldots, X_n/t_n\}$ and $\rho = \{Y_1/s_1, \ldots, Y_m/s_m\}$ is defined as follows:

$$\sigma\rho = \{X_i/t_i\rho \mid X_i \neq t_i\rho\} \cup \{Y_j/s_j \mid Y_j \notin \{X_1, \ldots, X_n\}\}.$$

A *unifier* of a nonempty set T of terms is a substitution σ such that $T\sigma$ consists of exactly one term. σ is a *most general unifier* (mgu) of T if the following is true: For every unifier τ of T there is a substitution θ such that $\tau = \sigma\theta$.

Unifiers and most general unifiers can be naturally extended to literals. A literal L is a *variant* of a literal L' iff there are substitutions σ_1 and σ_2 such that $L\sigma_1 = L'$ and $L'\sigma_2 = L$.

---

[1] Simultaneously refers to all $i = 1, \ldots, n$ and to all occurrences of one variable X_i.

2.2 The semantics of predicate logic

2.2.1 Interpretations and validity

An *interpretation* (also called an *algebra*) $\mathcal{A}$ consists of

- a non–empty set $dom(\mathcal{A})$, the *domain* of the interpretation.
- a function $f_{\mathcal{A}} : dom^n \to dom(\mathcal{A})$, for every function symbol f of arity n.
- a relation $r_{\mathcal{A}} \subseteq dom^n(\mathcal{A})$, for every predicate symbol r of arity n.

A *state* over an interpretation $\mathcal{A}$ is a function sta from the set of all variables to $dom(\mathcal{A})$. Given a variable X and a value $a \in dom(\mathcal{A})$, the modified state $sta(X/a)$ is defined like sta, with the only difference that X is assigned the value a.

Given an interpretation $\mathcal{A}$ and a state sta, the *value* of a term t can be defined inductively as follows:

- $val_{\mathcal{A},sta}(X) = sta(X)$
- $val_{\mathcal{A},sta}(f(t_1,\ldots,t_n)) = f_{\mathcal{A}}(val_{\mathcal{A},sta}(t_1),\ldots,val_{\mathcal{A},sta}(t_n))$.

We define when a formula χ is *true* in an interpretation $\mathcal{A}$ and a state sta, denoted by $\mathcal{A} \models_{sta} \chi$, inductively as follows:

- $\mathcal{A} \models_{sta} p(t_1,\ldots,t_n)$ iff $(val_{\mathcal{A},sta}(t_1),\ldots,val_{\mathcal{A},sta}(t_n)) \in p_{\mathcal{A}}$
- $\mathcal{A} \models_{sta} \neg\varphi$ iff $\mathcal{A} \not\models_{sta} \varphi$
- $\mathcal{A} \models_{sta} (\varphi \vee \psi)$ iff $\mathcal{A} \models_{sta} \varphi$ or $\mathcal{A} \models_{sta} \psi$
- $\mathcal{A} \models_{sta} (\varphi \wedge \psi)$ iff $\mathcal{A} \models_{sta} \varphi$ and $\mathcal{A} \models_{sta} \psi$
- $\mathcal{A} \models_{sta} (\varphi \to \psi)$ iff $\mathcal{A} \models_{sta} (\neg\varphi \vee \psi)$
- $\mathcal{A} \models_{sta} (\varphi \leftrightarrow \psi)$ iff $\mathcal{A} \models_{sta} (\varphi \wedge \psi)$ or $\mathcal{A} \models_{sta} (\neg\varphi \wedge \neg\psi)$
- $\mathcal{A} \models_{sta} \forall X\varphi$ iff $\mathcal{A} \models_{sta(X/a)} \varphi$ for all $a \in dom(\mathcal{A})$
- $\mathcal{A} \models_{sta} \exists X\varphi$ iff there is an $a \in dom(\mathcal{A})$ such that $\mathcal{A} \models_{sta(X/a)} \varphi$.

Note that the state sta is irrelevant if the formula is ground; in that case, the truth value depends only on $\mathcal{A}$.

If $\mathcal{A} \models_{sta} \varphi$ for all states sta over $\mathcal{A}$, then we say that φ is *valid* (or *true*) in $\mathcal{A}$. In this case, $\mathcal{A}$ is a *model* of φ, denoted by $\mathcal{A} \models \varphi$. $\mathcal{A}$ is a model of a set of formulae M ($\mathcal{A} \models M$) iff it is a model of every formula in M.

A set of formulae N follows from a set of formulae M (denoted by $M \models N$) iff every model of M is a model of N. $Th(M)$ denotes the set of all formulae that follow from M (called the *deductive closure* of M); if $M = Th(M)$ then M is called *deductively closed*. A deductively closed set of closed formulae is called a *theory*. Here are some more definitions:

- A formula is a *tautology* (or *valid*) iff it is valid in every interpretation. *True* or $\top$ denotes a tautology, and *false* or $\bot$ a formula whose negation is a tautology. For any formula φ and substitution σ, the formula $\forall X \varphi \to \varphi \sigma$ is a tautology provided that $\varphi \sigma$ is admissible.

- φ is *satisfiable* iff there is an interpretation $\mathcal{A}$ and a state sta such that $\mathcal{A} \models_{sta} \varphi$. A set of formulae M is satisfiable iff there are $\mathcal{A}$ and sta such that all formulae in M are true in $\mathcal{A}$ and sta ($\mathcal{A} \models_{sta} M$).

- The formulae φ and ψ are *equivalent* iff $\varphi \leftrightarrow \psi$ is a tautology.

- A set of formulae M is *consistent* iff M is satisfiable. A formula φ is *consistent with* M iff $M \cup \{\varphi\}$ is consistent.

In some cases the signature Σ contains a special predicate symbol $=$ to denote equality. Of course, this symbol can be interpreted in any way. If an algebra interprets $=$ as the equality, that means, according to the definition

$$\mathcal{A} \models_{sta} t_1 = t_2 \text{ iff } val_{\mathcal{A},sta}(t_1) = val_{\mathcal{A},sta}(t_2),$$

then $\mathcal{A}$ is called a *normal interpretation*.

2.2.2 Normal forms

A formula is in *prenex normal form* if it has the form $Q_1 X_1 \ldots Q_n X_n \varphi$, where the Q_i are quantifiers, X_i variables, and φ a formula not containing any quantifiers. For every formula φ we can effectively construct an equivalent formula in prenex normal form.

A formula is in *conjunctive normal form* if it has the form $\bigwedge \bigvee L_{ij}$ with literals L_{ij}. A formula is in *disjunctive normal form* if it has the form $\bigvee \bigwedge L_{ij}$ with literals L_{ij}. Given a formula φ we can effectively construct an equivalent formula in conjunctive normal form; the same is true for disjunctive normal form.

A formula is in *Skolem normal form* if it has the form $\forall X_1 \ldots \forall X_n \varphi$, where φ is a quantifier–free formula in conjunctive normal form. For every formula φ we can effectively construct a formula ψ in Skolem normal form such that ψ has a model iff φ has a model.

2.2.3 Herbrand algebras

A *Herbrand algabra* is an interpretation $\mathcal{A}$ with the following properties:

- $dom(\mathcal{A})$ is the set of all ground terms[2].
- Function symbols are interpreted in a fixed way: $f_{\mathcal{A}}(t_1,\ldots,t_n) = f(t_1,\ldots,t_n)$, for ground terms $t_1,\ldots,t_n$.

So, the only part of a Herbrand algebra that is not fixed is the interpretation of the predicate symbols. Therefore a Herbrand algebra can be represented as a set of ground literals.

Let M be a set of formulae of the form $\forall X_1 \ldots \forall X_n \psi$ with a quantifier–free formula ψ. $ground(M)$ is defined to be the set of all formulae $\psi\{X_1/t_1,\ldots,X_n/t_n\}$, where t_i are arbitrary ground terms. According to *Herbrand's Theorem*, the following statements are equivalent:

- M has a model.
- M has a Herbrand model.
- $ground(M)$ has a model.
- $ground(M)$ has a Herbrand model.

The *Compactness Theorem* for predicate logic says that a set M of formulae is satisfiable iff every finite subset of M is satisfiable.

2.3 Proof theory

There exist sound and complete calculi for propositional and predicate logic. Sometimes we use $\vdash$ to denote a syntactic inference relation that is equivalent to the semantic counterpart $\models$.

2.3.1 Sequent calculi

A *sequent* has the form $\Gamma \rightsquigarrow \Delta$, where Γ and Δ are finite sequences of formulae such that at least one of them is nonempty. $\Gamma \rightsquigarrow \Delta$ is *true* in an interpretation $\mathcal{A}$ and a state *sta* iff the following is true:

$\mathcal{A} \models_{sta} \gamma$ for all γ in Γ implies $\mathcal{A} \models_{sta} \delta$ for at least one δ in Δ.

---

[2]We assume that the signature Σ contains at least one constant.

In other words, the left hand side is interpreted conjunctively and the right hand side disjunctively. Proof systems working with sequents have been developed to check the validity of formulae. In the following we describe a simple proof system of this type, *Wang's algorithm*. It works for propositional formulae without occurrences of the logical symbols $\rightarrow$ and $\leftrightarrow$. The rules of the proof system correspond exactly to the following observations:

1. $\varphi_1, \ldots, \varphi_n \rightsquigarrow \psi_1, \ldots, \psi_m$ is a tautology if $\{\varphi_1, \ldots, \varphi_n\}$ and $\{\psi_1, \ldots, \psi_m\}$ contain a common element. If all formulae φ_i and ψ_j are atomic, then the converse is true, too.

2. $\varphi_1, \ldots, \neg\varphi, \ldots, \varphi_n \rightsquigarrow \psi_1, \ldots, \psi_m$ is a tautology iff $\varphi_1, \ldots, \varphi_n \rightsquigarrow \psi_1, \ldots, \psi_m, \varphi$ is a tautology.

3. $\varphi_1, \ldots, \varphi_n \rightsquigarrow \psi_1, \ldots, \neg\psi, \ldots, \psi_m$ is a tautology iff $\varphi_1, \ldots, \varphi_n, \psi \rightsquigarrow \psi_1, \ldots, \psi_m$ is a tautology.

4. $\varphi_1, \ldots, (\psi \wedge \chi), \ldots, \varphi_n \rightsquigarrow \psi_1, \ldots, \psi_m$ is a tautology iff $\varphi_1, \ldots, \varphi_n, \psi, \chi \rightsquigarrow \psi_1, \ldots, \psi_m$ is a tautology.

5. $\varphi_1, \ldots, \varphi_n \rightsquigarrow \psi_1, \ldots, (\psi \vee \chi), \ldots, \psi_m$ is a tautology iff $\varphi_1, \ldots, \varphi_n \rightsquigarrow \psi_1, \ldots, \psi_m,$ is a tautology.

6. $\varphi_1, \ldots, (\psi \vee \chi), \ldots, \varphi_n \rightsquigarrow \psi_1, \ldots, \psi_m$ is a tautology iff both $\varphi_1, \ldots, \varphi_n, \psi \rightsquigarrow \psi_1, \ldots, \psi_m$ and $\varphi_1, \ldots, \varphi_n, \chi \rightsquigarrow \psi_1, \ldots, \psi_m$ are tautologies.

7. $\varphi_1, \ldots, \varphi_n \rightsquigarrow \psi_1, \ldots, (\psi \wedge \chi), \ldots, \psi_m$ is a tautology iff both $\varphi_1, \ldots, \varphi_n \rightsquigarrow \psi_1, \ldots, \psi_m, \psi$ and $\varphi_1, \ldots, \varphi_n \rightsquigarrow \psi_1, \ldots, \psi_m, \chi$ are tautologies.

The rules 2–7 enable the algorithm to simplify successively composed formulae within the considered sequents. Having arrived at sequents including atomic formulae only, rule 1 finishes the game correctly.

2.3.2 Resolution

A *clause* C is a finite set of literals. The empty set is called the *empty clause* and is denoted by $\square$. An interpretation $\mathcal{A}$ is a *model* of $C = \{L_1, \ldots, L_n\}$ iff $\mathcal{A}$ is a model of $\forall(L_1 \vee \ldots \vee L_m)$. Concepts such as variants or logical entailment ('clause C follows from a set of clauses M') carry over from formulae in a natural way.

Given a set E of formulae let $clauses(E)$ denote the collection of all clauses $\{L_{i1}, \ldots, L_{in_i}\}$, where $\forall(\bigwedge_{i=1}^{m} \bigvee_{j=1}^{n_i} L_{ij})$ is the Skolem normal form of a formula in E.

The *resolution calculus* consists of the following rule:

$$\frac{\{L_1, \ldots, L_m\} \cup C_1 \qquad \{L_{m+1}, \ldots, L_{m+n}\} \cup C_2}{(C_1 \cup C_2)\mu}$$

for all $m \geq 1, n \geq 1$, literals L_i, clauses C_1 and C_2 and a most general unifier μ of $\{L_1, \ldots, L_m, \sim L_{m+1}, \ldots, \sim L_{m+n}\}$. It is assumed that the clauses $\{L_1, \ldots, L_m\} \cup C_1$ and $\{L_{m+1}, \ldots, L_{m+n}\} \cup C_2$ do not contain common variables; this can be achieved by renaming, that means, using suitable variants of the clauses.

Resolution is *sound*: If a clause C can be derived in the resolution calculus from a set of clauses M, then C follows from M. Resolution is *complete as a refutation calculus*: If the formula φ follows from the set of formulae E, then the empty clause can be derived from $Clauses(E \cup \{\neg\varphi\})$.

Part II

Default Logic

The first nonmonotonic logic we present is *Default Logic*. Introduced by Reiter in 1980, it has evolved as one of the main approaches to nonmonotonic reasoning and is (in the author's view) the most promising to be used for serious applications.

Default Logic distinguishes between two kinds of knowledge, usual predicate logic formulae (called *axioms* or *facts*) and rules of thumb called *defaults*. So, a *default theory* consists of a set of facts which represents certain, but usually incomplete information about the world; and a set of defaults that sanction plausible but not necessarily true conclusions. That means, some conclusions may have to be revised when more information becomes available. A simple example of a default is

$$\frac{bird(X) : flies(X)}{flies(X)}$$

which is read as 'If X is a bird and if it is consistent to assume that X flies, then conclude that X flies'. In the absence of knowledge to the contrary it is reasonable to assume that a particular bird can fly, more simply 'Usually (typically) birds fly'. Given the information that Tweety[3] is a bird we may conclude that he flies. But if later on we learn that he cannot fly, for example because he is a penguin, then the default becomes inapplicable: we are no longer allowed to assume that Tweety flies! Thus our behaviour is nonmonotonic. Chapter 3 introduces the notion of a default and gives an idea of possible application areas.

The operational semantics of Default Logic is defined in terms of so–called *extensions*, sets of beliefs one may hold about the domain described by the default theory under consideration. Their technical definition is complex and is presented in Chapter 4. Essentially, extensions are obtained by applying defaults as long as possible without running into inconsistencies.

One disappointing result is that some default theories may not possess any extensions; such theories are worthless because they don't provide any usable information. Therefore, various restricted classes of default theories have been analyzed.

---

[3]the most famous bird in the history of nonmonotonic reasoning!

Normal default theories are studied in Chapter 5, and it turns out that they always possess extensions. Normal theories have further desirable properties such as goal–driven query evaluation.

If normal defaults are so well–behaved why don't we restrict our attention to them alone? Unfortunately this is impossible because there are applications for which normal default theories are not expressive enough. Therefore Chapter 6 is devoted to a richer class of default theories, the so–called *semi–normal default theories*. One of the main results defines a sufficient condition for the existence of extensions.

In Chapter 7 we take a critical look at Default Logic both from the computational and the representational point of view. Default reasoning turns out to be harder than predicate logic in terms of complexity and computability. Also, some of the knowledge representation properties of Reiter's original presentation are controversial; alternative design decisions have led to the development of a number of alternative approaches. One of the representational issues is priorities among defaults. We consider this aspect to be so important that we have allocated Chapter 8 to it.

One final remark in order to avoid misunderstandings: Chapters 7 and 8 should not be interpreted in the form that the standard presentation of Default Logic is useless or 'wrong'. Reiter's ingenious contribution to the field is that he developed a formalism which is still very useful on its own, and which has led to a *family of logics*, all of them sharing the same ideas and techniques and being only slight variations of each other. In fact, some variants simply follow different intuitions rather than improve the original logic.

Chapter 3

Default Reasoning

In section 3.1 we begin the presentation of Default Logic by introducing the notion of a default and presenting a variety of examples that demonstrate the broad applicational scope of the concept. In section 3.2 we introduce the syntax of Default Logic while in section 3.3 we informally discuss the semantics of the logic. The formal definition of the (operational) semantics will be given in the next chapter.

3.1 The notion of a default

Suppose I am asked in the morning how I intend to go to work. My answer is 'By bus' because usually I go to work by bus. This rule of thumb is represented by the default

$$\frac{goToWork : useBus}{useBus}.$$

So I leave home, walk to the bus station and read a notice saying 'No buses today because we are on strike!'. Now I definitely know that I cannot use the bus to go to work, therefore the default is no longer applicable (now I cannot assume that I may use the bus). I have to revise my previous conclusion, so my behaviour is nonmonotonic.

Before proceeding with more examples let us first explain why classical logic is not appropriate to model this situation. Of course, I could use the rule

$$goToWork \land \neg strike \to useBus.$$

Except that this rule is still insufficient: another reason for not wanting to use the bus is that I am late and therefore in a hurry. Then the rule could be modified as follows:

$$goToWork \land \neg strike \land \neg inHurry \to useBus$$

But there are more conceivable reasons for my not using a bus, for example icy streets. A first difficulty of a predicate logic solution becomes apparent: we would have to list *all* possible obstacles, however unprobable they may be. Is this possible, especially in a rapidly changing environment?

But the real difficulty actually lies in the use of the rule: I would have to definitively establish that all the preconditions of the rule are true (that is that the obstacles are not given) before I could apply the rule. So every morning I would have to call news agencies, listen to the radio etc. to obtain all the information needed about weather, strikes etc., before making up my mind. It might be afternoon when I would finally arrive at work, only to be told that I am fired because I missed giving my lecture.

Let us now turn to more serious examples. Defaults can be used to model various forms of default reasoning. One such form is *prototypical reasoning* which means that most instances of a concept have some property. One example is the statement 'Typically, children have (living) parents' which may be expressed by the default

$$\frac{child(X) : hasParents(X)}{hasParents(X)}.$$

To give another example: typically, if someone has a birthday, their friends give them gifts. Formulated as a default:

$$\frac{birthday(X) \wedge friend(Y, X) : givesGift(Y, X)}{givesGift(Y, X)}.$$

A further form of default reasoning is *no–risk reasoning*. It concerns situations where we draw a conclusion even if it is not the most probable, because another decision could lead to a disaster. Perhaps the best example is the following main principle of justice in the Western cultures: 'In the absence of evidence to the contrary assume that the accused is innocent'. In default form:

$$\frac{accused(X) : innocent(X)}{innocent(X)}.$$

Best–guess reasoning is exemplified by the following situation: I know there are some shopping centers in my city, and some of them are open on Sundays but I don't know which one is. On a Sunday I would drive to the closest one though I do not have any evidence that it will be open; it is simply the most convenient conjecture I can make:

$$\frac{closest(S) : openSundays(S)}{openSundays(S)}.$$

Defaults naturally occur in many application domains. Let us give an example from legal reasoning. According to German law, a foreigner is usually expelled if they have committed a crime. One of the exceptions to this rule concerns political refugees. This information is expressed by the default

$$\frac{criminal(X) \wedge foreigner(X) : expell(X)}{expell(X)}$$

in combination with the rule

$$politicalRefugee(X) \rightarrow \neg expell(X).$$

Hierarchies with exceptions are commonly used in biology. Here is a standard example:

Typically, molluscs are shell–bearers.
Cephalopods are molluscs.
Cephalopods are not shell–bearers.

It is represented by the default

$$\frac{mollusc(X) : shellBearer(X)}{shellBearer(X)}$$

together with the rule

$$cephalopod(X) \rightarrow mollusc(X) \wedge \neg shellBearer(X).$$

In *diagnosis*, the task is to determine some explanation for the symptoms observed; diagnosis is common in areas like medicine or factory quality control. Here is a funny (silly, if you wish) example from an everyday situation: if the car cannot start and if it was inspected recently, then it is out of gas. In default form:

$$\frac{\neg starts(X) \wedge recentlyInspected(X) : outOfGas(X)}{outOfGas(X)}.$$

Defaults can be used naturally to model situations that are well–known in some fields of Computer Science and Artificial Intelligence. One such application is the *Closed World Assumption* which is used in database theory, algebraic specification, and logic programming. According to this assumption, an application domain is described by certain axioms (in form of relational facts, equations, rules etc.) with the following understanding: a ground fact (that is, a non–parameterized statement about single objects) is taken to be false in the problem domain if it does not follow from the axioms. To give an example, suppose you are consulting a database of scheduled flights. If a flight from London to Paris at 2am is not listed then it is natural to assume that it does not exist (even if this is wrong in case the database is incomplete). The closed world assumption has the simple default representation

$$\frac{true : \neg\varphi}{\neg\varphi}$$

for each ground atom φ. The explanation of the default is: if it is consistent to assume $\neg\varphi$ (which is equivalent to not having a proof for φ) then conclude $\neg\varphi$.

Finally we take a look at *reasoning about action*. Imagine a robot acting in an environment. For example, it may pick up a box and place it somewhere else. When actions are performed then some properties change but most properties remain unaffected. For instance, if the robot picks up block A and puts it on the table, then the formula $on(A, B)$ is no longer correct. On the other hand, neither the colour of the blocks nor the location of blocks B and C have been changed. To represent the invariant aspects of the world *explicitly* would require a huge number of axioms. This problem is known as the *frame problem*. Using defaults it is very easy to express: 'All aspects of the world remain unchanged except for those that are explicitly changed by the action'.

$$\frac{holds(\varphi, S) : holds(\varphi, act(S))}{holds(\varphi, act(S))}$$

for all formulae φ, situations S and actions act. If φ *is* affected by act then $holds(\varphi, act(S))$ will be *explicitly known* to be false (as a postcondition of the action), so the default will be blocked[1].

When a robot decides to take an action the question arises whether the action was carried out successfully. This is known as the *qualification problem*. Success of an action may depend on numerous factors. For instance, the success of an action 'Put block A on top of block B' depends on factors like A not being too heavy, the robot's arm not being broken, block A not being fluid etc. Again, the problem is naturally and simply represented using defaults.

---

[1]Unfortunately, this representation does not *automatically* give a satisfactory solution to the frame problem, but that is another story.

3.2   The syntax of Default Logic

A *default theory* T is a pair (W, D) consisting of a set W of predicate logic formulae (called the *facts* or *axioms* of T) and a countable set D of defaults. A *default* δ has the form

$$\frac{\varphi : \psi_1, \ldots, \psi_n}{\chi}$$

where $\varphi, \psi_1, \ldots, \psi_n, \chi$ are closed predicate logic formulae, and $n > 0$. The formula φ is called the *prerequisite*, $\psi_1, \ldots, \psi_n$ the *justifications*, and χ the *consequent* of δ. Sometimes φ is denoted by $pre(\delta)$, $\{\psi_1, \ldots, \psi_n\}$ by $just(\delta)$, and χ by $cons(\delta)$. For a set D of defaults, $cons(D)$ denotes the set of consequents of the defaults in D.

One point that needs some discussion is the requirement that the formulae in a default be closed. This implies that

$$\frac{bird(X) : flies(X)}{flies(X)}$$

is *not* a default according to the definition above. Let us call such 'defaults' *open defaults*. An open default is interpreted as a default schema meaning that it represents a *set of defaults* (this set may be infinite).

A *default schema* looks like a default, the only difference being that $\varphi, \psi_1, \ldots, \psi_n, \chi$ are arbitrary predicate logic formulae (i.e. they may contain free variables). A default schema defines a set of defaults, namely

$$\frac{\varphi\sigma : \psi_1\sigma, \ldots, \psi_n\sigma}{\chi\sigma}$$

for all ground substitutions σ that assign values to all free variables occurring in the schema. That means, free variables are interpreted as being universally quantified *over the whole default schema*. Given a default schema

$$\frac{bird(X) : flies(X)}{flies(X)}$$

and the facts $bird(tweety)$ and $bird(sam)$, the default theory represented is

$$(\{bird(tweety), bird(sam)\}, \{\frac{bird(tweety) : flies(tweety)}{flies(tweety)}, \frac{bird(sam) : flies(sam)}{flies(sam)}\})$$

In order to explain why we interpret open defaults as schemata let us briefly show that two straightforward alternative interpretations are inadequate. In the first one we interpret open formulae occurring in a default as in predicate logic, that means as being universally quantified. Consider the open default

$$\frac{bird(X) : flies(X)}{flies(X)}.$$

According to the interpretation proposed, the default would read as follows: *If all X are birds, and if for all X we may assume that they fly, then we conclude that all X fly.* Obviously this interpretation does not match our intuitive understanding. In fact, it would be useless: it could be applied only in the case that every object in the domain is a bird, and if no non–flying bird is known!

So let us interpret the formulae existentially. The same default would read as: *If there is a bird, and if there is an X that flies, then conclude that there is some flying object.* Using this interpretation, it would be impossible to conclude $flies(tweety)$ from $bird(tweety)$; instead, we could only conclude $\exists X flies(X)$.

We conclude the discussion of this point by noting that there is work being done to assign other interpretations to open defaults, but no satisfactory solution has been found to date.

3.3   Informal discussion of the semantics

Given a default $\frac{\varphi:\psi_1,\ldots,\psi_n}{\chi}$, its informal meaning is the following:

If φ is known, and if it is consistent to assume $\psi_1, \ldots, \psi_n$, then conclude χ.

In order to formalize this interpretation we must say where φ should be included and with what $\psi_1, \ldots, \psi_n$ should be consistent. A first guess would be the set of facts, but this turns out to be inappropriate. Consider the default schema

$$\frac{friend(X,Y) \land friend(Y,Z) : friend(X,Z)}{friend(X,Z)}$$

which says 'Usually my friends' friends are also my friends'. Given the information $friend(tom, bob), friend(bob, sally), friend(sally, tina)$, we would like to conclude $friend(tom, tina)$. But this is only possible if we apply the appropriate instance of the default schema to $friend(sally, tina)$ and $friend(tom, sally)$. The latter formula stems from a previous application of the default schema[2]. If we did not

---

[2] with other instantiations, of course.

admit this intermediate step and used the original facts only, then we could not get the expected result.

Another example in the same direction is the default theory $T = (W, D)$ with $W = \{green, aaaMember\}$ and $D = \{\delta_1, \delta_2\}$ with

$$\delta_1 = \frac{green : \neg likesCars}{\neg likesCars}, \quad \delta_2 = \frac{aaaMember : likesCars}{likesCars}.$$

If consistency of the justifications was tested against the set of facts, then both defaults could be subsequently applied. But then we would conclude both $likesCars$ and $\neg likesCars$ which is a contradiction. It is unintuitive to let the application of *rules of thumb* lead to an inconsistency, even if they contradict each other. Instead, if we applied the first default, and then checked application of the second with respect to the *current knowledge* collected so far, the second default would be blocked: from the application of the first default we know $\neg likesCars$, so it is not consistent to assume $likesCars$. After these examples let us give a somewhat more precise formulation of default interpretation.

> *If φ is currently known, and if all ψ_i are consistent with the current knowledge base, then conclude χ. The current knowledge base E is obtained from the facts and the consequents of some defaults that have been applied previously.*

Here is the formal definition:

$\delta = \frac{\varphi : \psi_1, \ldots, \psi_n}{\chi}$ is *applicable to* a deductively closed set of formulae E iff $\varphi \in E$ and $\neg\psi_1 \notin E, \ldots, \neg\psi_n \notin E$.

The example of Greens and AAA members indicates that there can be several competing current knowledge bases which may be inconsistent with each other. The semantics of Default Logic will be given in terms of *extensions* that will be defined as the current knowledge bases satisfying some conditions. Intuitively, extensions represent possible world views which are based on the given default theories; they seek to extend the set of known facts with 'reasonable' conjectures based on the available defaults. The formal definition will be given in the next chapter. Here we just collect some desirable properties of extensions.

- An extension should include the set W of facts since W contains the certain information.
- An extension should be deductively closed because we do not want to prevent classical logical reasoning. Actually, we want to draw *more* conclusions and that is why we apply default rules in addition.

- An extension E should be *closed under the application of defaults in D* (formally: if $\frac{\varphi : \psi_1, \ldots, \psi_n}{\chi} \in D$, $\varphi \in E$ and $\neg\psi_1 \notin E, \ldots, \neg\psi_n \notin E$ then $\chi \in E$). That is, we do not stop applying defaults until we are forced to. The explanation is that there is no reason to stop at some particular stage if more defaults might be applied; extensions are *maximal* possible world views.

These properties are certainly insufficient because they do not include any 'upper bound', that is, they don't provide any information about which formulae should be excluded from an extension. So we should require that an extension E be *minimal with respect to these properties*. Unfortunately, this requirement is still insufficient. To see this consider the default theory $T = (W, D)$ with $W = \{aussie\}$ and $D = \{\frac{aussie : drinksBeer}{drinksBeer}\}$. Let $E = Th(\{aussie, \neg drinksBeer\})$. It is easy to check that E is minimal with the three properties mentioned above, but it would be highly unintuitive to accept it as an extension, since that would support the following argument: 'If Aussies usually drink Beer and if somebody is an Aussie, then assume that she does not drink Beer'!

We conclude the discussion of extensions with an example which shows that finding the appropriate formal definition is not simple. This should not scare the reader, of course, because they must 'only' understand the definition given in Chapter 4; it was Reiter who did the job for them! Now to our example: imagine a bank's credit approval procedure. Among others, it could be based on the defaults

$$\frac{true : creditworthy}{approveCredit}, \quad \frac{true : \neg creditworthy}{\neg creditworthy}.$$

The defaults should have the effect that if an applicant may be assumed to be creditworthy then credit is approved. But the bank is cautious in that it assumes by default that somebody is not creditworthy unless evidence to the contrary is provided. So, if no further information apart from both defaults is given, we would expect that credit is not approved. Now suppose that the first default is applied; this may be done since we have no knowledge that *creditworthy* may not be assumed. Next we also apply the second default; this is possible since $\neg creditworthy$ is consistent with the current knowledge. As a consequence, its consequent $\neg creditworthy$ is included in the current knowledge base. We do not have an inconsistency, and yet something has gone wrong: inclusion of $\neg creditworthy$ in the knowledge shows *a posteriori* that we should not have assumed *creditworthy* as done when the first default was applied. According to the definition given in the next chapter, the current knowledge base $Th(\{approveCredit, \neg creditworthy\})$ is *not* an extension, and this is in accordance with our intuitive expectation.

Problems

3-1. In the Aussie/Beer example in section 3.3, verify that $E = Th(\{aussie,$ $\neg drinksBeer\})$ is a minimal set of formulae which is deductively closed, includes the default theory's facts, and is closed under the application of defaults. Can you think of an additional condition that would prevent E from being a candidate extension?

3-2.* Think of a problem domain other than those described here, and formulate some defaults within that domain.

Chapter 4

Operational Semantics of Default Logic

After having informally discussed the motivations and intuitions of Default Logic, in this chapter we present its formal operational semantics and derive some properties. The main focus is to provide a formal definition of the notion of an extension.

The definition we give in section 4.1 is operational in the sense that it is a procedure that can be applied to examples. The main idea consists of applying defaults as long as possible. If we find out that a default should not have been applied, then we have to backtrack and try some alternative. It is possible to give very simple prototype implementations of this procedure, and we do so in section 4.3 where we present a simple Prolog program that computes extensions. In section 4.4 we give an alternative characterization of extensions based on fixed–points; this characterization is the definition usually found in the literature. Finally, section 4.5 contains some theoretical results on Default Logic.

4.1   The definition of extensions

For a given default theory $T = (W, D)$ let $\Pi = (\delta_0, \delta_1, \ldots)$ be a finite or infinite sequence of defaults from D without multiple occurrences. Think of Π as a possible order in which we apply some defaults from D. Of course, we don't want to apply a default more than once within such a reasoning chain because no additional information would be gained by doing so. We denote by $\Pi[k]$ the initial segment of Π of length k by $\Pi[k]$, provided the length of Π is at least k (from now on, this assumption is always made when referring to $\Pi[k]$). With each such sequence Π we associate two sets of first–order formulae, $In(\Pi)$ and $Out(\Pi)$:

- $In(\Pi)$ is $Th(M)$, where $M = W \cup \{cons(\delta) \mid \delta \text{ occurs in } \Pi\}$. So, $In(\Pi)$ collects the information gained by the application of the defaults in Π and represents the *current knowledge base* after the defaults in Π have been applied.

- $Out(\Pi) = \{\neg\psi \mid \psi \in just(\delta) \text{ for some } \delta \text{ occurring in } \Pi\}$. So, $Out(\Pi)$ collects formulae that should not turn out to be true, i.e. that should not become part of the current knowledge base even after subsequent application of other defaults.

Let us give a simple example. Consider the default theory $T = (W, D)$ with $W = \{a\}$ and D containing the following defaults:

$$\delta_1 = \frac{a : \neg b}{\neg b}, \quad \delta_2 = \frac{b : c}{c}.$$

For $\Pi = (\delta_1)$ we have $In(\Pi) = Th(\{a, \neg b\})$ and $Out(\Pi) = \{b\}$. For $\Pi = (\delta_2, \delta_1)$ we have $In(\Pi) = Th(\{a, c, \neg b\})$ and $Out(\Pi) = \{\neg c, b\}$.

Up to now we have not assured that the defaults in Π can be applied in the order given. In the example above, (δ_2, δ_1) cannot be applied in this order. To be more specific, δ_2 cannot be applied, since $b \notin In(()) = Th(W) = Th(\{a\})$ which is the current knowledge before we attempt to apply δ_2. On the other hand, there is no problem with $\Pi = (\delta_1)$; in this case we say that Π is a *process of T* — the reader is asked to explain why $\Pi' = (\delta_1, \delta_2)$ is not a process. Here is the formal definition:

- Π is called a *process of T* iff δ_k is applicable to $In(\Pi[k])$, for every k such that δ_k occurs in Π.

Given a process Π of T we define the following:

- Π is *successful* iff $In(\Pi) \cap Out(\Pi) = \emptyset$, otherwise it is *failed*. Success captures the intuitive statement 'nothing has gone wrong' in the sense that it was okay to have assumed the justifications of the defaults that have been applied to be true: no formula $\neg\psi$ in the Out–set has become part of the current knowledge base, so it was consistent to assume ψ.

- Π is *closed* iff every $\delta \in D$ that is applicable to $In(\Pi)$ already occurs in Π. Closed processes correspond to the desired property of an extension E being closed under application of defaults in D.

The reader may already have the feeling that closed and successful processes will play an important role in the definition of extensions because they exhibit some of the ideas we informally developed in the previous chapter. But before we proceed let us look at an example. Consider the default theory $T = (W, D)$ with $W = \{a\}$ and D containing the following defaults:

$$\delta_1 = \frac{a : \neg b}{d}, \quad \delta_2 = \frac{true : c}{b}.$$

$\Pi_1 = (\delta_1)$ is successful but not closed since δ_2 may be applied to $In(\Pi_1) = Th(\{a, d\})$. $\Pi_2 = (\delta_1, \delta_2)$ is closed but not successful: both $In(\Pi_2) = Th(\{a, d, b\})$ and $Out(\Pi_2) = \{b, \neg c\}$ contain b. On the other hand, $\Pi_3 = (\delta_2)$ is a closed and successful process of T. According to the following definition, $In(\Pi_3) = Th(\{a, b\})$ is an extension of T, in fact its single extension.

Definition 4.1 (Extension) *A set of formulae E is an* extension of *the default theory T iff there is some closed and successful process Π of T such that $E = In(\Pi)$.*

The definition of extensions is operational in that it may be directly applied to concrete examples. Nevertheless we make some remarks and give some tips for determining extensions.

No care needs to be taken to ensure the success of a process. If, by applying defaults in a particular order, we reach a failed situation (nonempty intersection of *In*–set and *Out*–set) then we simply backtrack along the process we have just built up and try some other alternative.

In the case of finite default theories (theories with a finite set D of defaults) there is no problem ensuring closure: simply apply any applicable defaults (which haven't been applied yet) until no more are left. But in the case where the set D is infinite we should be more careful in order not to deliberately avoid some default. Let us formulate and prove a simple result.

Lemma 4.2 *An infinite process Π of a default theory $T = (W, D)$ is closed iff each default that is applicable to $In(\Pi[k])$, for infinitely many numbers k, is already contained in Π.*

Proof*: By definition of processes and using the Compactness Theorem of predicate logic, it is easy to see that the following statements are equivalent for each formula ψ (to be thought of as a justification of a default):

1. ψ is consistent with $In(\Pi)$.

2. ψ is consistent with $In(\Pi[k])$ for infinitely many k.

3. ψ is consistent with $In(\Pi[k])$ for all $k > k'$ (for some number k').

Likewise, the following statements are equivalent for each formula φ (to be thought of as the prerequisite of a default):

1. $\varphi \in In(\Pi)$.

2. $\varphi \in In(\Pi[k])$ for infinitely many k.

3. $\varphi \in In(\Pi[k])$ for all $k > k'$ (for some number k').

These equivalences obviously prove the claim of the lemma.   ∎

So, a strategy to guarantee the closure of an infinite process Π must take care that any default which, from some stage k on, constantly demands application will eventually be applied. This is nothing other than *fairness*, a well–known concept in the area of concurrent programming.

We conclude this section by describing a formal way of constructing a systematic overview of all closed and successful processes. One reason for doing so is that a common error when trying to determine the extensions of a default theory is that some extensions are overlooked.

We intend to arrange all possible processes in a canonical manner within a tree, called the *process tree* of the given default theory $T = (W, D)$. The nodes of the tree are labeled with two sets of formulae, an In–set (to the left of the node) and an Out–set (to the right of the node). The edges correspond to default applications and are labeled with the default that is being applied. The paths of the process tree starting at the root correspond to processes of T.

The root of the process tree is labeled with $Th(W)$ as In–set and $\emptyset$ as Out–set (it should be clear why we use these labels before any default has been applied yet; they correspond to $In(())$ and $Out(())$ where () is the empty sequence of defaults).

Now consider a node N labeled with sets In and Out. N is only expanded if $In \cap Out = \emptyset$ else it is marked as failed and is a leaf of the process tree. If N is expanded it possesses one successor node $N(\delta)$ for each default $\delta = \frac{\varphi : \psi_1, \ldots, \psi_n}{\chi}$ that does not appear on the path from the root to N and that is applicable to In. The edge from N to $N(\delta)$ is labeled with δ, and the labels of $N(\delta)$ are $Th(In \cup \{\chi\})$ and $Out \cup \{\neg\psi_1, \ldots, \neg\psi_n\}$.

In case a node N is allowed to be expanded but there are no applicable defaults left, N is marked as closed and successful. Of course, the In–set associated with N is an extension of the default theory.

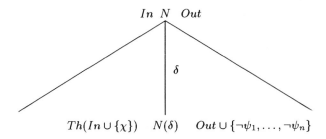

$$Th(In \cup \{\chi\}) \qquad N(\delta) \qquad Out \cup \{\neg\psi_1, \ldots, \neg\psi_n\}$$

Figure 4.1
Expanding a node in a process tree

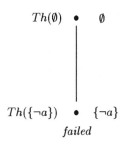

Figure 4.2

4.2 Some examples

Let $T = (W, D)$ with $W = \emptyset$ and $D = \{\frac{true:a}{\neg a}\}$. The process tree in Figure 4.2 shows that T has no extensions. Indeed, the default may be applied because there is nothing preventing us from assuming a. But when the default is applied, the negation of a is added to the knowledge base, so the default invalidates its own application because both the In and the Out–set contain $\neg a$. The reader hopefully agrees that this default exhibits a very strange behaviour. The example demonstrates that there need not always be an extension of a default theory.

Let $T = (W, D)$ with $W = \{\neg p, q\}$ and $D = \{\frac{q:\neg r}{p}\}$. Figure 4.3 shows that T has no extension. The default can be applied, but leads to a failed process: The In–set is inconsistent, therefore it includes r.

Let $T = (W, D)$ be the default theory with $W = \emptyset$ and $D = \{\delta_1, \delta_2\}$ with

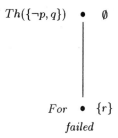

$Th(\{\neg p, q\})$ • $\emptyset$

For • $\{r\}$
$failed$

Figure 4.3

$$\delta_1 = \frac{true : p}{\neg q}, \quad \delta_2 = \frac{true : q}{r}.$$

The process tree of T is found in Figure 4.4 and shows that T has exactly one extension, namely $Th(\{\neg q\})$. The right path of the tree gives us an example where application of a default destroys the applicability of a previous default.

Reconsider the example of Greens who are members of AAA from Chapter 3. We have $T = (W, D)$ with $W = \{green, aaaMember\}$ and $D = \{\delta_1, \delta_2\}$ with

$$\delta_1 = \frac{green : \neg likesCars}{\neg likesCars}, \quad \delta_2 = \frac{aaaMember : likesCars}{likesCars}.$$

The process tree in Figure 4.5 shows that T has exactly two extensions. This example shows a situation where two defaults contradict one another. A consequence is that there are two extensions which, taken together, are inconsistent. In fact, one of the strengths of Default Logic (and Nonmonotonic Reasoning in general) is that potentially inconsistent information may be represented within the same knowledge base.

The examples discussed here show that a default theory may possess none, one or several extensions. We hope to have illustrated the basic concepts of Default Logic in a satisfactory way. From now on, we shall not draw process trees when discussing examples. The reader should consider it as a constant exercise to check the examples in subsequent sections and chapters by hand, in mind or using the prototype program of the following section. Who knows, maybe they will be rewarded by finding an error in one of the examples we will be discussing!

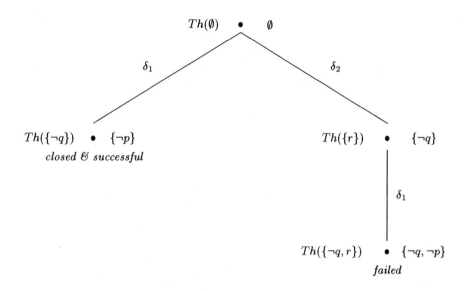

Figure 4.4

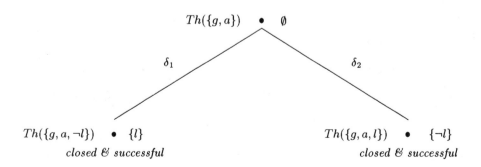

Figure 4.5

4.3   A prototype Prolog implementation

Even if the definition of an extension is operational and may, in principle, be applied without computer support, determining extensions becomes a tedious (though not intellectually demanding) task if the default theory is complicated and larger than the toy examples we have given so far. The reader who is not yet convinced is challenged to determine the extensions of the following theory by hand (and if they are successful and still not convinced they should contact the author for another try). $T = (W, D)$ with $W = \{b, c \to (d \lor a), a \land c \to \neg e\}$ and $D = \{\frac{c \lor \neg d : a}{a \lor \neg e}, \frac{true:c}{f \lor \neg b}, \frac{true:e}{\neg c}, \frac{(\neg c \lor d \lor a \lor e) \land f : \neg a, a \lor d}{\neg e}\}$.

Fortunately, the definition of an extension can be implemented in a straightforward way. We give a prototype implementation in Prolog which can then be used to check the accuracy of the examples to follow in subsequent sections and chapters. The main characteristics of this program are its simplicity and transparency rather than its efficiency. It contains many redundancies; see the *Problems* section at the end of the chapter for a brief discussion of some points.

The program is self–contained apart from making use of an external theorem prover **sequent**. The nature of sequent calculi was briefly explained in Chapter 2. In the case of propositional logic Wang's algorithm may be used.

The Prolog program we give works for default theories with one justification only. This restriction is unnecessary but simplifies the program. One of the exercises at the end of this chapter will be to extend the program to arbitrary default theories. Defaults are represented as terms **default(A,B,C)** where **A** is the prerequisite, **B** the justification, and **C** the consequent of the default. The logical connectives $\neg, \land, \lor, \to$ are represented by Prolog operators $\sim$, **&**, **v**, **->** respectively. So, the formula $((\neg a \land b) \to c)$ is represented by **((∼a & b) -> c)**.

The program is self–explanatory. Only one hint: the predicate **process** takes as input the set of defaults **D** (represented as a list), the current process **Pcurrent** along with the associated *In*–set **InCurrent** (represented as a list of formulae) and the *Out*–set **OutCurrent**, and tries to expand **Pcurrent** to a closed and successful process **P** with *In*–set **In** and *Out*–set **Out**. It does so by picking out a new default, testing for applicability, and, if successful, expanding **Pcurrent** and the associated sets with the new information and calling **process** recursively. The loop terminates when a closed and successful process is found.

```
extension(W,D,E) :- process(D,[ ],W,[ ],_,E,_).

process(D,Pcurrent,InCurrent,OutCurrent,P,In,Out) :-
   getNewDefault(default(A,B,C),D,Pcurrent),
   sequent(InCurrent,[A]),
   not sequent(InCurrent,[~B]),
   process(D,[default(A,B,C) | Pcurrent],
      [C | InCurrent],
      [~B | OutCurrent], P, In, Out).

process(D,P,In,Out,P,In,Out) :-
   closed(D,P,In),
   successful(In,Out).

closed(D,P,In) :-
   not(getNewDefault(default(A,B,C),D,P),
      sequent(In,[A]),
      not sequent(In,[~B])).

successful(In,Out) :- not (member(B,Out),sequent(In,[B])).

getNewDefault(default(A,B,C),D,P) :-
   member(default(A,B,C),D),
   not member(default(A,B,C),P).
```

4.4   An alternative characterization of extensions

Here we give an alternative characterization of extensions. Actually, it is the original definition given by Reiter and the one that is used in the literature. The reason we have given an alternative definition in section 4.1 is that Reiter's definition is based on fixed–point equations, so it is not constructive and therefore difficult to understand and apply. Furthermore, we have found our operational definition to be more suitable for proving theoretical results.

Let us try to motivate the classical definition. Once again we consider the example of Greens who are also members of AAA. We have $T = (W, D)$ with $W = \{green, aaaMember\}$ and $D = \{\delta_1, \delta_2\}$ with

$$\delta_1 = \frac{green : \neg likesCars}{\neg likesCars}, \quad \delta_2 = \frac{aaaMember : likesCars}{likesCars}.$$

Let us forget for the moment what we have learnt so far about extensions in this chapter. The discussion in Chapter 3 showed that when testing applicability of a default, the consistency of the justification should not be tested with respect to the facts W alone, because this may lead (as in our example) to a contradiction. But which theory should justifications be consistent with? Can this theory change within a proof?

The solution adopted by Reiter is to use some theory *beforehand*. That is, choose a theory which plays the role of a *context* or *belief set* and always check consistency against this context. Let us formalize this notion:

- A default $\delta = \frac{\varphi : \psi_1, \ldots, \psi_n}{\chi}$ *is applicable to* a deductively closed set of formulae F *with respect to belief set* E (the aforementioned context) iff $\varphi \in F$, and $\neg\psi_1 \notin E, \ldots, \neg\psi_n \notin E$ (that is, each ψ_i is consistent with E). Note that the concept 'δ is applicable to E' used so far is a special case where $E = F$.

The next question that arises is which contexts to use. Firstly note that when a belief set E has been established some formulae will become part of the knowledge base by applying defaults with respect to E. Therefore they should be believed, i.e. be members of E. On the other hand what would be a justification for a belief if it were not obtained from default application w.r.t. E? We require that E contain only formulae that can be derived from the axioms by default application w.r.t. E.

Let us now give a formal presentation of these ideas. For a set D of defaults, we say that F *is closed under D with respect to belief set E* iff, for every default δ in D that is applicable to F with respect to belief set E, its consequent χ is also contained in F.

According to these definitions, the bigger the set E the more difficult it is for a default to be applicable. Therefore we observe the following:

Lemma 4.3 *Suppose that $E' \subseteq E$ and F is closed under D w.r.t. E'. Then F is closed under D w.r.t. E.*

Given a default theory $T = (W, D)$ and a set of formulae E, let $\Lambda_T(E)$ be the least set of formulae that contains W, is closed under logical conclusion (i.e. first–order deduction), and closed under D with respect to E[1]. Informally speaking, $\Lambda_T(E)$ is

---

[1]It is left to the reader to verify that $\Lambda_T(E)$ is unique, thus justifying the name 'least' used.

the set of formulae that are sanctioned by the default theory T with respect to the belief set E.

Now, according to Reiter's definition, E is an extension of T iff $E = \Lambda_T(E)$. This fixed–point definition says that E is an extension iff by deciding to use E as a belief set, exactly the formulae in E will be obtained from default application. But please note the difficulty in applying this definition: we have to *guess* E and subsequently check for the fulfillment of the fixed-point equation. There are potentially infinitely many candidates. The reader may start appreciating the definition we gave in section 4.1![2] The following theorem shows that Reiter's extension concept is equivalent to our definition.

Theorem 4.4 *Let $T = (W, D)$ be a default theory. E is an extension of T (in the sense of definition 4.1) iff $E = \Lambda_T(E)$.*

Proof: Let Π be a closed and successful process of T with $E = In(\Pi)$. By definition of $In(\Pi)$, $W \subseteq E$ and $Th(E) = E$. Also, E is closed under D w.r.t. E because Π is closed. Since $\Lambda_T(E)$ is defined as the smallest set having these properties, we have shown $\Lambda_T(E) \subseteq E$.

In order to show $E \subseteq \Lambda_T(E)$, we prove by induction on k that $In(\Pi[k]) \subseteq \Lambda_T(E)$ for all k. Then we are done. The inclusion is trivial for $k = 0$. Now let the claim be true for k, and let $\delta = \frac{\varphi : \psi_1, \ldots, \psi_n}{\chi}$ be the $k + 1$-th default in Π. As Π is a process, we know that $\varphi \in In(\Pi[k]) \subseteq \Lambda_T(E)$, and $\neg\psi_1, \ldots, \neg\psi_n \in Out(\Pi[k + 1]) \subseteq Out(\Pi)$. Thus, $\neg\psi_1, \ldots, \neg\psi_n \notin In(\Pi) = E$ (because Π is successful). So, we have established that δ is applicable to $\Lambda_T(E)$ w.r.t. E. Therefore, $\chi \in \Lambda_T(E)$ and $In(\Pi[k + 1]) \subseteq \Lambda_T(E)$. Altogether, we have shown $E = \Lambda_T(E)$, so one direction of the theorem is proven.

For the opposite direction, suppose $E = \Lambda_T(E)$. Consider an arbitrary fixed enumeration $\{\delta^0, \delta^1, \ldots\}$ of D. In the following, we define a process Π of T with the properties (for all i such that $\Pi[i]$ is defined)

$In(\Pi[i]) \subseteq E$
$Out(\Pi[i]) \cap E = \emptyset$

as follows:

- *Case 1:* Every $\delta \in D$ which is applicable to $In(\Pi[i])$ is already contained in $\Pi[i]$. Then terminate the construction, and take $\Pi[i]$ as Π.

---

[2]Of course the price we have to pay for not having to guess is that we have to carry out a systematic search, in which some branches may not lead to an extension.

- *Case 2:* Else choose the smallest default in the fixed enumeration of D that is applicable to $In(\Pi[i])$, and attach it to $\Pi[i]$ to obtain $\Pi[i+1]$.

First, it is easy to see that the construction in case 2 preserves both conditions imposed on Π. Also, these conditions are trivially true for $i = 0$. Now, suppose the construction terminates in case 1. To show that $E = In(\Pi)$, it suffices to show the inclusion '$\subseteq$', since the other is already given by construction. Since $In(\Pi) \subseteq E = \Lambda_T(E)$, it suffices to show

$W \subseteq In(\Pi)$
$In(\Pi)$ is deductively closed
$In(\Pi)$ is closed under D w.r.t. $In(\Pi)$ (so w.r.t. E by lemma 4.3).

The first two properties are given by the construction of processes, the third by the definiton of case 1. This completes the proof in this case.

It remains to show what happens when the construction yields an infinite process Π. First, we note that $In(\Pi) \cap Out(\Pi) = \emptyset$ because $In(\Pi[i]) \subseteq E$ and $Out(\Pi[i]) \cap E = \emptyset$ for all i. Therefore Π is a successful process.

Next we show $In(\Pi) = E$. One inclusion holds by construction. To show the other inclusion, i.e. $E \subseteq In(\Pi)$, it suffices to show that $In(\Pi)$ is deductively closed, includes W, and is closed under D w.r.t. $In(\Pi)$ (by lemma 4.3). The first two properties are given by definition. To see the third one, consider a default $\delta = \frac{\varphi : \psi_1, \dots, \psi_n}{\chi}$ that is applicable to $In(\Pi)$. Now choose a number i such that $\varphi \in In(\Pi[i])$, and every $\delta' \in \Pi$ that appears before δ in the fixed enumeration of D is already contained in $\Pi[i]$. By definition of case 2, δ is the default that is chosen at stage $i+1$, so it is contained in Π, and its consequent is included in $In(\Pi)$.

The argument above together with the equation $E = In(\Pi)$ just proven shows that Π is also closed.   ■

Let us give a simple application of Reiter's characterization: we check whether the requirements on the concept of an extension that we developed in Chapter 3 are fulfilled. Let E be an extension. Since $E = \Lambda_T(E)$, E includes W, is deductively closed, and also closed under D w.r.t. E. Now we show that E is minimal with these properties. Consider a subset E' of E having these properties. Since $E' \subseteq E$, E' is closed under D not only w.r.t. E' but also w.r.t. E (by lemma 4.3). Therefore, by definition of $\Lambda_T(E)$, $E = \Lambda_T(E) \subseteq E'$, so $E = E'$. The following observation is a direct implication of this argument.

Corollary (Minimality of extensions) *If, for two extensions E and E' of a default theory T, $E \subseteq E'$ then $E = E'$.*

4.5   Some properties of Default Logic

Here we derive some simple properties of Default Logic that follow more or less directly from the basic definitions. Let us first explore the exact treatment of inconsistency; the following result shows that Default Logic is consistency preserving.

Theorem 4.5 (Consistency preservation) *A default theory $T = (W, D)$ has an inconsistent extension iff W is inconsistent.*

Proof: If W is inconsistent then $E = Th(W)$ coincides with $\Lambda_T(E)$; so E is an inconsistent extension of T. Let $E = In(\Pi)$ (for a closed and successful process Π of T) be an inconsistent extension of T. If Π is nonempty, then so is $Out(\Pi)$, in which case Π is failed (since $Out(\Pi) \neq \emptyset$ and every formula is included in the inconsistent set $In(\Pi)$). So, the only possibility is that Π is the empty process (). But then, $In(\Pi) = Th(W)$. Since $E = In(\Pi)$ is inconsistent this shows that W is inconsistent. ∎

Corollary *If a default theory T has an inconsistent extension E, then E is its only extension.*

We have mentioned occasionally that a default theory may have several extensions if there are some defaults that conflict one another. The next result shows that a form of the converse is also true: if there are no conflicts among justifications and consequents of all defaults in D, then the default theory has exactly one extension.

Theorem 4.6 *Let $T = (W, D)$ be a default theory such that the set of formulae $M = W \cup \{\psi_1 \wedge \ldots \wedge \psi_n \wedge \chi \mid \frac{\varphi : \psi_1, \ldots, \psi_n}{\chi} \text{ is a default in } D\}$ is consistent. Then T has exactly one extension.*

Proof*: It is easy to see that, by the consistency of M, all processes of T are successful. Therefore it is possible to obtain an extension of T simply by successively applying defaults in a fair way (to ensure closure in case D is infinite). This argument shows that T has at least one extension.

Now suppose that E_1 and E_2 are extensions of T. Let $\Pi = (\delta_0, \delta_1, \ldots)$ and $\Gamma = (\gamma_0, \gamma_1, \ldots)$ be closed and successful processes of T such that $E_1 = In(\Pi)$ and $E_2 = In(\Gamma)$. By induction on i we show that $\delta_i \in \{\gamma_0, \gamma_1, \ldots\}$. Suppose that this has been shown for all $j < i$, and let $\delta_i = \frac{\varphi : \psi_1, \ldots, \psi_n}{\chi}$.

We have $\varphi \in In(\Pi[i]) \subseteq In(\Gamma)$. Next we show that none of $\neg\psi_1, \ldots, \neg\psi_n$ is included in $In(\Gamma)$. Assume that $\neg\psi_k \in In(\Gamma)$. Since $In(\Gamma) \cup \{\psi_k\}$ is a subset of $Th(M)$, this would imply the inconsistency of M which is a contradiction. Altogether we showed that δ is applicable to $In(\Gamma)$. Γ is closed, therefore δ_i appears within Γ.

It follows that $E_1 = In(\Pi) \subseteq In(\Gamma) = E_2$. By symmetry (alternatively, by applying minimality of extensions) we also obtain $E_2 \subseteq E_1$.   ∎

Theorem 4.7 *Let E be an extension of the default theory $T = (W, D)$. Then E is also an extension of $T' = (W \cup W', D)$ for every subset W' of E.*

Proof*: E is a deductively closed set that contains $W \cup W'$ and is closed under D w.r.t. E; therefore $\Lambda_{T'}(E) \subseteq E$. Furthermore, $E = \Lambda_T(E) \subseteq \Lambda_{T'}(E) \subseteq E$. Therefore $\Lambda_{T'}(E) = E$.   ∎

But we should note that nothing more than the information contained in this theorem holds. Some extensions of T may disappear and new extensions may emerge that are not related to any extensions of T. This point is illustrated by the following example, borrowed from Marek and Truszczynski's book. Let $T = (W, D)$ be the default theory with $W = \emptyset$ and $D = \{\delta_1, \delta_2, \delta_3, \delta_4\}$ where

$$\delta_1 = \frac{true : \neg b, \neg d}{a}, \delta_2 = \frac{true : \neg b, \neg d}{c}, \delta_3 = \frac{true : \neg a, \neg c}{d}, \delta_4 = \frac{a : \neg c}{b}.$$

It is left to the reader as an exercise to check that T has two extensions, $E = Th(\{a, c\})$ and $F = Th(\{d\})$. Consider the subset $W' = \{a\}$ of E. The default theory $T' = (\{a\}, D)$ has two extensions, E as predicted by theorem 4.7, and $Th(\{a, b\})$ which is completely unrelated to F.

We conclude this chapter by briefly discussing the nonmonotonic nature of Default Logic. The reader may have noticed the absence of any nonmonotonic behaviour so far. The reason is quite simple: we concentrated on providing an operational semantics for a given default theory T. But if the default theory is fixed, then indeed there is no nonmonotonicity. The nonmonotonic behaviour may appear as soon as the default theory is *changed*. Changing either W or D can modify the set of extensions in an unpredictable way. Let us give some examples.

Let $T = (W, D)$ with $W = \emptyset$ and $D = \{\frac{true:a}{a}\}$. T has exactly one extension, namely $E = Th(\{a\})$. We expand D by four different defaults and see what happens:

- Let $\delta_1 = \frac{true:b}{\neg b}$. $T_1 = (W, D \cup \{\delta_1\})$ has no extensions.
- Let $\delta_2 = \frac{b:c}{c}$. $T_2 = (W, D \cup \{\delta_2\})$ still has E as the only extension.
- Let $\delta_3 = \frac{true:\neg a}{\neg a}$. $T_3 = (W, D \cup \{\delta_3\})$ has two extensions, E and $Th(\{\neg a\})$.
- Let $\delta_4 = \frac{a:b}{b}$. $T_4 = (W, D \cup \{\delta_4\})$ has the extension $Th(\{a, b\})$ that includes E.

So, expansion of D may lead to new extensions, destroy old ones or modify old extensions. Now let us see what may happen if W is expanded. Consider $T = (W, D)$ with $W = \emptyset$ and $D = \{\delta_1, \delta_2, \delta_3, \delta_4, \delta_5\}$ with

$$\delta_1 = \frac{true : a, \neg c}{a}, \delta_2 = \frac{a : b, \neg c}{b}, \delta_3 = \frac{true : \neg a, c}{c}, \delta_4 = \frac{d : e}{e}, \delta_5 = \frac{f : g}{\neg g}.$$

T has two extensions, $E_1 = Th(\{a, b\})$ and $E_2 = Th(\{c\})$. We expand W in the following ways:

- $W_1 = \{f\}$. (W_1, D) has no extension.
- $W_2 = \{\neg a\}$. (W_2, D) has the only extension $Th(\{\neg a, c\})$.
- $W_3 = \{\neg a, \neg c, d\}$. (W_3, D) has only the new extension $Th(\{\neg a, \neg c, d, e\})$.
- $W_4 = \{d\}$. (W_4, D) has the extensions $Th(E_1 \cup \{d, e\})$ and $Th(E_2 \cup \{d, e\})$.

Finally we note that usually, when speaking of the nonmonotonic nature of Default Logic, we mean nonmonotonicity in W. The reason is that defaults are seen as *long term* rules of thumb that we would like to keep as long as possible, whereas the set of facts may vary; a part of the set of facts W may be, for example, the observations for a concrete case, whereas the defaults determine the behaviour of the knowledge system for all possible cases.

Problems

4-1. Why is $Out(\Pi)$ not required to be deductively closed?

4-2. Show that if all defaults in Π occur in Π', then $In(\Pi) \subseteq In(\Pi')$ and $Out(\Pi) \subseteq Out(\Pi')$.

4-3.* Given a default theory $T = (W, D)$, we say that E *has a quasi–inductive definition in* T iff $E = \bigcup_i E_i$, where $E_0 = Th(W)$ and $E_{i+1} = Th(E_i \cup \{cons(\delta) \mid \delta \in D$ is applicable to E_i w.r.t. belief set $E\})$. Show: E is an extension of T iff E has a quasi–inductive definition in T.

4-4. In our definition of a default we required that there be at least one justification (which may be the formula *true*). Consider an alternative definition where defaults may have no justification. Would theorem 4.5 still be true?

4-5.* Extend the Prolog program of section 4.3 to treat defaults with arbitrarily many justifications. Also, write a user–friendly interface for the input of default theories and the output of extensions.

4-6. Compare the checks for success in the Prolog program and in the definition of process trees. Determine the difference and modify the program so that it reflects exactly the way process trees are built.

4-7. Consider the default theory $(\emptyset, \{\frac{true:a}{a}, \frac{true:b}{b}, \frac{true:c}{c}\})$. How many extensions does it have? How many answers does the Prolog program compute? Explain the difference!

4-8.* The Prolog program that computes the extensions of a default theory tests all possible orderings of defaults. That means, if D has n defaults then in the worst case we have a run–time $O(n!)$. But on the other hand, there are at most 2^n extensions (is it clear why?).

(a) Let Π be a closed and successful process of T which can be written in the form $\Pi_1 \circ \Pi_2 \circ (\delta) \circ \Pi_3$[3]. Further let $pre(\delta) \in In(\Pi_1)$. Show that $\Pi' = \Pi_1 \circ (\delta) \circ \Pi_2 \circ \Pi_3$ is a closed and successful process of T, and $In(\Pi') = In(\Pi)$.

(b) Explain how part (a) can be used to build a modified process tree of T that has at most $O(2^n)$ maximal paths without losing any extension of T.

4-9. Check that all the examples at the end of this chapter illustrating the non-monotonic behaviour of Default Logic were treated correctly.

---

[3]where ∘ denotes concatenation of sequences.

4-10.* Stratified default logic (Cholewinski). Suppose that the default theory $T = (W, D)$ is propositional, and that D is finite. Stratification is a powerful technique for cutting down the size of the process tree. It is based on a syntactic preprocessing of default theories which decomposes the theory into levels called strata; consequents of defaults in lower strata are used in higher strata but not vice versa.

Formally, a *stratification function* ρ assigns to every default in D a number i in such a way that the following condition is satisfied: For all defaults $\delta = \frac{\varphi : \psi_1, \ldots, \psi_n}{\chi}$ and $\delta' = \frac{\varphi' : \psi'_1, \ldots, \psi'_m}{\chi'}$ in D,

1. $Prop(\chi) \cap Prop(\chi') \neq \emptyset$ implies $\rho(\delta) = \rho(\delta')$[4].
2. $Prop(\{\psi_1, \ldots, \psi_n\}) \cap Prop(\chi') \neq \emptyset$ implies $\rho(\delta) \geq \rho(\delta')$.
3. $Prop(\varphi) \cap Prop(\chi') \neq \emptyset$ implies $\rho(\delta) \geq \rho(\delta')$.

T is *stratifiable* iff W is consistent and $Prop(W) \cap Prop(cons(D)) = \emptyset$. In the following we assume that T is stratifiable and ρ is a stratification function. Clearly, D is decomposed into partitions $D_1, \ldots, D_l$ of ascending value under ρ.

(a) We say that $\Pi = (\delta_0, \ldots, \delta_k)$ *respects* ρ iff $i < j$ implies $\rho(\delta_i) \leq \rho(\delta_j)$. Show that for every closed and successful process Π' of T we can construct a closed and successful process Π of T, such that Π is a permutation of Π' which respects ρ. *Hint:* Define Π such that the order in Π' is respected apart from cases where ρ is violated. Then show that Π has the form $\Pi_1 \circ \ldots \circ \Pi_l$, where Π_i contains only defaults from the i-th stratum D_i.

(b) Formalize and prove the following: Every extension E of T can be computed bottom–up 'stratum by stratum'. *Hint:* Show that the processes Π_i from part (a) are closed and successful processes of $(W \cup cons(\bigcup_{j<i} \Pi_j), D_i)$[5].

---

[4]$Prop(M)$ denotes the set of propositions occurring in M.
[5]Slightly abusing notation we consider Π_j as a *set* of defaults here.

Chapter 5

Normal Default Theories

Now that we have introduced Default Logic in its general form we turn our attention to a subclass of default theories, the so–called *normal* default theories. All defaults in such theories are normal which means their consequent is their only justification. A simple example is our familiar default

$$\frac{bird : flies}{flies}.$$

It turns out that normal defaults are very well–behaved. They always have extensions which is important since if T has no extensions then T is useless. Further advantages are monotonicity in D (one of the results in section 5.2) and the possibility of goal–driven query evaluation as shown in section 5.3. So why don't we exclusively use normal defaults if they are so well–behaved? Unfortunately, it turns out that they are not expressive enough to model some domains. Their main limitation is that they do not allow for the representation of priorities and other interactions among defaults. We discuss the limitations of normal defaults in section 5.4.

5.1 Normal defaults

A default is called *normal* iff its consequent is its only justification. So, normal defaults have the form

$$\frac{\varphi : \psi}{\psi}.$$

A default theory $T = (W, D)$ is called normal iff all defaults in D are normal.

A normal default draws the conclusion ψ when φ is known and it is consistent to conclude ψ. This idea is intuitively clear and avoids all kinds of undesirable effects like the 'strange default' $\frac{true:a}{\neg a}$. Let us investigate what processes of normal default theories look like. The case of W being inconsistent has been studied in the previous chapter: T has only the inconsistent extension which consists of all formulae. So let us assume that W is consistent.

If $\Pi = (\delta_0, \delta_1, \ldots)$ is a process of a normal default theory T and $\delta_i = \frac{\varphi_i : \psi_i}{\psi_i}$, then $In(\Pi)$ contains W and all ψ_i, and $Out(\Pi)$ consists of the formulae $\neg\psi_i$. Since Π is a process, each default in Π was applicable, so it was consistent to conclude ψ_i. Therefore $In(\Pi)$ is consistent. Can Π be failed? Suppose some $\neg\psi_k \in Out(\Pi)$ were in $In(\Pi)$. However, by definition, the consequent ψ_k of δ_k would also be in $In(\Pi)$. But this would imply that $In(\Pi)$ is inconsistent which is impossible, as we saw. Let us formulate this result.

Lemma 5.1 *Each process of a normal default theory is successful.*

The consequences of this fact are indeed desirable and far–reaching: given a finite process Π we are able to expand it in any possible way without ever running into failure. So, by expanding Π in a fair way we arrive at a closed and successful process which corresponds to an extension. This argument holds also for the empty process. Therefore we have established the following:

Theorem 5.2 (Existence of extensions) *Normal default theories always possess extensions. Every finite process Π may be expanded to a closed process Π'[1].*

5.2   Some theoretical properties

At the end of Chapter 4 we saw that Default Logic is nonmonotonic both with respect to W and D. For normal default theories, though, the following monotonicity result w.r.t. the set of defaults can be shown.

Theorem 5.3 (Semi–monotonicity) *Let $T = (W, D)$ and $T' = (W, D')$ be normal default theories such that $D \subseteq D'$. Then each extension of T is contained in an extension of T'.*

Proof[*]:* The statement is trivial if W is inconsistent, so in the following we assume that W is consistent. Let E be an extension of T and let $\Pi = (\delta_0, \delta_1, \ldots)$ be a closed process of T such that $E = In(\Pi)$ (recall that Π, as all other processes in this chapter, is successful by lemma 5.1). Obviously Π is also a process of T' but not necessarily a *closed* process.

---

[1]which is successful by lemma 5.1.

Our task is to transform Π to a closed process of T' by adding defaults from $D' - D$. In case Π is finite we simply expand Π by applying defaults from $D' - D$ in a fair way until a closed process of T' is reached. But when Π is infinite we cannot proceed in this simple way: there is no 'end' of Π where we could start applying defaults from $D' - D$.

The solution to this problem is not hard to see. We weave the new defaults into Π itself: after each default of Π we try to apply a default from $D' - D$. We must only take care not to destroy the applicability of a default of Π which appears *after* the insertion point under consideration. Technically we solve this problem by checking the consistency of a new default not only w.r.t. the defaults applied so far but also w.r.t. the *entire* E^2.

Now we formalize the idea outlined above. We define a process $\Gamma = (\gamma_0, \gamma_1, \ldots)$ of T' as follows:

1. Let γ_{2i} be δ_k with k minimal such that $\delta_k \notin \{\gamma_0, \ldots, \gamma_{2i-1}\}$.

2. Let γ_{2i+1} be the first default in $D' - \{\gamma_0, \ldots, \gamma_{2i}\}$ (referring to a fixed enumeration of D') which is applicable to $In(\Gamma[2i+1])$ w.r.t. belief set $Th(E \cup In(\Gamma[2i+1]))$; if no such default exists, then define γ_{2i+1} to be δ_k with k minimal such that $\delta_k \notin \{\gamma_0, \ldots, \gamma_{2i}\}$.

The definition of Γ implies the following properties (for all i):

- $\{\delta_0, \ldots, \delta_{i-1}\} \subseteq \{\gamma_0, \ldots, \gamma_{2i-1}\}$.
- The prerequisite of γ_i is included in $In(\Gamma[i])$.
- $In(\Gamma[i]) \cup E$ is consistent.

So Γ is a process of T' containing Π as a subsequence. We conclude the proof by showing that Γ is closed. Consider $\delta \in D'$ which is applicable to $In(\Gamma)$. Since $E \subseteq In(\Gamma)$, δ is applicable to $In(\Gamma[i])$ w.r.t. $Th(E \cup In(\Gamma[i]))$ for infinitely many i. Having chosen 'the first default that...' (to ensure fairness) in case 2 above we are sure that δ will be eventually selected at some stage, so $\delta \in \Gamma$. Note that fairness was essential in this proof. ∎

As already stated in Chapters 3 and 4, a default theory has more than one extension when defaults are in conflict with one other. A classical example is that

---

[2]To avoid misunderstandings: this is not a look ahead in the sense of Reiter's definition of extensions. E is the given extension of T; we do not use look ahead to the extension of T' yet to be constructed.

of Greens and AAA members. In that case, one extension contains the formula *likesCars* and the other ¬*likesCars*, so the union of the extensions is inconsistent. This observation is not coincidental but lies in the nature of normal defaults as the next result shows. Note, though, that this property does not hold for arbitrary defaults (because defaults may be in conflict in terms of justifications which do not appear in the extensions). For example consider $T = (W, D)$ with $W = \emptyset$ and $D = \{\frac{true:\neg p}{q}, \frac{true:\neg q}{p}\}$ (the consequent of each default conflicts with the justification of the other). T has two extensions, $E = Th(\{p\})$ and $F = Th(\{q\})$. $E \cup F$ is consistent.

Theorem 5.4 (Orthogonality of extensions) *Let E and F be different extensions of a normal default theory T. Then $E \cup F$ is inconsistent.*

Proof*: By the minimality of extensions, neither $E \subseteq F$ nor $F \subseteq E$. Suppose $E \cup F$ were consistent. Choose closed processes $\Pi = (\delta_0, \delta_1, \ldots)$ and $\Gamma = (\gamma_0, \gamma_1, \ldots)$ of T such that $E = In(\Pi)$ and $F = In(\Gamma)$. Consider the least i such that δ_i does not occur in Γ, and let δ_i be the default $\frac{\varphi:\psi}{\psi}$.

By the minimality of i, $\varphi \in In(\Pi[i]) \subseteq In(\Gamma)$ since $\delta_0, \ldots, \delta_{i-1}$ occur in Γ. Choose a number k such that $\varphi \in In(\Gamma[k])$ (k exists by the compactness of predicate logic). Also $\psi \in E$, $In(\Gamma) = F$ and $E \cup F$ is consistent, so $\neg\psi \notin In(\Gamma)$. This shows that δ_i is applicable to $In(\Gamma[k])$ w.r.t. belief set $In(\Gamma)$. We have chosen δ_i as a default of Π not included in Γ. The only possibility for this is that, for some $l > k$, $\neg\psi$ is included in $In(\Gamma[l])$. But then we would have $\psi \in E = In(\Pi)$ and $\neg\psi \in F = In(\Gamma)$. Therefore $E \cup F$ would be inconsistent which contradicts the assumption made above. ∎

Now we apply this result to establish another interesting property of normal default theories. Suppose $T = (W, D)$ has two different extensions E and F. In this case W must be consistent. Now let us expand D by some new normal defaults to obtain $T' = (W, D')$. We know that E and F may be expanded to extensions E' and F' of T' respectively. Is it possible that E' and F' are identical? Well, in that case $E \cup F$ would be a subset of $E' = F'$ and as such consistent (by consistency preservation, recalling that W is consistent). Orthogonality of extensions says that this case is impossible. So we have proven the following result.

Corollary *Expanding the set of defaults of a normal default theory by additional normal defaults does not decrease the number of extensions.*

At the end of Chapter 4 we gave an example which shows that this property does not hold for general default theories.

5.3   A proof theory for normal default theories

Until now we have investigated Default Logic based on extensions, and our primary concern was to determine extensions and study their properties. Indeed, if we are interested in finding the formulae that are supported by a given default theory all we have to do is determine the theory's extensions. But what if we are particularly interested in knowing whether a specific formula is included in an extension of T? It certainly seems inappropriate to answer such *queries* by determining extensions of T blindly.

The situation might be best described in terms of *backward chaining* or *goal–driven reasoning* on one side, and *forward chaining* on the other. In the former approach we start with the query given and try to reach the axioms using deduction; query evaluation in Prolog is an example of this approach. Forward chaining consists of deriving conclusions until a given goal (for example a given query) is found. This is the approach we have taken so far in Default Logic; it is a 'blind' search in the sense that it takes no advantage of the given goal to guide the search.

There is a good reason why we have not taken the former approach so far: in general, a goal–driven approach is simply impossible! To illustrate this claim let us look at an example. Consider the default theory $T = (W, D)$ with $W = \{p\}$ and $D = \{\delta_1, \delta_2, \delta_3\}$ with

$$\delta_1 = \frac{p : q}{r}, \delta_2 = \frac{r : q}{s}, \delta_3 = \frac{true : true}{\neg q}.$$

Suppose we are interested in testing whether the formula s is supported by T. We have not yet said anything about what this means. For the time being let us say that we are interested in finding out whether there exists an extension of T that contains s; we postpone a more thorough discussion of the notion 'a formula follows from a default theory' until the discussion of nonmonotonic inference relations in Chapter 13.

If we proceeded in a goal–driven way we would argue as follows: s is the consequent of δ_2, so let us try to derive the prerequisite of that default which is r. r is the consequent of δ_1 so let us try to derive its prerequisite p. p is included in W so we are done. Of course, we did not pay any attention to consistency but this is not the problem here because there are no conflicts among W, δ_1 and δ_2. So we would be tempted to answer the question positively. Unfortunately, though, the only extension of T is $Th(\{p, \neg q\})$ which does not include s, so our answer is wrong!

The problem in the example above stems from the fact that default δ_3, which had not occurred in the goal–driven argument, destroyed the process (δ_1, δ_2). But this problem cannot arise if only normal defaults are considered. We have seen that any finite process of a normal default theory T may be expanded to a closed process of T which, by definition, corresponds to an extension of T. So there is hope if we restrict attention to normal theories, and indeed goal–driven query evaluation *is* possible in this case!

Let us try to develop the notion of a *default proof* for a formula φ. First we must determine a set of defaults D_0 with the property that φ follows from $W \cup cons(D_0)$. To ensure applicability of the defaults in D_0 we then determine a set of defaults D_1 such that all prerequisites of defaults in D_0 follow from $W \cup cons(D_1)$. We proceed this way until some D_k is empty which means that the prerequisites of defaults in D_{k-1} follow from W. Then we have determined a proof provided that we have not run into a contradiction, meaning that W must be consistent with the set of consequents of all defaults involved in the proof. For example, given the default theory $T = (\{p\}, \{\delta_1 = \frac{p:r}{r}, \delta_2 = \frac{r:p \rightarrow s}{p \rightarrow s}\})$, $(\{\delta_2\}, \{\delta_1\}, \emptyset)$ is a default proof of s in T.

Formally: A *default proof* of φ in a normal default theory $T = (W, D)$ is a finite sequence $(D_0, D_1, \ldots, D_k)$ of subsets of D such that

- φ follows from $W \cup cons(D_0)$
- for all $i < k$, the prerequisites of defaults in D_i follow from $W \cup cons(D_{i+1})$
- $D_k = \emptyset$
- $W \cup cons(\bigcup_i D_i)$ is consistent.

Theorem 5.5 *A formula φ has a default proof in a normal default theory T iff there is an extension E of T such that $\varphi \in E$.*

Proof*: Suppose that φ is included in an extension E of T, and let Π be a closed process of T such that $E = In(\Pi)$. By the compactness of predicate logic there is a number k such that $\varphi \in In(\Pi[k])$. Define D_i to be the set of defaults occurring in $\Pi[k - i]$ (for all $0 \leq i \leq k$). Note that D_0 includes all defaults of $\Pi[k]$ and that $D_k = \emptyset$ since $\Pi[0]$ is the empty sequence. It is easy to verify the properties of a default proof for $(D_0, \ldots, D_k)$.

Conversely, let a default proof $(D_0, \ldots, D_k)$ of φ be given. For all $0 < i \leq k$ define Π_i to be any permutation of the defaults in D_{k-i} which do not already occur in some Π_j for $j < i$. Finally, define Π as the concatenation $\Pi_1 \circ \ldots \circ \Pi_k$. We make the following observations (for all $0 < i \leq k$):

- $In(\Pi_1 \circ \ldots \circ \Pi_i) = Th(W \cup cons(\bigcup_{j \geq k-i} D_j))$
- All defaults in D_0 appear in Π.

The first observation follows directly from the definitions. To see the second one, suppose δ is not included in any D_i for $i > 0$; then, by definition, δ occurs in Π_k. Else let i be the largest index such that $\delta \in D_i$. Then, again by definition, δ occurs in Π_{k-i}.

So we know that $\varphi \in In(\Pi)$. We conclude the proof by showing that Π is a process of T. Then we are done because Π may be expanded to a closed process Π' of T (then φ is included in the extension $In(\Pi')$ of T).

Let δ be a default $\frac{\varphi : \psi}{\psi}$ occurring in Π_i. Then $\delta \in D_{k-i}$ and, by definition of a default proof, $\varphi \in Th(W \cup cons(D_{k-i+1})) \subseteq In(\Pi_1 \circ \ldots \circ \Pi_{i-1})$. Also $\neg\psi \notin In(\Pi)$ since $W \cup cons(\bigcup_j D_j)$ is consistent. This shows that δ is applicable ever after the defaults of $\Pi_1 \circ \ldots \circ \Pi_{i-1}$ have been applied (formally: δ is applicable to $In(\Pi[l])$ for all $l \geq |\Pi_1| + \ldots + |\Pi_{i-1}|$). This shows that regardless of where δ occurs in Π_i its application is possible. ∎

We conclude this section with two examples that illustrate the goal–driven approach of default proofs. Consider the default theory $T = (W, D)$ with $W = \{q \wedge r \rightarrow p\}$ and $D = \{\delta_1, \delta_2, \delta_3, \delta_4, \delta_5, \delta_6\}$ with

$$\delta_1 = \frac{true : d}{d}, \delta_2 = \frac{d : \neg c \wedge b}{\neg c \wedge b}, \delta_3 = \frac{d : c}{c}, \delta_4 = \frac{true : a}{a}, \delta_5 = \frac{a \wedge b : q}{q}, \delta_6 = \frac{\neg c : r}{r}$$

Suppose we want to know whether p is included in some extension of T. We determine $D_0 = \{\delta_5, \delta_6\}$ and have to derive $a \wedge b$ and $\neg c$. We may prove these formulae using $D_1 = \{\delta_2, \delta_4\}$. Now our task is to prove d. $D_2 = \{\delta_1\}$ does the job and concludes the default proof of p since the prerequisite of δ_1 follows from W. $(D_0, D_1, D_2, \emptyset)$ is a default proof of p in T since there is no conflict among W and $cons(D_0 \cup D_1 \cup D_2)$.

Now consider the default theory $T = (W, D)$ with $W = \emptyset$ and $D = \{\delta_1, \delta_2, \delta_3\}$ with

$$\delta_1 = \frac{q : p}{p}, \delta_2 = \frac{\neg p : q}{q}, \delta_3 = \frac{true : \neg p}{\neg p}.$$

$(\{\delta_1\}, \{\delta_2\}, \{\delta_3\}, \emptyset)$ is not a default proof of p because $cons(\{\delta_1, \delta_2, \delta_3\})$ is inconsistent.

5.4   Limitations of normal default theories

Are normal defaults sufficient to represent knowledge in various problem domains?
At first sight it seems so, because the defaults that usually occur are of the form
'Typically birds fly' or 'Assume that the accused is innocent unless you know otherwise' or 'The meeting will be on Wednesday unless another decision is made'. If
normal defaults would turn out to be sufficient then we would end up with a very
nice logic which always has extensions, is semi–monotonic and allows for goal–driven
query evaluation.

Unfortunately it turns out that this expectation is too optimistic. The lesson
learned when the first attempts were made to formalize some knowledge in Default
Logic was the following: a default rule *on its own* is almost always normal, however
there are problems when *several defaults* have to interact within a default theory.
Let us give some examples to illustrate this point. Suppose we are given the information

Bill is a high school dropout.
Typically, high school dropouts are adults.
Typically, adults are employed.

These facts are naturally represented by the normal default theory

$$T = (\{dropout(bill)\}, \{\frac{dropout(X) : adult(X)}{adult(X)}, \frac{adult(X) : employed(X)}{employed(X)}\})$$

T has the single extension $Th(\{dropout(bill), adult(bill), employed(bill)\})$. It is
acceptable to assume that Bill is adult, but it is counterintuitive to assume that
Bill is employed! That is, whereas the second default *on its own* is accurate, we
want to prevent its application in case the adult X is a high school dropout. This
can be achieved if we change the second default to

$$\frac{adult(X) : employed(X) \wedge \neg dropout(X)}{employed(X)}.$$

This default is not normal! It is left as an exercise for the reader to find out why it
is not reasonable to add $\neg dropout(X)$ to the prerequisite of the default, in which
case it would have remained normal.

Here is an example that demonstrates the need for priorities among defaults.
Consider the default theory $T = (W, D)$ with $W = \{bird(X) \rightarrow animal(X),$
$bird(tweety)\}$ and $D = \{\delta_1, \delta_2\}$ with

$$\delta_1 = \frac{animal(X) : \neg flies(X)}{\neg flies(X)}, \delta_2 = \frac{bird(X) : flies(X)}{flies(X)}.$$

T has two extensions, one including $\neg flies(tweety)$ and one including $flies(tweety)$. Intuitively we would prefer the second one only, because we would give δ_2 higher priority over δ_1 (assumptions about birds are more specific and thus more reliable than assumptions about animals). This can be achieved if we replace δ_1 by

$$\delta_1' = \frac{animal(X) : \neg bird(X) \wedge \neg flies(X)}{\neg flies(X)}.$$

In both examples the modified defaults have the form $\frac{\varphi : \psi \wedge \chi}{\chi}$. Such defaults are called *semi-normal* and will be studied in the following chapter. Let us also note that in case some means for dealing with priorities among defaults is available ('Give δ_2 higher priority than δ_1'), normal defaults are appropriate to model most problem domains. We will come back to this point in Chapter 8 where we shall describe some ways of representing and reasoning about default priorities.

Problems

5-1. Fill in the technical details missing in the proof of theorem 5.5.

5-2. Reconsidering the last examples of section 5.4, explain why the defaults had to be turned into semi-normal form instead of putting the additional condition into the prerequisite of the defaults.

5-3. Give an example which demonstrates that expanding a set of normal defaults by additional normal defaults may increase the number of extensions.

5-4.* Show that every process Π of a normal default theory T is included in a closed process Π' of T. *Hint:* For an infinite process Π use the 'weaving' technique from the proof of theorem 5.3.

5-5. A class $\mathcal{C}$ of default theories is called *representationally complete* iff the following property is satisfied: For every default theory T there is a default theory T' in $\mathcal{C}$ such that T and T' have precisely the same extensions. Show that the class of normal default theories is not representationally complete. *Hint:* Consider T with two extensions E, F such that $E \cup F$ is consistent.

5-6. Build the process trees of all default theories discussed in this chapter.

Chapter 6

Semi-normal Default Theories

At the end of the last chapter we identified semi–normal default theories as a class which is sufficiently expressive to model domains where normal default theories have problems, without being too syntactically distant from normal defaults. In this chapter we shall investigate semi–normal defaults more thoroughly.

Our first concern will be the existence of extensions. Unfortunately it turns out that semi–normal theories do not necessarily possess extensions. To see this consider the default theory $T = (W, D)$ with $W = \emptyset$ and D consisting of the defaults

$$\frac{true : \neg q \wedge p}{p}, \quad \frac{true : \neg r \wedge q}{q}, \quad \frac{true : \neg p \wedge r}{r}.$$

The reader may build the process tree of T and check that T does not have any extensions. Fortunately, it is possible to identify a very broad class of semi–normal default theories, so–called *ordered theories*, which (under some additional conditions) do have extensions. Section 6.1 introduces this concept, and section 6.2 contains a proof of the existence of extensions.

Then we turn our attention to a knowledge representation issue: is it possible to transform defaults into semi–normal defaults while preserving their intuitive meaning? Section 6.3 describes such a translation and presents some formal properties.

6.1 Ordered, semi-normal default theories*

A default is called *semi–normal* iff it has the form $\frac{\varphi : \psi \wedge \chi}{\chi}$. A default theory (W, D) is called semi–normal iff all defaults in D are semi–normal. Normal defaults $\frac{\varphi : \psi}{\psi}$ can be regarded as semi–normal since they are equivalent to $\frac{\varphi : \psi \wedge \psi}{\psi}$.

In the following we introduce the concept of an ordered default theory so that we may define a class of default theories that always possess extensions. Ordered default theories are meant to avoid the circularity that is obvious in the example given in the introduction to this chapter. First we need some technical preliminaries.

A *clausal default theory* $T = (W, D)$ is a default theory in which all formulae occurring in D and W are clausal (i.e. quantifier–free formulae in conjunctive normal form $\bigwedge_i \bigvee_j \varphi_{ij}$). In a clausal formula φ, we write φ_{ij} for the j–th literal in the i–th conjunct of φ; $Literals(\varphi)$ is the set of literals φ_{ij} occurring in φ.

Definition 6.1 Let $T = (W, D)$ be a semi–normal, clausal default theory. The relations $\prec$ and $\preceq$ on literals occurring in T are defined as follows:

1. $\sim \varphi_{ij} \preceq \varphi_{ik}$ for each $\varphi \in W$ and $j \neq k$[1].

2. For each $\frac{\varphi : \psi \wedge \chi}{\chi}$ in D

   (a) $\varphi_{ij} \preceq \chi_{kl}$ if φ_{ij} is not the formula *true*.

   (b) $\sim \psi_{ij} \prec \chi_{kl}$

   (c) $\sim \chi_{ij} \preceq \chi_{ik}$ if $j \neq k$.

3. $\prec$ and $\preceq$ are the least relations satisfying

   (a) conditions 1 and 2.

   (b) $\varphi \preceq \psi$ and $\psi \preceq \chi$ implies $\varphi \preceq \chi$

   (c) $\varphi \prec \psi$ and $\psi \prec \chi$ implies $\varphi \prec \chi$

   (d) $\varphi \preceq \psi$ and $\psi \prec \chi$ implies $\varphi \prec \chi$

   (e) $\varphi \prec \psi$ and $\psi \preceq \chi$ implies $\varphi \prec \chi$.

T is called *ordered* iff there is no literal L such that $L \prec L$. Considering the example from the introduction to this chapter once again, we obtain $q \prec p$, $r \prec q$, and $p \prec r$ using condition (2b), so $q \prec q$ and the theory is not ordered. But orderedness of semi–normal default theories is still insufficient to ensure the existence of extensions as the following examples will illustrate. We need the following additional properties:

   (a) The set of defaults D is finite.

   (b) The default theory is propositional.

---

[1] Recall that for a literal L, we denote by $\sim L$ the literal $\neg L$, if L is a positive literal, and L', if $L = \neg L'$ and L' is a positive literal.

Let us call a default theory *plain* if it satisfies conditions (a) and (b). The main result concerning ordered default theories is stated below. We postpone its proof until the next section because it is lengthy and requires extensive preparations.

Theorem (Existence of extensions) *A semi–normal, plain, ordered default theory has at least one extension.*

First we note that the converse is not true. The following example even suggests that it would be naive to expect a result like that: the default theory includes a 'cyclical argument' that could cause trouble, but the defaults involved are made inapplicable, so there does exist an extension. Let $T = (W, D)$ with $W = \emptyset$ and D consisting of the defaults

$$\frac{f : \neg p \wedge q}{q}, \frac{f : \neg q \wedge r}{r}, \frac{f : \neg r \wedge p}{p}.$$

$Th(\emptyset)$ is an extension of T. The next example shows that restriction to propositional logic is essential for the existence of extensions. Let $T = (W, D)$ with $W = \{\forall X \forall Y (\neg p(X) \vee p(Y))\}$ and D consisting of the defaults

$$\frac{true : \neg q \wedge p(a)}{p(a)}, \frac{true : \neg r \wedge q}{q}, \frac{true : \neg p(b) \wedge r}{r}.$$

The reader is asked to build the process tree of T and verify that it does not have an extension. Now let us compute the relations $\prec$ and $\preceq$. We get

$$p(X) \preceq p(Y), \neg p(Y) \preceq \neg p(X)$$

from condition (1) in definition 6.1, and

$$q \prec p(a), r \prec q, p(b) \prec r$$

from condition (2b). Apparently, there does not exist a literal L such that $L \prec L$, so T is ordered. Note, though, that if we had used the ground instances of $(\neg p(X) \vee p(Y))$ instead of the universally quantified formula in W, we would have had $p(a) \preceq p(b)$ from which we would have concluded

$$q \prec p(a) \preceq p(b) \prec r \prec q.$$

Now consider the following example (from Besnard's book) which shows that restriction to finite sets of defaults is essential for the existence of extensions. Consider $T = (W, D)$ with $W = \{q_i \rightarrow q_{i+1} \mid i \geq 0\} \cup \{q_i \rightarrow \neg p_{i+1} \mid i \geq 0\}$ and $D = \{\frac{true : q_i \wedge p_i}{p_i} \mid i \geq 0\}$. First we compute the relations $\prec$ and $\preceq$. We have

$$q_i \preceq q_{i+1}, \neg q_{i+1} \preceq \neg q_i, q_i \preceq \neg p_{i+1}, p_{i+1} \preceq \neg q_i$$

from condition (1), and

$$\neg q_i \prec p_i$$

from condition (2b). By transitivity and the closure properties we obtain maximal sequences

$$q_i \preceq q_{i+1} \preceq \cdots \preceq q_{i+j} \preceq \neg p_{i+j+1}$$

and

$$\neg q_i \preceq \neg q_{i-1} \preceq \cdots \preceq \neg q_{i-j} \prec p_{i-j} \preceq \neg q_{i-j-1} \preceq \cdots \preceq \neg q_{i-j-k} \prec p_{i-j-k} \cdots$$

So there is no literal L such that $L \prec L$, and T is ordered. But T does not possess any extensions (see problem 6-1 at the end of this chapter).

We leave the discussion of the existence of extensions; a technical proof is found in the next section. Existence of extensions is one of the main desirable properties of normal default theories. Since semi–normal, ordered, plain default theories have this property, it is natural to ask whether they have other properties like

- semi–monotonicity
- orthogonality of extensions, or
- success of all processes as a prerequisite for goal–driven query evaluation.

Unfortunately it turns out that none of these properties is true. Consider $T = (W, D)$ with $W = \emptyset$ and $D = \{\frac{true:\neg q \land p}{p}\}$. T is ordered and has the unique extension $E = Th(\{p\})$. Now consider $T' = (W, D')$ with $D' = \{\frac{true:\neg q \land p}{p}, \frac{true:\neg r \land q}{q}\}$. T' is also ordered and has the unique extension $E' = Th(\{q\})$; E is not a subset of E', so semi–monotonicity is violated. In addition T' has a failed process.

A default theory that violates orthogonality of extensions is $T = (W, D)$ with $W = \emptyset$ and $D = \{\frac{true:p \land q}{q}, \frac{true:\neg q \land \neg p}{\neg p}\}$. T has two extensions, $E_1 = Th(\{q\})$ and $E_2 = Th(\{\neg p\})$. $E_1 \cup E_2$ is consistent.

6.2   Proof of the existence of extensions*

First we get an overview of interactions of defaults, as far as the destruction of applicability is concerned. Let $T = (W, D)$ be a default theory, and $\delta = \frac{\varphi:\psi}{\chi}$

a default in D. A *destruction process* of δ is a minimal process Π_{des} of T such that $In(\Pi_{des}) \cup \{\chi\} \models \neg\psi$ and $In(\Pi_{des}) \cup \{\chi\}$ is consistent. $Des(\delta, T)$ denotes the set of all destruction processes of δ for a default theory T. A *destruction sequence* in $T = (W, D)$ with *basis default* $\delta_1 \in D$ is a (finite or infinite) sequence $< \Pi^1_{des}, \Pi^2_{des}, \ldots >$ of processes of T such that

- $\Pi^i_{des} \in Des(\delta_i, T)$ (for all $i \geq 0$)
- δ_{i+1} occurs in Π^i_{des} (for all $i > 0$).

A finite destruction sequence $< \Pi^1_{des}, \ldots, \Pi^n_{des} >$ with basis default δ_1 is called a *destruction cycle* if δ_1 occurs in Π^n_{des}.

A circularity indicated by a destruction cycle is typical for semi–normal default theories without extensions. For example, consider the theory $T = (W, D)$ with $W = \{(h \wedge a) \rightarrow \neg g\}$ and $D = \{\delta_1, \delta_2, \delta_3, \delta_4, \delta_5\}$ with

$$\delta_1 = \frac{true : b \wedge a}{a}, \delta_2 = \frac{true : d \wedge c}{c}, \delta_3 = \frac{c : f \wedge \neg b}{\neg b}$$

$$\delta_4 = \frac{true : g \wedge \neg f}{\neg f}, \delta_5 = \frac{true : \neg b \wedge h}{\neg b \wedge h}$$

A destruction sequence of T is $< (\delta_2, \delta_3), (\delta_4), (\delta_1, \delta_5) >$: (δ_2, δ_3) destroys the applicability of δ_1 via $\neg b$; (δ_4) destroys the applicability of δ_3, and (δ_1, δ_5) destroys the applicability of δ_4. This destruction sequence is also a destruction cycle since the basis default δ_1 occurs in the last process (δ_1, δ_5). In the following we prove that semi–normal, plain, ordered default theories do not possess destruction cycles.

Lemma 6.2 *Let M be a consistent, finite set of propositional logic formulae in clausal form. Let φ be a propositional logic formula in clausal form, and assume that M is minimal with the property that $M \models \neg\varphi$. Finally, let $\preceq$ be any transitive relation on the literals in $M \cup \{\varphi\}$ satisfying the following:*

$$\sim \chi_{uv} \preceq \chi_{uw} \text{ for all } v \neq w \text{ and all formulae } \chi \text{ in } M \cup \{\varphi\}.$$

Then: For all $\psi \in M$ there exists $\psi_{ij} \in Literals(\psi)$ and $\varphi_{kl} \in Literals(\varphi)$ such that $\psi_{ij} \preceq \sim \varphi_{kl}$ or $\psi_{ij} = \sim \varphi_{kl}$.

Proof: By the completeness of linear resolution and the consistency of M there must be a linear refutation of the form shown in Figure 6-1; in this figure, $R_1 \in \{\varphi_i \mid i > 0\}$ and $C_n \in \{\chi_k \mid \chi \in M \cup \{\varphi\}\} \cup \bigcup_{l \leq n} C_l$. Since M is assumed to be

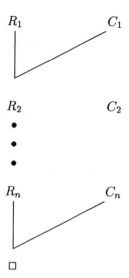

R_1 C_1

R_2 C_2

•

•

•

R_n C_n

□

Figure 6.1
A linear refutation

minimal with the property $M \models \neg\varphi$, there must be some ψ_i for each $\psi \in M$ such that $\psi_i \in \{C_1, \ldots, C_n\}$. The proof is completed by showing that for each C_i there is some C_{ij} and some φ_{kl} such that $C_{ij} \preceq \sim \varphi_{kl}$ or $C_{ij} = \sim \varphi_{kl}$.

The proof goes by induction on the height of the above deduction tree (i.e. on n). The base case is that R_1 is a literal L and C_1 the literal $\sim L$; the claim is trivial. Now assume that the claim has been proved for all $i < n$. Let L be the literal upon which C_n and R_n were resolved; let $L \in R_n$ and $\sim L \in C_n$. By the definition of resolvents, $L \in Literal(R_1)$ or $L \in Literal(C_i)$ for some $i < n$. In the first case we get immediately that $\sim L$ has the form $\sim \varphi_{uv}$.

Otherwise we apply induction hypothesis to C_i and conclude that there is a literal C_{ij} and some φ_{kl} such that $C_{ij} \preceq \sim \varphi_{kl}$ or $C_{ij} = \sim \varphi_{kl}$. By the main property of $\preceq$ we have $\sim L \preceq C_{ij}$ or $L = C_{ij}$. Putting everything together we conclude that for $\sim L \in Literals(C_n)$, $L \in Literals(\varphi)$ or $L \preceq \varphi_{kl}$ and we are finished. ∎

Lemma 6.3 Let $T = (W, D)$ be a semi–normal, plain default theory, and $\delta = \frac{\varphi:\psi\wedge\chi}{\chi}$ a default in D. Let $\delta' = \frac{\varphi':\psi'\wedge\chi'}{\chi'}$ be a default in a process Π_{des} occurring in $Des(\delta, T)$. Then there is a literal $\chi'_{kl} \in Literals(\chi')$ such that $\chi'_{kl} \prec \chi_{ij}$ for all $\chi_{ij} \in Literals(\chi)$.

Proof: Let W be consistent (otherwise the claim is trivial, as all processes are empty). $\Pi_{des} \in Des(\delta, T)$ means that Π_{des} is a minimal process of T such that $In(\Pi_{des}) \cup \{\chi\} \models (\neg\psi \vee \neg\chi)$ and $In(\Pi_{des}) \cup \{\chi\}$ is consistent. Therefore $In(\Pi_{des}) \models \neg\psi$.

We can split Π_{des} into two disjoint parts Π_1 and Π_2: Π_1 collects only the defaults that contribute to the deduction of $\neg\psi$, Π_2 collects the rest (by the minimality of Π_{des}, we know that defaults in Π_2 are necessary to apply some defaults in Π_1, i.e. to make Π_{des} a process).

1. case: δ' occurs in Π_1. We know: Π_1 is minimal with $In(\Pi_1) \models \neg\psi$. Applying lemma 6.2 we obtain the following:

> There exists $\chi'_{kl} \in Literals(\chi')$, $\psi_{ij} \in Literals(\psi)$ such that $\chi'_{kl} \preceq \sim \psi_{ij}$ or $\chi'_{kl} = \sim \psi_{ij}$.

2. case: δ' occurs in Π_2. By minimality of Π_{des} we know that there must be a default $\delta'' = \frac{\varphi'' : \psi'' \wedge \chi''}{\chi''}$ in Π_1 such that δ' is needed for the derivation of φ''. Applying lemma 6.2 we obtain

$$\chi'_{kl} \preceq \sim \varphi^*_{st} \text{ or } \chi'_{kl} = \sim \varphi^*_{st} \qquad (1)$$
(where φ^* is the formula $\neg\varphi''$ in clausal form; note that $\{\sim L \mid L \in Literals(\varphi^*)\} = Literals(\varphi'')$).

By definition of $\preceq$ we also know

$$\sim \varphi^*_{st} \preceq \chi''_{mn} \text{ for all } \chi''_{mn} \in Literals(\chi'') \qquad (2)$$

Finally, applying case 1 to δ'' we obtain

> There is $\chi''_{mn} \in Literals(\chi'')$ and $\psi_{ij} \in Literals(\psi)$ such that $\chi''_{mn} \preceq \sim \psi_{ij}$ or $\chi''_{mn} = \sim \psi_{ij}$. $\qquad (3)$

From (1), (2) and (3) we conclude as in the first case:

> There exists $\chi'_{kl} \in Literals(\chi')$, $\psi_{ij} \in Literals(\psi)$ such that $\chi'_{kl} \preceq \sim \psi_{ij}$ or $\chi'_{kl} = \sim \psi_{ij}$.

From the definition of the relation $\prec$ we know $\sim \psi_{ij} \prec \chi_{st}$ for all $\chi_{st} \in Literals(\chi)$. Using the definition of $\prec$ and $\preceq$ (clause 3), we finally derive $\chi'_{kl} \prec \chi_{st}$ for all $\chi_{st} \in Literals(\chi)$. ∎

Corollary 6.4 *A semi-normal, ordered, plain default theory T does not admit a destruction cycle.*

Proof: The previous lemma states that the relation $\prec$ is propagated through a destruction sequence. If a circularity occurs, e.g. if the basis default δ_1 occurs in Π_{des}^n, then $\chi_{ij} \prec \chi_{ij}$ for some literal χ_{ij} in the consequent of δ_1.   ∎

Theorem 6.5 (Existence of extensions) *A semi–normal, ordered, plain default theory has at least one extension.*

Proof: We construct a closed, successful process of T as follows:

```
T₀ := T;  i := 0;
W₀ := W;  D₀ := D;
WHILE
there is a nonempty, maximal (i.e.  not extendable)
destruction sequence < Π_des^{i1},…,Π_des^{ik_i} > of T_i
DO   W_{i+1}  := In(Π_des^{ik_i});
     D_{i+1}  := D_i - {δ_j | δ_j occurs in Π_des^{ik_i}};
     T_{i+1}  := (W_{i+1}, D_{i+1});
     i  := i+1
END;
Let Π̄ be a closed process of T_i;
Π := Π_des^{1k_1} ∘ Π_des^{2k_2} ∘ … ∘ Π_des^{i-1k_{i-1}} ∘ Π̄
```

The main idea in showing that Π is successful is the following: if we have a maximal (i.e. not extendable) destruction sequence $< \Pi^{1k_1} \dots, \Pi_{des}^{ik_i} >$ of T_i, then there is no default sequence that destroys the applicability of any default of $\Pi_{des}^{ik_i}$ at a later stage. Therefore, defaults appended to $\Pi_{des}^{ik_i}$ in the entire process Π do not destroy the applicability of the defaults in $\Pi_{des}^{ik_i}$. The proof of the theorem is completed by proving the following claims.

- *Claim 1:* All destruction sequences considered are finite.
- *Claim 2:* The above procedure terminates.
- *Claim 3:* After termination of the loop, $Des(\delta, T_i) = \emptyset$ for all $\delta \in D_i$.
- *Claim 4:* $\overline{\Pi}$ is successful.
- *Claim 5:* Π is a process of T.

- *Claim 6:* Π is successful.
- *Claim 7:* Π is closed under D.

Proof of Claim 1: D (and each D_i) is finite, therefore processes are always finite, and there exist finitely many different ones. If there were an infinite destruction sequence, then $\Pi^i_{des} = \Pi^j_{des}$ for some indices i, j. Then we would have a destruction cycle $< \Pi^i_{des}, \ldots, \Pi^j_{des} >$, thus contradicting corollary 6.4.

Proof of Claim 2: $|D_i| < |D_{i+1}|$ for all i such that $D_i \neq D_{i+1}$. The rest follows from the finiteness of D.

Proof of Claim 3: If $Des(\delta, T_i)$ is nonempty, then (by the maximality condition on the destruction sequence) there is a destruction cycle.

Proof of Claim 4: Suppose $\overline{\Pi}$ is failed. Then

$$W_i \cup \{cons(\delta_j) \mid \delta_j \text{ in } \overline{\Pi}\} \models \neg\psi_k \text{ for some } \delta_k = \frac{\varphi_k : \psi_k}{\psi_k} \text{ in } \overline{\Pi}.$$

This shows that $Des(\delta_k, T_i)$ is nonempty. Contradiction to Claim 3.

Proof of Claim 5: Follows immediately from the fact that W_{i+1} includes the consequents of the defaults from $\Pi^{i1}_{des}, \ldots, \Pi^{ik_i}_{des}$.

Proof of Claim 6: Suppose Π is not successful. Then

$$W \cup \{cons(\delta_j) \mid \delta_j \text{ in } \Pi\} \models \neg just(\delta) \text{ for some } \delta \text{ in } \Pi.$$

We know that $\overline{\Pi}$ is successful, so δ in not in $\overline{\Pi}$ but in some $\Pi^{nk_n}_{des}$. We have

$$W_n \cup \{cons(\delta_j) \mid \delta_j \text{ in } \Pi^{nk_n}_{des} \circ \ldots \circ \Pi^{i-1k_{i-1}}_{des} \circ \overline{\Pi}\} \models \neg just(\delta).$$

Therefore, $Des(\delta, T_n)$ is nonempty. But this contradicts the maximality of $\Pi^{nk_n}_{des}$ which was assumed in the condition of the WHILE loop.

Proof of Claim 7: Follows from the construction of T_j and the fact that $\overline{\Pi}$ is closed. $\blacksquare$

We conclude with an example illustrating the above procedure. Let T be the default theory (W, D) with $W = \emptyset$ and $D = \{\delta_1, \delta_2, \delta_3, \delta_4, \delta_5, \delta_6, \delta_7\}$ with

$$\delta_1 = \frac{true : a \wedge b}{b}, \delta_2 = \frac{true : d \wedge c}{c}, \delta_3 = \frac{c : \neg a}{\neg a}, \delta_4 = \frac{true : f}{f},$$

$$\delta_5 = \frac{f : \neg d}{\neg d}, \delta_6 = \frac{true : \neg a}{\neg a}, \delta_7 = \frac{true : g}{g}$$

1. Build a nonempty, maximal destruction sequence for $T_0 = T$

We have $(\delta_2, \delta_3) \in Des(\delta_1, T)$ and $(\delta_4, \delta_5) \in Des(\delta_2, T)$, whereas $Des(\delta_4, T)$ and $Des(\delta_5, T)$ are empty. Therefore, $< (\delta_2, \delta_3), (\delta_4, \delta_5) >$ is such a destruction sequence of T, and we 'save' (δ_4, δ_5) for the final process Π of T to be constructed.

2. Build a nonempty, maximal destruction sequence for the default theory $T_1 = (\{f, \neg d\}, \{\delta_1, \delta_2, \delta_3, \delta_6, \delta_7\})$

$(\delta_6) \in Des(\delta_1, T_1)$, and $Des(\delta_6, T_1)$ is empty, so $< (\delta_6) >$ is a destruction sequence we were looking for, and we save (δ_6) for further use.

3. Build a nonempty, maximal destruction sequence for the default theory $T_2 = (\{f, \neg d, \neg a\}, \{\delta_1, \delta_2, \delta_3, \delta_7\})$

There is no such destruction sequence.

4. Build a closed process of T_2

$\overline{\Pi} = (\delta_7)$

5. Build the entire process Π

$\Pi = (\delta_4, \delta_5, \delta_6, \delta_7)$. It is a closed, successful process of T, thus defining the extension $In(\Pi) = Th(\{f, \neg d, \neg a, g\})$ of T.

6.3 Translation into semi–normal form

Having seen that semi–normal defaults are well–suited to express desirable features of commonsense reasoning, it is interesting to ask for ways of translating more general defaults into this form. Here we present one such translation for defaults with one justification.

For a default $\delta = \frac{\varphi : \psi}{\chi}$ we define its *semi–normal transform* $\kappa(\delta)$ to be the semi–normal default $\frac{\varphi : \psi \wedge \chi}{\chi}$. For a default theory $T = (W, D)$ we define $\kappa(T) = (W, \{\kappa(\delta) \mid \delta \in D\})$. For a process $\Pi = (\delta_0, \delta_1, \ldots)$ of T define $\kappa(\Pi)$ to be the sequence of defaults $(\kappa(\delta_0), \kappa(\delta_1), \ldots)$.

The default $\kappa(\delta)$ is more cautious than δ: whereas δ checks consistency of ψ only, $\kappa(\delta)$ tests additionally for the consistency of its consequent. Indeed, if $\kappa(\delta)$ is not applicable whereas $\delta = \frac{\varphi : \psi}{\chi}$ is, then ψ is consistent with the current knowledge base and $\psi \wedge \chi$ is not. So, after application of δ, χ and the current knowledge, i.e. the new In–set, contradict ψ, the justification of δ, in which case we have run into a failed process. The following lemma shows that every consistent conclusion based on T can be maintained in $\kappa(T)$.

Lemma 6.6 *Let $T = (W, D)$ be a default theory such that all defaults in D have one justification, and let $\Pi = (\delta_0, \delta_1, \ldots)$ be a sequence of defaults in D without multiple occurrences.*

(a) *Π is a successful process of T iff $\kappa(\Pi)$ is a successful process of $\kappa(T)$.*

(b) *If Π is closed then $\kappa(\Pi)$ is closed, too.*

Proof*: (a): We note that $In(\Pi[i]) = In(\kappa(\Pi)[i])$ for all i (such that $\Pi[i]$ is defined) since δ and $\kappa(\delta)$ have the same consequent.

Let Π be a successful process of T. First we show that $\kappa(\Pi)$ is a process of $\kappa(T)$. Let $\delta_i = \frac{\varphi:\psi}{\chi}$; we shall show that $\kappa(\delta_i) = \frac{\varphi:\psi\wedge\chi}{\chi}$ is applicable to $In(\kappa(\Pi)[i]) = In(\Pi[i])$. $\varphi \in In(\Pi[i])$ because δ_i is applicable to $In(\Pi[i])$ (since Π is a process). Now assume that $\neg(\psi \wedge \chi) = \neg\psi \vee \neg\chi \in In(\Pi[i])$. Then $\neg\psi \vee \neg\chi \in In(\Pi)$. By definition we also know $\chi \in In(\Pi)$ (as the consequent of a default occurring in Π). So we obtain $\neg\psi \in In(\Pi)$. But we also have $\neg\psi \in Out(\Pi)$ (as a justification of a default occurring in Π). This shows that Π is not successful which is a contradiction.

Next we show that $\kappa(\Pi)$ is successful. Suppose that some element of $Out(\kappa(\Pi))$, say $\neg(\psi \wedge \chi)$ for a default $\frac{\varphi:\psi}{\chi}$ in Π, is included in $In(\kappa(\Pi)) = In(\Pi)$. Since $\chi \in In(\Pi)$ we conclude that $\neg\psi \in In(\Pi)$. Using $\neg\psi \in Out(\Pi)$ we get a contradiction to the assumption that Π is successful.

Conversely, suppose that $\kappa(\Pi)$ is a successful process of $\kappa(T)$. Let $\delta_i = \frac{\varphi:\psi}{\chi}$. Since $\kappa(\Pi)$ is a process we know $\varphi \in In(\kappa(\Pi)[i]) = In(\Pi[i])$ and $\neg\psi \vee \neg\chi \notin In(\Pi[i])$. Therefore $\neg\psi \notin In(\Pi)$, and δ_i is applicable to $In(\Pi[i])$.

Next we show that Π is successful. Assume that some element of $Out(\Pi)$, say $\neg\psi$ for a default $\frac{\varphi:\psi}{\chi}$, is included in $In(\Pi) = In(\kappa(\Pi))$. Then $\neg(\psi\wedge\chi) \in In(\kappa(\Pi))$. This contradicts the assumption that $\kappa(\Pi)$ be successful since $\neg(\psi \wedge \chi) \in Out(\kappa(\Pi))$.

(b): This is left as an exercise to the reader. ∎

Corollary 6.7 *Let T be a default theory in which all defaults have one justification. Then every extension of T is also an extension of $\kappa(T)$.*

So, $\kappa(T)$ has a smaller process tree but still has all the extensions of T. The following example shows that $\kappa(T)$ may possess more extensions than T. Consider $T = (W, D)$ with $W = \emptyset$ and $D = \{\delta_1 = \frac{true:p}{p}, \delta_2 = \frac{true:q}{\neg p}\}$. T has the only extension $Th(\{\neg p\})$, whereas $\kappa(T)$ has the additional extension $Th(\{p\})$. The reason is that after $\kappa(\delta_1)$ has been applied, the default $\kappa(\delta_2) = \frac{true:q\wedge\neg p}{\neg p}$ is not applicable and therefore does not lead to a failed process as δ_2 in T does. This example shows that the converse of claim (b) in lemma 6.6 is not true in general.

Finally let us note that another relationship between T and $\kappa(T)$ will be derived in section 7.2 when we introduce the concept of a *modified extension*. It will turn out that T and $\kappa(T)$ have the same modified extensions.

Problems

6-1. Consider the default theory $T = (W, D)$ with $W = \{q_i \rightarrow q_{i+1} \mid i \geq 0\} \cup \{q_i \rightarrow \neg p_{i+1} \mid i \geq 0\}$ and $D = \{\frac{true:q_i \wedge p_i}{p_i} \mid i \geq 0\}$.

   a) Show that the empty process of T is not closed.

   b) Show that any process of T which contains exactly one default is not closed.

   c) Show that any process of T containing exactly two defaults is failed.

   d) Conclude that T has no extension.

6-2. Prove part (b) of lemma 6.6.

6-3.* Show that the following equivalence is not true: Π is a process of T iff $\kappa(\Pi)$ is a process of $\kappa(T)$.

6-4.* The transformation presented in section 6.3 and the results drawn suggest that semi–normal default theories can adequately model any commonsense setting that can be expressed in terms of defaults *with one justification only*. The question arises whether more than one justification are necessary at all.

   a) Give an informal argument why a default with two justifications (*Hint:* $p, \neg p$) might be reasonable.

   b) Prove the following: there is a default $\delta = \frac{\varphi:\psi_1,\psi_2}{\chi}$ such that there exists no default $\delta' = \frac{\varphi':\psi'}{\chi'}$ with the property

   δ is applicable to E w.r.t. F iff δ' is applicable to E w.r.t. F, for all sets of formulae E and F.

Chapter 7

Alternative Approaches

In this chapter we take a critical look at Default Logic; in particular we look at some properties which are controversial. Some of these properties can be interpreted as deficiencies, or they highlight some of Reiter's original 'design decisions' and show alternative ideas that could be followed instead. In this sense the discussion section 7.1 motivates alternative approaches that will be presented in subsequent sections. One point that should be stressed is that there is not a 'correct' default logic approach, but rather the most appropriate for the concrete problem at hand. Different intuitions lead to different approaches that may work better for some applications and worse for others.

One problem (or property), namely the possibility that a default theory does not have any extensions, was identified in Chapter 4 and was a driving force behind many considerations in the previous chapters. Further properties are identified in section 7.1, one of them being *non–commitment to justifications*. Consider, for example, the default theory T consisting only of the defaults

$$\frac{true : p}{q}, \frac{true : \neg p}{r}.$$

T has the single extension $E = Th(\{q, r\})$. The set of assumptions that were used to compute this extension consists of p and $\neg p$, so it is inconsistent. Of course, it may be argued that it is not unintuitive to assume both p and $\neg p$ even within one logical argument, as long as nothing concerning p is known. But we show in section 7.1 that this approach may lead to undesirable conclusions.

Several variants of Default Logic have been proposed as alternatives to Reiter's approach; we present two of them in this chapter. In section 7.2 we introduce a modified concept of extensions, and show that the existence of such extensions is always guaranteed. The main purpose of this approach is to avoid running into failed processes.

In section 7.3 we introduce *Constrained Default Logic* which respects the commitment to justifications. This is achieved by enforcing *joint consistency* of the justifications of defaults involved in a process.

Section 7.4 discusses some interconnections between the various default logic variations and gives more examples. Finally section 7.5 presents some results from the complexity and computability point of view. It turns out that default reasoning is harder than classical reasoning; this is primarily due to the necessity of consistency checks when defaults are tested for application.

7.1 Properties of Default Logic

7.1.1 Existence of extensions

We saw that a default theory may not have any extensions. Is this a shortcoming of Default Logic? One might hold the view that if the default theory includes 'nonsense' (for example $\frac{true:p}{\neg p}$), then the logic should indeed be allowed to provide no answer. According to this view, it is up to the user to provide meaningful information in the form of meaningful facts and defaults; after all, if a program contains an error, we don't blame the programming language.

The opposite view regards nonexistence of extensions as a drawback, and would prefer a more 'fault–tolerant' logic; one which works even if some pieces of information are deficient. This viewpoint is supported by the trend towards heterogeneous information sources, where it is not easy to identify which source is responsible for the deficiency, or where the single pieces of information are meaningful, but lead to problems when put together.

A more technical argument in favour of the second view is the concept of *semi–monotonicity*. Default Logic is a method for performing nonmonotonic reasoning, so we cannot expect it to be monotonic when new knowledge is added to the set of facts. Nevertheless, we would expect that the addition of new defaults would yield more, and not less information. As we saw in section 5.2, the well–behaved part of Default Logic, namely normal default theories, respects semi–monotonicity, while arbitrary default theories do not necessarily. Even though the concept of semi-monotonicity is not equivalent to the existence of extensions, these two properties usually come together.

If we adopt the view that the possible nonexistence of extensions is a problem, then there are two alternative solutions. The first one consists in restricting attention to those classes of default theories for which the existence of extensions is guaranteed. In fact this has been the driving force in Chapters 5 and 6.

Instead of imposing restrictions on the form of defaults in order to guarantee the existence of extensions, the other principle way is to modify the concept of an extension in such a way that all default theories have at least an extension, and that semi–monotonicity is guaranteed. We will discuss two important variants with these properties, Lukaszewicz' Justified Default Logic and Schaub's Constrained Default Logic.

7.1.2   Joint consistency of justifications

It is easy to see that the default theory consisting of the defaults $\frac{true:p}{q}$ and $\frac{true:\neg p}{r}$ has the single extension $Th(\{q, r\})$. This shows that the *joint consistency* of justifications is not required. Justifications are *not* supposed to form a set of supporting beliefs, rather they are used to sanction 'jumping' into conclusions.

This design decision is natural and makes sense for many cases, but for others it may lead to unintuitive results. As an example consider the default theory, due to Poole, which says that, by default, a robot's arm (say a or b) is usable unless it is broken; further we know that either a or b is broken. Given this information, we would not expect both a and b to be usable.

Let us see how Default Logic treats this example. Consider the default theory $T = (W, D)$ with $W = \{broken(a) \vee broken(b)\}$ and D consisting of the defaults

$$\frac{true : usable(a) \wedge \neg broken(a)}{usable(a)}, \quad \frac{true : usable(b) \wedge \neg broken(b)}{usable(b)}.$$

Since we do not have definite information that a is broken we may apply the first default and obtain $E' = Th(W \cup \{usable(a)\})$. Since E' does not include $broken(b)$ or $\neg usable(b)$ we may apply the second default and get $Th(W \cup \{usable(a), usable(b)\})$ as an extension of T. This result is undesirable, as we know that either a or b is broken.

In section 7.3 we shall discuss Constrained Default Logic as a prototypical default logic approach that enforces joint consistency of justifications of defaults involved in an extension.

The joint consistency property gives up part of the expressive power of default theories: under this property any default with several justifications $\frac{\varphi:\psi_1,...,\psi_n}{\chi}$ is equivalent to the modified default $\frac{\varphi:\psi_1 \wedge ... \wedge \psi_n}{\chi}$ which has one justification. This is in contrast to the fact that in Reiter's Default Logic, defaults with several justifications are strictly more expressive than defaults with just one justification (see problem 6.4). Essentially, in default logics adopting joint consistency it is impossible to express default rules of the form 'In case I am ignorant about p (meaning that I know neither p nor $\neg p$) I conclude q'. The natural representation in default form would be $\frac{true:p,\neg p}{q}$, but this default can never be applied if joint consistency is required, because its justifications contradict one another; on the other hand it is applicable in the sense of Reiter's Default Logic.

Another example for which joint consistency of justifications is undesirable is the following[1]. When I prepare for a trip then I use the following default rules:

If I may assume that the weather will be bad I'll take my sweater.

If I may assume that the weather will be good then I'll take my swimsuit.

In the absence of any reliable information about the weather I am cautious enough to take both with me. But note that I am not building a consistent belief set upon which I make these decisions; obviously the assumptions of the default rules contradict each other. So Reiter's default logic will treat this example in the intended way whereas joint consistency of justifications will prevent me from taking both my sweater and my swimsuit with me.

7.1.3   Cumulativity and Lemmas

Cumulativity is, informally speaking, the property that allows for the safe use of lemmas. Formally: Let D be a fixed, countable set of defaults. For a formula φ and a set of formulae W we define $W \vdash_D \varphi$ iff φ is included in all extensions of the default theory (W, D). Now, cumulativity is the following property:

$$If\ W \vdash_D \varphi,\ then\ for\ all\ \psi:\ W \vdash_D \psi \Longleftrightarrow W \cup \{\varphi\} \vdash_D \psi.$$

If we interpret φ as a lemma, cumulativity says that the same formulae can be obtained from W as from $W \cup \{\varphi\}$. This is the standard basis of using lemmas in, say, mathematics. Default logic does not respect cumulativity: consider $T = (W, D)$ with $W = \emptyset$ and D consisting of the defaults

$$\frac{true : a}{a}, \quad \frac{a \vee b : \neg a}{\neg a}$$

(this example is due to Makinson). The only extension of T is $Th(\{a\})$. Obviously, $W \vdash_D a$. From $a \vee b \in Th(\{a\})$ we get $W \vdash_D a \vee b$. If we take $W' = \{a \vee b\}$, then the default theory (W', D) has two extensions, $Th(\{a\})$ and $Th(\{\neg a, b\})$; therefore $W \cup \{a \vee b\} \not\vdash_D a$.

One might argue that the property is rather unintuitive because it requires a *defeasible* conclusion which was based on some assumptions to be represented by a *certain* piece of information, that means a fact, and yet exhibit the same behaviour.

---

[1]My thanks go to an anonymous referee.

From the practical point of view the really important issue is whether we are able to represent and use lemmas in a safe way. In section 7.3 we show that lemmas in Constrained Default Logic can be represented as *defaults* (rather than facts), and this representation works properly. In problem 7-15 it is shown that the same idea works for Reiter's Default Logic.

7.2   Justified Default Logic

After we recognized the problem with the nonexistence of extensions in Chapter 4, we tried to overcome this difficulty by restricting the class of default theories considered, as done in Chapters 5 and 6. In this and the next section we take an alternative approach: we consider all classes of default theories but modify the definition of an extension in such a way that the existence of extensions is always guaranteed.

An additional justification of the alternative extension concepts we shall present is that they can lead to more intuitive conclusions than the extension concept we have been using so far. For example, consider the following piece of information:

Usually I go fishing on Sundays unless I wake up late.
When I am on holidays I usually wake up late.

Suppose it is Sunday and I am on holidays. Then, of course, both default rules cannot be applied in conjunction. Instead we would expect two alternative possibilities, depending on whether I wake up late or not. The information above is expressed by the default theory $T = (W, D)$ with $W = \{holidays, sunday\}$ and D consisting of the defaults

$$\delta_1 = \frac{sunday : goFishing \land \neg wakeUpLate}{goFishing}, \quad \delta_2 = \frac{holidays : wakeUpLate}{wakeUpLate}.$$

It is easily seen that T has only one extension, namely $Th(\{holidays, sunday, wakeUpLate\})$. The other expected outcome, $Th(\{holidays, sunday, goFishing\})$ is not an extension because it is not closed under application of defaults in D: δ_2 can be applied and leads to a failed process. The technical definition presented below aims at avoiding this 'destruction' of a previously constructed In–set.

Let T be a default theory, and let Π and Γ be processes of T. We define $\Pi < \Gamma$ iff the set of defaults occurring in Π is a proper subset of the defaults occurring in Γ. Π is called a *maximal process of T*, iff Π is successful and there is no successful process Γ such that $\Pi < \Gamma$. A set of formulae E is called a *modified extension* of T iff there is a maximal process Π of T such that $E = In(\Pi)$.

In the example above $\Pi = (\delta_1)$ is a maximal process: the only process that strictly includes Π is $\Gamma = (\delta_1, \delta_2)$, but it is not successful. Since every maximal process is successful, it is interesting to determine the relationship between maximal processes, and closed and successful processes, i.e. the extensions of T.

Theorem 7.1 *Every closed and successful process of default theory T is a maximal process of T. Therefore, every extension of T is a modified extension of T.*

Proof: Let $\Pi = (\delta_0, \delta_1, \ldots)$ be a closed and successful process of T, and suppose that Π is not maximal. Then there is a successful process $\Gamma = (\gamma_0, \gamma_1, \ldots)$ of T such that $\{\delta_0, \delta_1, \ldots\} \subset \{\gamma_0, \gamma_1, \ldots\}$. Let i be the smallest index such that $\gamma_i = \frac{\varphi : \psi_1, \ldots, \psi_n}{\chi}$ does not occur in Π. $\varphi \in In(\Gamma[i]) \subseteq In(\Pi)$ (by the choice of i). $\{\neg\psi_1, \ldots, \neg\psi_n\} \subseteq Out(\Gamma)$, therefore $\neg\psi_1 \notin In(\Gamma), \ldots, \neg\psi_n \notin In(\Gamma)$ because Γ is successful. Since $In(\Pi) \subseteq In(\Gamma)$ we obtain $\neg\psi_1 \notin In(\Pi), \ldots, \neg\psi_n \notin In(\Pi)$. So we have established that γ_i is applicable to $In(\Pi)$. Since γ_i was defined not to occur in Π, we have a contradiction to Π being closed. ∎

The converse of this result is not true, as shown by the following example. Consider $T = (W, D)$ with $W = \emptyset$ and $D = \{\delta_1 = \frac{true:p}{\neg q}, \delta_2 = \frac{true:q}{r}\}$. There are two closed processes of T, $\Pi_1 = (\delta_1)$ and $\Pi_2 = (\delta_2, \delta_1)$. Π_1 is also successful, so $In(\Pi_1) = Th(\{\neg q\})$ is an extension of T, but Π_2 is failed. On the other hand, there are two maximal processes of T, (δ_1) as predicted by theorem 7.1, and (δ_2). Therefore T has two modified extensions, $Th(\{\neg q\})$ and $Th(\{r\})$.

Given that a process Π is successful, the difference between Π being closed and Π being maximal is the following: in the former case Π must be closed under application of all defaults, however the maximality concept requires Π to be closed only under the application of defaults *which preserve success*. In the example above, δ_1 is applicable to $Th(\{r\})$, but its application would lead to a failed process. Therefore δ_1 is disregarded and (δ_2) is a maximal process.

With this in mind, it is not surprising that the existence of modified extensions is always guaranteed. It is instructive to look at the 'classical' default theory without an extension, $T = (W, D)$ with $W = \emptyset$ and $D = \{\frac{true:p}{\neg p}\}$. The empty process is maximal (though not closed), because the application of the 'strange default' would lead to a failed process. It is left as an easy exercise to the reader to prove the following result.

Theorem 7.2 (Existence of modified extensions) *Every default theory has at least one modified extension.*

Whenever the default theory is normal, the application of a default can never lead to a failed process. Therefore, maximality and closure of a process are equivalent concepts.

Theorem 7.3 *Let T be a normal default theory. Then E is an extension of T iff E is a modified extension of T.*

Let us for the moment look back at section 6.3. There we presented a translation of defaults $\delta = \frac{\varphi:\psi}{\chi}$ to semi–normal defaults $\kappa(\delta) = \frac{\varphi:\psi\wedge\chi}{\chi}$. It turned out that the extensions of T are also extensions of $\kappa(T)$ but not vice–versa. The intention of translating arbitrary defaults into semi–normal form was to avoid running into failed processes. The idea behind the definition of modified extensions is similar. In fact, the relationship between both approaches is established by the following result.

Theorem 7.4 *Let $T = (W, D)$ be a default theory such that all defaults in D have one justification. Then T and $\kappa(T)$ have the same modified extensions.*

Proof*:   Let Π be a maximal process of T, and suppose that $\kappa(\Pi)$ is not a maximal process of $\kappa(T)$. By lemma 6.6 we know that $\kappa(\Pi)$ is successful. Therefore there must be a successful process Γ' of $\kappa(T)$ such that $\kappa(\Pi) < \Gamma'$. By lemma 6.6 Γ' has the form $\kappa(\Gamma)$ for a successful process Γ of T. Obviously, $\Pi < \Gamma$ which contradicts the maximality of Π.

Conversely, let $\kappa(\Pi)$ be a maximal process of $\kappa(T)$ (by lemma 6.6 this is the only possibility of a successful process of $\kappa(T)$), and suppose that Π is not a maximal process of T. By lemma 6.6 we know that Π is successful. Therefore there must be a successful process Γ of T with $\Pi < \Gamma$. Hence $\kappa(\Pi) < \kappa(\Gamma)$, and $\kappa(\Gamma)$ is successful by lemma 6.6. Thus we have a contradiction to the maximality of $\kappa(\Pi)$.   ∎

We note that the process tree for Default Logic can be used for Justified Default Logic, too. Maximal processes correspond either to closed and successful nodes, or to nodes n such that all immediate children of n are failed.

We conclude this section by giving an alternative characterization of modified extensions. This characterization is the original definition given by Lukaszewicz. It is based on fixed–point equations and is thus difficult to apply to concrete examples. Let $T = (W, D)$ be a default theory, and E, F, E' and F' sets of formulae. We say that a default $\delta = \frac{\varphi : \psi_1, \ldots, \psi_n}{\chi}$ is *applicable to* E' *with respect to* E *and* F iff $\varphi \in E'$ and $E \cup \{\chi\} \not\models \neg\psi$ for all $\psi \in F \cup \{\psi_1, \ldots, \psi_n\}$.

E' and F' are *closed under* the application of defaults in D *with respect to* E *and* F iff, whenever a default $\delta = \frac{\varphi : \psi_1, \ldots, \psi_n}{\chi}$ in D is applicable to E' with respect to E and F, $\chi \in E'$ and $\{\psi_1, \ldots, \psi_n\} \subseteq F'$.

Define $\Lambda_T^1(E, F)$ and $\Lambda_T^2(E, F)$ to be the smallest sets of formulae such that $\Lambda_T^1(E, F)$ is deductively closed, $W \subseteq \Lambda_T^1(E, F)$, and $\Lambda_T^1(E, F)$ and $\Lambda_T^2(E, F)$ are closed under D with respect to E and F.

The following theorem shows that modified extensions correspond exactly to sets E and F satisfying the fixed–point equations $E = \Lambda_T^1(E, F)$ and $F = \Lambda_T^2(E, F)$. This is not surprising: intuitively, the idea behind the complicated definition of the Λ–operators is to maintain the set of justifications of defaults that have been applied (i.e. the sets F and F' which, in fact, correspond to $\neg Out(\Pi)$), and to avoid applications of defaults if they lead to an inconsistency with one of these justifications. Our approach of using processes where the Out–set contains the justifications, and requiring maximality to avoid inconsistencies, follows similar ideas although it is technically simpler.

Theorem 7.5 *Let T be a default theory. For every modified extension E of T there is a set of formulae F such that $E = \Lambda_T^1(E, F)$ and $F = \Lambda_T^2(E, F)$.*

Conversely, let E and F be sets of formulae such that $E = \Lambda_T^1(E, F)$ and $F = \Lambda_T^2(E, F)$. Then E is a modified extension of T.

The proof of this theorem is tedious, but analogous to the proof of theorem 4.4. Therefore it is left to the reader as an exercise.

7.3   Constrained Default Logic

The approach of the previous section avoids running into inconsistencies and can therefore guarantee the existence of modified extensions. On the other hand, it does not commit to default justifications. The default theory $T = (W, D)$ with $W = \emptyset$ and $D = \{\frac{true:p}{q}, \frac{true:\neg p}{r}\}$ has the modified extension $Th(\{q, r\})$. In order to avoid this kind of reasoning we have to ensure the *joint consistency* of all justifications involved in a process; this is the main idea of *Constrained Default Logic* (*CDL*). According to this approach, after the application of the first default in the example above, the second default may not be applied because $\{p, \neg p\}$ is inconsistent.

Furthermore, since the justifications are consistent with each other, we test the consistency of their conjunction with the current knowledge base. In the terminology of processes, we require the consistency of $In(\Pi) \cup \neg Out(\Pi)$.

Finally, we adopt the idea from the previous section, namely a default may only be applied if it does not lead to a contradiction a posteriori. That means, if $\frac{\varphi : \psi_1, \ldots, \psi_n}{\chi}$ is tested for application to a process Π, then $In(\Pi) \cup \neg Out(\Pi) \cup \{\psi_1, \ldots, \psi_n, \chi\}$ must be consistent. We note that the set Out no longer makes sense since we require joint consistency. Instead we have to maintain the set of formulae which consists of W, all consequents *and all justifications* of the defaults that have been applied.

- Given a default theory $T = (W, D)$ and a sequence Π of defaults in D without multiple occurrences, we define $Con(\Pi) = Th(W \cup \{\varphi \mid \varphi$ is the consequent or a justification of a default occurring in $\Pi\})$. Sometimes we refer to $Con(\Pi)$ as the *set of constraints* or the *set of supporting beliefs*.

$Con(\Pi)$ represents the set of beliefs supporting Π. For the default theory $T = (W, D)$ with $W = \emptyset$ and $D = \{\delta_1 = \frac{true : p}{q}, \delta_2 = \frac{true : \neg p}{r}\}$ let $\Pi_1 = (\delta_1)$. Then $Con(\Pi_1) = Th(\{p, q\})$.

We say that a default $\delta = \frac{\varphi : \psi_1, \ldots, \psi_n}{\chi}$ *is applicable* to a pair of deductively closed sets of formulae (E, C) iff $\varphi \in E$ and $\psi_1 \wedge \ldots \wedge \psi_n \wedge \chi$ is consistent with C. A pair (E, C) of deductively closed sets of formulae is called *closed under* D if, for every default $\frac{\varphi : \psi_1, \ldots, \psi_n}{\chi} \in D$ that is applicable to (E, C), $\chi \in E$ and $\{\psi_1, \ldots, \psi_n, \chi\} \subseteq C$.

In the example above, δ_2 is not applicable to $(In(\Pi_1), Con(\Pi_1)) = (Th(\{q\}), Th(\{p, q\}))$ because $\{\neg p \wedge r\} \cup Th(\{p, q\})$ is inconsistent.

Let $\Pi = (\delta_0, \delta_1, \ldots)$ be a sequence of defaults in D without multiple occurrences.

- Π is a *constrained process* of the default theory $T = (W, D)$ iff, for all k such that $\Pi[k]$ is defined, δ_k is applicable to $(In(\Pi[k]), Con(\Pi[k]))$.

- A *closed constrained process* Π is a constrained process such that every default δ which is applicable to $(In(\Pi), Con(\Pi))$ already occurs in Π.

- A pair of sets of formulae (E, C) is a *constrained extension of* T iff there is a closed constrained process Π of T such that $(E, C) = (In(\Pi), Con(\Pi))$.

Note that we do not need a concept of success here because of the definition of default applicability we adopted: δ is only applicable to (E, C) if it does not lead to a contradiction. The following observation follows directly from the definitions: the consistency checks required in a constrained process are stronger than those required in a process (in the sense of the usual Default Logic), while the default prerequisites are treated in the same way.

Lemma 7.6 *Let T be a default theory. Every constrained process of T is a successful process of T. Conversely, every process Π of T such that $In(\Pi) \cup \neg Out(\Pi)$ is consistent, is a constrained process of T.*

Let us reconsider the 'broken arms' example: $T = (W, D)$ with $W = \{broken(a) \vee broken(b)\}$, and D consisting of the defaults

$$\delta_1 = \frac{true : usable(a) \wedge \neg broken(a)}{usable(a)}, \delta_2 = \frac{true : usable(b) \wedge \neg broken(b)}{usable(b)}.$$

It is easily seen that there are two closed constrained processes, (δ_1) and (δ_2), leading to two constrained extensions:

$(Th(W \cup \{usable(a)\}), Th(\{broken(b), usable(a), \neg broken(a)\}))$, and
$(Th(W \cup \{usable(b)\}), Th(\{broken(a), usable(b), \neg broken(b)\}))$.

The effect of the definitions above is that it is impossible to apply both defaults together: after the application of, say, δ_1, $\neg broken(a)$ is included in the Con-set; together with $broken(a) \vee broken(b)$ it follows $broken(b)$, therefore δ_2 is blocked. The two alternative constrained extensions describe the two possible cases we would have intuitively expected.

For another example consider $T = (W, D)$ with $W = \{p\}$ and $D = \{\frac{p : \neg r}{q}, \frac{p : r}{r}\}$. T has two constrained extensions, $(Th(\{p, q\}), Th(\{p, q, \neg r\}))$ and $(Th(\{p, r\}), Th(\{p, r\}))$. Note that for both constrained extensions, the second component collects the assumptions supporting the first component.

So CDL commits to justifications. Apart from that, CDL has further advantages as a knowledge representation method:

- Default theories always possess constrained extensions.

- Constrained Default Logic is semi–monotonic.

- CDL satisfies the following orthogonality property: if (E, C) and (E', C') are different constrained extensions of a default theory T, then $C \cup C'$ is inconsistent.

The proofs of these results are left to the reader as exercises (see problems 7-7 – 7-9). The underlying technical reason for these desirable properties is that there does not exist any failed constrained process; the proofs are straightforward adaptions of the proofs of similar results for normal default theories given in Chapter 5.

Finally we turn our attention to cumulativity. For a countable set D of defaults we define $W \vdash_D \varphi$ iff, for all constrained extensions (E, C) of (W, D), $\varphi \in E$. CDL does not respect cumulativity of $\vdash_D$, and we may use the same counterexample as for Default Logic. Consider the default theory $T = (W, D)$ with $W = \emptyset$ and D consisting of the defaults

$$\frac{true : a}{a}, \quad \frac{a \vee b : \neg a}{\neg a}.$$

T has only the constrained extension $(Th(\{a\}), Th(\{a\}))$, so $W \vdash_D a$. In addition, from $a \vee b \in Th(\{a\})$ we get $W \vdash_D a \vee b$. If we take $W' = \{a \vee b\}$, then the default theory (W', D) has two constrained extensions, $(Th(W' \cup \{a\}), Th(W' \cup \{a\}))$ and $(Th(W' \cup \{\neg a\}), Th(W' \cup \{\neg a\}))$; obviously, $W' \not\vdash_D a$.

What went wrong in this example? In particular, what is the difference between $a \vee b$ being included in W and $a \vee b$ being derived by the first default? Well, in the former case, the set of constraints is still empty, whereas in the latter case it contains a. This difference is crucial: in the former case $\frac{a \vee b : \neg a}{\neg a}$ can be applied, however in the latter case it is blocked.

So, when adding a formula ξ to the set of axioms, we must also take care to 'store' the assumptions that led to the deduction of ξ. The correct place would be the Con–set associated with the constrained processes, but this is impossible because according to the definition we gave, $Con(()) = Th(W)$, where $()$ is the empty process. One possibility to overcome this difficulty is to define another variant of CDL (see problem 7-11).

Another way is to represent a lemma as a default. As we said above, it is insufficient to consider a *lemma* as a formula ξ only; we must also take into consideration the set of assumptions J that led to its derivation. Using a default δ to represent the lemma, we take ξ as the consequent of δ, and the conjunction of all formulae in J as the justification of δ; the default will be prerequisite–free. This lemma representation has the additional advantage that it appeals to our intuition: a lemma that is derived using default consequents *is defeasible in nature* and should be represented as such. We formalize this idea below.

Let $T = (W, D)$ be a default theory. A formula ξ is a *lemma* of T if there is a constrained extension (E, C) of T such that $\xi \in E$. Let Γ_ξ be a minimal constrained process of T such that $\xi \in In(\Gamma_\xi)$; by the compactness of predicate logic Γ_ξ is finite. Let $M_\xi = \{\varphi \mid \varphi$ is the consequent or a justification of a default in $\Gamma_\xi\}$. We say that the default

$$\delta_\xi = \frac{true : \bigwedge_{\varphi \in M_\xi} \varphi}{\xi}$$

is *associated with* ξ. The following theorem shows that adding δ_ξ to a default theory T (for a lemma ξ of T) does not alter the constrained extensions of T. Informally, the reason is that the presence of δ_ξ in a closed constrained process enforces the presence of all defaults of Γ_ξ in that constrained process, without providing any new information (remember that $\xi \in In(\Gamma_\xi)$).

Theorem 7.7 (Lemma Handling) *Let* $T = (W, D)$ *be a default theory, and* ξ *a lemma of* T. (E, C) *is a constrained extension of* T *iff it is a constrained extension of* $T' = (W, D \cup \{\delta_\xi\})$.

Proof*: Let (E, C) be a constrained extension of T, and Π a closed constrained process of T such that $(E, C) = (In(\Pi), Con(\Pi))$. Suppose that (E, C) is not a constrained extension of T'. The only possibility for this is that δ_ξ is applicable to (E, C) and $\xi \notin E$. By the applicability of δ_ξ to (E, C) we know that $M_\xi \cup C$ is consistent. Then $M_\xi \cup Con(\Pi)$ is also consistent.

Now we show that all defaults in $\Gamma_\xi = (\gamma_0, \dots, \gamma_m)$ occur in Π. Suppose this were not the case, and let i be the least number such that $\gamma_i = \frac{\varphi : \psi_1, \dots, \psi_n}{\chi}$ does not occur in Π. $\{\psi_1, \dots, \psi_n, \chi\} \cup Con(\Pi)$ is consistent because $M_\xi \cup Con(\Pi)$ is consistent. Also, $\varphi \in In(\Gamma[i]) \subseteq In(\Pi)$ (by the choice of i). So we have established that γ_i is applicable to $(In(\Pi), Con(\Pi))$ which is a contradiction to Π being closed. From $In(\Gamma_\xi) \subseteq In(\Pi)$ and $\xi \in In(\Gamma_\xi)$ we get $\xi \in In(\Pi) = E$ which contradicts our assumption.

Conversely, let (E, C) be a constrained extension of T', and let $\Pi = (\delta_0, \delta_1, \dots)$ be a closed constrained process of T' such that $(E, C) = (In(\Pi), Con(\Pi))$. If δ_ξ does not occur in Π then Π is a closed constrained process of T and we are finished. Otherwise $M_\xi \cup Con(\Pi)$ is consistent. It follows (as shown above) that all defaults in $\Gamma_\xi = (\gamma_0, \dots, \gamma_m)$ occur in Π.

Now we define $\Pi' = (\delta'_0, \delta'_1, \dots)$ to be the following permutation of the defaults in Π except for δ_ξ: the beginning sequence of Π' is Γ_ξ, the other defaults remain in their old order. Formally:

$$\delta'_i = \begin{cases} \gamma_i & \text{for } i \leq m \\ \delta_{j(i)} & \text{otherwise} \end{cases}$$

where $j(i)$ is the smallest number j such that $\delta_j \neq \delta_\xi$ and δ_j does not occur in $\Pi'[i]$. By definition, $In(\Pi') = In(\Pi)$ and $Con(\Pi') = Con(\Pi)$ (note that δ_ξ does not contribute anything new when Γ_ξ is included in a constrained process). So, $(E, C) = (In(\Pi'), Con(\Pi'))$.

We conclude the proof by showing that Π' is a closed constrained process of T. Π' contains only defaults from D; the closure property is inherited from Π. Finally, joint consistency of the consequents and justifications of all defaults in Π' is inherited from Π. So we must only show that the defaults can be applied in the given order.

For $i \leq m$, δ_i' is applicable to $(In(\Pi'[i]), Con(\Pi'[i]))$ because Γ_ξ is a constrained process of T. For $i > m$ let δ_i' be the default δ_j. By construction, for all $k < j$ there is $l < i$ such that $\delta_k = \delta_l'$ (for $\delta_k \neq \delta_\xi$). Furthermore, $\xi \in In(\Pi'[i])$ by the definition of Π', since $i > m$. Therefore $In(\Pi[j]) \subseteq In(\Pi'[i])$. δ_j is applicable to $(In(\Pi[j]), Con(\Pi))$, therefore δ_i' is applicable to $(In(\Pi'[i]), Con(\Pi'[i]))$. ∎

7.4 Interconnections and examples

Let us now establish some relationships between constrained extensions and the other extension concepts we have seen so far. The following result is a straightforward implication of lemma 7.6.

Theorem 7.8 *Let T be a default theory and $E = In(\Pi)$ an extension of T, where Π is a closed and successful process of T. If $E \cup \neg Out(\Pi)$ is consistent, then $(E, Th(E \cup \neg Out(\Pi)))$ is a constrained extension of T.*

The converse does not hold since the existence of an extension is not guaranteed. For example $T = (\emptyset, \{\frac{true:p}{\neg p}\})$ has the single constrained extension $(Th(\emptyset), Th(\emptyset))$, but no extension.

Theorem 7.9 *Let T be a default theory and $E = In(\Pi)$ a modified extension of T, where Π is a maximal process of T. If $E \cup \neg Out(\Pi)$ is consistent, then $(E, Th(E \cup \neg Out(\Pi)))$ is a constrained extension of T.*

Proof*: By lemma 7.6, if $E \cup \neg Out(\Pi)$ is consistent then Π is a constrained process of T. Suppose Π is not a closed constrained process of T. Then there must exist a default $\delta = \frac{\varphi:\psi_1,...,\psi_n}{\chi}$ which is applicable to $(In(\Pi), Con(\Pi))$ and does not occur in Π. Then

$$\varphi \in In(\Pi) \text{ and } \{\psi_1, \ldots, \psi_n, \chi\} \cup Con(\Pi) \text{ is consistent.} \tag{$*$}$$

Since $In(\Pi) \subseteq Con(\Pi)$, we obtain that $In(\Pi) \cup \{\psi_i\}$ is consistent, for all $i \in \{1, \ldots, n\}$. This shows that δ is applicable to $In(\Pi)$. Furthermore, $(*)$ implies that $Th(In(\Pi) \cup \{\chi\}) \cup \{\psi_i\}$ is consistent, for all $i \in \{1, \ldots, n\}$. This contradicts the maximality of Π: if Π is finite simply add δ at the end of Π. If Π is infinite, apply δ the first time it becomes applicable[2], and then apply the remaining defaults of Π. In both cases, the new process is successful and includes more defaults than Π, contradicting the maximality of Π.   ∎

The example $T = (W, D)$ with $W = \emptyset$ and $D = \{\frac{true:p}{q}, \frac{true:\neg p}{r}\}$ shows that we cannot expect the first component of a constrained extension to be a modified extension: T has the single modified extension $Th(\{q, r\})$, but possesses two constrained extensions, $(Th(\{q\}), Th(\{p, q\}))$ and $(Th(\{r\}), Th(\{\neg p, r\}))$. As the following result demonstrates, it is not accidental that for both constrained extensions, the first component is included in the modified extension.

Theorem 7.10 *Let T be a default theory and (E, C) a constrained extension of T. Then there is a modified extension F of T such that $E \subseteq F$.*

Proof: Let Π be a closed constrained process of T such that $(E, C) = (In(\Pi), Con(\Pi))$. By lemma 7.6 Π is a successful process of T. If Π is a maximal process we are finished. Otherwise there is a maximal process Π' of T such that $\Pi < \Pi'$ (see problem 7-12). Then $E = In(\Pi)$ is contained in the modified extension $In(\Pi')$ of T.   ∎

Let us now look at some more examples, taken from a paper by Delgrande *et al.* Let $T = (W, D)$ with $W = \{p\}$ and $D = \{\frac{p:q \wedge \neg r}{q}, \frac{p:r}{r}\}$. T has the single extension $Th(\{p, r\})$, two modified extensions $Th(\{p, r\})$ and $Th(\{p, q\})$, and two constrained extensions, $(Th(\{p, q\}), Th(\{p, q, \neg r\}))$ and $(Th(\{p, r\}), Th(\{p, r\}))$. In the case of Default Logic, the application of the second default after the first one leads to a failed process, therefore there is just one extension. When computing modified extensions, we avoid destroying the success of a process by running into failure, therefore there is a second modified extension. In Constrained Default Logic the two defaults cannot be applied within the same constrained process since their justifications conflict one another.

Which result is intuitively preferable? We argue that the syntactic form of the default theory is not sufficient to answer this question. Interpreting

---

[2]Compactness of predicate logic ensures that there is such a finite stage k.

p by 'It is Sunday',
q by 'I go fishing',
and r by 'I wake up late',

we have exactly the example that was used to motivate modified extensions. On the other hand, if we interpret

p as 'The television receives SBS',
q as 'I watch World Sport', and
r as 'SBS reception is poor',

then we observe the following: The first default can be applied, suggesting that I should decide to watch World Sport. But if I am living in an area where SBS reception is usually poor, then clearly this should override the first default. So, this interpretation supports Default Logic.

What can we learn from this example? There is no 'right' default logic variant, but rather alternative approaches following somewhat different intuitions. The suitability of a logic will vary from situation to situation, and it is up to the knowledge engineer to determine which logic is most suitable to the problem at hand.

Next we consider the following example. A family may decide to do one of two things on the weekend, either go to the beach or to a movie, depending on whether it is sunny or not. Of the two children, Chris doesn't like the beach and would be happy if the family didn't make that choice, while Leslie doesn't like movies and would be happy if that choice were not taken. Intuitively, when the family is planning ahead it has the following three alternatives: If it is sunny then the family goes to the beach and Leslie is happy; if it is not sunny then the family goes to a movie and Chris is happy; or, the parents decide to sacrifice their pleasure to keep both children happy, and the family does nothing special on the weekend, with the children playing computer games at home. Let us see how this example works formally. Consider the default theory $T = (W, D)$ with $W = \{\neg goMovie \vee \neg goBeach\}$ and D consisting of the defaults

$$\frac{true : sunny}{goBeach}, \quad \frac{true : \neg sunny}{goMovie}, \quad \frac{true : \neg goBeach}{happyChris}, \quad \frac{true : \neg goMovie}{happyLeslie}.$$

T has no extension (check!), so Default Logic operates in an unsatisfactory way. On the other hand, T has three constrained extensions, as desired:

$(Th(\{goBeach, \neg goMovie, happyLeslie\}),$
$Th(\{goBeach, \neg goMovie, happyLeslie, sunny\}))$

$(Th(\{goMovie, \neg goBeach, happyChris\}),$
$Th(\{goMovie, \neg goBeach, happyChris, \neg sunny\}))$

$(Th(\{happyChris, happyLeslie, \neg goMovie \lor \neg goBeach\}),$
$Th(\{happyChris, happyLeslie, \neg goBeach, \neg goMovie\})).$

Finally consider the default theory $T = (W, D)$ with $W = \emptyset$ and

$$D = \{\frac{true : p}{q}, \frac{true : \neg p}{r}, \frac{true : \neg q, \neg r}{s}\}.$$

T has the single extension
$Th(\{q, r\}),$

two modified extensions,

$Th(\{q, r\})$
$Th(\{s\}),$

and three constrained extensions

$(Th(\{q\}), Th(\{q, p\}))$
$(Th(\{r\}), Th(\{r, \neg p\}))$
$(Th(\{s\}), Th(\{s, \neg q, \neg r\})).$

This theory illustrates the essential differences of the three approaches discussed. Default Logic does not care about inconsistencies among justifications and may run into inconsistencies. Thus the first two defaults can be applied together, while if the third default is applied first, then the process is not closed and subsequent application of another default leads to failure. Justified Default Logic avoids the latter situation, so we obtain an additional modified extension. Constrained Default Logic avoids running into failure, too, but additionally requires joint consistency of justifications, therefore the two first defaults cannot be applied in conjunction, as in the other two approaches. Thus we get three constrained extensions.

7.5 Computability and complexity considerations

In this section we present some theoretical results which show that default reasoning is harder than reasoning in classical logic. The results should not be interpreted to mean that default reasoning is hopeless as far as implementation and applications are concerned. Rather they explain why it is hard to come up with good implementations of Default Logic. And, as usual with theoretical results, they are based on a *worst case analysis*, while the picture can be quite different when practical problems are considered. So the reader should not be discouraged when faced with the results of this section, but rather should consider them as a challenge. After all, the most interesting problems in Computer Science and Artificial Intelligence *are* intractable and/or undecidable!

From the *computability* point of view, it is clear that default reasoning is undecidable since predicate logic is undecidable. Predicate logic is at least semi–decidable (if φ is a theorem then a proof will be found eventually), however Default Logic is not even semi–decidable. To see this think back to the default proofs in Chapter 5. Clearly, if a formula does not have a default proof, then the search for a proof may take forever (just as in predicate logic). But even if a default proof exists, it is necessary to carry out consistency tests, and some of these tests may not terminate; so termination is not guaranteed even if a default proof exists.

The reader should note that this argument is informal and very superficial; the formal results and their proofs can be found in the literature. But let us at least formulate this result:

- Predicate logic is semi–decidable.

- Default Logic is not semi–decidable (even in the case of normal theories).

Now we look at default reasoning from the *computational complexity* point of view. Restricting attention to propositional theories, it turns out that Default Logic problems are one level higher on the polynomial hierarchy than problems of propositional logic.

- The satisfiability problem in propositional logic is NP–complete.

We give a summary of some known complexity results. Let T be a finite, propositional default theory, and φ a propositional formula. Then the following problems are Σ_2^P–complete:

- Deciding whether T has an extension.

- Deciding whether φ is contained in an extension of T.

- Deciding whether there is an extension of T that does not contain φ.

The following problems are Π_2^P–complete:

- Deciding whether φ is contained in all extensions of T.

- Deciding whether φ is not contained in an extension of T.

Problems

7-1. Default Logic does not support *reasoning by cases*. For example, consider the default theory $T = (W, D)$ with $W = \{emu \vee ostrich\}$ and $D = \{\frac{emu:runs}{runs}, \frac{ostrich:runs}{runs}\}$. Then *runs* is not contained in any extension of T because none of the defaults can be applied. Now let's reformulate the default theory, and consider $T' = (W, D')$ with $D' = \{\frac{true:emu \rightarrow runs}{emu \rightarrow runs}, \frac{true:ostrich \rightarrow runs}{ostrich \rightarrow runs}\}$.

(a) Compute the extensions of T'. Compare the result with that of T, and try to explain the difference.

(b) Given a normal default $\delta = \frac{\varphi:\psi}{\psi}$, define $\lambda(\delta)$ to be $\frac{true:\varphi \rightarrow \psi}{\varphi \rightarrow \psi}$. For a normal default theory $T = (W, D)$ let $\lambda(T) = (W, \{\lambda(\delta) \mid \delta \in D\})$. Show that every extension of T is contained in an extension of $\lambda(T)$.

7-2. Prove theorem 7.2.

7-3.* Show that if E is an extension of $\kappa(T)$, then E is a modified extension of T.

7-4. Show that the converse of problem 7-3 is not true, that is, a modified extension of T is not necessarily an extension of $\kappa(T)$. *Hint:* Use a default theory T such that the semi–normal theory $\kappa(T)$ has no extension.

7-5.* Prove the following *semi–monotonicity* result for modified extensions: If $T = (W, D)$ and $T' = (W, D')$ are default theories with $D \subseteq D'$, then each modified extension of T is included in a modified extension of T'. *Hint:* Use the same idea as in the proof of semi–monotonicity for normal default theories.

7-6.* Prove theorem 7.5.

7-7. Show that the existence of constrained extensions is always guaranteed.

7-8.* Show that CDL is semi–monotonic: Let $T = (W, D)$ and $T' = (W, D')$ be default theories with $D \subseteq D'$. Then every constrained extension of T is contained in a constrained extension of T'.

7-9. Prove the following weak orthogonality result for CDL: If (E, C) and (E', C') are different constrained extensions of a default theory T, then $C \cup C'$ is inconsistent. Does a similar result hold for E and E'?

7-10.* As with the other notions of an extension, there is a fixed–point characterization of constrained extensions. Let $T = (W, D)$ be a default theory. For a set C of formulae let $\Theta_T(C)$ be the pair of smallest sets of formulae (E', C') such that

1. $W \subseteq E' \subseteq C'$
2. E' and C' are deductively closed
3. For every $\frac{\varphi : \psi_1, \ldots, \psi_n}{\chi} \in D$, if $\varphi \in E'$ and $C \cup \{\psi_1, \ldots, \psi_n, \chi\}$ is consistent, then $\chi \in E'$ and $\{\psi_1, \ldots, \psi_n, \chi\} \subseteq C'$.

Show that (E, C) is a constrained extension of T iff $(E, C) = \Theta_T(C)$.

7-11. A *default theory with constraints* is a tuple $T = (W, D, C)$ such that (W, D) is a default theory, and C is a set of closed formulae. For a sequence Π of defaults in D without multiple occurrences, the definition of $Con(\Pi)$ is modified to include C (that means, in all consistency checks, consistency with C is additionally required). Apart from this modification, constrained processes and constrained extensions are defined as before.

(a) Show: (E, C) is a constrained extension of $(W, D, \emptyset)$ iff it is a constrained extension of (W, D).

(b) Discuss how lemmas of default theories with constraints can be represented directly as formulae instead of using defaults as done in section 7.3.

7-12. Given a default theory T, show that for every non–maximal successful process Π of T there is a maximal process Π' of T such that $\Pi < \Pi'$.

7-13. In Chapter 4 we saw that no extension E of T can be a proper subset of another extension E' of T. Is this true for constrained and modified extensions?

7-14.   Let T be a normal default theory. Show that E is an extension of T iff (E, E) is a constrained extension of T.

7-15.   In section 7.3 we showed how a lemma in CDL can be represented by a default. Give a similar lemma representation for Default Logic and prove a result analogous to theorem 7.7.

7-16.   Define a process tree for CDL similar to that for Default Logic, and use it to illustrate some of the examples in this chapter.

Chapter 8

Priorities Among Defaults

As we have already seen defaults may conflict with one another, and this is the reason why some default theories have more than one extension. Sometimes it is desirable to have an overview of all possible world views (extensions) supported by the default theory given, but there are situations where we would like to give some defaults higher priority over others. In medical diagnosis, for example, usually doctors begin with treatment making conjectures about the most probable cause for the observed symptoms, disregarding theoretically possible, but unlikely alternative causes. In legal reasoning, laws may contradict each other, but some laws may have higher priority than others (for example, a more recent law may override an older one, or federal law may override state law).

In this chapter we shall discuss two alternative approaches to priorities in default reasoning. Section 8.1 introduces *Prioritized Default Logic (PDL)*, a version of Default Logic in which the user provides priority information in the form of a partial order on the defaults. This method works well in cases where the priority information is clear and does not change over time.

But there are cases where the user does not have the information needed to provide all the priorities, or where dynamic changes of the priority relationships are necessary. In section 8.2 we present the logic *PRDL*, introduced by Brewka, which allows for reasoning about priorities *within* Default Logic, thus treating priorities as another piece of knowledge. According to this approach, it is possible to express statements like: *'If A is true, then default 1 usually has higher priority than default 2'*. Section 8.3 shows an example where this expressive power is used. Section 8.4 gives an alternative characterization of extensions in *PRDL*.

The expressive power of *PRDL* is high, but there is, as always, a price to pay in the form of a more difficult implementation, and the violation of some desirable theoretical properties, as discussed in section 8.5.

In both logics we shall only consider normal defaults. As pointed out in Chapter 5, normal default theories on their own are insufficient because they do not allow for the representation of interactions among defaults. But since we provide extra mechanisms for dealing with priorities here, normal defaults seem to be expressive enough for many practical purposes. And it is possible to extend the approaches to non–normal default theories in a straightforward way.

8.1   PDL: Prioritized Default Logic

In PDL the user explicitly provides the priority order in which defaults are supposed to be applied. In the simplest case a strict well order is used (that is, an irreflexive total order in which every subset of D has a smallest element). Let us consider the default theory $T = (W, D)$ with $W = \{bird, penguin\}$ and D consisting of the defaults

$$\delta_1 = \frac{penguin : \neg flies}{\neg flies}, \ \delta_2 = \frac{bird : flies}{flies}.$$

Suppose a total order $\ll$ is given according to which δ_1 is preferred over δ_2, i.e. $\delta_1 \ll \delta_2$. Then T together with $\ll$ should only admit the extension

$$Th(\{bird, penguin, \neg flies\}).$$

Let $T = (W, D)$ be a normal default theory, and $\ll$ a strict well order on D. A process $\Pi = (\delta_0, \delta_1, \ldots)$ of T is *generated by* $\ll$ iff, for all i, δ_i is the $\ll$–minimal default in $\Pi - \Pi[i]$ that is applicable to $In(\Pi[i])$, provided that such a δ_i exists. Clearly, Π is closed; it is also successful since T is a normal default theory. We say that E is *generated by* $\ll$ iff $E = In(\Pi)$ for a process Π that is generated by $\ll$.

It is left as an exercise to the reader to verify that Π and E, as defined above, are uniquely determined. In the previous example, $\ll$ is defined by $\delta_1 \ll \delta_2$. (δ_1) is the process generated by $\ll$, and $Th(\{bird, penguin, \neg flies\})$ is the extension generated by $\ll$.

Of course, we cannot expect the defaults in all problem domains to be ordered in a total way. Often defaults should be left incomparable with one another. In other words, requiring a total ordering of defaults will often be a kind of overspecification. Here is a simple example from politics.

According to conservative politicians, taxes should be cut without cutting spending; the latter is unnecessary because reduced taxes are supposed to lead to increased economic growth. Radical conservatives proclaim tax cuts and spending cuts because the government should be as lean as possible. According to social democrats, neither taxes nor spendings should be cut because they believe government should afford welfare programs and create additional demand. This information can be expressed by the following defaults:

$$\delta_1 = \frac{conservative : taxCut \wedge \neg spendingsCut}{taxCut \wedge \neg spendingsCut}$$

$$\delta_2 = \frac{conservative \wedge radical : taxCut \wedge spendingsCut}{taxCut \wedge spendingsCut}$$

$$\delta_3 = \frac{socialDemocrat : \neg taxCut \wedge \neg spendingsCut}{\neg taxCut \wedge \neg spendingsCut}$$

Intuitively it is clear that δ_2 should be given higher priority than δ_1 because the information that somebody is a radical conservative is more specific than the information that she is a conservative. But there is no reason to prescribe any order between δ_1 and δ_3, or between δ_2 and δ_3.

Technically speaking, the priority information will be given in the form of a *strict partial order* $<$ on the set of defaults. The definition of the semantics will make use of all strict well orders that contain $<$. This approach resembles the treatment of concurrency in computer science, where meaning is assigned by considering all possible linearizations.

Definition 8.1 (PDL–extension) *$T = (W, D, <)$ is a prioritized default theory if (W, D) is a normal default theory and $<$ a strict partial order on D. E is a PDL–extension of T iff there is a strict well order $\ll$ on D which contains $<$ and generates E.*

Consider the prioritized default theory $T = (W, D, <)$ with $W = \{politician\}$, D consisting of the defaults

$$\delta_1 = \frac{politician : \neg respected}{\neg respected}, \quad \delta_2 = \frac{politician : wellPayed}{wellPayed},$$

$$\delta_3 = \frac{\neg respected : \neg wellPayed}{\neg wellPayed},$$

and $<$ defined by $\delta_2 < \delta_3$. Now there are three strict well orders on D that contain $<$, namely

$\delta_1 \ll \delta_2 \ll \delta_3$
$\delta_2 \ll \delta_1 \ll \delta_3$, and
$\delta_2 \ll \delta_3 \ll \delta_1$.

The first one generates the process (δ_1, δ_2) and the extension

$$Th(\{politician, \neg respected, wellPayed\}).$$

The reader is asked to verify that the two other strict well orders lead to the same PDL–extension.

By definition of a PDL–extension E, $E = In(\Pi)$ for a closed and successful process Π. Therefore we make the following observation:

Theorem 8.2 *If E is a PDL–extension of the prioritized default theory $T = (W, D, <)$ then E is an extension of (W, D).*

The next result follows from the observation that given a finite set M, every strict partial order on M is included in a strict well order on M. A strict partial order $<$ defines some constraints about which elements should precede which other elements. A strict total order $\ll$ respecting these constraints can always be constructed. Since M is finite, a minimal element exists. Therefore the extension generated by $\ll$ is a PDL–extension.

Theorem 8.3 *A prioritized default theory $T = (W, D, <)$ always has a PDL–extension if D is finite.*

Theorem 8.3 is not true for infinite sets of defaults. Let $D = \{\delta_i \mid i \geq 0\}$, and $<$ the strict partial order on D determined by $\delta_i < \delta_0$ for all $i > 0$. Then there is no strict well order of D containing $<$; there are, of course, strict total orders, but the existence of minimal elements cannot be established.

Note that PDL allows the user to specify priorities among defaults, but only in a rigid, predefined form. In contrast to this, the logic we shall present in the following section provides far greater flexibility in specifying and reasoning about priorities. We call that logic $PRDL$ for 'Priority Reasoning in Default Logic'.

8.2   PRDL: Reasoning about priorities

In PDL the priority information was *extralogical*, i.e. outside the standard Default Logic. Here we describe an approach where priority information will be part of the logical language. The information 'δ_1 has higher priority than δ_2' will be a formula as every other assertion, and will be included in the default theory given[1]. For the

---

[1] Of course, priority information will be treated differently from the *semantic* point of view.

sake of technical simplicity we restrict our presentation to finite sets D of (normal) defaults.

To be able to reason about default priorities, defaults are augmented by a (unique) name; so, named defaults have the form $d \equiv \frac{\varphi:\psi}{\psi}$. Whenever confusion does not arise, we shall assume that d_i is the name of δ_i, and that δ_i is the default with name d_i. Please notice the difference between d_i and δ_i: d_i is a default name *within the logical language*, whereas δ_i is used *on the meta–level*, that means outside the logical language, to refer to a default.

Also we introduce a special symbol $\prec$ representing default priorities and acting on default names. $d_1 \prec d_2$ is to be read as 'give the default (with name) d_1 priority over (the default with name) d_2'.

A *named default theory* T is a tuple (W, D) consisting of a set of first order formulae W and a finite set D of named normal defaults $d \equiv \frac{\varphi:\psi}{\psi}$. It is implicitly assumed that W contains axioms expressing the transitivity and irreflexivity of $\prec$:

$$\forall X \forall Y \forall Z \ (X \prec Y \wedge Y \prec Z \to X \prec Z), \ \forall X \ \neg \ X \prec X.$$

Therefore, if both assertions $d_1 \prec d_2$ and $d_2 \prec d_1$ are included in a set E containing W, then E is inconsistent.

- For a named default theory T, let T' denote the unnamed version of T (in which the defaults are as defined in section 3.2). A *DL–extension of T* is defined as an extension of T'.

So far there is no semantic difference between priority statements and other formulae. But, of course, priority statements will be taken into consideration by ruling out the application of a default if there exists another applicable default with higher priority. We consider some examples to illustrate and collect some desirable properties of the subsequent formal definition of priority extensions. First we use the well–known birds domain, and consider the named default theory $T = (W, D)$ with W consisting of the formulae

penguin
bird
$d_2 \prec d_1$

and D consisting of the defaults

$$d_1 \equiv \frac{bird:flies}{flies}, \ d_2 \equiv \frac{penguin:\neg flies}{\neg flies}.$$

The unnamed default theory T' has two extensions: $E_1 = Th(\{penguin, bird, d_2 \prec d_1, flies\})$, and $E_2 = Th(\{penguin, bird, d_2 \prec d_1, \neg flies\})$. Intuitively, only E_2 should be a priority extension of T, since we have to prefer d_1 over d_2 to derive E_1, and that is not consistent with W. The definition to follow will ensure that this outcome is indeed produced.

In this example all priority information was given in W, in which case it is quite easy to deal with. The situation becomes more complicated when *different processes (and thus extensions) contain different priority information*. Consider, for example, the named default theory $T = (W, D)$ with $W = \emptyset$ and W consisting of the defaults

$$d_1 \equiv \frac{true : d_2 \prec d_1}{d_2 \prec d_1}, \ d_2 \equiv \frac{true : d_1 \prec d_2}{d_1 \prec d_2}.$$

There are two closed and successful processes of T', $\Pi_1 = (\delta_1)$ and $\Pi_2 = (\delta_2)$ (they are closed because of the implicitly given irreflexivity of $\prec$). Note that $In(\Pi_1) = Th(\{d_2 \prec d_1\})$ and $In(\Pi_2) = Th(\{d_1 \prec d_2\})$ contain mutually inconsistent priority information (recall that $\prec$ is reflexive and transitive). Furthermore, if the first default is applied then it turns out that the second default should have been applied instead ($d_1 \prec d_2$), and vice versa. Therefore we wouldn't expect T to have any priority extensions. Again this will be achieved by the formal definition of priority extensions.

The interpretation of $PRDL$ is similar to that for Default Logic. In fact, the only thing we must additionally take care of is the priority information. If a default δ is applied instead of some others, it should not turn out at a later stage that δ should not have been applied. Stated another way: when a default is applied, we decide to give it higher priority than all other defaults that are applicable at the time. This decision should remain consistent even after application of further defaults.

Since we restrict attention to *normal* defaults augmented by priority information, the Out–set is unnecessary (since always $In(\Pi) \cap Out(\Pi) = \emptyset$). Instead, in the following we shall associate with process Π a set $Pri(\Pi)$ which collects the priority decisions made while building Π. The following figure shows the modified process tree for the example from the previous section. The left–hand branch leads to a failed situation because $In \cup Pri$ is inconsistent (it includes both $d_1 \prec d_2$ and $d_2 \prec d_1$, thus contradicting the irreflexivity and transitivity of $\prec$).

In the following we shall give the formal definition of a (modified) process tree. The definition here concerns the entire process tree and not one process as in Default Logic. The reason is clear: in Default Logic we may analyze a process stand alone, whilst in $PRDL$ we must take alternative defaults into consideration. This means that at each node, we have to determine all applicable defaults before proceeding

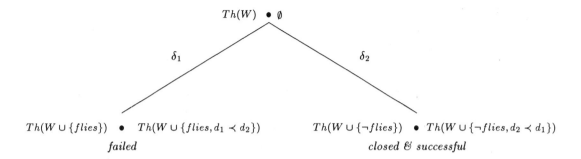

$Th(W) \bullet \emptyset$

δ_1 δ_2

$Th(W \cup \{flies\}) \bullet Th(W \cup \{flies, d_1 \prec d_2\})$ $Th(W \cup \{\neg flies\}) \bullet Th(W \cup \{\neg flies, d_2 \prec d_1\})$

failed   *closed & successful*

Figure 8.1

along one choice.

The *process tree* $proc(T)$ of $T = (W, D)$ consists of nodes n and edges e. With each node n, we associate sets of formulae $In(n)$ and $Pri(n)$. Also, with each edge e we associate a default $def(e)$. The root of $proc(T)$ is the node n_0 with $In(n_0) = Th(W)$ and $Pri(n_0) = \emptyset$.

Let n be any node that has already been constructed. The tree can be expanded at n in the following way: let $\delta_1, \ldots, \delta_k$ be the unnamed defaults that are applicable to $In(n)$ and have not been used as labels of edges on the path connecting n with the root. Then, the process tree is expanded by inserting child nodes n_i corresponding to the application of $\delta_i \in \{\delta_1, \ldots, \delta_k\}$. For each of the nodes n_i we define the *In* and *Pri*-set as follows:

$$In(n_i) = Th(In(n) \cup \{cons(\delta_i)\})$$
$$Pri(n_i) = Pri(n) \cup \{d_i \prec d_j \mid j \in \{1, \ldots, k\}, j \neq i\}.$$

The node n is *closed* if it is a leaf, i.e. if $k = 0$, and n is *successful* iff $In(n) \cup Pri(n)$ is consistent, otherwise it is *failed*. Finally, one notational convention: we denote the path within $proc(T)$ from the root to a node n_m by $\Pi = (n_0, < \delta_1, n_1 >, \ldots, < \delta_m, n_m >)$, whereby δ_i is $def(e_i)$ for the edge e_i connecting n_{i-1} with n_i. Note that all paths are finite since we only consider finite sets D of defaults.

Definition 8.4 (priority extension) *E is a priority extension of a named default theory T iff there is a closed and successful node n in $proc(T)$ such that $E = In(n)$.*

We conclude this section with an example. Reconsider $T = (W, D)$ with $W = \emptyset$ and $D = \{d_1 \equiv \frac{true : d_2 \prec d_1}{d_2 \prec d_1}, d_2 \equiv \frac{true : d_1 \prec d_2}{d_1 \prec d_2}\}$. As stated before, we do not expect T to have any priority extensions. The following process tree shows that the definition above matches this intuition.

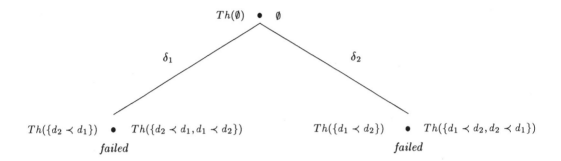

$$Th(\emptyset) \quad \bullet \quad \emptyset$$

$$\delta_1 \qquad\qquad\qquad\qquad \delta_2$$

$$Th(\{d_2 \prec d_1\}) \quad \bullet \quad Th(\{d_2 \prec d_1, d_1 \prec d_2\}) \qquad\qquad Th(\{d_1 \prec d_2\}) \quad \bullet \quad Th(\{d_1 \prec d_2, d_2 \prec d_1\})$$

$$failed \qquad\qquad\qquad\qquad\qquad\qquad failed$$

Figure 8.2

8.3 An example from legal reasoning

This example is due to Brewka. If a person possesses a ship and wants to find
out whether his security interest in the ship is perfected, there is a relevant law,
the Uniform Commercial Code (UCC), which lays down that a security interest is
perfected by taking possession of the collateral. However there is a federal law, the
Ship Mortgage Act (SMA), according to which a security interest in a ship can only
be perfected by filing a financing statement, something which in our case has not
been done.

Obviously the two laws are in conflict with one another. How can the conflict
be resolved? According to a legal principle, *Lex Posterior*, a more recent law over-
rides an older one; in our case, UCC is more recent than SMA. However, according
to another legal principle, *Lex Superior*, a law is preferred to a conflicting one by
the higher authority. In our case, SMA is a federal law and has therefore higher
authority than UCC. This information is expressed by the named default theory
$T = (W, D)$ with W consisting of the formulae

> *possession*
> *ship*
> $\neg financialStatement$
> $moreRecent(UCC, SMA)$
> $higherAuthority(SMA, UCC)$

and D consisting of the defaults (and default schemas)

$$UCC \equiv \frac{possession:perfected}{perfected}$$

$$SMA \equiv \frac{ship \land \neg financialStatement : \neg perfected}{\neg perfected}$$
$$LexPosterior(X,Y) \equiv \frac{moreRecent(X,Y) : X \prec Y}{X \prec Y}$$
$$LexSuperior(X,Y) \equiv \frac{higherAuthority(X,Y) : X \prec Y}{X \prec Y}.$$

The reader is asked to build the process tree of T and verify that T has two priority extensions, namely

$$E_1 = Th(W \cup \{perfected, UCC \prec SMA\}), \text{ and}$$
$$E_2 = Th(W \cup \{\neg perfected, SMA \prec UCC\}).$$

Still we don't have a definite answer to the question of whether the security interest in the ship is perfected or not. This should not be surprising since there are two conflicting principles, Lex Superior and Lex Posterior. If we decided to give one of them higher priority, for example by adding the formula

$$\forall X \forall Y \forall U \forall V \, LexSuperior(X,Y) \prec LexPosterior(U,V)$$

to W, then only E_2 remains a priority extension (again the reader is asked to verify this). Please notice the different levels of conflict resolution: there was a conflict between UCC and SMA, therefore some higher principles (Lex Superior, Lex Posterior) were used. But because they led to contradictory results as well, their conflict had to be resolved on yet a higher level. In more complicated examples more layers might have to be used.

8.4   An alternative characterization of extensions*

Brewka's original presentation of PRDL was different; instead of using the operational definition we gave above, it makes use of PDL concepts.

Let $T = (D, W)$ be a named default theory, E a set of formulae including W, and $\ll$ a strict well order on D' (the set of unnamed defaults). Then, $\ll$ is *compatible with* E iff

$$E \cup \{d_i \prec d_j \mid d_i \equiv \delta_i \in D, d_j \equiv \delta_j \in D, \delta_i \ll \delta_j\}$$

is consistent[2]. E is a *B–priority extension* of T iff there is a strict well order $\ll$ on D' that is compatible with E, such that E is the DL–extension of T generated by

---

[2]Recall that $\ll$ is an order on unnamed defaults, whereas $\prec$ is an order on default names *and is part of the logical language.*

$\ll$. The following theorem states the equivalence between the two priority extension concepts.

Theorem 8.5 *Let $T = (W, D)$ be a named default theory. E is a priority extension of T iff E is a B–priority extension of T.*

Proof: Let n be a closed and successful node in $proc(T)$, and $\Pi = (n_0, < \delta_1, n_1 > , \ldots, < \delta_m, n_m >)$ the associated path. First note that $In(n)$ is a DL–extension of T; this is a direct implication of the fact that the In–set is defined as for Default Logic, and that all defaults are normal.

Consider the set $M = \{d_i \prec d_j \mid In(n) \cup Pri(n) \models d_i \prec d_j\} \cup IRREF \cup TRANS$, where $IRREF$ and $TRANS$ are the irreflexivity and transitivity axiom for $\prec$ respectively. Since n is successful, M is consistent. Therefore, there is a total ordering $\ll$ on unnamed defaults which is consistent with M. Taking such a total ordering, we show that $In(n_m)$ is the PDL–extension generated by $\ll$; then we are finished.

δ_1 is the $\ll$–minimal default applicable to $Th(W)$. To see this, suppose that $\delta^1, \ldots, \delta^k$ are the other applicable defaults. Then $d_1 \prec d^i \in Pri(n_1)$ and $d_1 \prec d^i \in M$, so $\delta_1 \ll \delta^i$ (for all $i = 1, \ldots, k$). The same argument shows that δ_2 is the next applicable default etc.

Conversely let E be a B–priority extension of T. Then E is a DL–extension of T, and also a PDL–extension of T generated by a total order $\ll$ compatible with E. Let $(\delta_1, \ldots, \delta_m)$ be the process generated by $\ll$. Then, there is a path $(n_0, < \delta_1, n_1 >, \ldots, < \delta_m, n_m >)$ in $proc(T)$. Further, $In(n_m) = E$. Now, n_m is closed since E is a DL–extension of T. Finally, n_m is also successful. Otherwise, $In(n_m) \cup Pri(n_m)$ would include some information stating that some default δ'_k should have been preferred to δ_k for a $k \in \{1, \ldots, m\}$. But δ_k was defined to be the $\ll$–minimal default not in $\{\delta_1, \ldots, \delta_{k-1}\}$, applicable to $In(n_{k-1})$. This means that $\ll$ is inconsistent with $In(n_m) = E$ which is a contradiction. ∎

8.5 Properties of PRDL*

In Default Logic, normal default theories have some very desirable properties. These include existence of extensions, semi–monotonicity, and goal–driven query evaluation. Unfortunately, none of these properties are preserved when reasoning about priorities is added. The last example in section 8.2 shows that a named default theory may not possess a priority extension.

Here is an example which shows that $PRDL$ is not semi–monotonic. Consider the theory $T = (W, D)$ with $W = \emptyset$ and $D = \{d_1 \equiv \frac{true:a}{a}, d_2 \equiv \frac{true:\neg a}{\neg a}\}$. T has two priority extensions, $E_1 = Th(\{\neg a\})$ and $E_2 = Th(\{a\})$. Now expand D as follows: $D' = D \cup \{d_3 \equiv \frac{true:d_1 \prec d_2}{d_1 \prec d_2}\}$. The named default theory $T' = (W, D')$ has the single priority extension $E = Th(\{a, d_1 \prec d_2\})$. The priority extension E_1 of (W, D) is not included in a priority extension of (W, D').

The theory T' of the example above shows that the straightforward goal–driven query evaluation known from normal default theories is not possible here: The query ?– $\neg a$ fails, although we would be tempted to give a positive answer if we thought in a naive goal–driven way.

Finally we give some simple sufficient conditions for the existence of priority extensions of a named default theory $T = (W, D)$. In the following, we shall consider named default theories with the following restriction: For each default δ, its consequent either contains no occurrence of $\prec$, or it is an atomic formula of the form $d_i \prec d_j$. We call such theories *restricted*. If additionally the only occurrences of $d_i \prec d_j$ in W are as elements of W, then T is called *strongly restricted*.

Theorem 8.6 *Let T be a restricted named default theory. Suppose that $M = W \cup \{d_i \prec d_j \mid d_i \prec d_j$ is the consequent of some default in $D\}$ is consistent. Then T has a priority extension.*

Proof: If M is consistent, then there is a total order $\ll$ consistent with M. Let E be the PDL–extension of T generated by $\ll$. If $\Pi = (\delta_1, \delta_2, \ldots, \delta_n)$ is the sequence of defaults used in constructing E, then $E = In(\Pi)$, and E is a DL–extension of T: Π is successful (as all defaults are normal), closed (since, by definition, no more default can be applied), and a process (since the defaults $\delta_1, \delta_2, \ldots, \delta_n$ may be applied in this order). Finally, $\ll$ is consistent with E since it is already consistent with M.   ∎

Theorem 8.7 *Let T be a strongly restricted named default theory. If no atomic formula $d_i \prec d_j$ is included in any default consequent in D, then T has a priority extension.*

Proof: Suppose W is inconsistent. Then T has as (the only) extension the set of all formulae. So, suppose that W is consistent. Then, the set of formulae $d_i \prec d_j$ included in $Th(W)$ is also consistent. This means that there is some total ordering $\ll$ on the unnamed defaults of D such that

$$W \cup \{d_i \prec d_j \mid d_i \equiv \delta_i \in D, d_j \equiv \delta_j \in D, \delta_i \ll \delta_j\}$$

is consistent. Define E as the PDL–extension generated by $\ll$. E is a DL–extension of T. It remains to show that $\ll$ is compatible with E. Because of the imposed restrictions on T, the information on $\prec$ contained in E is the same as in W. By construction, $\ll$ is compatible with E.   ∎

We must be very careful about the sufficient conditions. For example, the result above is not even true for restricted default theories: consider the restricted named default theory $T = (W, D)$ with $W = \{a \rightarrow d_1 \prec d_2, \neg a \rightarrow d_2 \prec d_1\}$ and $D = \{d_1 \equiv \frac{true:\neg a}{\neg a}, d_2 \equiv \frac{true:a}{a}\}$. T has no priority extension, although it satisfies the other condition of theorem 8.7.

Theorem 8.8 *Let T be a restricted named default theory such that $\prec$ does not occur in W. Let $E = In(\delta_1, \ldots, \delta_k)$ be a DL–extension of T. If no formula $d \prec d_i$ (for $i \in \{1, \ldots, k\}$) is the consequent of a default δ_j ($j \in \{1, \ldots, k\}$), then E is also a priority extension of T.*

Proof: On the corresponding path in $proc(T)$, Pri collects formulae of the form $d_i \prec d$ while defaults $\delta_1, \ldots, \delta_k$ are being applied. If E were not a priority extension of T, then $In(n_k) \cup Pri(n_k)$ would be inconsistent for the leaf node n_k of the path in $proc(T)$. By the restrictions imposed on T, this can only happen if $d \prec d_i \in In(n_k)$ for some $d_i \prec d \in Pri(n_k)$. Where could this $d_i \prec d \in Out(n_k)$ come from? By the restrictions imposed on T, it can only be a member of W, a consequent of some default δ_j for $j \in \{1, \ldots, k\}$, or be derived using the transitivity of $\prec$. The first two cases are impossible (due to the conditions of the theorem); a simple inductive argument shows then that $d_i \prec d \in Out(n_k)$ could not have been introduced through transitivity. Therefore, we are finished.   ∎

If $\prec$ occurs in W, the conclusion of theorem 8.8 may be wrong. Consider the strongly restricted named theory $T = (W, D)$ with $W = \{d_2 \prec d_1\}$ and $D = \{d_1 \equiv \frac{true:a}{a}, d_2 \equiv \frac{true:\neg a}{\neg a}\}$. $E = Th(\{a\})$ fulfills the other conditions on E and T, but is not a priority extension of T.

We note that the sufficient conditions above are indeed very strong. This is an indication that while PRDL is expressive, it is also 'dangerous' in the sense that it will often exhibit unexpected behaviour if the user is not very cautious.

Problems

8-1. Show that a strict well order on D determines a unique process Π and a unique extension of a default theory $T = (W, D)$.

8-2. Give a prioritized default theory with more than one PDL–extension.

8-3. Let (W, D) be a normal default theory, and $\ll$ a strict well order on D. Show that the prioritized default theory $(W, D, \ll)$ has exactly one PDL–extension, which is the extension of (W, D) generated by $\ll$.

8-3 Develop a Prolog implementation of PDL.

8-4. Work out the example in section 8.3.

8-5.* Discuss the generalization of $PRDL$ to include the case of infinite sets of defaults.

8-6. Check all examples from section 8.5 using process trees.

8-7.* Write down default theories with priorities in several problem domains. Determine the outcomes you would intuitively expect, and check formally whether they are indeed produced by PDL or PRDL.

References for Part II

Reiter's classical paper [71] introducing Default Logic is still worth reading. It presents the ideas, the basic technicalities and the main results. In that work, Reiter expressed his belief that normal defaults would be sufficient for practical purposes. Later Etherington studied semi–normal default theories [23] as a way of overcoming the limitations of normal theories that had become apparent in the meantime; ordered default theories were introduced in that paper. Our presentation of Default Logic and its variants is based on a series of technical papers [5, 6, 7, 8].

Justified Default Logic was introduced by Lukaszewicz [46, 47], and Constrained Default Logic by Schaub [77]; most theorems (but not the proofs) of sections 7.2–7.4 can be found in these works. An excellent overview paper on different default logics is [18], which is the basis of parts of Chapter 7, including some examples in section 7.4. An exposition of computational issues of nonmonotonic reasoning can be found in [34, 54]. Our presentation of priorities among defaults is based on a paper by Brewka [16], from which the example in section 8.3 is borrowed.

Default Logic has been covered in several books, including [11, 15, 47, 54]. They include a broad variety of the standard examples (such as our friend Tweety), some of which are used in this book without referring to the original source, simply because they belong to the folklore of the area. [47] contains a classification of forms of default reasoning which was partially used in section 3.1. [54] includes an excellent in–depth treatment of Default Logic based on an operational interpretation of Default Logic similar to our processes, but does not discuss the variants of Chapters 7 and 8. The monograph complements this book rather well.

Recently implementation issues attracted attention; the interested reader may consult [17, 44, 63, 75].

Part III

Classical Approaches to Nonmonotonic Reasoning

In the previous part we presented Default Logic as one major approach for non-monotonic reasoning. Its idea is to use first–order logic for representing certain information, and enhance it by rules of inference called defaults that can be used to make plausible assumptions. In this part we present the two other important classical approaches of nonmonotonic reasoning, Moore's Autoepistemic Logic and McCarthy's Circumscription.

The idea of *Autoepistemic Logic (AEL)* is to extend the logic language by an operator of knowledge or belief $L\varphi$, which is interpreted as 'I believe in φ' or 'I know φ'. By extending the language itself, Autoepistemic Logic departs radically from first–order logic (if we disregard the fact that predicate logic is included as part of the new formalism). Chapter 9 discusses the intuitive idea of AEL which is based on introspection (that means, assumptions are made based on one's own knowledge or beliefs). The chapter also describes the syntax and semantics of the logic.

The meaning of a knowledge base is given in terms of so–called *expansions*, which are 'world views' sanctioned by the knowledge. The idea is similar to the notion of extensions of default theories although the technicalities are quite different. Expansions are defined using fixed–point equations just as default logic extensions were. This raises once again the question of computing extensions. Chapter 10 introduces an operational method for computing expansions of autoepistemic theories.

Though the motivations of Default and Autoepistemic Logic are different, AEL can be used for default reasoning. In fact, as shown in Chapter 11, Default Logic can be embedded in a variant of AEL. But it turns out that Autoepistemic Logic offers greater semantic flexibility than Default Logic (in the sense that the translation of a default theory allows more conclusions to be drawn). Most of Chapter 11 is devoted to showing that a specific subset of all expansions of the translation corresponds exactly to the extensions of the original default theory.

So, AEL is stronger than Default Logic. A word of caution is necessary at this point: contrary to widespread claims, the two logics are *not* equivalent. These claims stem simply from a misinterpretation of results. Autoepistemic Logic is strictly stronger than Default Logic.

The other major approach, *Circumscription*, takes a different standpoint from Autoepistemic Logic. Instead of regarding predicate logic as inappropriate and extending its language, it considers it to be sufficient for default reasoning; it is only the way it is used that has to be changed. Chapter 12 is devoted to this formalism.

It should be noted that Autoepistemic Logic and Circumscription are covered to a lesser extent than Default Logic was – actually, Circumscription is discussed only superficially. The reason is that the author is a supporter of Default Logic. But this is only the biased opinion of a person who does not expect anybody to believe in what he says! The reader is encouraged to take a closer look at the bibliographical remarks at the end of this part and draw their own conclusions, possibly disregarding the author's humble opinion.

Chapter 9

Autoepistemic Logic

One of the most prominent methods for nonmonotonic reasoning is Autoepistemic Logic, a formalism that was developed by Moore in the early 80s. Its main idea is to give a formal account of an agent reasoning about his own knowledge or beliefs. Consider the following dialog:

Are the Rolling Stones giving a concert in Newcastle next week?
No, because otherwise I would have heard about it.

We can illustrate some interesting points using this example. First, it is clear that I don't have any definite knowledge that the Rolling Stones are not giving a concert in Newcastle next week. In this sense, my knowledge is incomplete and, by giving a negative answer, I am making a conjecture. This conjecture is based on reflection upon the knowledge I have (if something so important is happening in my city, then I will know about it). The word *autoepistemic* means reflection upon self–knowledge.

To proceed with the example, suppose that I buy the Newcastle Herald the morning after the conversation above, and read the head title:

The concert of the century: The Rolling Stones in Newcastle next week!

The situation has changed: Now I do know that the Stones are giving a concert, so my answer to the question above would be 'Yes'. This means that the old conclusion I had drawn by introspection is no longer valid and must be revised. So my reasoning is nonmonotonic (new information has invalidated a previous conclusion). Note, though, that my long–term knowledge has not changed: I can still argue *'If something so important is taking place in my city, then I will know about it'*. The only difference is that now I know that the concert will take place, so I cannot conclude the contrary based on introspection.

Autoepistemic Logic formalizes this kind of reasoning. The approach it takes is to introduce a so–called modal operator L that is applied to first–order sentences (i.e. closed formulae).

$L\varphi$

has the meaning

I know φ (or *I believe in φ*).

Our concert example is formulated as follows:

$concert \rightarrow Lconcert$ ('If a concert takes place then I know about it')
$\neg Lconcert$ ('I don't know that a concert will take place')

The L–operator may be applied in a nested way, for example, I may know that I don't know something. Thus, the following are formulae of Autoepistemic Logic: LLp, $L\neg Lq$, $\neg LL(\neg p \vee Lr)$ etc.

The semantics of Autoepistemic Logic is given in terms of so–called *expansions*, pieces of knowledge defining 'world views' compatible with and based on the given knowledge. One of the main properties of expansions is stability: A deductively closed set E of autoepistemic formulae is called *stable* if the following conditions hold:

- $\varphi \in E$ implies $L\varphi \in E$.
- $\varphi \notin E$ implies $\neg L\varphi \in E$.

The concept of stability clearly reflects introspection, i.e. autoepistemic reasoning: if A is in my knowledge, then I know A, I know that I know A etc. On the other hand, if I do not know B, then I know that I do not know B etc.

The chapter is organized as follows: Section 9.1 describes the syntactical concepts of Autoepistemic Logic, section 9.2 its semantics. Section 9.3 introduces the notion of an expansion, while section 9.4 studies the properties of stable sets (and thus of expansions).

9.1   The language of autoepistemic logic

As already stated, the language of Autoepistemic Logic is the language of predicate logic extended by a modal operator L. *Autoepistemic formulae (AE–formulae)* are defined as the smallest set satisfying the following:

- Each closed first–order formula is an AE–formula.

- If φ is an AE–formula, then $L\varphi$ is also an AE-formula.

- If φ and ψ are AE–formulae, then so are the following: $\neg\varphi$, $(\varphi \vee \psi)$, $(\varphi \wedge \psi)$, $(\varphi \rightarrow \psi)$.

The set of all AE–formulae is denoted by *For*. An *autoepistemic theory* (*AE–theory*) is a set of AE–formulae.

We point out that the definition above allows the application of the L–operator to a quantified first–order formula (if it is closed!), but not vice versa: it is impossible to quantify over beliefs. So, whereas $L\forall X\exists Y\ X < Y$ ('I know that for all natural numbers X there is a number Y greater than X') is an autoepistemic formula, $\forall X L\exists Y\ X < Y$ ('For all natural numbers X, I know that there is a number Y greater than X') is not an AE–formula, because $\exists Y\ X < Y$ is not closed. The reason for this restriction is that it is difficult to define the meaning of quantification over knowledge or beliefs; current research is addressing this restriction.

In some examples it may be convenient to use open first–order formulae within the scope of an L–operator. In this case a AE–formula must be read as a schema, that means as the collection of all ground instances (just like open defaults). For example,

$aussie(X) \wedge \neg L\neg drinksBeer(X) \rightarrow drinksBeer(X)$
$aussie(bob)$
$aussie(lisa)$

must be read as the autoepistemic theory

$aussie(bob) \wedge \neg L\neg drinksBeer(bob) \rightarrow drinksBeer(bob)$
$aussie(lisa) \wedge \neg L\neg drinksBeer(lisa) \rightarrow drinksBeer(lisa)$
$aussie(bob)$
$aussie(lisa)$

Note the occurrence of $\neg L\neg$ in this example. It has the meaning 'it is consistent to believe' ($\neg L\neg\varphi$ is read as: 'I do not know (believe in) $\neg\varphi$').

Let us now introduce some syntactic concepts that we will use in the sequel. Given an AE–theory T, $sub(T)$ is the union of $sub(\varphi)$, for all $\varphi \in T$, where $sub(\varphi)$ is defined as follows:

- $sub(\varphi) = \emptyset$ for first–order formulae φ
- $sub(\neg\varphi) = sub(\varphi)$
- $sub(\varphi \vee \psi) = sub(\varphi \wedge \psi) = sub(\varphi \rightarrow \psi) = sub(\varphi) \cup sub(\psi)$
- $sub(L\varphi) = \{\varphi\}$.

The last item in this definition lays down that we do not go further into the structure of a formula after the outermost occurrence of L. So, if $T = \{L\neg Lq, L(Lp \vee r), \neg Lr, s\}$, then $sub(L) = \{\neg Lq, (Lp \vee r), r\}$.

The *degree* of an AE–formula φ is the maximal depth of L–nesting that occurs in φ; it is denoted by $degree(\varphi)$. For example, $degree(\neg L\neg L(a \vee Lb)) = 3$. Given an autoepistemic theory T, T_n denotes the set of AE–formulae in T with degree less or equal n.

When studying AE–theories it is often useful to investigate the *predicate logic part* of them. The *kernel* of an AE–theory T is defined as the set of all first–order formulae that are members of T, i.e. T_0. So, if $T = \{p, \neg Lq, \neg Lq \rightarrow s, L\neg Lr, r\}$, then $T_0 = \{p, r\}$.

We conclude the syntax section by defining the normal form for AE–formulae. It will be the basis for several proofs that follow in subsequent sections. An autoepistemic formula is said to be *in normal form* if it has the form

$$\varphi_1 \wedge \ldots \wedge \varphi_n$$

where each φ_i has the form

$$\beta \vee L\gamma_1 \vee \ldots \vee L\gamma_p \vee \neg L\delta_1 \vee \ldots \vee \neg L\delta_q$$

with a first–order formula β. Each AE–formula φ may be transformed into a semantically equivalent formula $nf(\varphi)$ in normal form such that $degree(\varphi) = degree(nf(\varphi))$. The proof is left as an exercise to the reader (which, of course, can only be solved after we have defined the semantics of Autoepistemic Logic in the next section).

9.2   The semantics of autoepistemic formulae

The semantics of Autoepistemic Logic is readily defined if we lay down that $L\varphi$ be treated as a new atom (for every AE–formula φ). To be more precise, an *autoepistemic interpretation* (*AE–interpretation*) $\mathcal{A}$ over a signature Σ provides

- a non–empty domain $dom(\mathcal{A})$

- an interpretation $f_{\mathcal{A}}$ of appropriate functionality for each function symbol f in Σ (like in predicate logic)
- an interpretation $r_{\mathcal{A}}$ of appropriate functionality for every predicate symbol p in Σ (like in predicate logic)
- a truth value $(L\varphi)_{\mathcal{A}}$ for every AE–formula $L\varphi$.

Based on this definition, the concept of the *validity* of an AE–formula in $\mathcal{A}$ is carried over from predicate logic. We write $\mathcal{A} \models \varphi$ to denote that φ is valid in an AE–interpretation $\mathcal{A}$ (or, stated another way, that $\mathcal{A}$ is an *AE–model* of φ).

We say that φ *logically follows* from a set M of AE–formulae (denoted by $M \models \varphi$) iff φ is valid in all AE–models of M. For a set of AE–formulae M, let $Th(M)$ denote the set of autoepistemic formulae that logically follow from M.

According to this definition, validity of φ in $\mathcal{A}$ and validity of $L\varphi$ in $\mathcal{A}$ are totally unrelated because $L\varphi$ is treated as a new atom (that is, as a 0–ary predicate). Intuitively, φ expresses *truth* of φ whereas $L\varphi$ expresses *belief in* (or knowledge of) φ. We are allowed to believe in something false, or not to believe in something that is true. The following alternative definition of AE–interpretations underlies this observation.

An *algebra with belief set* is a pair $(\mathcal{B}, Bel)$ consisting of a first–order interpretation $\mathcal{B}$, and a set Bel of AE–formulae. Validity of AE–formulae in $(\mathcal{B}, Bel)$ is defined as follows:

- $(\mathcal{B}, Bel) \models \varphi$ iff $\mathcal{B} \models \varphi$ for a closed first–order formula φ
- $(\mathcal{B}, Bel) \models \neg\varphi$ iff $(\mathcal{B}, Bel) \not\models \varphi$
- $(\mathcal{B}, Bel) \models (\varphi \vee \psi)$ iff $(\mathcal{B}, Bel) \models \varphi$ or $(\mathcal{B}, Bel) \models \psi$
- $(\mathcal{B}, Bel) \models (\varphi \wedge \psi)$ iff $(\mathcal{B}, Bel) \models \varphi$ and $(\mathcal{B}, Bel) \models \psi$
- $(\mathcal{B}, Bel) \models (\varphi \to \psi)$ iff $(\mathcal{B}, Bel) \models \varphi$ implies $(\mathcal{B}, Bel) \models \psi$
- $(\mathcal{B}, Bel) \models L\varphi$ iff $\varphi \in Bel$.

Algebras with belief set are related to AE–interpretations $\mathcal{A}$ in an obvious way. Given an AE–interpretation $\mathcal{A}$, $(\mathcal{B}, Bel)$ can be defined as follows:

- The domain of $\mathcal{B}$ and the interpretation of function and predicate symbols are precisely those of $\mathcal{A}$.
- $Bel = \{\varphi \mid (L\varphi)_{\mathcal{A}} = true\}$.

In the opposite direction, given an algebra with belief set $(\mathcal{B}, Bel)$, an AE–interpretation $\mathcal{A}$ may be defined as follows:

- The domain of $\mathcal{A}$ and the interpretation of function and predicate symbols are precisely those of $\mathcal{B}$.

- $(L\varphi)_{\mathcal{A}} = true$ iff $\varphi \in Bel$.

In the following we shall use the two concepts interchangeably. So when speaking of an 'AE–interpretation with belief set Bel' we mean that $Bel = \{\varphi \mid (L\varphi)_{\mathcal{A}} = true\}$.

We say that φ *follows from T with respect to belief set E*, denoted by $T \models_E \varphi$, iff φ is valid in every AE–model of T with belief set E.

9.3   Expansions of autoepistemic theories

What knowledge would an agent with introspection have, given a set of facts (AE–formulae) T? It will be a set E of AE-formulae that

- includes T

- allows introspection

- is grounded in T in the sense that the knowledge in E must be reconstructable using T, belief in (knowledge of) E, and non–belief in (non–knowledge of) E.

These ideas are formalized as follows. Let T and E be sets of AE–formulae. We denote the set $\{L\varphi \mid \varphi \in E\}$ as LE, and the set $\{\neg L\psi \mid \psi \notin E\}$ as $\neg LE^C$. Define $\Omega_T(E) = \{\varphi \mid T \cup LE \cup \neg LE^C \models \varphi\}$.

Definition 9.1

- E is T–*sound* iff $E \subseteq \Omega_T(E)$.

- E is T–*complete* iff $\Omega_T(E) \subseteq E$.

- E is an *expansion* of T iff $E = \Omega_T(E)$.

Let us look at the definition of an expansion. What it essentially says is the following: imagine that you decide to believe (include in your knowledge) a set of AE–formulae T. Given this decision, a set of AE–formulae can be deduced from the given theory T and the belief we adopted (represented as $LE \cup \neg LE^C$). If this way it turns out that we obtain the belief set E we adopted ('Truth implies belief'), and only E ('Belief implies truth'), then E is an expansion of T.

An alternative characterization of expansions follows from the following observation: the AE–models of $T \cup LE \cup \neg LE^C$ are just the AE–models of T with belief set E. Hence we have the following result:

Corollary E *is an expansion of an AE–theory* T *iff* $E = \{\varphi \mid T \models_E \varphi\}$.

We conclude this section by giving two examples of expansions. Consider the following AE–theory:

$(aussie \wedge \neg L \neg drinksBeer) \rightarrow drinksBeer$
$aussie$

This AE–theory has exactly one expansion. There is no possibility of deriving $\neg drinksBeer$, therefore $\neg L \neg drinksBeer$ is contained in the expansion. Thus, the first rule is applicable and gives $drinksBeer$. The only expansion of this theory has the kernel $Th(\{aussie, drinksBeer\})$. But if we extend the theory by adding

$(eatsPizza \wedge \neg LdrinksBeer) \rightarrow \neg drinksBeer$
$eatsPizza$

then the new theory has two expansions: the kernel of one expansion contains $aussie$, $eatsPizza$, and $drinksBeer$, the kernel of the other expansion contains $aussie, eatsPizza$ and $\neg drinksBeer$.

The reader is encouraged to prove the claims about the expansions of the two theories. But even if this task is carried out, the question remains whether there are more expansions! And it is probably not completely clear how we arrived at the expansion candidates above. Even if the reader is quite uneasy by now, we encourage him/her to continue reading. The problem of determining the expansions of an autoepistemic theory will be addressed in Chapter 10 where we present a method that is as easily to follow and apply as processes in Default Logic.

9.4   Stable sets and their properties

Let E be a set of autoepistemic formulae. E is called *stable* iff

- E is deductively closed, i.e. $E = Th(E)$
- $\varphi \in E$ implies $L\varphi \in E$, for all AE–formulae φ
- $\varphi \notin E$ implies $\neg L\varphi \in E$, for all AE–formulae φ.

Expansions are stable sets by definition, therefore they are sometimes called stable expansions. As a consequence, expansions have all the properties of stable sets that we shall derive in this section. But first we give an alternative characterization of expansions using stable sets.

Theorem 9.2* *For an AE–theory T and a set of AE–formulae E the following statements are equivalent:*

(a) E *is an expansion of* T.

(b) E *is stable, contains* T *and is* T*–sound.*

Proof: (a) implies (b) by definition. Conversely, assume that E is stable, contains T and is T–sound. Stability implies $LE \cup \neg LE^C \subseteq E$. Using $T \subseteq E$ it follows that $\Omega_T(E) = Th(T \cup LE \cup \neg LE^C) \subseteq Th(E) = E$. This shows that E is T–complete; together with the T–soundness of E we have shown that E is an expansion of T. ∎

Lemma 9.3* *For a stable set E and an AE–formula φ the following statements are equivalent:*

(a) $E \models_E \varphi$

(b) $E \models \varphi$

(c) $\varphi \in E$.

For a first–order formula φ, (a)–(c) are equivalent to

(d) $E_0 \models \varphi$.

Proof: Stability of E implies $LE \cup \neg LE^C \subseteq E$. Therefore, $E \models_E \varphi$ iff $E \cup LE \cup \neg LE^C \models \varphi$ iff $E \models \varphi$ iff $\varphi \in E$ (because E is deductively closed). For a first–order formula φ, $\varphi \in E$ iff $\varphi \in E_0$ iff $E_0 \models \varphi$. ∎

For a stable set E, the decision we make to include or not to include some first–order formula in E has far reaching consequences: if, for example, a stable set contains p, then it contains also Lp, LLp, $LLLp$, $(p \vee q)$ (by deductive closure), $L(p \vee q)$ etc. Similarly, if a stable set does not contain q, then it contains $\neg Lq$, $L\neg Lq$, $(r \vee LL\neg Lq)$ etc. In fact, the two following results show that a stable set is uniquely determined by the set of first–order formulae it contains, that is by its kernel.

Theorem 9.4 *For stable sets E and F, $E_0 = F_0$ implies $E = F$.*

Proof*: Let E and F be stable sets with $E_0 = F_0$. By induction on the degree of AE–formulae we show that $\varphi \in E$ iff $\varphi \in F$. In the following we make use of the normal form of AE–formulae that was introduced in section 9.1. It is a fundamental technical tool for proofs in Autoepistemic Logic, and we will make use of it on several other occasions. Its essential idea is to reduce claims on AE–formulae to claims on first–order formulae.

For a given φ let its normal form $nf(\varphi)$ be $\varphi_1 \wedge \ldots \wedge \varphi_n$. Since E and F are deductively closed it suffices to show that $\varphi_i \in E$ iff $\varphi_i \in F$ for all $i \in \{1, \ldots, n\}$. Let φ_i be the formula $\beta \vee L\gamma_1 \vee \ldots \vee L\gamma_p \vee \neg L\delta_1 \vee \ldots \vee \neg L\delta_q$.

Case 1: $\gamma_j \in E$ for some $j \in \{1, \ldots, p\}$. By the induction hypothesis we know $\gamma_j \in F$ (induction hypothesis is applicable because $degree(\gamma_j) < degree(\varphi_i) \leq degree(nf(\varphi)) = degree(\varphi)$). By stability of E and F we have $L\gamma_j \in E$ and $L\gamma_j \in F$. E and F are deductively closed, therefore $\varphi_i \in E$ and $\varphi_i \in F$.

Case 2: $\delta_k \notin E$ for some $k \in \{1, \ldots, q\}$. By the induction hypothesis we know $\delta_k \notin F$. By stability of E and F we have $\neg L\delta_k \in E$ and $\neg L\delta_k \in F$. E and F are deductively closed, so $\varphi_i \in E$ and $\varphi_i \in F$.

Case 3: $\gamma_j \notin E$ and $\delta_k \in E$ for all $j \in \{1, \ldots, p\}$ and $k \in \{1, \ldots, q\}$. Using the induction hypothesis and the stability of E and F we obtain $\neg L\gamma_j \in E$, $\neg L\gamma_j \in F$, $L\delta_k \in E$ and $L\delta_k \in F$ for all $j \in \{1, \ldots, p\}$ and $k \in \{1, \ldots, q\}$. Now we may successively conclude: $\varphi_i \in E$ iff $\beta \in E$ iff $\beta \in E_0$ iff $\beta \in F_0$ iff $\beta \in F$ iff $\varphi_i \in F$.
∎

Theorem 9.5 *Let T be a first–order theory[1]. Then there is a stable set E with $E_0 = T$.*

Proof*: We define sets $E(n)$ inductively as follows:

$$E(0) = T$$
$$E(n+1) = \{\varphi \in For_{n+1} \mid T \models_{E(n)} \varphi\}.$$

Let $E = \bigcup_n E(n)$. We show by induction on n that $E(n) = E(n+1)_n$.

$$E(1)_0 =$$
$$\{\varphi \in For_1 \mid T \models_{E(0)} \varphi\}_0 =$$

---

[1]that is, T is a deductively closed set containing only closed formulae.

$$\{\varphi \in For_0 \mid T \models_{E(0)} \varphi\} =$$
(since T is first–order)

$$\{\varphi \in For_0 \mid T \models \varphi\} =$$
(since T is deductively closed)

$$T = E(0).$$

Assume that $E(n) = E(n+1)_n$. Then we conclude

$$E(n+2)_{n+1} =$$
$$\{\varphi \in For_{n+2} \mid T \models_{E(n+1)} \varphi\}_{n+1} =$$
$$\{\varphi \in For_{n+1} \mid T \models_{E(n+1)} \varphi\} =$$
(since φ has degree at most $n+1$)

$$\{\varphi \in For_{n+1} \mid T \models_{E(n+1)_n} \varphi\} =$$
(by induction hypothesis)

$$\{\varphi \in For_{n+1} \mid T \models_{E(n)} \varphi\} =$$
$$E(n+1).$$

In particular, $E(n) = E(n+1)_n \subseteq E(n+1)$ for all n. By the compactness of predicate logic E is deductively closed. Also, it is easy to see that $T = E_0$.

We conclude the proof by showing the stability of E. Let $\varphi \in E$; then, by definition, $\varphi \in E(n)$ for some n. Hence $T \models_{E(n)} L\varphi$, so $L\varphi \in E(n+1) \subseteq E$. Let $\psi \notin E$ and assume $\psi \in For_{n+1}$. Since $\psi \notin E(n)$ we conclude that $T \models_{E(n)} \neg L\psi$, therefore $\neg L\psi \in E(n+1) \subseteq E$.   ∎

We conclude this chapter with two interesting properties of stable sets.

Theorem 9.6 (Orthogonality of stable sets) *Let E and F be different stable sets. Then $E \cup F$ is inconsistent.*

Proof: Since $E \neq F$ there must be at least one AE–formula φ that is included in one set but not in the other; say $\varphi \in F$ and $\varphi \notin E$. By stability of E and F we conclude $L\varphi \in F$ and $\neg L\varphi \in E$, so $E \cup F$ is inconsistent.   ∎

Theorem 9.7 *If E is a stable set then it is an expansion of E_0.*

Proof*: By theorem 9.2 it suffices to show that E is E_0–sound, that is, $E \subseteq \{\varphi \mid E_0 \cup LE \cup \neg LE^C \models \varphi\}$. Consider a formula $\varphi \in E$ and its normal form $nf(\varphi) = \varphi_1 \wedge \ldots \wedge \varphi_n$. Since E is deductively closed, it suffices to show that each φ_i (which has the form $\beta \vee L\gamma_1 \vee \ldots \vee L\gamma_p \vee \neg L\delta_1 \vee \ldots \vee \neg L\delta_q$ and is also an element of E) follows from $E_0 \cup LE \cup \neg LE^C$. This is trivially the case if $\gamma_j \in E$ for some $j \in \{1, \ldots, p\}$, or $\delta_k \notin E$ for some $k \in \{1, \ldots, q\}$. Otherwise we know by the stability of E that $\neg L\gamma_j \in E$ and $L\delta_k \in E$ for all $j \in \{1, \ldots, p\}$ and

$k \in \{1, \ldots, q\}$. Then we successively get $\beta \in E$, $\beta \in E_0$, $E_0 \cup LE \cup \neg LE^C \models \beta$, $E_0 \cup LE \cup \neg LE^C \models \varphi_i$. ∎

Problems

9-1. Give a formal proof of the equivalence of the concepts AE–interpretation and algebra with belief set.

9-2. Give an inductive definition of $degree(\varphi)$.

9-3.* Show that for each AE–formula φ there is a semantically equivalent formula $nf(\varphi)$ in normal form such that $degree(\varphi) = degree(nf(\varphi))$.

9-4. Show that the equivalences given in lemma 9.3 do not hold for arbitrary sets E of AE–formulae.

9-5. Show that the only possible inclusion relationships between stable sets are $E = F$ and $E \subseteq For$.

9-6. For a stable set E show that E is the unique expansion of E_0.

9-7. E is called *semantically complete* iff $\{\varphi \mid \models_E \varphi\} \subseteq E$. Show that E is semantically complete iff it is a stable set.

9-8. E is called *semantically sound w.r.t.* T iff $T \models_E E$. Show that E is semantically sound w.r.t. T iff E is T–sound. Based on this and the previous exercise, establish an alternative definition of expansions, and prove its equivalence to the definition given in section 9.3.

9-9. If E is a stable set then, for every AE–formula φ, either $\neg L\varphi \in E$ or $\neg L\neg\varphi \in E$.

9-10. Try to express some examples from Default Logic in the language of Autoepistemic Logic.

Chapter 10

Computing Expansions of AE-Theories

The syntax and semantics of Autoepistemic Logic were introduced in the previous chapter. The basic semantic notion was that of an expansion and it was defined as a solution to a fixed–point equation. Though mathematically elegant and simple, this definition is difficult to apply to concrete theories. In order to reassure the reader that this difficulty is not experienced by novices alone, we give the following, admittedly early, statement by Moore, the developer of Autoepistemic Logic: *'One of the problems with our original presentation of autoepistemic logic was that, since both logic and semantics were defined nonconstructively, we were unable to easily prove the existence of stable expansions of nontrivial sets of premises...'*

In this chapter we present a simple operational method for determining the expansions of an autoepistemic theory. Its main idea is to guess a set of beliefs and to check whether this decision leads to a solution of the fixed–point equation. An important feature is that decisions on belief or non–belief may be restricted to some specific subformulae of the autoepistemic theory given.

Section 10.1 presents and explains the method for determining expansions. Section 10.2 demonstrates the application of the method using some examples, while section 10.3 contains a formal correctness proof. Finally, a prototype Prolog implementation is given in section 10.4.

10.1 Motivation and description of the method

Let T be an autoepistemic theory. Since all expansions of T are stable, we must include in each of them LT, LLT, ..., $(\varphi \vee \psi)$ for each $\varphi \in T$ and each ψ, etc. The approach so far is monotonic.

Since Autoepistemic Logic is a nonmonotonic formalism, we are allowed to make conjectures and include some AE–formulae or their negation in some expansion even if we are not forced to. In this case, some other AE–formulae must be included, too. For example, if we decide not to believe in χ, then $\neg L\chi$, $L\neg L\chi$ etc. will be included in the expansion. Different conjectures may lead to different expansions. Now, what are the obstacles in determining the expansions of T?

1. Nested occurrences of the L–operator make candidate expansions hard to deal with.

2. There are potentially infinitely many conjectures that can be made, so how can we compute all expansions?

The first problem can be treated using theorem 9.4: we may concentrate on potential *kernels of expansions*, since the expansions are determined by their kernels.

The second problem is eased by establishing a *Coincidence Lemma* which says that it suffices to consider belief or non–belief in formulae from $sub(T)$ in order to determine the expansions of T (see section 10.3 for the technical details). Recall that $sub(T)$ is the set of formulae φ such that $L\varphi$ has an occurrence in T at the 'top level'; it collects those AE–formulae whose belief or non–belief plays a role in the interpretation of T. As $sub(T)$ is finite, the second problem mentioned above is solved, too. The procedure for determining expansions may be summarized as follows:

- Partition $sub(T)$ into a part $E(+)$ you believe in, and a part $E(-)$ you do not believe in.

- Compute the corresponding kernel $E(0)$ of a potential expansion, using T, belief in $E(+)$, and non–belief in $E(-)$.

- Check whether the stable set determined by $E(0)$ is indeed an expansion (this test is carried out in a simpler way than in the original definition; see the subsequent description for details).

First let us look at an example. Consider the autoepistemic theory $T = \{Lp \rightarrow p\}$. We note that Lp is the only AE–formula occurring (at the top level) in T, therefore $sub(T) = \{p\}$. There are two possible decompositions of $sub(T) = \{p\}$: we either decide to believe in p or not. Each possibility leads to a different line in the following table.

Line 1: We believe in p, so Lp is known. Using the formula in T we derive p. No other predicate logic formula can be derived from $T \cup LE(+) \cup \neg LE(-)$, so

$E(0) = Th(\{p\})$. The test goes through, therefore $E(0)$ is an expansion of T. Line 2 is explained in a similar way, leading to a second expansion with kernel $Th(\emptyset)$.

$E(+)$	$E(-)$	$E(0)$	$E(+) \subseteq E(0)$	$E(-) \cap E(0) = \emptyset$	expansion
$\{p\}$	$\emptyset$	$Th(\{p\})$	yes	yes	yes
$\emptyset$	$\{p\}$	$Th(\emptyset)$	yes	yes	yes

To simplify the situation, we first treat autoepistemic theories without nested occurrences of the L-operator. In this case, $sub(T)$ consists only of first-order formulae by definition.

10.1 Procedure for AE-theories without L-nesting

Expansions := $\emptyset$
FORALL partitions $E(+)$ and $E(-)$ of $sub(T)$ DO
    BEGIN
        $E(0) := \{\varphi \in For_0 \mid T \cup LE(+) \cup \neg LE(-) \models \varphi\}$
        IF $E(+) \subseteq E(0)$ AND $E(-) \cap E(0) = \emptyset$
        THEN *Expansions* := *Expansions* $\cup \{E(0)\}$
    END
    END

Some short comments on this procedure: $E(0)$ is the set of first-order formulae that follow from T, belief in $E(+)$ and non-belief in $E(-)$. The condition $E(+) \subseteq E(0)$ tests whether $E(0)$ includes what we decided to believe in, while the condition $E(-) \cap E(0) = \emptyset$ ensures that $E(0)$ does not include something we decided not to believe in. If both conditions are passed, then we have determined an expansion (actually the kernel of an expansion). The set *Expansions* contains the kernels of all expansions of T.

Now we turn to the general case. First we look at an example. Let $T = \{Lp \rightarrow p, \neg L \neg Lp\}$. Then, $sub(T) = \{p, \neg Lp\}$. The only difference in the table below is the following: since T contains nested occurrences of the L-operator, the decomposition sets $E(+)$ and $E(-)$ are no longer sets of first-order formulae. Therefore, it is impossible to compare them with $E(0)$ which is still a potential kernel of an expansion. So, in columns 4 and 5 we have to use E instead of $E(0)$; E is hereby the uniquely determined stable set with kernel $E(0)$.

$E(+)$	$E(-)$	$E(0)$	$E(+) \subseteq E$	$E(-) \cap E = \emptyset$	expansion
$\{p, \neg Lp\}$	$\emptyset$	For_0	yes	yes	yes
$\{p\}$	$\{\neg Lp\}$	$Th(\{p\})$	yes	yes	yes
$\{\neg Lp\}$	$\{p\}$	For_0	yes	no	no
$\emptyset$	$\{p, \neg Lp\}$	$Th(\emptyset)$	yes	no	no

Unfortunately, we pay a price for allowing L–nesting. It was easy to read and understand the table in the example preceding the procedure 10.1 (everything referred to classical logic), here however we have to take stability into consideration when testing columns 4 and 5. We give some hints to help in understanding the entries in these columns:

- **1. line:** $E(0)$ is inconsistent since $L\neg Lp \in LE(+)$ and $\neg L\neg Lp \in T$. The entries in the last three columns follow directly.

- **2. line:** $T \cup LE(+) \cup \neg LE(-) = \{Lp \rightarrow p, \neg L\neg Lp, Lp\}$, therefore $E(0) = Th(\{p\})$. To establish the answer in the fifth column, note that $p \in E$, and E is stable and consistent. So, $Lp \in E$ and therefore $\neg Lp \notin E$.

- **3. line:** $T \cup LE(+) \cup \neg LE(-)$ contains both $L\neg Lp$ and $\neg L\neg Lp$, therefore $E(0) = For_0$.

- **4. line:** $T \cup LE(+) \cup \neg LE(-) = \{Lp \rightarrow p, \neg L\neg Lp, \neg Lp\}$, so $E(0) = Th(\emptyset)$. Since p is not member of E, it follows $\neg Lp \in E$ and therefore $E(-) \cap E \neq \emptyset$.

10.2 Procedure for general autoepistemic theories

```
Expansions := ∅
FORALL partitions E(+) and E(−) of sub(T) DO
    BEGIN
        E(0) := {φ ∈ For₀ | T ∪ LE(+) ∪ ¬LE(−) ⊨ φ}
        Let E be the unique stable set with kernel E(0)
        IF E(+) ⊆ E AND E(−) ∩ E = ∅
        THEN Expansions := Expansions ∪ {E(0)}
        END
END
```

10.2 Some examples

Here we will apply the method of the previous section to a number of simple examples. The AE–theories have been chosen such that some interesting properties of Autoepistemic Logic can be illustrated. None of them include any L-nesting to keep the discussion as simple as possible.

Consider the theory $T = \{p \to L\neg p\}$. The following table shows that none of the decompositions of $sub(T) = \{\neg p\}$ passes both tests. Therefore, this theory does not possess any expansions.

$E(+)$	$E(-)$	$E(0)$	$E(+) \subseteq E(0)$	$E(-) \cap E(0) = \emptyset$	expansion
$\{\neg p\}$	$\emptyset$	$Th(\emptyset)$	no	yes	no
$\emptyset$	$\{\neg p\}$	$Th(\{\neg p\})$	yes	no	no

Let $T = \{\neg Lp \to q, Lq \to p, Lq \to q\}$; $sub(T) = \{p, q\}$. The following table shows that $Th(\{p, q\})$ is the kernel of the only expansion of T. Note that this set occurs twice in the third column, in line 1 and in line 3. Line 3 fails, but line 1 succeeds; therefore $E(0)$ is the kernel of an expansion, obtained from the decomposition in line 1. So, an entry 'no' in the last column means that the decomposition *corresponding to that line* does not lead to an expansion; it does *not* mean that $E(0)$ is definitely not the kernel of an expansion (as this example shows).

$E(+)$	$E(-)$	$E(0)$	$E(+) \subseteq E(0)$	$E(-) \cap E(0) = \emptyset$	expansion
$\{p, q\}$	$\emptyset$	$Th(\{p, q\})$	yes	yes	yes
$\{p\}$	$\{q\}$	$Th(\emptyset)$	no	yes	no
$\{q\}$	$\{p\}$	$Th(\{p, q\})$	yes	no	no
$\emptyset$	$\{p, q\}$	$Th(\{q\})$	yes	no	no

Let $T = \{\neg Lp\}$. The following table shows that T has two expansions, one of which is inconsistent (i.e. the set of all AE-formulae). The example shows that a consistent theory may have an inconsistent expansion.

$E(+)$	$E(-)$	$E(0)$	$E(+) \subseteq E(0)$	$E(-) \cap E(0) = \emptyset$	expansion
$\{p\}$	$\emptyset$	For_0	yes	yes	yes
$\emptyset$	$\{p\}$	$Th(\emptyset)$	yes	yes	yes

Here is an informal attempt to explain the existence of two expansions: T says 'Do not believe in p'. Now, the 'cautious' approach is to 'obey' (line 2). But there is also a 'courageous' approach in which I say 'Well, I decide to believe in p' and look for trouble!

Let $T = \{Lp \to q, Lq \to p\}$. The table below shows that T has two expansions. This is quite clear on the intuitive level: if I decide to believe in either p or q, the rules in T force me to include the other atom in my knowledge, too. So, either I believe in both or in neither of p nor q.

$E(+)$	$E(-)$	$E(0)$	$E(+) \subseteq E(0)$	$E(-) \cap E(0) = \emptyset$	expansion
$\{p,q\}$	$\emptyset$	$Th(\{p,q\})$	yes	yes	yes
$\{p\}$	$\{q\}$	$Th(\{q\})$	no	no	no
$\{q\}$	$\{p\}$	$Th(\{p\})$	no	no	no
$\emptyset$	$\{p,q\}$	$Th(\emptyset)$	yes	yes	yes

Consider the example from the introduction to Chapter 9. $T = \{con \to Lcon\}$ has a unique expansion which includes $\neg con$, but the unique expansion of $T = \{con \to Lcon, con\}$ includes con.

$E(+)$	$E(-)$	$E(0)$	$E(+) \subseteq E(0)$	$E(-) \cap E(0) = \emptyset$	expansion
$\{con\}$	$\emptyset$	$Th(\emptyset)$	no	yes	no
$\emptyset$	$\{con\}$	$Th(\neg con)$	yes	yes	yes

$E(+)$	$E(-)$	$E(0)$	$E(+) \subseteq E(0)$	$E(-) \cap E(0) = \emptyset$	expansion
$\{con\}$	$\emptyset$	$Th(\{con\})$	yes	yes	yes
$\emptyset$	$\{con\}$	For_0	yes	no	no

Finally we reconsider the example concerning beer drinkers from section 9.3. Let $T = \{a, e, a \wedge \neg L\neg d \to d, e \wedge \neg Ld \to \neg d\}$ (where a stands for *aussie*, e for *eatsPizza* and d for *drinksBeer*). $sub(T) = \{d, \neg d\}$. The following table shows that T has exactly two expansions, as claimed in section 9.3.

$E(+)$	$E(-)$	$E(0)$	$E(+) \subseteq E(0)$	$E(-) \cap E(0) = \emptyset$	expansion
$\{d, \neg d\}$	$\emptyset$	$Th(\{a,e\})$	no	yes	no
$\{d\}$	$\{\neg d\}$	$Th(\{a,e,d\})$	yes	yes	yes
$\{\neg d\}$	$\{d\}$	$Th(\{a,e,\neg d\})$	yes	yes	yes
$\emptyset$	$\{d, \neg d\}$	For_0	yes	no	no

10.3   Correctness proofs*

Preservation Lemma 10.3 *Let E be a stable set and T an AE–theory. If $E_0 = \{\varphi \in For_0 \mid T \cup LE \cup \neg LE^C \models \varphi\}$ then $T \subseteq E$ and $E = \{\varphi \in For \mid T \cup LE \cup \neg LE^C \models \varphi\}$.*

Proof: First we show $T \subseteq E$. Consider an arbitrary AE–formula φ in T and let $\varphi_1 \wedge \ldots \wedge \varphi_n$ be its normal form. It suffices to show $\varphi_i \in E$ for all $i \in \{1, \ldots, n\}$. Let

φ_i be $\beta \vee L\gamma_1 \vee \ldots \vee L\gamma_p \vee \neg L\delta_1 \vee \ldots \vee \neg L\delta_q$ with a first–order formula β. We may assume $\gamma_j \notin E$ (for all $j \in \{1, \ldots, p\}$) and $\delta_k \in E$ (for all $k \in \{1, \ldots, q\}$) because otherwise the claim is trivially true. Consequently we obtain $T \cup LE \cup \neg LE^C \models \beta$, $\beta \in E_0$, $\beta \in E$, $\varphi_i \in E$, and finally $\varphi \in E$.

Secondly, we use the stability of E to conclude $\{\varphi \in For \mid E \models_E \varphi\} \subseteq E$ by applying lemma 9.3. Using the inclusion $T \subseteq E$ we just proved we obtain $\{\varphi \in For \mid T \models_E \varphi\} \subseteq E$.

Finally we show $T \models_E \varphi$ for every AE–formula $\varphi \in E$. Given φ, we use its normal form $\varphi_1 \wedge \ldots \wedge \varphi_n$ once again. We know $\varphi_i \in E$ (for all $i \in \{1, \ldots, n\}$) because E is deductively closed. It is sufficient to show $T \models_E \varphi_i$. This is obvious if $\gamma_j \in E$ for some j or $\delta_k \notin E$ for some k, so we disregard these cases. Stability of E implies $\neg L\gamma_1, \ldots, \neg L\gamma_p, L\delta_1, \ldots, L\delta_q \in E$, so $\beta \in E$ and $\beta \in E_0$. By assumption we know $T \cup LE \cup \neg LE^C \models \beta$. Therefore we have also $T \cup LE \cup \neg LE^C \models \varphi_i$. ∎

Coincidence Lemma 10.4 *Let T be an AE–theory. Consider sets of AE–formulae $E(+)$, $E(-)$, $F(+)$ and $F(-)$ with the following properties:*

- $sub(T) \subseteq E(+) \cup E(-)$, $E(+) \cap E(-) = \emptyset$
- $sub(T) \subseteq F(+) \cup F(-)$, $F(+) \cap F(-) = \emptyset$
- $E(+) \cap sub(T) = F(+) \cap sub(T)$
- $E(-) \cap sub(T) = F(-) \cap sub(T)$

Then the same first–order formulae follow from $T \cup LE(+) \cup \neg LE(-)$ as from $T \cup LF(+) \cup \neg LF(-)$.

Proof: Suppose $T \cup LE(+) \cup \neg LE(-) \models \varphi$ for a first–order formula φ. Let $(\mathcal{A}, Bel)$ be an arbitrary AE–model of $T \cup LF(+) \cup \neg LF(-)$; recall that in this case $(\mathcal{A}, Bel)$ is a model of T, $F(+) \subseteq Bel$ and $F(-) \cap Bel = \emptyset$. Now we consider the AE–interpretation $(\mathcal{A}, E(+))$. Then $(\mathcal{A}, E(+)) \models LE(+)$. Also, since $E(+) \cap E(-) = \emptyset$, we know $(\mathcal{A}, E(+)) \models \neg LE(-)$. Finally, we conclude $(\mathcal{A}, E(+)) \models T$ from the equivalence $\psi \in Bel$ iff $\psi \in E(+)$ for all $\psi \in sub(T)$. Altogether we have shown $(\mathcal{A}, E(+)) \models T \cup LE(+) \cup \neg LE(-)$.

Since φ is a first–order formula we consequtively conclude $(\mathcal{A}, E(+)) \models \varphi$, $\mathcal{A} \models \varphi$, and $(\mathcal{A}, Bel) \models \varphi$. $(\mathcal{A}, Bel)$ was an arbitrary model of $T \cup LF(+) \cup \neg LF(-)$, therefore $T \cup LF(+) \cup \neg LF(-) \models \varphi$.

By symmetry, the opposite direction also holds (first–order consequents of $T \cup LF(+) \cup \neg LF(-)$ follow from $T \cup LE(+) \cup \neg LE(-)$). ∎

Therefore, in determining the first–order consequences of an AE-theory T with respect to a belief set E only belief or nonbelief in members of $sub(T)$ is relevant. The following two theorems show the correctness of the procedures 10.1 and 10.2.

Theorem 10.5 *Let T be an AE–theory of degree ≤ 1, and suppose that $sub(T)$ (which, by definition, is a set of first–order formulae) is partitioned into disjoint subsets $E(+)$ and $E(-)$. We consider the two following steps:*

1. Compute $E(0) = \{\varphi \in For_0 \mid T \cup LE(+) \cup \neg LE(-) \models \varphi\}$.
2. Check *whether $E(+) \subseteq E(0)$ and $E(-) \cap E(0) = \emptyset$.*

If the check in step 2 ends positively then the unique stable set E with kernel $E(0)$ is an expansion of T. Conversely, for every kernel E_0 of an expansion E of T there is a partition of $sub(T)$ into $E(+)$ and $E(-)$ such that $E(0) = E_0$ and the check in step 2 succeeds.

Proof: Consider a partition of $sub(T)$: $sub(T) = E(+) \cup E(-)$ and $E(+) \cap E(-) = \emptyset$. Let $E(0)$ be defined as in step 1, and let E be the unique stable set with kernel $E(0)$. Suppose that step 2 is successful, i.e. $E(+) \subseteq E(0)$ and $E(-) \cap E(0) = \emptyset$. Then $E(+) \cap sub(T) = E \cap sub(T)$ and $E(-) \cap sub(T) = E^C \cap sub(T)$. By lemma 10.4 we may replace $E(+)$ by E and $E(-)$ by E^C in the equation that defines $E(0)$ and obtain $E_0 = E(0) = \{\varphi \in For_0 \mid T \cup LE \cup \neg LE^C \models \varphi\}$. By lemma 10.3 we conclude that E is an expansion of T.

Conversely let E be an expansion of T. Define $E(+) = sub(T) \cap E$ and $E(-) = sub(T) \cap E^C$. Using lemma 10.4 we obtain

$$E(0) =$$
$$\{\varphi \in For_0 \mid T \cup LE(+) \cup \neg LE(-) \models \varphi\} =$$
$$\{\varphi \in For_0 \mid T \cup LE \cup \neg LE^C \models \varphi\} = E_0.$$

So $E(+) = sub(T) \cap E \subseteq E_0 = E(0)$ and $E(-) \cap E(0) = sub(T) \cap E^C \cap E(0) = \emptyset$. Therefore the check in step 2 is successful. ∎

Theorem 10.6 *Let T be an AE–theory, and suppose that $sub(T)$ is partitioned into disjoint subsets $E(+)$ and $E(-)$. We consider the two following steps:*

1. Compute $E(0) = \{\varphi \in For_0 \mid T \cup LE(+) \cup \neg LE(-) \models \varphi\}$. *Let E be the unique stable set with kernel $E(0)$.*

2. Check *whether* $E(+) \subseteq E$ *and* $E(-) \cap E = \emptyset$.

If the check in step 2 ends positively then E is an expansion of T. Conversely, for every expansion E of T there is a decomposition of $sub(T)$ into $E(+)$ and $E(-)$ such that $E(0) = E_0$ and the check in step 2 succeeds.

Proof: Consider a partition of $sub(T)$: $sub(T) = E(+) \cup E(-)$ and $E(+) \cap E(-) = \emptyset$. Let E be the stable set defined in step 1. Suppose that step 2 is successful, i.e. $E(+) \subseteq E$ and $E(-) \cap E = \emptyset$. Then $E(+) \cap sub(T) = E \cap sub(T)$ and $E(-) \cap sub(T) = E^C \cap sub(T)$. By lemma 10.4 we may replace $E(+)$ by E and $E(-)$ by E^C in the equation defining $E(0)$ and obtain $E_0 = \{\varphi \in For_0 \mid T \cup LE \cup \neg LE^C \models \varphi\}$. By lemma 10.3 we obtain that E is an expansion of T.

Conversely let E be an expansion of T. Define $E(+) = sub(T) \cap E$ and $E(-) = sub(T) \cap E^C$. Using lemma 10.4 we obtain

$$E(0) =$$
$$\{\varphi \in For_0 \mid T \cup LE(+) \cup \neg LE(-) \models \varphi\} =$$
$$\{\varphi \in For_0 \mid T \cup LE \cup \neg LE^C \models \varphi\} =$$
$$E_0.$$

So $E(+) \subseteq E$ and $E(-) \cap E = sub(T) \cap E^C \cap E = \emptyset$. Therefore the check in step 2 is successful.   ∎

10.4   A prototype implementation in Prolog

In this section we present the core of a prototype Prolog implementation. We do not claim that it is an efficient implementation of Autoepistemic Logic, but rather, it is a straightforward encoding of the procedure in section 10.1. Nevertheless it is capable of computing the examples we gave in this chapter and those usually found in the literature.

We have restricted our attention to autoepistemic theories without L-nesting so that a theorem prover on the propositional or first-order level is sufficient (the predicate *sequent* stands for a sequent-style theorem prover; in the simplest case, it may be Wang's algorithm for propositional logic). The predicates `followAll` and `followNone` are left as easy exercises.

The L-operator is represented by the function symbol l, logical negation by ∼. The rest have the meaning suggested by their names. An expansion E is represented as `exp(Epos,Eneg)` corresponding to the decomposition of $sub(T)$ into $E(+)$ and

$E(-)$ which leads to the construction of E (more precisely, of the kernel of E). The implementation of the predicates `partition` and `occursAsSubformula` is left to the reader as a simple exercise.

```
expansion(T, exp(Epos, Eneg)) :-
    setof(Formula, occursAsSubformula(l(Formula), T), SubT),
    partition(SubT,Epos,Eneg),
    setof(l(F), member(F, Epos), Tpos),
    setof(~ l(F), member(F,Eneg),Tneg),
    append(Tpos,Tneg,Tposneg),
    append(T, Tposneg, Tall),
    followAll(Tall, Epos),
    followNone(Tall, Eneg).
```

Problems

10-1. Give an intuitive explanation of the expansions of $T = \{\neg Lp \to q, Lq \to p, Lq \to q\}$.

10-2. Determine the expansions of $T = \{Lp \to q, L(q \vee r) \to s\}$.

10-3. Implement the predicates `partition`, `followAll`, `followNone` and `occursAsSubformu`. that have been omitted in the Prolog program in section 10.4.

10-4. In the Prolog program, an expansion E is represented as `exp(Tpos,Eneg)`. Modify the program so that E is represented by its kernel.

10-5. Determine the expansions of $T = \{con \to Lcon, \neg Lcon\}$.

Chapter 11

Embedding Default Logic into Variants of AE–Logic

Having studied Default Logic and Autoepistemic Logic we turn our attention to relationships between the two formalisms. Their motivations are different: the idea of Default Logic is to use default rules, whereas Autoepistemic Logic is based on introspection. Nevertheless it is possible to translate default theories into the language of Autoepistemic Logic. Consider, for example, the default

$$\frac{aussie : drinksBeer}{drinksBeer}.$$

Its meaning is

If aussie is known, and if it is consistent to assume drinksBeer,
i.e. if ¬drinksBeer is not known, then conclude drinksBeer.

Now, interpreting $L\varphi$ as 'φ is known', it is natural to express the default above as the AE–formula

$$Laussie \wedge \neg L\neg drinksBeer \rightarrow drinksBeer.$$

This translation is of a syntactic nature, and the main theme of this chapter will be to establish a *semantic* relationship between the default theory T and its translation $trans(T)$.

In section 11.1 we define the syntax of the translation and point out that extensions of the default theory will be compared to *the kernels* of the expansions of the translation. It turns out that Autoepistemic Logic provides a broader semantic variety than Default Logic in the sense that expansions need not be as well 'grounded' in the given knowledge as extensions of a default theory. Sections 11.2 and 11.3 show two ways of strengthening the definition of an expansion which are still insufficient to establish an equivalence to default extensions.

Section 11.4 introduces *strongly grounded expansions* which have the desired property: the extensions of a default theory T are exactly the kernels of the strongly grounded expansions of $trans(T)$. The technical proof of this result is found in section 11.5.

11.1   Expressing default theories as AE-theories

Our first aim is to express default theories in the language of Autoepistemic Logic. One idea for the translation is to express the consistency of ψ (a justification of some default) by $\neg L\neg\psi$: $\neg\psi$ is not known (not believed).

So, given a default $\delta = \frac{\varphi:\psi_1,\ldots,\psi_n}{\chi}$, we define $trans(\delta)$ to be the AE–formula $L\varphi \wedge \neg L\neg\psi_1 \wedge \ldots \wedge \neg L\neg\psi_n \rightarrow \chi$. Given a default theory $T = (W, D)$ we define $trans(T)$ as the AE–theory $W \cup \{trans(\delta) \mid \delta \in D\}$[1].

We are interested in comparing the extensions of T with the expansions of $trans(T)$. Note that the extensions are sets of first–order formulae, whilst expansions include occurrences of the L–operator. Therefore we shall compare the extensions of T with the *kernels* (first–order portions) of the expansions of $trans(T)$. This approach is justified because an expansion is uniquely determined by its kernel, as shown in section 9.4.

The reader might hope that there is an equivalence between extensions of T and kernels of expansions of $trans(T)$, in which case we would conclude this chapter and move to the next one. But, unfortunately, things are not always that easy in life! In particular, Autoepistemic Logic admits more expansions than Default Logic admits extensions. Consider the default theory $T = (W, D)$ with $W = \emptyset$ and $D = \{\frac{p:true}{p}\}$. The AE–theory $trans(T)$ consists of the single AE–formula $Lp \wedge \neg Lfalse \rightarrow p$. The only extension of T is $Th(\emptyset)$. However $trans(T)$ has two expansions, one with kernel $Th(\emptyset)$ and the other with kernel $Th(\{p\})$.

How can this difference be explained? Where does the second expansion of $trans(T)$ come from? The answer is obtained if we look at the definition of an expansion E:

$$E = \{\varphi \mid T \cup LE \cup \neg LE^C \models \varphi\}.$$

According to this fixed–point equation a formula φ may be included in an expansion

---

[1]We assume that all formulae in W are closed so that they are AE–formulae, too. In case this is not the case, simply use their universal closure.

E if it can be derived *using the decision to believe in E*, in particular using the decision to believe in φ. This self–referential argument is used to obtain the second expansion in the example above: if we decide to believe in p (and not to believe in *false*, of course) then p can be derived! Note the difference in the definition of default logic extensions: there p must already be known *using other information*, which is not the case in the example given. We summarize the discussion so far by pointing out that expansions

- are not necessarily minimal with respect to kernel inclusion (as seen in the example above); in contrast, no default logic extension can be proper subset of another extension, as shown in Chapter 4.

- may not be 'well grounded' in the given knowledge, in the sense that they may include AE–formulae based solely on the argument that it was decided to believe in them.

Clearly we must strengthen the definition of an expansion to obtain the desired correspondence between the extensions of T and the expansions of $trans(T)$. This is achieved in the following sections.

11.2   Minimal expansions

Our first attempt to overcome the problem outlined in the previous section is to impose a minimality condition on expansions (of course referring to their kernels; is it clear why?).

Let T be an AE–theory and E an expansion of T. We say that E is an *AE–minimal expansion of T* iff there is no expansion F of T such that $F_0 \subset E_0$.

Now let us look back at the example from the previous section, i.e. the default theory $T = (W, D)$ with $W = \emptyset$ and $D = \{\frac{p:true}{p}\}$. The AE–theory $trans(T)$ has a single AE–minimal expansion, namely the one with kernel $Th(\emptyset)$ which corresponds exactly to the extension of T.

But AE–minimality is still insufficient to ensure equivalence with the extension notion of Default Logic. Consider the default theory $T = (W, D)$ with $W = \emptyset$ and $D = \{\frac{true:\neg p}{q}, \frac{p:true}{p}\}$. T has the single extension, $Th(\{q\})$. Now consider $trans(T)$. It consists of the AE–formulae $Ltrue \wedge \neg L\neg\neg p \to q$ and $Lp \wedge \neg Lfalse \to p$. The reader is asked to verify that $trans(T)$ has two expansions, E with kernel $Th(\{q\})$ (as expected), and F with kernel $Th(\{p\})$. Both E and F are obviously AE–minimal, so there isn't a one–to–one correspondence with the extensions of T.

11.3 Moderately grounded expansions*

Our next attempt is to further strengthen the minimality concept defined in the previous section. Let T be an AE–theory and E an expansion of T. E is called an *SS–minimal expansion of T* iff there is no stable set F such that $T \subseteq F$ and $F_0 \subset E_0$.

SS–minimality implies AE–minimality since expansions are stable sets. The converse is not true: consider the AE–theory $T = \{\neg Lp \to q, Lq \to p, Lq \to q\}$. In section 10.2 we showed that T has only the expansion E with kernel $Th(\{p, q\})$, so E is AE–minimal. But E is not SS–minimal. To see this consider the stable set F with kernel $Th(\{p\})$. Obviously, $F_0 \subset E_0$. We show that F includes T. From $p \in F_0$ we conclude $Lp \in F$, and from the deductive closure of F we obtain $\neg Lp \to q \in F$. Also, from $q \notin F$ we obtain $\neg Lq \in F$, $Lq \to p \in F$, and $Lq \to q \in F$.

There is an interesting counterpart of SS–minimality which we present in the following. Recall that in the summary of the discussion in section 11.1 we mentioned two reasons for the non–equivalence between extensions of a default theory T and the kernels of expansions of $trans(T)$: expansions are not minimal, and they are not well grounded in the given AE–theory. Up till now we have focused on minimality only. Let us now switch views. In section 11.1 we said that the reason for the non–groundedness of expansions is the appearance of LE in the definition of an expansion E. In the following we try to address this problem.

First we make a technical observation. Let SS denote the class of all stable sets. We define $T \models_{SS} \varphi$ iff $T \models_E \varphi$ for all stable sets E. Thus $\models_{SS}$ restricts the AE–interpretations considered to those with a stable belief set. Since $\models_{SS}$ is stronger than $\models$, it allows us to weaken the premises used in the definition of an expansion without losing any information.

Lemma 11.1 *A set of AE–formulae E is an expansion of an AE–theory T iff*
$$E = \{\varphi \mid T \cup LE_0 \cup \neg L(For_0 - E_0) \models_{SS} \varphi\}.$$

The proof is left as an exercise for the reader; she may find lemma 11.5 in section 11.4 helpful. Lemma 11.1 shows that the self–referentiality in the definition of expansions has been restricted to first–order beliefs.

Since our aim is to eliminate the self–referentiality of expansions let us restrict the concept of expansions by replacing LE_0 by LT in the definition above. This approach makes sense since the only beliefs we admit are those in the *given knowledge T*. Formally: E is a *moderately grounded expansion* of an AE–theory T iff $E = \{\varphi \mid T \cup LT \cup \neg L(For_0 - E_0) \models_{SS} \varphi\}$. The following theorem shows that moderately grounded expansions correspond to SS-minimal expansions precisely.

Theorem 11.2 *Let T be an AE-theory and E a set of AE-formulae. E is a moderately grounded expansion of T iff E is an SS-minimal expansion of T.*

The proof of this theorem is lengthy and will be presented in section 11.5. Since we have identified a strengthened definition of expansions which addresses both minimality and groundedness in the given knowledge, we may hope that it is the one we are looking for. Unfortunately, this hope is once again not fulfilled. Let us consider the default theory $T = (W, D)$ with $W = \emptyset$ and $D = \{\frac{true:\neg p}{q}, \frac{p:true}{p}\}$ once again. We saw in the previous section that $trans(T)$ has two expansions, E with kernel $Th(\{q\})$ which corresponds to the single extension of T, and F with kernel $Th(\{p\})$. We saw that E and F are AE-minimal. In the following we show that they are even SS-minimal (so moderately grounded expansions), which destroys our hopes of an equivalence to the extensions of T.

Let S be a stable set with $trans(T) \subseteq S$. Suppose $S_0 \subset F_0$. Then $p \notin S$, $\neg\neg p \notin S$, therefore $\neg L\neg\neg p \in S$, so $q \in S$ and $q \in S_0$. But then $S_0 \not\subseteq F_0$ which is a contradiction.

Now suppose that $S_0 \subset E_0$. Then $p \notin S$ and $\neg\neg p \notin S$, therefore $\neg L\neg\neg p \in S$, so $q \in S$ and $q \in S_0$. Since S is deductively closed (as a stable set), S_0 is deductively closed, too. With $q \in S_0$ we conclude that S_0 cannot be a proper subset of E_0 which is a contradiction.

Let us try to determine what went wrong with the example. In particular, we analyze the way p is derived from $T \cup LT \cup \neg(For_0 - F_0)$. Let $(\mathcal{A}, S)$ be an AE-model of $T \cup LT \cup \neg(For_0 - F_0)$, where S is a stable set. Then $L(\neg L\neg\neg p \to q) \in S$. Stability and consistency (is it clear why S is consistent?) of S imply that $\neg L\neg\neg p \to q \in S$. So $L\neg\neg p \in S$ or $q \in S$ (see problem 11-5). Since $(\mathcal{A}, S) \models \neg Lq$ (because $q \notin F_0$) we know that $q \notin S$. Successively we conclude $L\neg\neg p \in S$, $\neg\neg p \in S$, $p \in S$, and $(\mathcal{A}, S) \models Lp$. Using $(\mathcal{A}, S) \models Lp \wedge \neg Lfalse \to p$ and $(\mathcal{A}, S) \models \neg Lfalse$, we finally get $(\mathcal{A}, S) \models p$.

Note that in this argument $L\neg\neg p$ was obtained *before* $\neg\neg p$, an indication that we relied on a self-referential argument once again. The crucial point is that $L\neg\neg p$ was obtained from the rule $\neg L\neg\neg p \to q$ via $L(\neg L\neg\neg p \to q)$ which is SS-equivalent to $\neg L\neg\neg p \to Lq$, that is $\neg Lq \to L\neg\neg p$. See problem 11-6 for some explanations regarding this argument.

The rule $\neg L\neg\neg p \to Lq$ was applied *using contraposition*, that means from right to left ($\neg Lq$ implied $L\neg\neg p$). On the other hand, the corresponding default $\frac{true:\neg p}{q}$ is only used from the top to the bottom, or, in terms of the AE-formula, from left to right! To be more specific, it is not possible to obtain the inconsistency of $\neg p$ from not knowing q.

Now we have finally identified the cause of our problems: the AE–formulae may be used in both directions whereas defaults are strictly unidirectional. The main idea of the definition of *strongly grounded expansions* in the next section is to enforce the application of AE–rules in the 'correct direction' only. After having achieved this, the equivalence to the extensions in Default Logic can be established.

11.4   Strongly grounded expansions*

AE–formulae in default normal form are AE–formulae $L\varphi \wedge \neg L\neg\psi_1 \wedge \ldots \wedge \neg L\neg\psi_n \rightarrow \chi$ where $\varphi, \psi_1, \ldots, \psi_n, \chi$ are first–order formulae; they are the translations of defaults into the language of AE–logic.

Let T be an AE–theory consisting of first–order formulae and AE–formulae in default normal form. Further let E be an expansion of T. T^E denotes the set of AE–formulae $L\varphi \wedge \neg L\neg\psi_1 \wedge \ldots \wedge \neg L\neg\psi_n \rightarrow \chi$ in T such that $\neg\psi_1 \notin E, \ldots, \neg\psi_n \notin E$. We say that E is *strongly grounded in T* iff the following equation holds:

$$E = \{\varphi \mid T^E \cup LT^E \cup \neg L(For_0 - E_0) \models_{SS} \varphi\}.$$

Note that the definition above avoids arguments like the one that led to the problems in the example of the previous section: for a strongly grounded expansion E it is impossible to obtain $L\psi_i$ from not knowing the consequent χ. Before we formulate the main result let us first show that strongly grounded expansions are always moderately grounded.

Lemma 11.3 *Let E be a strongly grounded expansion of an AE–theory T. Then E is a moderately grounded (and thus SS–minimal) expansion of T.*

Proof: We know that $T^E \subseteq T$, $T \subseteq E$ and E is stable, therefore

$E =$
$\{\varphi \mid T^E \cup LT^E \cup \neg L(For_0 - E_0) \models_{SS} \varphi\} \subseteq$
$\{\varphi \mid T \cup LT \cup \neg L(For_0 - E_0) \models_{SS} \varphi\} \subseteq$
$\{\varphi \mid E \models_{SS} \varphi\} \subseteq$
$\{\varphi \mid E \models_E \varphi\} = E.$ ∎

The main theorem of this section (and this chapter) is shown below. Its proof is found in the next section.

Theorem 11.4 *Let $T = (W, D)$ be a default theory. For every extension E of T there is a strongly grounded expansion F of $trans(T)$ such that $E = F_0$. Conversely, the kernel of every strongly grounded expansion of $trans(T)$ is an extension of T.*

Let us reconsider the continuing example from the previous sections. $T = (W, D)$ with $W = \emptyset$ and $D = \{\frac{true:\neg p}{q}, \frac{p:true}{p}\}$ has the single extension $Th(\{q\})$, whereas $trans(T)$ has two expansions, E with kernel $Th(\{q\})$ which corresponds to the only extension of T, and F with kernel $Th(\{p\})$. F should turn out not to be strongly grounded. Indeed, $trans(T)^F$ contains only the rule $Lp \wedge \neg Lfalse \rightarrow p$. We have already shown that $Th(\{p\})$ is not an AE-minimal (or SS-minimal) expansion of $\{Lp \wedge \neg Lfalse \rightarrow p\}$, therefore F is not a strongly grounded expansion of $trans(T)$. On the other hand, E is strongly grounded, as expected: $trans(T)^E = trans(T)$, and E is an SS-minimal expansion of $trans(T)$, as we already know.

11.5 Proofs*

This section contains the proofs of theorems 11.2 and 11.4 with the necessary technical preparations.

Theorem 11.2 *Let T be an AE-theory and E a set of AE-formulae. E is a moderately grounded expansion of T iff E is an SS-minimal expansion of T.*

Proof: Let E be an SS-minimal expansion of T. Then the only stable set S with $T \subseteq S$ and $(For_0 - E_0) \cap S = \emptyset$ is $S = E$. Therefore $T \cup LT \cup \neg L(For_0 - E_0) \models_{SS} \varphi$ is equivalent to $T \models_E \varphi$. Hence $E = \{\varphi \mid T \models_E \varphi\} = \{\varphi \mid T \cup LT \cup \neg L(For_0 - E_0) \models_{SS} \varphi\}$, and E is a moderately grounded expansion of T.

Conversely, let E be a moderately grounded expansion of T. Then

$$E = \{\varphi \mid T \cup LT \cup \neg L(For_0 - E_0) \models_{SS} \varphi\} \tag{1}$$

First we show

$$T \cup LT \cup \neg L(For_0 - E_0) \models_{SS} LE_0 \tag{2}$$

Consider an AE-model $(\mathcal{A}, S)$ of $T \cup LT \cup \neg L(For_0 - E_0)$ with stable S. We must show that $(\mathcal{A}, S)$ is an AE-model of LE_0, that means $E_0 \subseteq S$. Let $\psi \in E_0$.

We know $(\mathcal{A}, S) \models LT \cup \neg L(For_0 - E_0)$, therefore $T \subseteq S$ and $A \cap (For_0 - E_0) = \emptyset$. Then also $LT \subseteq S$ and $\neg L(For_0 - E_0) \subseteq S$. So we have:

$$T \cup LT \cup \neg L(For_0 - E_0) \subseteq S \tag{3}$$

From theorem 9.7 we know that S is an expansion of S_0, that is

$$S = \{\varphi \mid S_0 \cup LS_0 \cup \neg L(For_0 - S_0) \models_{SS} \varphi\} \tag{4}$$

Using (3) and (4) we conclude $S_0 \cup LS_0 \cup \neg L(For_0 - S_0) \models_{SS} T \cup LT \cup \neg L(For_0 - E_0)$. Using (1) and $\psi \in E$ we conclude $T \cup LT \cup \neg L(For_0 - E_0) \models_{SS} \psi$. Altogether we obtain $S_0 \cup LS_0 \cup \neg L(For_0 - S_0) \models_{SS} \psi$. Applying (4) we obtain $\psi \in S$, so (2) is shown. Now we are ready to show that E is an expansion of T:

$$
\begin{aligned}
E &= \\
&\{\varphi \mid T \cup LT \cup \neg L(For_0 - E_0) \models_{SS} \varphi\} = &\text{(using (2))} \\
&\{\varphi \mid T \cup LT \cup LE_0 \cup \neg L(For_0 - E_0) \models_{SS} \varphi\} = \\
&\{\varphi \mid T \cup LT \models_E \varphi\} = &\text{(since } T \subseteq E) \\
&\{\varphi \mid T \models_E \varphi\} = \\
&\{\varphi \mid T \models_E \varphi\}.
\end{aligned}
$$

Finally we show that E is SS–minimal. Let S be a stable set such that $T \subseteq S$ and $S_0 \subseteq E_0$. Then

$$T \cup LT \cup \neg L(For_0 - E_0) \subseteq S \tag{5}$$

We conclude

$$
\begin{aligned}
E &= \\
&\{\varphi \mid T \cup LT \cup \neg L(For_0 - E_0) \models_{SS} \varphi\} \subseteq &\text{(by (5))} \\
&\{\varphi \mid S \models_{SS} \varphi\} \subseteq &\text{(by the stability of } S) \\
&\{\varphi \mid S \models_S \varphi\} \subseteq &\text{(by lemma 9.3)} \\
&S.
\end{aligned}
$$

Therefore $E_0 \subseteq S_0$. Together with the assumption $S_0 \subseteq E_0$ we get $E_0 = S_0$ and, by theorem 9.4, $E = S$. ∎

Lemma 11.5 *Let F be a stable set and T an AE–theory. Define $E = \{\varphi \mid T \models_F \varphi\}$. Then $E_0 = F_0$ implies $E = F$.*

Proof: We know $T \models_F E$. By theorem 9.7 F is an expansion of F_0, that is, $F = \{\varphi \mid F_0 \models_F \varphi\}$. If $F_0 \subseteq E_0$ then $F = \{\varphi \mid F_0 \models_F \varphi\} \subseteq \{\varphi \mid E_0 \models_F \varphi\} \subseteq \{\varphi \mid E \models_F \varphi\} \subseteq \{\varphi \mid T \models_F \varphi\} = E$.

Conversely, assume $E_0 \subseteq F_0$, and let $\varphi \in E$, i.e. $T \models_F \varphi$. Consider $nf(\varphi) = \bigwedge_i \varphi_i$. Consider some φ_i which has the form $\beta \vee L\gamma_1 \vee \ldots \vee L\gamma_p \vee \neg L\delta_1 \vee \ldots \vee \neg L\delta_q$ for a first-order formula β. If some γ_j is an element of F or some δ_k is not an element of F then we are done using the stability of F. Otherwise we get $T \models_F \neg(L\gamma_1 \vee \ldots \vee L\gamma_p \vee \neg L\delta_1 \vee \ldots \vee \neg L\delta_q)$, so $T \models_F \beta$. Therefore $\beta \in E_0 \subseteq F_0$, $\beta \in F$ and $\varphi \in F$. ∎

Lemma 11.6 *Let $T = (W, D)$ be a default theory and E an extension of T. The stable set S with kernel E is the only stable set with $trans(T) \subseteq S$ and $S \cap (For_0 - E) = \emptyset$.*

Proof: Let S be the stable set with kernel E. Obviously, $S \cap (For_0 - E) = \emptyset$. Next we show $trans(T) \subseteq S$. $W \subseteq S$ is trivial because $W \subseteq E = S_0$. Let $\delta = \frac{\varphi : \psi_1, \ldots, \psi_n}{\chi}$ be a default in D, and suppose that $trans(\delta) = L\varphi \wedge \neg L\neg\psi_1 \wedge \ldots \wedge \neg L\neg\psi_n \to \chi$ is not included in S. Then $(\neg L\varphi \vee L\neg\psi_1 \vee \ldots \vee L\neg\psi_n \vee \chi) \notin S$. By the stability of S we get $\varphi \in S, \neg\psi_1 \notin S, \ldots, \neg\psi_n \notin S, \chi \notin S$. So, $\varphi \in E, \neg\psi_1 \notin E, \ldots, \neg\psi_n \notin E, \chi \notin E$. But this means that E is not closed under application of defaults in D w.r.t. belief set E, which is a contradiction to E being an extension of T.

Now we show that S is unique with the properties $trans(T) \subseteq S$ and $S \cap (For_0 - E) = \emptyset$. Let S' be a stable set with these properties; we shall prove that $S'_0 = E$. One inclusion is already given by the second property, so we show $E \subseteq S'_0$. Since E is an extension of T, it is sufficient to show that S'_0 includes W, is deductively closed, and is closed under the application of defaults in D w.r.t. belief set E. The first two properties are clearly given: S'_0 is deductively closed because S' is a stable set, $W \subseteq S'_0$ because $W \subseteq trans(T)$. Consider a default $\frac{\varphi : \psi_1, \ldots, \psi_n}{\chi}$ in D such that $\varphi \in S'_0$ and $\neg\psi_1 \notin E, \ldots, \neg\psi_n \notin E$. From $S'_0 \subseteq E$ we get $\neg\psi_1 \notin S', \ldots, \neg\psi_n \notin S'$. Therefore $L\varphi \in S'$ and $\neg L\neg\psi_1 \in S', \ldots, \neg L\neg\psi_n \in S'$. Since $(L\varphi \wedge \neg L\neg\psi_1 \wedge \ldots \wedge \neg L\neg\psi_n \to \chi) \in trans(T) \subseteq S'$, we get $\chi \in S'$ and $\chi \in S'_0$. ∎

Lemma 11.7 *Let $T = (W, D)$ be a default theory. If S is a stable set with $S_0 = E$ and $trans(T) \subseteq S$, then $\Lambda_T(E) \subseteq \{\alpha \in For_0 \mid trans(T)^E \models_S \alpha\}$[2].*

---

[2]Recall that Λ was the operator used in Reiter's definition of extensions in section 4.4.

Proof: It suffices to show that $\{\alpha \in For_0 \mid trans(T)^E \models_S \alpha\}$ is deductively closed, includes W, and is closed under the application of defaults in D w.r.t. belief set E. The first two properties are clearly given. Let $\delta = \frac{\varphi : \psi_1, \ldots, \psi_n}{\chi}$ be a default in D such that $trans(T)^E \models_S \varphi$ and $\neg\psi_1 \notin E, \ldots, \neg\psi_n \notin E$. Then $\neg\psi_1 \notin S, \ldots, \neg\psi_n \notin S$. $trans(T)^E \models_S \varphi$ and $trans(T) \subseteq S$ imply $S \models_S \varphi$, and, by lemma 9.3, $\varphi \in S$. So $\models_S L\varphi \wedge \neg L\neg\psi_1 \wedge \ldots \wedge \neg L\neg\psi_n$. Using $(L\varphi \wedge \neg L\neg\psi_1 \wedge \ldots \wedge \neg L\neg\psi_n \rightarrow \chi) \in trans(T)^E$ we finally obtain $trans(T)^E \models_S \chi$.
■

Theorem 11.4 *Let $T = (W, D)$ be a default theory. For every extension E of T there is a strongly grounded expansion F of $trans(T)$ such that $E = F_0$. Conversely, the kernel of every strongly grounded expansion of $trans(T)$ is an extension of T.*

Proof: Let E be an extension of T. Define $D^E = \{\frac{\varphi : \psi_1, \ldots, \psi_n}{\chi} \in D \mid \neg\psi_1 \notin E, \ldots, \neg\psi_n \notin E\}$. Obviously, $trans(T)^E = W \cup \{trans(\delta) \mid \delta \in D^E\}$. Since only defaults from D^E can occur in a closed and successful process of T defining E, E is also an extension of (W, D^E). Define $F = \{\alpha \mid trans(T)^E \cup Ltrans(T)^E \cup \neg L(For_0 - E) \models_{SS} \alpha\}$. By lemma 11.6 there is a unique stable set S such that $trans(T)^E \subseteq S$ and $S \cap (For_0 - E) = \emptyset$; furthermore $S_0 = E$. Therefore, the definition of F may be equivalently written as $F = \{\alpha \mid trans(T)^E \models_S \alpha\}$. By lemma 11.7 we obtain $E = \Lambda_T(E) \subseteq F_0$.

Also, $F_0 = \{\alpha \in For_0 \mid trans(T)^E \models_S \alpha\} \subseteq \{\alpha \in For_0 \mid S \models_S \alpha\} \subseteq S_0$, so $F_0 \subseteq S_0 = E$. So we have established $S_0 = F_0$. Using lemma 11.5 we conclude $F = S$. Therefore $S = \{\alpha \mid trans(T)^E \cup Ltrans(T)^E \cup \neg L(For_0 - E) \models_{SS} \alpha\}$, so S is a strongly grounded expansion of $trans(T)$.

Conversely, let S be a strongly grounded expansion of $trans(T)$ with kernel E. Then $trans(T) \subseteq S$ and $S = \{\alpha \mid trans(T)^S \cup Ltrans(T)^S \cup \neg L(For_0 - E) \models_{SS} \alpha\}$. We show that E is an extension of T.

First note that E is deductively closed and includes W because $W \subseteq trans(T) \subseteq S$. Let $\delta = \frac{\varphi : \psi_1, \ldots, \psi_n}{\chi}$ be a default in D such that $\varphi \in E$ and $\neg\psi_1 \notin E, \ldots, \neg\psi_n \notin E$. By the stability of S we get $(L\varphi \wedge \neg L\neg\psi_1 \wedge \ldots \wedge \neg L\neg\psi_n) \in S$. Using $trans(\delta)$ we obtain $\chi \in S$ and $\chi \in E$. So, $\Lambda_T(E) \subseteq E$.

To show the opposite inclusion which completes the proof, consider the unique stable set F with kernel $\Lambda_T(E)$. We show $trans(T)^E \subseteq F$. Then we are finished: by lemma 11.3, S is moderately grounded, therefore S is SS–minimal. If we can prove $trans(T)^E \subseteq F$, then SS–minimality shows that F_0 is not a proper subset of S_0, i.e. $E \subseteq \Lambda_T(E)$.

F obviously contains W. Consider a rule $L\varphi \wedge \neg L\neg\psi_1 \wedge \ldots \wedge \neg L\neg\psi_n \rightarrow \chi$ in $trans(T)$ with $\neg\psi_1 \notin E, \ldots, \neg\psi_n \notin E$. If $\varphi \notin F$ then $\neg L\varphi \in F$, so $(L\varphi \wedge \neg L\neg\psi_1 \wedge \ldots \wedge \neg L\neg\psi_n \rightarrow \chi) \in F$. If, on the other hand, $\varphi \in F$ then $\varphi \in \Lambda_T(E)$. Together with $\neg\psi_1 \notin E, \ldots, \neg\psi_n \notin E$ we get $\chi \in \Lambda_T(E)$, therefore $\chi \in F$ and $(L\varphi \wedge \neg L\neg\psi_1 \wedge \ldots \wedge \neg L\neg\psi_n \rightarrow \chi) \in F$. ∎

Problems

11-1. Why do the minimality definitions of sets of AE–formulae refer to the minimality of kernels instead of the minimality of the full sets?

11-2. Let T be a default theory and E an extension of T. Show that there is an expansion F of $trans(T)$ such that $F_0 = E$. You should prove this result directly and not using theorem 11.4!

11-3. Determine the expansions of $T = \{Ltrue \wedge \neg Lp \rightarrow q, Lp \wedge \neg Lfalse \rightarrow p\}$.

11-4.* Prove lemma 11.1.

11-5. Let S be a stable set. If $\neg Lp \rightarrow q \in S$, then $Lp \in S$ or $q \in S$.

11-6. Two AE–formulae φ and ψ are called *SS–equivalent* iff $\models_{SS} \varphi \leftrightarrow \psi$. Show that $L(\neg Lp \rightarrow q)$ and $\neg Lp \rightarrow Lq$ are SS–equivalent.

11-7.* Formulate some examples from Default Logic as autoepistemic theories, compute their expansions, and compare them with the default logic extensions. Summarize the feeling you develop as to which approach matches better your intuition.

Chapter 12

Circumscription

Developed by McCarthy, Circumscription is the third main formalism for nonmonotonic reasoning, besides Default Logic and Autoepistemic Logic. Nonmonotonic reasoning is intended to draw conclusions from incomplete information in cases where classical logic is insufficient. Both formalisms we have seen so far achieve this by departing from predicate logic: Default Logic augments predicate logic with default rules, Autoepistemic Logic extends the language of predicate logic to include the modal operator L.

Circumscription in its simplest forms sticks to predicate logic using a very simple idea: given a first–order theory T, it enhances T by a set of additional formulae; for the time being, let us denote it by $circ(T)$. Then usual reasoning in the sense of classical logic is used. Let us look at a very simple example, our fine–feathered friend Tweety. Consider the first–order theory T consisting of the formulae

$\forall X(bird(X) \land \neg abnormal(X) \rightarrow flies(X))$
$bird(tweety)$.

The rule says: 'All birds that are not abnormal fly'; this is a way of representing the usual default rule 'Birds normally fly'. We want to deduce

$flies(tweety)$

from T, but this does not follow from T in predicate logic because we cannot prove that Tweety is not abnormal, indeed Tweety may be abnormal, after all. The idea of circumscription is the following: minimize the set of objects for which the predicate *abnormal* is true to those objects a for which there is definite information that $abnormal(a)$ is true. In our case, there is no evidence about any bird being abnormal. Therefore we add the formula

$\forall X \neg abnormal(X)$

to the set $circ(T)^1$. Now it is easy to see that the desired conclusion $flies(tweety)$ follows from $T \cup circ(T)$. Note what happened on the semantic side: we eliminated all models of T in which the interpretation of *abnormal* is nonempty. The models that are left are *minimal* in the interpretation of *abnormal*. In general, the idea of circumscription consists of minimizing the interpretation of specific predicates, thus eliminating many models of T and enabling more logical conclusions.

In this chapter we shall give a brief, rather superficial presentation of circumscription: we highlight some basic ideas and properties without going into details. The reason we do not treat the logic in more detail is twofold. On the theoretical side, circumscription reaches its full strength when second–order logic is used. We avoid discussion of second–order variants because they are beyond the scope of this book. On the practical side, it is very difficult to see how circumscription could be implemented efficiently and used in applications (especially if second–order logic is used). In the words of Marek and Truszczynski: 'Without entering into details, let us express the conviction that this goes beyond currently accepted notions of reasonable computability'.

The reason that we still regard circumscription as a useful technique to confront the reader with is that it provides the opportunity for her to clearly see the idea of minimal models behind a nonmonotonic system. The idea of minimal models is an underlying principle of nonmonotonicity and some of its important applications.

In section 12.1 we introduce the simplest form of circumscription, called predicate circumscription. Section 12.2 describes the relationship to minimal models, while section 12.3 discusses aspects of consistency preservation, and shows some serious limitations of predicate circumscription regarding its expressive power. Sections 12.4 and 12.5 briefly introduce two further variants of circumscription which are improvements of predicate circumscription.

12.1   Predicate circumscription

In this section we present the simplest, and historically first, variant of circumscription. As already stated, the main idea is to minimize the interpretation of some predicates; for simplicity we start by considering the minimization of one predicate only. Suppose that the formula

$$isBlock(a) \wedge isBlock(b)$$

---

[1]This is a simplistic statement; actually, some other formulae are added to $circ(T)$ which imply $\forall X \neg abnormal(X)$.

is given. If we decide to minimize the predicate *isBlock* we intuitively expect that the only blocks are a and b, that is those that are already known. Thus we want to establish a correspondence between

$$isBlock(X)$$

and

$$X = a \vee X = b^2.$$

That means, we want $isBlock(X)$ to be true iff X equals a or X equals b. In a way, the formula $X = a \vee X = b$ is supposed to replace the predicate $isBlock(X)$, therefore it is called a predicate expression.

Formally, a *predicate expression of arity* n consists of a formula ψ and the distinguished variables $X_1, \ldots, X_n$. A predicate expression is sometimes called a *λ-expression* and is denoted by $\lambda X_1, \ldots, X_n.\psi$.

Such an expression is a possible candidate for 'replacing' an n–ary predicate symbol. It is clear what replacement means on the intuitive level; here is the formal definition: Let φ be a closed formula, p an n–ary predicate symbol, and ψ a predicate expression of arity n with distinguished variables $X_1, \ldots, X_n$. We define the result of substituting ψ for p in φ, denoted as $\varphi[p/\psi]$, inductively as follows:

- $q(t_1, \ldots, t_k)[p/\psi] = q(t_1, \ldots, t_k)$ for a predicate symbol q other than p
- $p(t_1, \ldots, t_n)[p/\psi] = \psi\{X_1/t_1, \ldots, X_n/t_n\}$
- $(\varphi_1 * \varphi_2)[p/\psi] = \varphi_1[p/\psi] * \varphi_2[p/\psi]$, for $* \in \{\vee, \wedge, \rightarrow\}$
- $(\neg\varphi)[p/\psi] = \neg(\varphi[p/\psi])$
- $(QX\varphi)[p/\psi] = QX(\varphi[p/\psi])$ for $Q \in \{\forall, \exists\}$.

We say that $\varphi[p/\psi]$ *is admissible* iff no occurrence of a variable of ψ other than $X_1, \ldots, X_n$ is placed into the scope of a quantifier in φ. Admissibility resembles a similar condition on substitution applicability in predicate logic, and is introduced to prevent some unintuitive semantic effects. We exclude $X_1, \ldots, X_n$ because they are supposed to be treated exactly as the n arguments of p. Admissibility can be enforced by renaming variables.

Generalization of the definition above to *simultaneous substitution* of several predicates in φ is straightforward, and is left as an exercise for the reader. Also, if T

---

[2]In this chapter we make use of the equality symbol and assume that the usual equality axioms are implicitly present.

is a finite first–order theory, $T[p/\psi]$ denotes the set $\{\varphi[p/\psi] \mid \varphi \in T\}$. After these technicalities let us return to the 'blocks world example'. The result of substituing

$$X = a \vee X = b$$

for

$$isBlock(X)$$

in the formula

$$isBlock(a) \wedge isBlock(b)$$

is

$$(a = a \vee a = b) \wedge (b = a \vee b = b).$$

The latter formula is obviously valid, and this is a desirable property. After all, we wish to minimize the predicate *isBlock* in such a way that the given information is not violated. To illustrate what we mean, suppose that we decided to minimize *isBlock* radically: nothing is a block. Would this decision be acceptable? Certainly not, given the information $isBlock(a) \wedge isBlock(b)$. Look at what happens if we substitute *false* for $isblock(X)$ in $isBlock(a) \wedge isBlock(b)$:

$$false \wedge false,$$

a false formula. Now we are ready to motivate and define circumscription. Suppose we know that a predicate expression ψ_p is 'smaller than' a predicate p, that means ψ_p implies p (ψ_p is smaller than p in the sense that whenever ψ_p is true of a tuple, p is also true of that tuple; of course, p may be true in other cases as well). Then ψ_p is a candidate predicate expression to minimize p. If additionally ψ_p 'satisfies' the given information, say the formula φ (satisfies in the sense explained above: $\varphi[p/\psi_p]$ must be true), then we may indeed restrict p in φ to ψ_p: p is not allowed to satisfy any more tuples than ψ_p does.

Definition 12.1 Let φ be a closed first–order formula containing an n–ary predicate p, and let ψ_p be a predicate expression of arity n with distinguished variables $X_1, \ldots, X_n$ such that $\varphi[p/\psi_p]$ is admissible. The *circumscription of p in φ by ψ_p* is the following formula:

$$\varphi[p/\psi_p] \wedge \forall X_1 \ldots \forall X_n (\psi_p \to p(X_1, \ldots, X_n)) \to \forall X_1 \ldots \forall X_n (p(X_1, \ldots, X_n) \to \psi_p)$$

If we let ψ_p vary, then the formula above is actually a *schema* which we call the *circumscription of p in φ*. Let $Circum(\varphi, p)$ denote the set of all formulae of the form above for varying ψ_p. A formula χ is *derivable from φ with circumscription of p*, denoted as $\{\varphi\} \vdash_{Circ(p)} \chi$, iff $\{\varphi\} \cup Circum(\varphi, p) \models \chi$. The concepts above can be easily generalized to a finite set T of closed predicate logic formulae.

Now we look at some examples, beginning with our familiar blocks. Circumscription of $isBlock$ in $isBlock(a) \wedge isBlock(b)$ yields the schema

$$\psi(a) \wedge \psi(b) \wedge \forall X(\psi(X) \rightarrow isBlock(X)) \rightarrow \forall X(isBlock(X) \rightarrow \psi(X)).$$

This schema includes, of course, many formulae that are useless for our purpose (for example: take $X = a \vee X = b \vee X = c$ for $\psi(X)$), but also the following ψ: $X = a \vee X = b$ (from now on we use the following notation: $\psi(X) \Longleftrightarrow X = a \vee X = b$). We have already seen that both premises of the schema are fulfilled. Therefore we may conclude

$$\forall X(isBlock(X) \rightarrow \psi(X))$$

which in our case reads

$$\forall X(isBlock(X) \rightarrow (X = a \vee X = b)).$$

Therefore we have

$$\{isBlock(a) \wedge isBlock(b)\} \vdash_{Circ(isBlock)} \forall X(isBlock(X) \rightarrow (X = a \vee X = b))$$

which is what we had expected: the only blocks are a and b. Before we proceed with more examples, let us briefly explain why circumscription is a *nonmonotonic* formalism. The reason is that when a given theory T is extended, some previous conclusions via circumscription no longer hold. For example, suppose that we learn that c is also a block. It is left to the reader to check that then $\forall X(isBlock(X) \rightarrow X = a \vee X = b)$ cannot be derived in the way described above, and this is good because it would be highly counterintuitive to conclude that the only blocks are a and b, given the information that c is also a block. Is it clear which conclusion could be drawn instead?

As another example consider the formula $\neg p(a)$. Equipped with this knowledge exclusively, it is impossible to derive $p(t)$ for any term t, so we would expect the minimization of p to yield $\forall X \neg p(X)$. Let us check that this is indeed possible: circumscription of p in $\neg p(a)$ produces the schema

$$\neg \psi_p(a) \wedge \forall X(\psi_p(X) \rightarrow p(X)) \rightarrow \forall X(p(X) \rightarrow \psi_p(X)).$$

Since we do not want p to be true for any argument we choose $\psi_p \iff false$. Then we have

$$\neg false \wedge \forall X (false \rightarrow p(X)) \rightarrow \forall X(p(X) \rightarrow false).$$

On the left side of the main implication we find only tautologies, so we can derive

$$\forall X (p(X) \rightarrow false)$$

which is equivalent to

$$\forall X \neg p(X).$$

The *Closed World Assumption* (*CWA*) is another formalism based on the idea of minimizing the interpretation of predicates, and is used in logic programming and database systems. According to the CWA we obtain $\neg p(t)$ for every ground term t such that $p(t)$ does not follow from the given knowledge. The CWA and circumscription share the same fundamental ideas, and there exist connections between them. Nevertheless, the two systems exhibit a different behaviour. To see this, consider the formula

$$\varphi = isBlock(a) \vee isBlock(b).$$

That is, we know that either a or b is a block, but we do not know exactly which is a block. If we minimize the interpretation of $isBlock$ in the formula above we would expect the following conclusion: *there is one block, and it is either a or b.* First let us see what happens when circumscription is applied. Using $\psi_{isBlock}(X) \iff X = a$ in the circumscription schema of $isBlock$ in φ we get

$$isBlock(a) \rightarrow \forall X(isBlock(X) \rightarrow X = a).$$

Using $\psi_{isBlock}(X) \iff X = b$ in the circumscription schema of $isBlock$ in φ we get

$$isBlock(b) \rightarrow \forall X(isBlock(X) \rightarrow X = b).$$

Together with φ, these two formulae give us

$$\forall X(isBlock(X) \rightarrow X = a) \vee \forall X(isBlock(X) \rightarrow X = b)$$

which is exactly what we intuitively expected. Now we apply the closed world assumption to φ. Since neither $isBlock(a)$ nor $isBlock(b)$ follow from φ, we may imply both $\neg isBlock(a)$ and $\neg isBlock(b)$ which, together with φ, lead to a contradiction. The CWA misbehaves in this example whereas circumscription derives the expected result.

One (actually the) main disadvantage of circumscription becomes obvious if we look back at the examples of this section. In each of them, we had the expected conclusion in mind and chose suitable formulae from the circumscription schema which gave us the result we had expected. But is this reasonable in practice? Do we always know the expected result a priori? The situation is compounded if we want to implement circumscription, since machines lack human intuition. It is very difficult for an automated program to determine the most suitable predicate expression from the vast number of possibilities. References to some implementation works are found at the end of Part III.

We conclude this section by noting that predicate circumscription may be easily generalized to allow the minimization of several predicates simultaneously. For example, circumscription of p and q in φ is given by the schema

$$(\varphi[p/\psi_p, q/\psi_q] \wedge$$
$$\forall X_1 \ldots \forall X_n (\psi_p \rightarrow p(X_1, \ldots, X_n)) \wedge$$
$$\forall Y_1 \ldots \forall Y_m (\psi_q \rightarrow q(Y_1, \ldots, Y_m))) \rightarrow$$
$$(\forall X_1 \ldots \forall X_n (p(X_1, \ldots, X_n) \rightarrow \psi_p) \wedge$$
$$\forall Y_1 \ldots \forall Y_m (q(Y_1, \ldots, Y_m) \rightarrow \psi_q))$$

where ψ_p and ψ_q are suitable predicate expressions of the same arity as p and q respectively, such that $\varphi[p/\psi_p, q/\psi_q]$ is admissible. For a finite set P of predicate symbols, $\vdash_{Circ(P)}$ is defined in the obvious way.

12.2 Minimal models

In this section we shall describe semantic facets of minimizing the meaning of some predicates. Once again, we consider the example

$$\varphi = isBlock(a) \wedge isBlock(b).$$

We saw in the previous section that circumscription of $isBlock$ in φ derives

$$\forall X (isBlock(X) \rightarrow (X = a \vee X = b))$$

which is equivalent to

$$\forall X ((\neg X = a \wedge \neg X = b) \rightarrow \neg isBlock(X)).$$

So, of all models $\mathcal{A}$ of φ, only those which interpret $isBlock$ as being true of the elements $a_{\mathcal{A}}$ and $b_{\mathcal{A}}$ exclusively, are models of $\{\varphi\} \cup Circum(\varphi, isBlock)$. Consider the algebra $\mathcal{B}$ defined as follows:

- $dom(\mathcal{B}) = \{1, 2, 3, 4\}$
- $a_{\mathcal{B}} = 1, b_{\mathcal{B}} = 2$
- $isBlock_{\mathcal{B}} = \{(1), (2), (3)\}$.

Obviously, $\mathcal{B}$ is a model of φ but not a model of $Circum(\varphi, isBlock)$. Now we observe that we can make it 'smaller' in the following sense: define $\mathcal{C}$ exactly as $\mathcal{B}$, with the only difference that $isBlock_{\mathcal{C}} = \{(1), (2)\}$; thus $isBlock_{\mathcal{C}} \subset isBlock_{\mathcal{B}}$. $\mathcal{C}$ is a model of both φ and $circum(\varphi, isBlock)$. Can the interpretation of $isBlock$ be restricted further while the overall algebra still remains a model of φ? Obviously not, otherwise either $isBlock(a)$ or $isBlock(b)$ would be false.

The algebra $\mathcal{C}$ is minimal in the sense that it is impossible to restrict the interpretation of *isBlock while keeping all other parts of $\mathcal{C}$ unchanged*. Algebras like $\mathcal{C}$ are the interesting ones in our quest of characterizing circumscription semantically: they restrict the interpretation of some predicates as far as possible, which is also the intention of the circumscription schema. Now for the formal definition.

Let T be a finite first–order theory in a signature which contains at least the predicate symbols $P = \{p_1, \ldots, p_k\}$. Let $\mathcal{A}$ and $\mathcal{B}$ be models[3] of T. $\mathcal{A}$ is called a *P–submodel of $\mathcal{B}$*, denoted by $\mathcal{A} \leq^P \mathcal{B}$, iff the following conditions hold:

- $dom(\mathcal{A}) = dom(\mathcal{B})$
- $f_{\mathcal{A}} = f_{\mathcal{B}}$ for all function symbols f
- $p_{\mathcal{A}} = p_{\mathcal{B}}$ for all predicate symbols $p \notin P$
- $p_{\mathcal{A}} \subseteq p_{\mathcal{B}}$ for all $p \in P$.

A model $\mathcal{A}$ of T is called *P–minimal* iff every model of T which is a P–submodel of $\mathcal{A}$ is identical with $\mathcal{A}$. The following theorem states the soundness of predicate circumscription with respect to the minimal model semantics just presented.

Theorem 12.2 *Let T be a finite set of closed formulae, $P = \{p_1, \ldots, p_k\}$ a set of predicate symbols, and χ a formula. If $T \vdash_{Circ(P)} \chi$ then every P–minimal model of T is a model of χ.*

Proof: Let $T \vdash_{Circ(P)} \chi$. If χ is an implication of T in predicate logic then the claim is trivial. Therefore it suffices to show the validity of $Circum(T, P)$ in

---

[3]Since the equality axioms are implicitly present, the algebras we will be considering in this chapter are assumed to be *normal*, that means they interpret = as the equality relation on their domain.

all P–minimal models of T. Assume, to the contrary, that one of the formulae of $Circum(T, P)$ is not valid in some P–minimal model $\mathcal{A}$ of P. Then there is a state sta in $\mathcal{A}$ such that

(1) $\mathcal{A} \models_{sta} T[p_1/\psi_1, \ldots, p_k/\psi_k]$

(2) $\mathcal{A} \models_{sta} \bigwedge_{i=1,\ldots,k} \forall X_{i1} \ldots \forall X_{in_i}(\psi_i \rightarrow p_i(X_{i1} \ldots, X_{in_i}))$

(3) $\mathcal{A} \not\models_{sta} \bigwedge_{i=1,\ldots,k} \forall X_{i1} \ldots \forall X_{in_i}(p_i(X_{i1} \ldots, X_{in_i}) \rightarrow \psi_i)$

where ψ_i are suitable predicate expressions for p_i such that $T[p_1/\psi_1, \ldots, p_k/\psi_k]$ is admissible. Let ψ_i be the predicate expression $\lambda X_{i1}, \ldots, X_{in_i}.\varphi_i$. Then define $\psi_{i_{\mathcal{A},sta}}$ to be the set of tuples $(d_1, \ldots, d_{n_i}) \in dom(\mathcal{A})^{n_i}$ such that

$$\mathcal{A} \models_{sta(X_{i1}/d_1, \ldots, X_{in_i}/d_{n_i})} \varphi_i.$$

Now define a new (normal) algebra $\mathcal{B}$ as follows:

- $dom(\mathcal{B}) = dom(\mathcal{A})$

- $f_{\mathcal{B}} = f_{\mathcal{A}}$ for all function symbols f

- $p_{\mathcal{B}} = p_{\mathcal{A}}$ for all predicate symbols $p \notin P$

- $p_{i_{\mathcal{B}}} = \psi_{i_{\mathcal{A},sta}}$ for all $p_i \in P$.

It is left as an exercise for the reader to verify that

$$\mathcal{A} \models_{sta} T[p_1/\psi_1, \ldots, p_k/\psi_k] \iff \mathcal{B} \models_{sta} T.$$

Then, by (1), $\mathcal{B} \models_{sta} T$, so $\mathcal{B}$ is a model of T, since T consists of closed formulae only. Points (2), (3) and the construction of $\mathcal{B}$ show that $\mathcal{B} \leq^P \mathcal{A}$, and $\mathcal{B}$ is different from $\mathcal{A}$. This is a contradiction to the assumed P–minimality of $\mathcal{A}$. ∎

The converse, that is completeness, does not hold, in general. It may happen that a formula χ is true in all P–minimal models of T, yet it does not follow from $T \cup Circum(T, P)$. From the syntactic point of view $T \cup Circum(T, P)$ is too weak; from the semantic point of view, $T \cup Circum(T, P)$ still admits too many models.

To make it clear what these models are, let us look for a moment at the algebras in predicate logic. Every predicate symbol in the signature is interpreted by a relation on the domain of the algebra. But *the converse is not true*: some relations on the domain of the algebra may not be expressible by first–order formulae. This phenomenon is well–known and causes incompleteness results in other areas such as program verification.

Turning our attention back to the circumscription schema, it is clear that $Circum(T, P)$ describes P–minimality only for relations that are expressible in predicate logic. There may be some relations, though, that are missing, and this can result in an incompleteness situation.

What can be done to avoid the incompleteness of circumscription? One elegant way (from the theoretical standpoint) is to go to second–order logic in which *it is possible to quantify over arbitrary relations*. The circumscription schema becomes a single formula $Circum2(\varphi, P)$ of second–order logic:

$$\forall\psi(\varphi[p/\psi] \wedge \forall X_1 \ldots \forall X_n(\psi \rightarrow p(X_1, \ldots, X_n)) \\ \rightarrow \forall X_1 \ldots \forall X_n(p(X_1, \ldots, X_n) \rightarrow \psi)).$$

Notice that now we can quantify over ψ instead of having to use predicate expressions. Therefore the second–order formula additionally covers relations that are not first–order expressible. In fact, the second–order models of $T \cup Circum2(T, p)$ are exactly the second–order P–minimal models of T. So, completeness has been established. This observation is of a general nature and is not restricted to predicate circumscription only. Usually other variants of circumscription found in the literature are incomplete (with respect to the appropriate minimal model concept that has been developed for each of them) if a first–order schema is used, and complete if a second–order formula is used.

As already indicated in the introduction, we shall abandon the discussion at this point. From the practical standpoint the price we have to pay in moving to second–order logic is far too high: it is hard to imagine a successful implementation. And from the methodological point of view, we would have to give an exposition of second–order logic before we could proceed with providing details of second–order variants of circumscription. This would need too much space and would disturb the flow of the book since second–order logic is not used elsewhere. The interested reader can find relevant references at the end of Part III.

12.3   Consistency and expressive power

An interesting question that arises is whether predicate circumscription is consistency preserving, that means whether $T \cup Circum(T, P)$ is always consistent whenever T is consistent. In the previous chapters we saw that Default Logic is consistency preserving in the sense that if the set of axioms is consistent then every extension is consistent[4], while Autoepistemic Logic is not (we gave an example of a consistent AE–theory with an inconsistent expansion).

It turns out that predicate circumscription is not consistency preserving. A concrete example is shown in problem 12-4. By theorem 12.2 inconsistency can only occur when T does not have a minimal model. For some classes of finite theories existence of minimal models can be shown, in which case consistency is preserved. Here is one: a set of closed formulae is called *universal* iff the prenex normal form of all its formulae does not contain any existential quantifier. An example of universal theories are definite logic programs (see section 18.1).

Theorem 12.3 *Let T be finite, consistent, universal set of closed formulae, and P a finite set of predicate symbols. Then there exists a P–minimal model of T. Consequently $T \cup Circum(T, P)$ is consistent.*

Finally we discuss the expressive power of predicate circumscription. The following result gives a surprising and very disappointing insight: we cannot derive anything new about predicates not being circumscribed, as far as ground terms are concerned. In other words, new information regarding ground terms can only be obtained for circumscribed predicates!

Theorem 12.4 *Let T be a finite, universal set of closed formulae, P a finite set of predicate symbols, p an n–ary predicate symbol not in P, and $t_1, \ldots, t_n$ ground terms. Then*

(a) $T \vdash_{Circ(P)} p(t_1, \ldots, t_n)$ *iff* $T \models p(t_1, \ldots, t_n)$.

(b) $T \vdash_{Circ(P)} \neg p(t_1, \ldots, t_n)$ *iff* $T \models \neg p(t_1, \ldots, t_n)$.

Proof*: (a): One direction is trivial. For the other assume that $T \not\models p(t_1, \ldots, t_n)$. Then $T \cup \{\neg p(t_1, \ldots, t_n)\}$ is a finite, consistent, universal set of closed formulae. By theorem 12.3 it has a P–minimal model $\mathcal{A}$. Obviously, $\mathcal{A}$ is a model of T; furthermore it can be compared to another model $\mathcal{B}$ of T along $\leq^P$ only if $p_{\mathcal{A}} = p_{\mathcal{B}}$ since $p \notin P$. Therefore $\mathcal{A}$ is also a P–minimal model *of* T. By theorem 12.2 it follows $T \not\vdash_{Circ(P)} p(t_1, \ldots, t_n)$.

(b): One direction is trivial. For the other suppose that $T \not\models \neg p(t_1, \ldots, t_n)$. Then $T \cup \{p(t_1, \ldots, t_n)\}$ is consistent and universal and has, by theorem 12.3, a P–minimal model $\mathcal{A}$. We conclude as above that $\mathcal{A}$ is a P–minimal model of T,

---

[4]This notion should be distinguished from the possibility that a default theory T has no extension; in such a case we may argue that an inconsistency of another kind has occurred, since any formula is included in all extensions of T.

therefore $T \not\vdash_{Circ(P)} \neg p(t_1, \ldots, t_n)$.   ∎

Let us reconsider the Tweety example. T consists of the formulae

  $bird(tweety)$
  $\forall X (bird(X) \wedge \neg abnormal(X) \rightarrow flies(X))$.

Theorem 12.4 says that circumscription of *abnormal* in T cannot derive $flies(tweety)$ which is very strange indeed! Let us check that this prediction is true nevertheless. Consider the algebra $\mathcal{A}$ with $dom(\mathcal{A}) = \{1\}$, $tweety_{\mathcal{A}} = 1$ and predicate interpretations $bird_{\mathcal{A}} = abnormal_{\mathcal{A}} = \{(1)\}$ and $flies_{\mathcal{A}} = \emptyset$. It is immediately checked that $\mathcal{A}$ is a model of T, and that $flies(tweety)$ is not true in $\mathcal{A}$. Also $\mathcal{A}$ is $\{abnormal\}$–minimal, since it is impossible to make $abnormal_{\mathcal{A}}$ smaller while preserving both $flies_{\mathcal{A}}$ and validity of T. By theorem 12.2 $T \not\vdash_{Circ(abnormal)} flies(tweety)$.

So predicate circumscription is not sufficient to realize default reasoning. Before the reader starts tearing up the book wishing the author to hell for having wasted her time, we urge her to read the next section; there she will be rewarded by a modification of predicate circumscription which will allow Tweety to fly! After having this rare insight into the wonderland of scientific achievement, we hope that the reader will then calm down (if not, we prescribe two shots of whiskey).

12.4   Variable circumscription

Let us reconsider the Tweety example which demonstrated a serious limitation of predicate circumscription. Consider the theory T consisting of the formulae

  $bird(tweety)$
  $\forall X (bird(X) \wedge \neg abnormal(X) \rightarrow flies(X))$.

Our intuition tells us that when circumscribing *abnormal* in T we should take $\psi_{abnormal} \Longleftrightarrow false$ in the circumscription schema since no information about an abnormal bird is included in T. Unfortunately we are unable to derive $T[abnormal/ \psi_{abnormal}]$ from T in classical logic, since this would mean that we could prove $\forall X (bird(X) \rightarrow flies(X))$. We cannot expect this formula to be derivable from T in classical logic, of course. So, predicate circumscription does not work well for this example, as shown in the previous section.

Variable circumscription is an improved version which avoids this problem by allowing some predicates in the given theory to *vary*, that means to substitute the predicates by some suitable predicate expressions within the circumscription schema. Looking at the example above we may decide to let the predicate *flies* vary and substitute it by *bird*. Now, $T[abnormal/\psi_{abnormal}, flies/bird]$ is valid, and we get successively

$$\forall X (abnormal(X) \rightarrow false)$$
$$\forall X \neg abnormal(X)$$
$$\forall X (bird(X) \rightarrow flies(X)), \text{ and finally}$$
$$flies(tweety).$$

Note that substitution of *flies* by *bird* matches our intuition that in case *abnormal* is 'empty' (*abnormal* is true of no element), the meanings of *bird* and *flies* coincide.

A new problem arises: which predicates should we let vary? There exists no definite rule, in general, but note that in our example *flies* is the predicate that is affected by the circumscription of *abnormal* in T. We can formulate the following guideline:

> *Let those predicates vary that are expected to be affected by circumscription (in the form of new ground instances).*

Now we are prepared to give the formal definition of variable circumscription. Let φ be a closed formula containing different predicates $p_1, \ldots, p_k, q_1, \ldots, q_l$ of arity $n_1, \ldots, n_k, m_1, \ldots, m_l$ respectively. Let ψ_{p_i} and ψ_{q_j} be predicate expressions of arity n_i and m_j respectively (for all $i = 1, \ldots, k$ and $j = 1, \ldots, l$) such that $\varphi[p_1/\psi_{p_1}, \ldots, p_k/\psi_{p_k}, q_1/\psi_{q_1}, \ldots, q_l/\psi_{q_l}]$ is admissible. The *circumscripton of $p_1, \ldots, p_k$ in φ with varying $q_1, \ldots, q_l$* is the following schema:

$$\varphi[p_1/\psi_{p_1}, \ldots, p_k/\psi_{p_k}, q_1/\psi_{q_1}, \ldots, q_l/\psi_{q_l}] \wedge$$
$$\bigwedge_{i=1,\ldots,k} \forall X_{i1} \ldots \forall X_{in_i}(\psi_{p_i} \rightarrow p_i(X_{i1}, \ldots, X_{in_i})) \rightarrow$$
$$\bigwedge_{i=1,\ldots,k} \forall X_{i1} \ldots \forall X_{in_i}(p_i(X_{i1}, \ldots, X_{in_i}) \rightarrow \psi_{p_i}).$$

The set of all formulae given by this schema is denoted by $Circum(\varphi, P, Q)$ (where $P = \{p_1, \ldots, p_k\}$ and $Q = \{q_1, \ldots, q_l\}$). A formula ψ is *derivable from φ by circumscription of P with varying Q*, denoted by $\{\varphi\} \vdash_{Circ(P,Q)} \psi$, iff $\{\varphi\} \cup Circum(\varphi, P, Q) \models \psi$. As before, generalization to finite sets T of closed formulae is trivial.

Now let us see how this definition works for a concrete example. Let T be the theory consisting of the following formulae:

$\forall X (creature(X) \land \neg abnormal1(X) \rightarrow \neg flies(X))$
$\forall X (bird(X) \rightarrow creature(X) \land abnormal1(X))$
$\forall X (bird(X) \land \neg abnormal2(X) \rightarrow flies(X))$
$\forall X (penguin(X) \rightarrow bird(X) \land \neg flies(X)).$

First let us point out the use of different *abnormality predicates*; each of them refers to a different aspect of abnormality. Flying creatures are abnormal creatures, while nonflying birds are abnormal birds. The use of abnormality predicates is typical when default rules are to be treated using circumscription.

Now, what are the conclusions we would intuitively expect from the knowledge above if we decided to minimize *abnormal1* and *abnormal2* in T? Creatures that are not birds should be nonflying, and birds should be flying except for penguins.

Technically this is achieved by minimizing *abnormal1* to *bird* and *abnormal2* to *penguin*. Which predicates should we let vary? The predicate we expect to be affected by circumscription is *flies*, so according to the guideline above, we decide to let it vary. The reader is asked to verify that using

$\psi_{abnormal1}(X) \Longleftrightarrow bird(X)$
$\psi_{abnormal2}(X) \Longleftrightarrow penguin(X)$
$\psi_{flies}(X) \Longleftrightarrow bird(X) \land \neg penguin(X)$

in the circumscription schema we may derive

$\forall X (abnormal1 \rightarrow bird(X))$
$\forall X (abnormal2(X) \rightarrow penguin(X)).$

Finally, using T we deduce

$\forall X (creature(X) \land \neg bird(X) \rightarrow \neg flies(X))$
$\forall X (bird(X) \land \neg penguin(X) \rightarrow flies(X))$

which is the desired result. Next we give a semantic characterization of variable circumscription. The concept of a P-minimal model must be modified in a way that reflects the fact that the predicates in Q may vary. Since these predicates can be replaced by any predicate expression (which meets the usual conditions concerning arity and admissibility), they will simply be disregarded when two models are compared.

Now for the formal definition. Let T be a finite set of closed formulae in a signature which contains at least the predicate symbols $P = \{p_1, \ldots, p_k\}$ and $Q =$

$\{q_1, \ldots, q_l\}$. Let $\mathcal{A}$ and $\mathcal{B}$ be models of T. $\mathcal{A}$ is called a (P,Q)–submodel of $\mathcal{B}$, denoted by $\mathcal{A} \leq^{P,Q} \mathcal{B}$, iff the following conditions hold:

- $dom(\mathcal{A}) = dom(\mathcal{B})$
- $f_\mathcal{A} = f_\mathcal{B}$ for all function symbols f
- $p_\mathcal{A} = p_\mathcal{B}$ for all predicate symbols $p \notin P \cup Q$
- $p_\mathcal{A} \subseteq p_\mathcal{B}$ for all $p \in P$.

We write $\mathcal{A} <^{P,Q} \mathcal{B}$ if $\mathcal{A} \leq^{P,Q} \mathcal{B}$ and not $\mathcal{B} \leq^{P,Q} \mathcal{A}$. A model $\mathcal{A}$ of T is called (P,Q)–minimal iff there is no model $\mathcal{B}$ of T such that $\mathcal{B} <^{P,Q} \mathcal{A}$.

Obviously it is possible that $\mathcal{A} \leq^{P,Q} \mathcal{B}$ and $\mathcal{B} \leq^{P,Q} \mathcal{A}$, but $\mathcal{A}$ and $\mathcal{B}$ are different models; this can happen when they interpret predicates from Q in a different way. So, $\leq^{P,Q}$ needs not be antisymmetric. On the other hand it is reflexive and transitive, therefore it makes sense to speak of minimality with respect to $\leq^{P,Q}$.

The following theorem states the soundness of variable circumscription w.r.t. the minimal model semantics just introduced. Its proof is very similar to the proof of theorem 12.2 and is left to the reader. Since we defined variable circumscription by a first–order schema instead of a second–order formula, completeness does not hold for the same reasons as for the incompleteness of predicate circumscription.

Theorem 12.5 *Let T be a finite set of closed formulae, P and Q two distinct finite sets of predicate symbols, and χ a formula. If $T \vdash_{Circ(P,Q)} \chi$ then every (P,Q)–minimal model of T is a model of χ.*

12.5 Prioritized circumscription

We saw in Chapters 7 and 8 that priorities among defaults are an important representational issue. Since default rules may be expressed in circumscription using abnormality predicates, we are confronted with priorities again, this time in a different setting. Consider the first–order theory T consisting of the formulae

$\forall X(adult(X) \land \neg abnormal1(X) \rightarrow employed(X))$
$\forall X(student(X) \land \neg abnormal2 \rightarrow \neg employed(X))$
$\forall X(student(X) \rightarrow adult(X))$
$student(mary)$.

When we try to minimize both *abnormal1* and *abnormal2* we make the following observation: there are two 'concurring' $\{abnormal1, abnormal2\}$–minimal models of T, one satisfying

$$\neg abnormal1(mary) \wedge abnormal2(mary) \wedge employed(mary)$$

and the other

$$\neg abnormal2(mary) \wedge abnormal1(mary) \wedge \neg employed(mary).$$

Therefore variable circumscription can only produce

$$\neg abnormal1(mary) \vee \neg abnormal2(mary).$$

This is not very helpful in determining Mary's employment status, of course. Actually we would like to give the information regarding students higher weight than the more general information about adults, and conclude that Mary is not employed. One way of doing this would be to add the rule

$$\forall X(student(X) \rightarrow abnormal1(X))$$

to T. This approach is inappropriate for practical applications, of course, for the same reasons we did not want to deal with priorities in Default Logic by 'patching' the priority information into the defaults: the knowledge base would tend to become unpredictable and unmanageable.

There is a variant of circumscription which can deal with priorities that are given explicitly. Let the set P of predicates to be circumscribed be partitioned into $(P_1, \ldots, P_n)$ with the intended meaning that minimization of predicates in P_i should have higher priority than minimization of some other predicate in P_j for $j > i$ (P_1 is the subset with highest priority).

Given a finite first–order theory T, the set $P = P_1 \cup \ldots \cup P_n$ and a set Q of predicates that may vary (Q is distinct from P), the *prioritized circumscription of P in T with varying Q* is given by the set

$$\bigcup_{i=1,\ldots,n} Circum(T, P_i, P_{i+1} \cup \ldots \cup P_n \cup Q).$$

In the example above, if we assign *abnormal2* higher priority than *abnormal1* then *abnormal2* is minimized with varying *abnormal1*[5], but not vice versa. It is left

---

[5]and *employed*

to the reader to check that prioritized circumscription indeed yields the desired conclusion $\neg employed(mary)$, using

$$\psi_{abnormal1}(X) \Longleftrightarrow student(X)$$
$$\psi_{abnormal2}(X) \Longleftrightarrow false$$
$$\psi_{employed} \Longleftrightarrow adult(X) \wedge \neg student(X).$$

Problems

12-1. Define $\varphi[p_1/\psi_1, \ldots, p_n/\psi_n]$, the simultaneous substitution of the predicates p_i by the predicate expressions ψ_i in φ.

12-2 Consider the circumscription schema for $isBlock$ and the given formula $isBlock(a) \wedge isBlock(b)$.

(a) Explain what happens when the predicate expression $\psi(X) \Longleftrightarrow X = a$ is used.

(b) Do the same for $\psi(X) \Longleftrightarrow X = a \vee X = b \vee X = c$.

(c) What happens if $isBlock(c)$ is added to the given knowledge?

12-3. Verify the equivalence used in the proof of theorem 12.2.

12-4.* Let T be the first–order theory consisting of the formulae

$$\forall X_1 \forall X_2 (p(X_1, X_2) \rightarrow \exists X_3 p(X_2, X_3))$$
$$\exists X_2 \exists X_3 (p(X_2, X_3) \wedge \forall X_1 \neg p(X_1, X_2))$$
$$\forall X_1 \forall X_2 \forall X_3 (p(X_2, X_1) \wedge p(X_3, X_1) \rightarrow X_3 = X_1)$$

Consider the circumscription of p using the predicate expression $\psi_p(X_1, X_2) \Longleftrightarrow p(X_1, X_2) \wedge \exists X_3 p(X_3, X_1)$.

(a) Verify that all three formulae in $T[p/\psi_p]$ follow from T.

(b) Show that $\forall X_1 \forall X_2 (\psi_p(X_1, X_2) \rightarrow p(X_1, X_2))$ is a tautology.

(c) Derive $\forall X_1 \forall X_2 (p(X_1, X_2) \rightarrow \psi_p)$ and show that an inconsistency has occurred.

12-5. Let T be a finite, universal set of closed formulae, P a finite set of predicate symbols, p an n–ary predicate symbol in P, and $t_1, \ldots, t_n$ ground terms. Show that $T \vdash_{Circ(P)} p(t_1, \ldots, t_n)$ iff $T \models p(t_1, \ldots, t_n)$.

12-6. Work out what exactly happens when *abnormal* is minimized in the usual Tweety example using predicate circumscription.

12-7.* Prove theorem 12.5.

12-8. Work out the example on prioritized circumscription.

12-9.* Reformulate some examples from Default Logic in Circumscription using abnormality predicates, and try to draw conclusions that were possible in Default Logic.

References for Part III

Autoepistemic Logic was developed by Moore [57, 58] and studied in depth by other researchers, for example [51, 33]. It has been deeply studied in [54] along with other nonmonotonic modal logics.

Our presentation of AEL is based on the paper [4]. The relationship between Default and Autoepistemic Logic was studied by Konolige [38] and Marek and Truszczynski [52]. The presentation of Chapter 11 is based on lecture notes by Sperschneider.

Predicate circumscription was introduced by McCarthy in [55] and studied by Etherington, Mercer and Reiter [22]. Variable circumscription was introduced by McCarthy [56], and ideas of prioritized circumscription can be found in [41, 56]. A thorough presentation of the basic forms of circumscription can be found in Lukaszewicz' book [47]. Also in Lifschitz' papers [42, 43]. Implementations of circumscription include SCAN [26] and DLS [20].

Part IV

Abstract and Dynamic Approaches to Nonmonotonic Reasoning

In the previous chapters we described some important methods for nonmonotonic reasoning: Default Logic, Autoepistemic Logic and Circumscription. For each of them there exist several variations, some of which we described and most of which we omitted. And there are other approaches to nonmonotonicity that we did not cover at all.

Given the diversity of specific forms of nonmonotonic reasoning methods that have been developed, the question naturally arises whether we can study the notion of nonmonotonic reasoning from a more general perspective, abstracting from approach–specific characteristics. Such a study is conducted in Chapter 13 which investigates *nonmonotonic inference relations* and their properties. For a nonmonotonic inference relation $\mathrel{|\!\sim}$,

$$M \mathrel{|\!\sim} \varphi$$

means that φ is a nonmonotonic consequence of the set of premises (formulae) M. One example of such an inference relation is the following: Let D be a countable set of defaults. Then $W \mathrel{|\!\sim} \varphi$ iff φ is included in all extensions of the default theory (W, D). The properties of $\mathrel{|\!\sim}$ studied in Chapter 13 hold trivially for the classical inference relation $\vdash$ of predicate logic, so we have to be very careful with nonmonotonic relations: Properties which look 'innocent' may infer monotonicity!

Then we turn our attention to the *dynamics of nonmonotonic reasoning*. Nonmonotonic reasoning methods usually take a static viewpoint in that they assume knowledge does not change over time. If this does happen, then the nonmonotonic conclusions have to be recomputed from scratch. In Chapter 14 we discuss *Belief Revision* which is devoted to the study of modeling changes to repositories of information. In particular we present the so–called *AGM paradigm* which introduces insertion, deletion and revision operators, and describes their intended meaning by logical postulates. These postulates turn out to be too weak to characterize the operators uniquely, therefore we use additionally a *preference criterion* which determines the formulae that should preferably be kept when changes become necessary.

Chapter 15 is devoted to the development of a computational model for belief revision. The questions addressed include finite representation and iterated belief change, that means, the iterated application of belief revision functions. Based on the techniques developed, a prototype program for belief revision that makes use of a standard theorem prover is provided.

As stated before, nonmonotonic reasoning methods are intended to work with *incomplete information* whereas belief revision deals with *changing information*. Despite this difference in intuition and intention, the two fields turn out to be very closely related via the common underlying principle of minimality, and we outline some aspects of this relationship in Chapter 16. In particular, the relationship between belief change functions and abstract properties of nonmonotonic inference relations is highlighted, and we demonstrate that a limited kind of default reasoning can be performed in the belief revision framework.

Chapter 13

Nonmonotonic Inference Relations

This chapter studies nonmonotonic reasoning from an abstract perspective. Section 13.1 describes the fundamental concept of this study, namely inference relations. Sections 13.2 and 13.3 discuss some basic conditions on inference relations, and define a core of desirable properties, namely cumulativity, supraclassicality and distribution. In section 13.4 we discuss these properties in the framework of Default Logic, while in section 13.5 we give a semantics for a class of nonmonotonic inference relations. Finally section 13.6 introduces some further properties which are more controversial.

13.1 The notion of an inference relation

As we have seen there exist many different approaches to nonmonotonic reasoning, and all of them aim to provide the barebone of a useful procedure to draw conclusions. Even though much work has been done in establishing interconnections between different approaches, there is a need to compare the approaches from a more abstract viewpoint.

A central concept in classical predicate logic is that of entailment or inference. The syntactic relation $\vdash$ (and the equivalent semantic relation $\models$) provides us with a possibility to determine whether a formula φ follows from a set of premises M. In a sense, $\vdash$ describes the behaviour (or *output*) of the logical machinery of predicate logic. In the following we take up this idea and use it in the context of nonmonotonicity. In particular, we decide to focus on the *inference relation* $\mid\!\sim$ generated by the various formalisms; that means, we are interested in the question which formulae follow nonmonotonically from a piece of information M. In Default Logic, for example, we can define an inference relation as follows: Given a countable set D of defaults,

$$W \hspace{0.2em}\vdash\hspace{-0.6em}\sim \varphi \text{ iff } \varphi \text{ is included in all extensions of } (W, D).$$

An alternative might be:

$$W \hspace{0.2em}\vdash\hspace{-0.6em}\sim \varphi \text{ iff } \varphi \text{ is included in some extension of } (W, D).$$

What we are going to do in the following sections is to look in a general manner at various desirable properties of nonmonotonic inference relations. We note that all of these properties hold for the classical inference relation $\vdash$; on the other hand, many properties of $\vdash$ have to be omitted because they are related to the property of monotonicity.

In this chapter we restrict our attention to propositional logic. We also use another notation interchangeably with $\hspace{0.2em}\vdash\hspace{-0.6em}\sim$, and that is the associated *inference operation* C defined as follows:

$$C(M) = \{\varphi \mid M \hspace{0.2em}\vdash\hspace{-0.6em}\sim \varphi\}.$$

For example, the property '$M \hspace{0.2em}\vdash\hspace{-0.6em}\sim \varphi$ if $\varphi \in M$' can be formulated as $M \subseteq C(M)$. Apart from some theoretical reasons[1] this representation tends to be more compact for many purposes such as composition. We shall switch freely between the two notations according to our needs.

13.2 Basic properties: pure conditions

Consider the following conditions on an inference operation C:

$M \subseteq C(M)$	*Inclusion*
$C(M) = C(C(M))$	*Idempotence*
$M \subseteq N \subseteq C(M)$ implies $C(N) \subseteq C(M)$	*Cut*
$M \subseteq N \subseteq C(M)$ implies $C(M) \subseteq C(N)$	*Cautious Monotony*
$M \subseteq N \subseteq C(M)$ implies $C(M) = C(N)$	*Cumulativity*
$M \subseteq N$ implies $C(M) \subseteq C(N)$	*Monotony*

---

[1]which we disregard here; essentially they have to do with being able to represent infinite sets of premises.

The meaning of inclusion and idempotence is clear. Cut says the following: If we expand the information M by some propositions which are included in the closure $C(M)$, then we don't obtain new conclusions. Stated another way, if we add a conclusion as a lemma to the set of premises we don't obtain additional inferences.

Cautious monotony is the converse of cut: The addition of a lemma does not decrease the set of conclusions. The combination of cut and cautious monotony gives us the property of cumulativity, which says that we can use lemmas safely without affecting the supported conclusions.

Of course we have to give up monotony to be able to study nonmonotonic inference relations. We consider the remaining properties to be important, because they appear to describe natural and useful ways of reasoning. A consequence relation satisfying these properties is called a *cumulative inference relation*.

It is interesting to determine relationships among the conditions above. This way we can determine a minimal set of conditions that should be satisfied for an inference relation to be cumulative.

Theorem 13.1 *Cut and inclusion imply idempotence. Cautious monotony and idempotence imply cut.*

Proof: For the first claim we note that $C(M) \subseteq C(C(M))$ follows directly from inclusion. Inclusion also gives us $M \subseteq C(M)$. Applying cut with $N = C(M)$ we obtain $C(C(M)) \subseteq C(M)$ and we are finished.

For the second claim suppose that $M \subseteq N \subseteq C(M)$. Then by cautious monotony we have $C(M) \subseteq C(N)$. Using our assumption $N \subseteq C(M)$ and cautious monotony once again we obtain $C(N) \subseteq C(C(M))$ which means $C(N) \subseteq C(M)$ because of idempotence. ∎

In summary, this section has identified the concept of a *cumulative inference relation (operation)* to be natural and useful; inclusion and cumulativity form a sufficient condition for an inference relation to be cumulative, as shown by theorem 13.1. We conclude this section by introducing a property which will also turn out to be useful. Problem 13-1 shows that, given inclusion, this condition is equivalent to cumulativity.

$M \subseteq C(N)$ and $N \subseteq C(M)$ implies $C(M) = C(N)$ *Reciprocity*

13.3 Basic properties: interaction with logical connectives

The properties in the previous section did not refer to any features of propositional logic formulae such as the logical connectives. Instead they can apply to any language L, therefore they are called *pure*. In the following we refer to the language of propositional logic, and introduce conditions which interact with this language. A natural condition which links nonmonotonic inference with classical inference is the following:

$$Th(M) \subseteq C(M) \qquad\qquad\qquad\qquad\qquad\qquad \textit{Supraclassicality}$$

This condition says that the classical logical consequences of M follow from M nonmonotonically, too. In other words, nonmonotonic inference is supposed to support *more* conclusions (to cope with incomplete information) but certainly not less. Theorem 13.2 shows interesting consequences of supraclassicality, and makes use of the following properties:

$$Th(C(M)) = C(M) \qquad\qquad\qquad\qquad\qquad\qquad \textit{Left Absorption}$$
$$C(Th(M)) = C(M) \qquad\qquad\qquad\qquad\qquad\qquad \textit{Right Absorption}$$
$$Th(C(M)) = C(M) = C(Th(M)) \qquad\qquad\qquad\qquad \textit{Full Absorption}$$

Theorem 13.2 *Let C be a supraclassical inference relation. If C satisfies idempotence then it satisfies left absorption. If C is cumulative then it satisfies full absorption.*

Proof: $C(M) \subseteq Th(C(M))$ by definition of Th. Conversely, $Th(C(M)) \subseteq C(C(M)) \subseteq C(M)$ using supraclassicality and idempotence.

For the second claim, we use supraclassicality to get $M \subseteq Th(M) \subseteq C(M)$, and then cumulativity to obtain $C(M) = C(Th(M))$. ∎

The absorption properties can be used to establish further relationships between nonmonotonic inference and logical connectives. Consider the following conditions.

$$\{\varphi, \psi\} \subseteq C(M) \text{ implies } \varphi \wedge \psi \in C(M) \qquad\qquad \textit{Right And}$$
$$\varphi \in C(M) \text{ and } \{\varphi\} \vdash \psi \text{ implies } \psi \in C(M) \qquad \textit{Right Weakening}$$
$$Th(M) = Th(N) \text{ implies } C(M) = C(N) \qquad \textit{Left Logical Equivalence}$$

These conditions are better understood in their inference relation representation:

$M \hspace{1pt}\vdash\hspace{-7pt}\sim \varphi$ and $M \hspace{1pt}\vdash\hspace{-7pt}\sim \psi$ implies $M \hspace{1pt}\vdash\hspace{-7pt}\sim \varphi \wedge \psi$ *Right And*

$M \hspace{1pt}\vdash\hspace{-7pt}\sim \varphi$ and $\{\varphi\} \vdash \psi$ implies $M \hspace{1pt}\vdash\hspace{-7pt}\sim \psi$ *Right Weakening*

$M \hspace{1pt}\vdash\hspace{-7pt}\sim \varphi$ and $Th(M) = Th(N)$ implies $N \hspace{1pt}\vdash\hspace{-7pt}\sim \varphi$ *Left Logical Equivalence*

Problem 13-3 shows that these properties are direct consequences of absorption. It is worth taking a closer look at right weakening. Notice that the second premise of the rule demands that ψ be a *classical* conclusion of φ, not a nonmonotonic one. In fact, if we would have used C instead of Th then we would have had a kind of transitivity: If φ is a nonmonotonic consequence of M and ψ a nonmonotonic consequence of φ, then ψ is a nonmonotonic consequence of M.

Transitivity clearly holds for the classical inference relation $\vdash$, and appears to be natural for nonmonotonic inference relations as well. But beware: A supraclassical and transitive inference relation satisfies a form of monotony, as shown below. Therefore, if we want to abandon monotony but wish to retain supraclassicality, we must be prepared to give up transitivity.

Theorem 13.3 *Suppose $\hspace{1pt}\vdash\hspace{-7pt}\sim$ is transitive and supraclassical. Then $\{\varphi\} \hspace{1pt}\vdash\hspace{-7pt}\sim \chi$ implies $\{\varphi \wedge \psi\} \hspace{1pt}\vdash\hspace{-7pt}\sim \chi$.*

Proof: We have $\{\varphi \wedge \psi\} \vdash \varphi$, so by supraclassicality $\{\varphi \wedge \psi\} \hspace{1pt}\vdash\hspace{-7pt}\sim \varphi$. Also $\{\varphi\} \hspace{1pt}\vdash\hspace{-7pt}\sim \chi$, therefore by transitivity $\{\varphi \wedge \psi\} \hspace{1pt}\vdash\hspace{-7pt}\sim \chi$.   ∎

Supraclassicality is one of the central properties that establish interactions with the language of classical logic and its machinery. Next we turn our attention to another important condition:

$C(M) \cap C(N) \subseteq C(Th(M) \cap Th(N))$ *Distribution*

Lemma 13.4 *If C satisfies absorption, then distribution is equivalent to the following conditions:*

(a) *If $M = Th(M)$ and $N = Th(N)$ then $C(M) \cap C(N) \subseteq C(M \cap N)$.*

(b) $C(T \cup M) \cap C(T \cup N) \subseteq C(T \cup (Th(M) \cap Th(N)))$.

The proof is left as an exercise to the reader (problem 13-5). An inference operation C (or inference relation $\hspace{1pt}\vdash\hspace{-7pt}\sim$) is called *distributive* iff it satisfies distribution.

It is easier to demonstrate the power and use of distribution rather than give an intuitive justification. So we describe some properties that follow from distribution plus some other basic properties.

$$C(M \cup \{\varphi\}) \cap C(M \cup \{\psi\}) \subseteq C(M \cup \{\varphi \vee \psi\}) \qquad\qquad \textit{Left Or}$$
$$C(M \cup \{\varphi\}) \cap C(M \cup \{\neg\varphi\}) \subseteq C(M) \qquad\qquad \textit{Proof By Cases}$$

Again, these properties can be more easily understood in the inference relation representation:

$$M \cup \{\varphi\} \mathrel{\vdash\mkern-9mu\sim} \chi \text{ and } M \cup \{\psi\} \mathrel{\vdash\mkern-9mu\sim} \chi \text{ implies } M \cup \{\varphi \vee \psi\} \mathrel{\vdash\mkern-9mu\sim} \chi \qquad \textit{Left Or}$$
$$M \cup \{\varphi\} \mathrel{\vdash\mkern-9mu\sim} \chi \text{ and } M \cup \{\neg\varphi\} \mathrel{\vdash\mkern-9mu\sim} \chi \text{ implies } M \mathrel{\vdash\mkern-9mu\sim} \chi. \qquad \textit{Proof By Cases}$$

Theorem 13.5 *If C satisfies distribution, supraclassicality and absorption, then C satisfies Left Or and Proof By Cases.*

Proof: In propositional logic $Th(\{\varphi\}) \cap Th(\{\psi\}) = Th(\{\varphi \vee \psi\})$. Left Or is shown as follows:

$$
\begin{aligned}
&C(M \cup \{\varphi\}) \cap C(M \cup \{\psi\}) \\
&\subseteq C(M \cup (Th(\{\varphi\}) \cap Th(\{\psi\}))) && \text{(lemma 13.4)} \\
&= C(M \cup Th(\{\varphi \vee \psi\})) && \text{(property above)} \\
&= C(Th(M \cup Th(\{\varphi \vee \psi\}))) && \text{(by absorption)} \\
&= C(Th(M \cup \{\varphi \vee \psi\})) && \text{(property of } Th) \\
&= C(M \cup \{\varphi \vee \psi\}). && \text{(by absorption)}
\end{aligned}
$$

Proof by cases is shown as follows:

$$
\begin{aligned}
&C(M \cup \{\varphi\}) \cap C(M \cup \{\neg\varphi\}) \\
&\subseteq C(M \cup \{\varphi \vee \neg\varphi\}) && \text{(by Left Or)} \\
&= C(Th(M \cup \{\varphi \vee \neg\varphi\})) && \text{(by absorption)} \\
&= C(Th(M)) = C(M). && \text{(by absorption)}
\end{aligned}
$$

∎

A central property of the classical inference relation $\vdash$ is given by the Deduction Theorem: $M \vdash \varphi \to \psi$ iff $M \cup \{\varphi\} \vdash \psi$. If we wish to give up monotony then we must abandon at least one direction of the deduction theorem: Suppose that the inference relation $\mathrel{\vdash\mkern-9mu\sim}$ is supraclassical and satisfies the following direction of the deduction theorem:

If $M \mathrel{\vrule height 1.4ex depth 0pt width 0pt}\!\!\sim \varphi \to \psi$ then $M \cup \{\varphi\} \mathrel{\vrule height 1.4ex depth 0pt width 0pt}\!\!\sim \psi$. $(*)$

Suppose $M \mathrel{\vrule height 1.4ex depth 0pt width 0pt}\!\!\sim \psi$. Then, by right weakening, $M \mathrel{\vrule height 1.4ex depth 0pt width 0pt}\!\!\sim \varphi \to \psi$. Therefore, by $(*)$, $M \cup \{\varphi\} \mathrel{\vrule height 1.4ex depth 0pt width 0pt}\!\!\sim \psi$. In other words we have a kind of finitary monotony. Therefore we are forced to give up this direction of the deduction theorem. But the other direction can be kept; indeed, it follows from the basic properties established so far (the proof is left to the reader as an exercise).

Theorem 13.6 *Let $\mathrel{\vrule height 1.4ex depth 0pt width 0pt}\!\!\sim$ be a distributive supraclassical inference relation satisfying absorption.*

(a) *If $M \cup \{\varphi\} \mathrel{\vrule height 1.4ex depth 0pt width 0pt}\!\!\sim \psi$ then $M \mathrel{\vrule height 1.4ex depth 0pt width 0pt}\!\!\sim \varphi \to \psi$.*   *Conditionalization*

(b) *If $M \mathrel{\vrule height 1.4ex depth 0pt width 0pt}\!\!\sim \psi$ and $M \cup \{\varphi\} \mathrel{\vrule height 1.4ex depth 0pt width 0pt}\!\!\sim \neg\psi$ then $M \mathrel{\vrule height 1.4ex depth 0pt width 0pt}\!\!\sim \neg\varphi$.*

Finally we look at the property of *loop*. An inference relation $\mathrel{\vrule height 1.4ex depth 0pt width 0pt}\!\!\sim$ satisfies loop iff $C(M_i) = C(M_j)$ for all $i, j \in \{1, \ldots, n\}$ whenever $M_1 \mathrel{\vrule height 1.4ex depth 0pt width 0pt}\!\!\sim M_2 \mathrel{\vrule height 1.4ex depth 0pt width 0pt}\!\!\sim \ldots \mathrel{\vrule height 1.4ex depth 0pt width 0pt}\!\!\sim M_n \mathrel{\vrule height 1.4ex depth 0pt width 0pt}\!\!\sim M_1$. An interesting feature of loop is that it does not refer to the underlying language, that is, it is a pure condition; loop does not follow from the basic pure properties of inclusion and cumulativity. On the other hand it can be derived using the *non–pure* conditions of supraclassicality and distribution, as shown below!

Theorem 13.7 *Let C be a cumulative, supraclassical and distributive inference operation. Then C satisfies loop.*

Proof*:   Let $M_1 \mathrel{\vrule height 1.4ex depth 0pt width 0pt}\!\!\sim M_2 \mathrel{\vrule height 1.4ex depth 0pt width 0pt}\!\!\sim \ldots \mathrel{\vrule height 1.4ex depth 0pt width 0pt}\!\!\sim M_n \mathrel{\vrule height 1.4ex depth 0pt width 0pt}\!\!\sim M_1$. In the following we show that $C(M_1) = C(M_n)$. Then we are finished, because the loop can begin anywhere. For example, another loop is $M_2 \mathrel{\vrule height 1.4ex depth 0pt width 0pt}\!\!\sim M_3 \mathrel{\vrule height 1.4ex depth 0pt width 0pt}\!\!\sim \ldots \mathrel{\vrule height 1.4ex depth 0pt width 0pt}\!\!\sim M_n \mathrel{\vrule height 1.4ex depth 0pt width 0pt}\!\!\sim M_1 \mathrel{\vrule height 1.4ex depth 0pt width 0pt}\!\!\sim M_2$.

To prove $C(M_1) = C(M_n)$, it suffices to show $M_1 \mathrel{\vrule height 1.4ex depth 0pt width 0pt}\!\!\sim M_n$; then we are finished, by reciprocity, using $M_n \mathrel{\vrule height 1.4ex depth 0pt width 0pt}\!\!\sim M_1$. We show $M_1 \mathrel{\vrule height 1.4ex depth 0pt width 0pt}\!\!\sim M_n$ by induction on n, that means, on the length of the loop. The induction base case is trivial since we have immediately $M_1 \mathrel{\vrule height 1.4ex depth 0pt width 0pt}\!\!\sim M_2$.

Assume that the property is true for all loops of length k, and consider the loop $M_1 \mathrel{\vrule height 1.4ex depth 0pt width 0pt}\!\!\sim M_2 \mathrel{\vrule height 1.4ex depth 0pt width 0pt}\!\!\sim \ldots \mathrel{\vrule height 1.4ex depth 0pt width 0pt}\!\!\sim M_{k+1} \mathrel{\vrule height 1.4ex depth 0pt width 0pt}\!\!\sim M_1$ of length $k + 1$. Using problem 13-8 we may assume without loss of generality that all M_i are deductively closed. Then $M_{k+1} \mathrel{\vrule height 1.4ex depth 0pt width 0pt}\!\!\sim M_1$ implies

$$C(M_1) = C(M_{k+1} \cap M_1) \qquad (*)$$

using problem 13-7. $M_1 \mathbin{|\!\sim} M_2$ gives us $M_{k+1} \cap M_1 \mathbin{|\!\sim} M_2$, and $M_k \mathbin{|\!\sim} M_{k+1}$ gives us $M_k \mathbin{|\!\sim} M_{k+1} \cap M_1$. Therefore we have the following loop:

$$M_{k+1} \cap M_1 \mathbin{|\!\sim} M_2 \mathbin{|\!\sim} \ldots \mathbin{|\!\sim} M_k \mathbin{|\!\sim} M_{k+1} \cap M_1.$$

This loop has length k, so we may use induction hypothesis and conclude $M_{k+1} \cap M_1 \mathbin{|\!\sim} M_k$. Using $M_k \mathbin{|\!\sim} M_{k+1} \cap M_1$, reciprocity implies $C(M_k) = C(M_{k+1} \cap M_1)$. Using $(*)$ we have $C(M_1) = C(M_{k+1} \cap M_1) = C(M_k)$. From the original loop considered we have $M_k \mathbin{|\!\sim} M_{k+1}$, so $M_1 \mathbin{|\!\sim} M_{k+1}$ and we are through. ∎

In summary, we have identified some central properties of inference relations which appear to be natural and desirable, and that play an important role in deriving further properties. These conditions are:

- The pure condition of *cumulativity* introduced in section 13.2. It does not refer to the underlying language.

- The conditions of *supraclassicality* and *distribution* which define interactions with the logical connectives in propositional logic[2].

13.4   Inference relations in default logic

We have already described how Default Logic can be used to define inference relations (or operations): Let D be a countable set of defaults. In the skeptical (resp. credulous) approach, $C(M)$ is defined to be the intersection (resp. union) of all extensions of the default theory (M, D).

The credulous inference relation tends to be very irregular, and violates most properties apart from those which follow trivially from the definition of extensions (such as Left Logical Equivalence or Right Weakening; see problem 13-9). Therefore in the following we restrict our attention to skeptical inference. We begin with some positive results.

Theorem 13.8 *The skeptical inference relation of Default Logic satisfies cut and absorption.*

---

[2]Notice that supraclassicality implies inclusion.

Proof*:   Let D be a countable set of defaults, and C the associated skeptical inference operation. For a sequence of defaults Π without repetition, $In_M(\Pi)$ denotes the In–set of Π *interpreted over the default theory* (M, D).

For absorption we have to show $Th(C(M)) = C(M) = C(Th(M))$. The left equality follows directly from the observation that extensions are deductively closed (w.r.t. classical inference $\vdash$), taking into account that the intersection of deductively closed sets is deductively closed. For the right equality it suffices to show that E is an extension of (M, D) iff E is an extension of $(Th(M), D)$. This is trivial, noting that, by definition, $In_M(\Pi) = In_{Th(M)}(\Pi)$ (the In–sets are always deductively closed).

Next we show cut: If $M \subseteq N \subseteq C(M)$ then $C(N) \subseteq C(M)$. Obviously it suffices to prove that every extension of (M, D) is also an extension of (N, D). Let E be an extension of the default theory (M, D), and let $\Pi = (\delta_0, \delta_1, \ldots)$ be a closed and successful process of (M, D) such that $E = In_M(\Pi)$. We complete the proof by showing that Π is a closed and successful process of (N, D), too, and $In_M(\Pi) = In_N(\Pi)$.

First we notice that $In_M(\Pi) \subseteq In_N(\Pi)$ because $M \subseteq N$. Also $In_N(\Pi) = Th(N \cup cons(\Pi)) \subseteq Th(E \cup cons(\Pi)) = E = In_M(\Pi)$[3] (we used $N \subseteq E$ which holds because $N \subseteq C(M)$, meaning that N is included in all extensions of (M, D)). So $In_M(\Pi) = In_N(\Pi)$. Also, by definition, the Out–set of Π does not depend on the given set of facts. Therefore we have immediately that Π is a closed and successful process of the default theory (N, D) as well. Finally we show that Π is a process of (N, D).

Consider $\delta_i = \frac{\varphi : \psi_1, \ldots, \psi_n}{\chi}$. Since Π is a process of (M, D) we know that $\varphi \in In_M(\Pi[i])$. Using $M \subseteq N$ we conclude $\varphi \in In_N(\Pi[i])$. Further we know that Π is successful, so $In_M(\Pi) \cap Out(\Pi) = \emptyset$. Using $\{\neg\psi_1, \ldots, \neg\psi_n\} \subseteq Out(\Pi)$ and $In_N(\Pi[i]) \subseteq In_N(\Pi) = In_M(\Pi)$ we conclude that $\neg\psi_1 \notin In_N(\Pi[i]), \ldots, \neg\psi_n \notin In_N(\Pi[i])$. This shows that δ_i is applicable to $In_N(\Pi[i])$, so Π is a process of (N, D). ∎

Now for some negative results. Recall that cut is half of the cumulativity property. We have already seen in Chapter 7 that Default Logic violates cumulativity. Distribution is violated as well: Let $D = \{\frac{\varphi : \chi}{\chi}, \frac{\neg\varphi : \chi}{\chi}\}$. Then $\chi \in C(\{\varphi\})$ and $\chi \in C(\{\neg\varphi\})$, but $\chi \notin C(Th(\{\varphi\}) \cap Th(\{\neg\varphi\})) = C(Th(\emptyset))$.

In other words, two of the three basic properties, cumulativity, distribution and supraclassicality, are violated. But let us make some comments. Firstly, the prop-

---

[3]Slightly abusing notation Π has been used as a *set* of defaults.

erties on nonmonotonic inference relations are given from a theoretical viewpoint, but do not necessarily indicate that a specific formalism is wrong or useless. Take, for example, the case of cumulativity. It seems to be very important in that it allows one to use lemmas in a safe way. But its violation does not mean that lemmas cannot be used in Default Logic. After all, the definition of C forces us to represent lemmas *as facts*. This appears to be rather counterintuitive. If a conclusion was derived using defeasible knowledge (defaults), then it is defeasible as well. It appears natural to represent a lemma *as a default*. In Chapter 7 we saw that this idea works for Constrained Default Logic, and so it does for Default Logic.

The second comment is that if we restrict attention to 'well–behaved' classes of default theories, then the situation improves significantly. In particular, if all defaults are supernormal (normal defaults with the prerequisite *true*), then the three basic properties do hold.

Theorem 13.9 *Let D be a countable set of normal defaults with the prerequisite true. Then the associated inference operation C is cumulative, supraclassical and distributive.*

Proof*: Supraclassicality follows immediately from the observation that extensions are deductively closed. Distribution is left as an exercise to the reader. In the following we prove cumulativity.

Since all defaults have the prerequisite *true* the ordering of the defaults in a process is irrelevant. Therefore we may interpret processes as *sets* of defaults. Also we make use of the notation $In_M(\Pi)$ to denote the In–set of Π as a process of the default theory (M, D).

One direction of cumulativity is given by cut (theorem 13.8). In the opposite direction (i.e. cautious monotony) we have to show that $M \subseteq N \subseteq C(M)$ implies $C(M) \subseteq C(N)$. It is sufficient to show that every extension of (N, D) is an extension of (M, D).

Let $E = In_N(\Pi) = Th(N \cup cons(\Pi))$ be an extension of (N, D), for a closed and successful process Π of (N, D). Consider $E' = Th(M \cup cons(\Pi))$. By $M \subseteq N$ we get immediately $E' \subseteq E$. From $N \subseteq C(M)$ we know $N \subseteq E'$, therefore $E = Th(N \cup cons(\Pi)) \subseteq Th(E' \cup cons(\Pi)) = E'$. So we have shown $E = E'$.

Suppose Π is not a closed process of (M, D), and let $\Pi \subset \Pi''$ with a process Π'' of (M, D). Then $E'' = Th(M \cup cons(\Pi''))$ is consistent. As above we can show that $Th(N \cup cons(\Pi''))$ is consistent. That shows that Π'' is a process of (N, D) with $\Pi \subset \Pi''$, which is a contradiction to Π being closed. ∎

13.5   Preferential models

In this section we give a semantic counterpart to the properties of inference relations which we studied purely from the syntactic viewpoint. Roughly speaking, the idea will be similar to the semantics of circumscription, in that we consider a kind of minimal models instead of all models as in classical logic. Since the ordering used indicates preference among models, we refer to the minimal models as *preferential models*.

The following definition abstracts from the underlying language L (whose elements we call propositions). In a sense, it is 'pure' and will be contrasted with the pure conditions on inference relations introduced in section 13.2. When we turn our attention to the language of propositional logic, we shall impose some conditions on our models. Technically, a *preferential model structure* is a triple $(A, \models, <)$ where

- A is an arbitrary set, whose members are called *models*.
- $\models \subseteq A \times L$ is an arbitrary relation between members of A and propositions of the language L, called the *satisfaction relation* of the structure. It lays down which propositions are satisfied by which models.
- $< \subseteq A \times A$ is an arbitrary relation between elements of A. It is the *preference relation* of the structure and lays down which models are preferred over which other models.

For $b \in A$ and $M \subseteq L$ we say that b *preferentially satisfies* M, denoted by $b \models_< M$, iff $b \models M$[4] and there is no $c \in A$ such that $c < b$ and $c \models M$. We call b a *minimal* (or *preferential*) *model of* M. Using this notion we define an inference relation *determined* by the preferential model structure $(A, \models, <)$:

$$M \mathrel{\vdash\!\!\!\sim}_< x \text{ iff for all } a \in A, a \models_< M \text{ implies } a \models x.$$

In the alternative notation using inference operations:

$$C_<(M) = \{x \in L \mid \text{For all } a \in A, a \models_< M \text{ implies } a \models x\}.$$

In other words, x follows nonmonotonically from M if it is satisfied by all minimal models of M. The reader can see how similar this idea is to the semantics of circumscription, where the meaning of some predicates was 'minimized' by restricting attention to minimal models.

---

[4]As always, $b \models M$ means $b \models m$ for all $m \in M$.

We note that our notation is slightly imprecise since $\mid\!\sim$ resp. C depends on A, $\models$ as well as on $<$. Nevertheless usually there will be no confusion because A and $\models$ will be clear from the context.

Before imposing any conditions on preferential model structures let us check that in their bare form, the inference relation they determine possesses some of the pure properties from section 13.2. In this case, we use the term that '*a preferential model structure satisfies these conditions*'.

Theorem 13.10 *Every preferential model structure satisfies inclusion, idempotence and cut.*

Proof: Theorem 13.1 shows that it suffices to show inclusion and cut. Let $(A, \models, <)$ be a preferential model structure and $C = C_<$ the inference relation it determines. Suppose $x \in M$. Let $a \in A$ such that $a \models_< M$. Then, by definition of $\models_<$, $a \models M$, therefore $a \models x$. This means $x \in C(M)$, and inclusion has been shown.

To show cut, suppose $M \subseteq N \subseteq C(M)$; we must show $C(N) \subseteq C(M)$. Suppose $x \notin C(M)$. Then there is $a \in A$ such that $a \models_< M$ and $a \not\models x$. Next we show $a \models_< N$ which completes the proof since then $x \notin C(N)$.

We know $a \models_< M$ and $N \subseteq C(M)$, therefore $a \models N$. Now consider a model $b < a$. $a \models_< M$ means that $b \not\models M$, therefore $b \not\models N$ (because $M \subseteq N$). So, a is a minimal model of N and we are finished.   ∎

The other basic pure property, namely cautious monotony, may not hold for an inference relation generated by a preferential model structure. Here is a counterexample. Let A be the infinite set $\{a_1, a_2, \ldots\}$, and define $a_i < a_j$ iff $j < i$. Consider x, y, z to be members of the underlying language L such that

$a_i \models x$ for all $i > 0$
$a_i \not\models y$ for all $i > 0$
$a_i \models z$ iff i=1.

There is no minimal model satisfying x, therefore $\{x\} \mid\!\sim y$ and $\{x\} \mid\!\sim z$. But a_1 is a minimal model satisfying $\{x, z\}$, and $a_1 \not\models y$, so $\{x, z\} \mid\!\sim y$ is wrong and cautious monotony (and thus cumulativity) is violated. We can overcome this problem by imposing a condition which requires the existence of minimal models satisfying a set M (for the cases that there exists any model satisfying M). Technically, we call a preferential model structure $(A, \models, <)$ *stopped* iff the following holds:

If $a \models M$ then there is $b \in A$ such that $b \leq a$ and $b \models_< M$.

$b \leq a$ means $b < a$ or $b = a$. In case $<$ is transitive this condition says that there is no infinitely descending chain under $<$. It is easy to prove the following theorem:

Theorem 13.11 *Every stoppered preferential model structure satisfies cumulativity.*

The discussion of pure properties is completed now, and we turn our attention to the properties from section 13.3 which establish interactions with the logical connectives of propositional logic. In order to satisfy these properties we have to impose some conditions on preferential model structures. In particular, we have to ensure that they interact well with the logical connectives. A preferential model structure $(A, \models, <)$ is called *classical* iff the following is true:

- $a \models \neg\varphi$ iff $a \not\models \varphi$.
- $a \models \varphi \vee \psi$ iff $a \models \varphi$ or $a \models \psi$.
- $a \models \varphi \wedge \psi$ iff $a \models \varphi$ and $a \models \psi$.
- $a \models \varphi \to \psi$ iff $a \models \neg\varphi \vee \psi$.
- $a \models \varphi \leftrightarrow \psi$ iff $a \models \varphi \wedge \psi$ or $a \models \neg\varphi \wedge \neg\psi$.

Theorem 13.12 *A classical and stoppered preferential model structure is supra-classical and distributive.*

Proof: Supraclassicality follows easily using the classicality of $\models$. For distribution, suppose $x \notin C(Th(M) \cap Th(N))$; we must show $x \notin C(M) \cap C(N)$. We know there exists $a \in A$ such that $a \models_< Th(M) \cap Th(N)$ and $a \not\models x$. We complete the proof by showing that a is a minimal model of M or a minimal model of N; then we are finished because $a \not\models x$.

First we note that either $a \models M$ or $a \models N$. Otherwise pick $z \in M$ and $y \in N$ such that $a \not\models z$ and $a \not\models y$. Since $\models$ is classical we have also $a \not\models z \vee y$. But this contradicts $a \models Th(M) \cap Th(N)$, given that $z \vee y \in Th(M) \cap Th(N)$.

So assume $a \models M$ (the other case goes exactly the same way). Suppose there is $b \in M$ such that $b < a$ and $b \models M$. Then $b \models Th(M)$ and $b \models Th(M) \cap Th(N)$. This gives us a contradiction to a being a minimal model of $Th(M) \cap Th(N)$. ∎

Theorems 13.11 and 13.12 tell us that the inference relation determined by a classical stoppered preferential model structure satisfies the basic conditions of cumulativity, supraclassicality and distribution. The question arises whether the converse is true as well. The following result gives a positive answer for the finite case (reference hints regarding its proof are found at the end of Part IV). In the general case the answer is negative: There exist cumulative, supraclassical and distributive inference relations that cannot be determined by any classical and stoppered preferential model structure.

Theorem 13.13 *Let C be a cumulative, supraclassical and distributive inference operation. Then there is a classical and stoppered preferential model structure $(A, \models, <)$ such that for all finite $M \subseteq L$, $C(M) = C_<(M)$.*

13.6 Further properties of inference relations

We begin by mentioning a property which concerns consistency. It says that a consistent set of formulae M cannot have inconsistent nonmonotonic conclusions.

If M is consistent then $C(M)$ is consistent.   *Consistency Preservation*

Consistency preservation does not follow from the 'basic properties' of cumulativity, distribution and supraclassicality (simply define $C(M) = For$ for all sets of formulae M). As we saw Default Logic violates this condition, but only in cases where a default theory has no extensions. If we extend the usual (skeptical) definition $C(M)$ by

$C(M) = M$ if (M, D) has no extension,

then indeed we achieve consistency preservation. Next we discuss briefly some *rationality conditions*. Once we give up monotony we can no longer expect to have the same set of nonmonotonic conclusions if we add formulae to the premises. So, even though $M \mathrel{|\!\sim} \varphi$, we cannot expect $M \cup \{\psi\} \mathrel{|\!\sim} \varphi$ to be true. The rationality conditions given below establish conditions under which this should be possible.

If $M \mathrel{|\!\sim} \chi$ and $M \cup \{\neg\varphi\} \mathrel{|\!\not\sim} \chi$
     then $M \cup \{\varphi\} \mathrel{|\!\sim} \chi$ *Negation Rationality*
If $M \cup \{\varphi \vee \psi\} \mathrel{|\!\sim} \chi$ and $M \cup \{\psi\} \mathrel{|\!\not\sim} \chi$
     then $M \cup \{\varphi\} \mathrel{|\!\sim} \chi$ *Disjunctive Rationality*
If $M \mathrel{|\!\sim} \chi$ and $M \mathrel{|\!\not\sim} \neg\varphi$ then $M \cup \{\varphi\} \mathrel{|\!\sim} \chi$ *Rational Monotony*

The intuitive idea of the first condition is the following: If χ follows nonmonotonically from M, then we should still get χ either by adding φ to M, or its negation $\neg\varphi$, since these are the two possibilities. This condition seems to be very natural, but it may be undesirable if the nonmonotonic reasoning allows introspection. Then a plausible conclusion may be based on the assumption that we are ignorant concerning φ. By adding φ or its negation to our knowledge, this nonmonotonic inference is lost. So we cannot expect Autoepistemic Logic and its kin to satisfy this condition.

Rational monotony allows one to expand the set of premises by a formula φ, provided that $\neg\varphi$ is not inferred nonmonotonically by the old premises. It is the strongest of these rationality conditions, as shown by the following result.

Theorem 13.14 *Let $\mid\sim$ be a cumulative, supraclassical and distributive inference relation. Then disjunctive rationality implies negation rationality, and rational monotony implies disjunctive rationality.*

Proof*: Assume disjunctive rationality, and suppose $M \mid\sim \chi$. Then $\chi \in C(M) = C(Th(M)) = C(Th(M \cup \{\varphi \vee \neg\varphi\})) = C(M \cup \{\varphi \vee \neg\varphi\})$ using absorption. Now we apply disjunctive rationality and obtain $M \cup \{\varphi\} \mid\sim \chi$ or $M \cup \{\neg\varphi\} \mid\sim \chi$. So negation rationality has been shown.

Assume rational monotony and suppose that $M \cup \{\varphi \vee \psi\} \mid\sim \chi$ and $M \cup \{\varphi\} \not\mid\sim \chi$. We have to show $M \cup \{\psi\} \mid\sim \chi$ to establish disjunctive rationality. Rational monotony gives us $M \cup \{\varphi \vee \psi\} \cup \{\varphi\} \mid\sim \chi$ or $M \cup \{\varphi \vee \psi\} \mid\sim \neg\varphi$. The former case is impossible because $M \cup \{\varphi\} \not\mid\sim \chi$, using right absorption.

Another application of rational monotony gives us $M \cup \{\varphi \vee \psi\} \cup \{\psi\} \mid\sim \chi$ or $M \cup \{\varphi \vee \psi\} \mid\sim \neg\psi$. In the former case we are finished since, by absorption, $C(M \cup \{\varphi \vee \psi, \psi\}) = C(M \cup \{\psi\})$.

So the case that remains to be considered is that both $M \cup \{\varphi \vee \psi\} \mid\sim \neg\varphi$ and $M \cup \{\varphi \vee \psi\} \mid\sim \neg\psi$. By Right And (problem 13-3) $M \cup \{\varphi \vee \psi\} \mid\sim \neg\varphi \wedge \neg\psi$. But $\mid\sim$ is supraclassical, therefore $M \cup \{\varphi \vee \psi\} \mid\sim \varphi \vee \psi$. Then $M \cup \{\varphi \vee \psi\} \mid\sim (\varphi \vee \psi) \wedge \neg\varphi \wedge \neg\psi$.

The right hand side is a contradiction from which everything follows classically. Consequently we can use Right Weakening and get $M \cup \{\varphi \vee \psi\} \mid\sim \psi$. Additionally we know by hypothesis $M \cup \{\varphi \vee \psi\} \mid\sim \chi$. Hence we can apply cautious monotony and get $M \cup \{\varphi \vee \psi, \psi\} \mid\sim \chi$. Using absorption to simplify the left hand side we finally conclude $M \cup \{\psi\} \mid\sim \chi$ which is what we had to show. ∎

Default Logic violates all rationality conditions we described. To see this, consider the set of defaults $D = \{\frac{true:\chi}{\chi}, \frac{\varphi:\neg\chi}{\neg\chi}, \frac{\neg\varphi:\neg\chi}{\neg\chi}\}$. The default theory $(\emptyset, D)$ has the single extension $Th(\{\chi\})$, so $C(\emptyset) = Th(\{\chi\})$. On the other hand, if we add φ or $\neg\varphi$ to the facts we get an additional extension $Th(\{\neg\chi\})$. Therefore $\chi \notin C(\{\varphi\})$ and $\chi \notin C(\{\neg\varphi\})$. So negation rationality is violated, and by the previous theorem, disjunctive rationality and rational monotony as well.

Preferential entailments may violate the rationality conditions, too, even if they are determined by a finite, stoppered classical preferential model structure $(A, \models, <)$ with an asymmetric transitive relation $<$. Here is a counterexample: Let $A = \{a_1, a_2, b_1, b_2\}$ and $<$ the transitive relation determined by $a_1 < b_1$ and $a_2 < b_2$. Further let

$$a_1 \models \{\varphi, \psi\}$$
$$a_2 \models \{\neg\varphi, \psi\}$$
$$b_1 \models \{\neg\varphi, \neg\psi\}$$
$$b_2 \models \{\varphi, \neg\psi\}$$

The minimal models of $\emptyset$ are a_1 and a_2, hence $\emptyset \hspace{1pt}\vdash\hspace{-6pt}\sim \psi$. On the other hand, b_1 is a minimal model of $\neg\varphi$ and $b_1 \not\models \psi$, while b_2 is a minimal model of φ and $b_2 \not\models \psi$. Therefore $\varphi \hspace{1pt}\not\vdash\hspace{-6pt}\sim \psi$ and $\neg\varphi \hspace{1pt}\not\vdash\hspace{-6pt}\sim \psi$, so negation rationality is violated.

This example shows that we have to impose additional conditions on preferential model structures to obtain the desired outcome. We define a preferential model structure $(A, \models, <)$ to be *modular* iff the following holds:

For $a, b, b' \in A$, if $a < b, b \not< b'$ and $b' \not< b$ then $a < b'$.

With this condition we can show the following result (its converse is true, too).

Theorem 13.15 *Every classical and modular preferential model structure $(A, \models, <)$ satisfies rational monotony.*

Proof: Let $\hspace{1pt}\vdash\hspace{-6pt}\sim$ be the inference relation determined by $(A, \models, <)$, and suppose that $M \cup \{\varphi\} \hspace{1pt}\not\vdash\hspace{-6pt}\sim \chi$ and $M \hspace{1pt}\not\vdash\hspace{-6pt}\sim \neg\varphi$. We must show that $M \hspace{1pt}\vdash\hspace{-6pt}\sim \chi$ is wrong.

Since $M \cup \{\varphi\} \hspace{1pt}\not\vdash\hspace{-6pt}\sim \chi$ we know that there is $a \in A$ such that $a \models_< M \cup \{\varphi\}$ and $a \not\models \chi$. For this a we show $a \models_< M$.

Obviously $a \models M$. We have to show $c \not\models M$ for all $c < a$. Consider such a model c. From $M \hspace{1pt}\not\vdash\hspace{-6pt}\sim \neg\varphi$, and by using classicality of $\models$ we conclude that there is a $b \in A$ such that $b \models_< M$ and $b \models \varphi$. So $b \models M \cup \{\varphi\}$, and from $a \models_< M \cup \{\varphi\}$ we get $b \not< a$. On the other hand it follows from $b \models_< M$ and $a \models M$ that $a \not< b$. Therefore, by modularity, $c < b$. Since $b \models_< M$ we conclude $c \not\models M$ which is what we had to show. ∎

Problems

13-1. Show that, given inclusion, cumulativity is equivalent to reciprocity.

13-2. Show that a supraclassical inference relation always satisfies inclusion.

13-3. Show that absorption implies Right And, Right Weakening, and Left Logical Equivalence.

13-4. A nonmonotonic inference relation is called *contrapositive* iff $\{\varphi\} \mathrel{|\!\sim} \psi$ implies $\{\neg\psi\} \mathrel{|\!\sim} \neg\varphi$. Show that a supraclassical contrapositive inference relation satisfies finitary conjunctive monotony (as in theorem 13.3).

13-5. Prove lemma 13.4.

13-6. Prove theorem 13.6.

13-7. Let C be a cumulative, supraclassical and distributive inference operation. Then $M \subseteq C(N)$ implies $C(M) = C(Th(M) \cap Th(N))$. *Hint:* Use reciprocity!

13-8. Let $\mathrel{|\!\sim}$ be a supraclassical inference relation. Show that for sets of formulae M and N, $M \mathrel{|\!\sim} N$ iff $Th(M) \mathrel{|\!\sim} Th(N)$. *Hint:* Use absorption!

13-9. Determine which conditions hold for the inference relation based on the credulous approach of Default Logic, by giving proofs or counterexamples.

13-10. Complete the proof of theorem 13.9.

13-11. Show that every stoppered preferential model with transitive relation $<$ satisfies loop.

13-12. Prove theorem 13.11.

13-13. Consider the following property:

   If $N \subseteq C(M)$ and $N \vdash \varphi$ then $\varphi \in C(M)$.   *Closure*

(a) Show that Reflexivity, Left Logical Equivalence, and Closure imply Supra-classicality, Right Weakening and Right And.

(b) Show that Conditionalization, Right And and Right Weakening imply Cut.

(c) Show that Rational Monotony and Consistency Preservation imply Cautious Monotony.

Chapter 14

Belief Revision

Most of this book is dedicated to nonmonotonic reasoning; a process that allows a reasoner to make plausible conjectures in the absence of complete information. If an intelligent information system is to exhibit common sense reasoning it must be capable of making decisions with incomplete information. Likewise an intelligent system must be adept at *changing* its knowledge base when it acquires *new information*. This is particularly important when the acquired information is in conflict with the current knowledge base.

In this chapter we explore the process of belief revision. Our purpose is to lay the foundations of principled mechanisms for modifying a knowledge base in a rational and coherent way. Some important issues concerning changing information and the process of belief revision are discussed in section 14.1. There are essentially two approaches to belief revision; the axiomatic and the constructive. We explore both approaches. First we describe several change functions axiomatically using rationality postulates, and second we demonstrate that a preference relation, called an epistemic entrenchment ordering, contains sufficient information to construct these change functions. The change functions *expansion, contraction, withdrawal* and *revision* are described using rationality postulates in sections 14.2 - 14.4. Interconnections between these change functions are highlighted in section 14.5. An *epistemic entrenchment ordering* is defined in section 14.6 where it is also shown to be capable of constructing change functions. In section 14.7 we calculate the number of possible change functions that satisfy the rationality postulates.

This chapter provides the theoretical underpinnings for the following chapter where the focus is on solutions to problems that arise when one attempts to develop a computer-based implementation of change functions.

14.1   Introduction

Belief revision is a process that can be used to modify a knowledge base when new information is acquired. If the new information is consistent with the knowledge base then this process is straightforward; simply incorporate the new information. On the other hand, if the new information contradicts the knowledge base then great care must be exercised. The introduction of inconsistency will comprise the integrity of the knowledge base.

Inconsistency is a grave, sometimes life-threatening, problem. It is well known, though perhaps not so well appreciated, that one can deduce *anything* from a set of inconsistent premises. For the sake of emphasis, let me tell you a story. On April 26, 1994 a Taiwanese commercial jet crashed during a landing attempt at Nagoya Airport in Japan killing 261 people on board. After analyzing the in-flight recorder, the engineers discovered that as the jet approached the runaway the pilot informed the aircraft landing system that *the jet was to land.* However due to poor weather conditions the co-pilot indicated that *the jet was not to land*, instead it was to make another approach. As a consequence of this inconsistency the engines exploded.

For the purpose of the discussion we will use the terms information, knowledge, and belief interchangeably; we say an information system believes a particular fact whenever it resides in its knowledge base, and the knowledge base represents the information the system accepts.

In order to incorporate new information which is inconsistent with the knowledge base, the system or agent must *decide* what information it is prepared to give up. Belief revision is a mechanism for modeling rational decisions concerning modifications to a knowledge base. One would expect a rational reasoner to modify its knowledge base as *little as possible* in order to accommodate new information.

Let us say that we are very naive and believe that *all birds fly* and that *Tweety is a bird*; consequently we also believe that *Tweety can fly*. This is *honkydori* until we discover that we were horribly mistaken because *Tweety cannot fly* at all. How should we modify our knowledge in view of this revelation? We must of course retract *Tweety can fly*, but we must also remove other beliefs which are also in conflict with the new information. We appear to have several possible courses of action to follow in this regard: (i) retract the information that *Tweety is a bird*, (ii) retract that *all birds fly*, or (iii) retract both of these facts. The choice we make will depend upon the relative importance we attribute to the two pieces of information in question. If we are rational and have less confidence that *Tweety is a bird* than *all birds fly* we would probably prefer the solution that (i) offers, conversely if we believe *Tweety is a bird* more strongly than *all birds fly* then we might prefer (ii). If we cannot decide which to prefer, or if they are causally linked then we might relinquish both beliefs to make way for the acceptance of the new information. From this we see, at least intuitively, how a preference ordering of facts in our knowledge base might help resolve the nontrivial problem of choosing what information to surrender in order to avoid inconsistency.

The belief revision framework restricts itself to modeling changes to knowledge bases that involve the addition and removal of facts. Therefore, we do not consider the possibility of explicitly modifying individual facts, such as transforming *all birds fly* to *all birds except Tweety fly*, as a primitive operation. Modifying individual facts is often seen in machine learning for example, and can be modelled in the belief revision framework by observing that *all birds fly* entails *all birds except Tweety fly*, therefore removing *all birds fly* and retaining *all birds except Tweety fly* achieves the same result.

Our aim is to study *rational modifications* to knowledge bases guided by the *Principle of Minimal Change*; regrettably the notions of *rationality* and *minimality*, in the sense we would like to capture, defy explicit definition. Intuitively, by rational we mean things like: the reasoner realizes that inconsistency is problematical and thus actively seeks to avoid it, and that given our example it is not sufficient to retract only the fact that *Tweety can fly* because it is derivable from the remaining information. The Principle of Minimal Change says that as much information should be conserved as is possible in accordance with an underlying preference relation. The underlying preference relation is used to capture the information *content* of the knowledge base, the reasoning agent's *commitment* to this information, and how the information should behave under *change*.

It has often been incorrectly argued that the choices (i) and (ii) are more minimal than (iii), because only *two* basic facts are jettisoned as opposed to *three*. The problem with this argument is that the interdependencies among our beliefs might force us to discard more than the minimal *number* of beliefs. The web of *causal* interdependencies is enmeshed in the preference relation, and cardinality measures are not the only, nor necessarily the most appropriate, when it comes to measuring the *magnitude of change*. For instance, to stretch our example a little further, it might have been that the only reason for believing that *all birds fly* is that *Tweety can fly*, so if we contract *Tweety can fly* then it should be permissible to retract *all birds fly* in the process. What we are saying is that cardinality is not the only allowable measure of change. Sometimes the most rational response is to forfeit more than the minimal number of beliefs. For instance, is it better to yield a single strongly held belief or several weakly held beliefs?

Notice that all three possibilities described above are minimal in the sense that they do not introduce extraneous information not entailed by the knowledge base. For instance incorporating the fact that *Tweety cannot fly* does not result in the acceptance of superfluous information like *birds have reptilian feet, 747's fly,* or *I like Chinese gooseberries.*

The framework for belief revision developed in this chapter is known as the AGM paradigm, so-called after its founders Carlos Alchourrón, Peter Gärdenfors and David Makinson. It is a formal framework for modeling ideal and rational changes to repositories of information under the Principle of Minimal Change. In particular, it provides mechanisms for modeling the coherent retraction and incorporation of information. For the example above the AGM paradigm allows all three choices discussed, and furthermore they are the *only* allowable ones.

Technically, the framework models corpora of information as logical theories, and changes in information content as functions that take a theory (the current knowledge base) and a logical sentence (the new information) to another theory (the new knowledge base). In this chapter we investigate four types of change functions: *contraction, withdrawal, expansion,* and *revision.* Contraction and withdrawal functions model the retraction of information, whilst expansion and revision model various ways of incorporating information. All four functions are interrelated.

Change functions can be described either *axiomatically* using rationality postulates, or *constructively* using certain preference relations. The rationality postulates are properties that we would expect rational change functions to satisfy and they characterize various classes of change functions. Moreover they may be satisfied by more than one function. In order to single out an individual function it is usual to make use of a preference relation such as an *epistemic entrenchment ordering* which provides the extralogical information required to make necessary choices concerning what information should be given up.

14.2   Expansion

Expansion models the simplest change to a knowledge base, it involves the acceptance of information without the removal of any previously accepted information, and as a consequence it may lead to an inconsistent knowledge base.

The *expansion* of a theory T[1] with respect to a sentence φ is the logical closure of T and φ. The set of all theories of a language $\mathcal{L}$[2] is denoted by $\mathcal{K}_{\mathcal{L}}$, and formally,

---

[1] Not to be confused with expansions of autoepistemic theories!

[2] In Chapters 14–16 the language used is the set of closed formulae (sentences) over a fixed signature Σ.

an expansion function $^+$ is a function from $\mathcal{K}_\mathcal{L} \times \mathcal{L}$ to $\mathcal{K}_\mathcal{L}$, mapping (T, φ) to T_φ^+ where $T_\varphi^+ = \text{Th}(T \cup \{\varphi\})$.

Clearly, expansion is a monotonic operation, that is, $T \subseteq T_\varphi^+$, and if $\neg\varphi \in T$, then T_φ^+ is inconsistent. Certainly if $\neg\varphi \notin T$, then we can accept that the Principle of Minimal Change is at work, since T_φ^+ would be the *smallest* change we can logically make to T in order to incorporate φ.

In contradistinction to expansion, it turns out that both contraction and revision are non-unique operations and cannot be realized using logical and set theoretical notions alone.

14.3   Contraction

Contraction of a knowledge base involves the retraction of information, the difficulty, as we noted in the introduction, is in determining those sentences that should be given up. We are usually presented with a choice. For example, perhaps our reasoner erroneously believed that *Tweety is a sulphur-crested cockatoo* and subsequently wished to retract it, this may or may not involve the removal of other beliefs, such as *Tweety has yellow and white feathers*, depending on how he views the causal dependencies, etc.

A *contraction* of T with respect to φ involves the removal of a set of sentences from T so that φ is no longer implied, provided φ is not a tautology. Formally, a contraction function $^-$ is any function from $\mathcal{K}_\mathcal{L} \times \mathcal{L}$ to $\mathcal{K}_\mathcal{L}$, mapping (T, φ) to T_φ^- which satisfies the following postulates. For any φ, $\psi \in \mathcal{L}$ and any $T \in \mathcal{K}_\mathcal{L}$:

($^-$1) $T_\varphi^- \in \mathcal{K}_\mathcal{L}$

($^-$2) $T_\varphi^- \subseteq T$

($^-$3) If $\varphi \notin T$ then $T \subseteq T_\varphi^-$

($^-$4) If $\nvdash \varphi$ then $\varphi \notin T_\varphi^-$

($^-$5) $T \subseteq (T_\varphi^-)_\varphi^+$ (*recovery*)

($^-$6) If $\vdash \varphi \leftrightarrow \psi$ then $T_\varphi^- = T_\psi^-$

($^-$7) $T_\varphi^- \cap T_\psi^- \subseteq T_{\varphi \wedge \psi}^-$

($^-$8) If $\varphi \notin T_{\varphi \wedge \psi}^-$ then $T_{\varphi \wedge \psi}^- \subseteq T_\varphi^-$

The postulates embody the *Principle of Minimal Change*, and act as integrity constraints for change functions. They do not uniquely determine a change function, rather their purpose is to identify the set of possible new knowledge bases that might reasonably result when information is retracted from the current knowledge base, T. The postulates themselves are explained in various works by Gärdenfors and are motivated via the criterion of informational economy.

The first postulate $(^-1)$ simply says that the result of a contraction is a theory, so that contracting information results in a theory, i.e. the new knowledge base is logically closed. Essentially the change functions described in this chapter model the processes of an ideal reasoning agent. Since theories are typically infinite structures the first postulate will not usually be satisfied by our implementation described in the next chapter. Postulate $(^-2)$ says that contracting a theory only involves the removal of old information and never the incorporation of new information, therefore when information is contracted no spurious information is added. Postulate $(^-3)$ says when the information φ is not accepted then taking it away should have no effect, indeed $(^-2)$ and $(^-3)$ considered together say that if φ is not in T, then $T_\varphi^- = T$. Postulate $(^-4)$, says if φ is not a tautology then it must be removed in the contraction T_φ^-. Postulate $(^-5)$ together with the previous four, says if $\varphi \in T$ then $T = (T_\varphi^-)_\varphi^+$. In other words, no more information is lost than can be reincorporated by an expansion with respect to the explicit information contracted, that is, if we contract φ and then immediately replace it using expansion then we obtain the theory we started with. Intuitively then, this postulate forces a *minimal* amount of information to be lost during a contraction. Postulate $(^-6)$ says that the same result is obtained whenever we contract with respect to equivalent logical sentences, that is, contraction is not dependent on the syntax of the information to be contracted. The last two postulates deal with the association of contracting a conjunction $\varphi \wedge \psi$ and the contraction of each conjunct, φ and ψ, individually. In order to contract $\varphi \wedge \psi$ we *must* at the very least contract either φ or ψ, and we might also consider contracting both of them depending on the mechanism we adopt to help us make the choice. Postulate $(^-7)$ says that the theory that results from contracting with respect to $\varphi \wedge \psi$ should never be *smaller* than taking the intersection of T_φ^- and T_ψ^-. That is to say, beliefs in both T_φ^- and T_ψ^- should always be contained in $T_{\varphi \wedge \psi}^-$. Postulate $(^-8)$ says that if φ is not contained in the contraction with respect to the conjunction $\varphi \wedge \psi$ then the contraction with respect to this conjunction cannot be larger that the theory obtained by contraction φ alone. Given postulates $(^-1)$ and $(^-6)$, postulates $(^-7)$ and $(^-8)$ together imply that $T_{\varphi \wedge \psi}^-$ is equivalent to either T_φ^-, T_ψ^- or $T_\varphi^- \cap T_\psi^-$.

The postulates for contraction identify a class of functions for a knowledge base and for each one of these functions we will show in section 14.6 that there is a preference criterion that can be used to construct it.

The most controversial of these postulates is *recovery*, $(^-5)$, because one can argue that it is not always an appropriate requirement, especially for a limited reasoning agent like the one we model in the next chapter.

In a convincing argument against recovery, Niederée shows that a consequence of theory closure and recovery is that for all $\psi \in \mathcal{L}$, whenever a sentence φ is contained in the theory T then $\psi \to \varphi \in T^-_{\varphi \vee \psi}$, and the consequences, $\varphi \in (T^-_{\varphi \vee \psi})^+_\psi$ and $\neg \psi \in (T^-_{\varphi \vee \psi})^+_{\neg \varphi}$, are not necessarily desirable for a limited reasoner.

Sven Ove Hansson provides the following example, which illustrates his objection to recovery by displaying a case where recovery is contrary to intuition. "As an example, suppose that I have read in a book about Cleopatra that she had both φ and ψ, where φ denotes that Cleopatra had a son and ψ that she had a daughter. I then learn from a knowledgeable friend that the book was in fact a historical novel, and that much of it does not correspond to what actually happened. I therefore retract $\varphi \vee \psi$ from my set of beliefs, that is, I do not any longer believe that Cleopatra had a child. Soon after that, however, I learn from a reliable source that Cleopatra had a child. It seems perfectly reasonable for me to add $\varphi \vee \psi$ to my set of beliefs without also reintroducing either φ or ψ."

A withdrawal function is similar to a contraction function with the exception that it may not satisfy recovery. In particular, a *withdrawal function* satisfies $(^-1)$ – $(^-4)$ and $(^-6)$ – $(^-8)$, but not necessarily $(^-5)$. Withdrawal functions will play an important role in the next chapter.

14.4   Revision

Revision attempts to change a knowledge base as *little as possible* in order to incorporate newly acquired information. This new information may be inconsistent with the knowledge base. In order to maintain consistency some old information may need to be retracted. Thus revision functions are nonmonotonic in nature, and related to withdrawal and contraction functions.

The process of revision was discussed in the introduction where our reasoner, if you recall, was mistaken about Tweety's power of flight, and had to revise his knowledge by accepting that *Tweety cannot fly.*

Formally, a revision function * is any function from $\mathcal{K}_\mathcal{L} \times \mathcal{L}$ to $\mathcal{K}_\mathcal{L}$, mapping (T, φ) to T^*_φ which satisfies the following postulates. For any φ, $\psi \in \mathcal{L}$ and any $T \in \mathcal{K}_\mathcal{L}$:

$(^*1)$ $T^*_\varphi \in \mathcal{K}_\mathcal{L}$

$(^*2)$ $\varphi \in T^*_\varphi$

$(^*3)$ $T^*_\varphi \subseteq T^+_\varphi$

(*4) If $\neg\varphi \notin T$ then $T_\varphi^+ \subseteq T_\varphi^*$

(*5) If $T_\varphi^* = \perp$ then $\vdash \neg\varphi$

(*6) If $\vdash \varphi \leftrightarrow \psi$ then $T_\varphi^* = T_\psi^*$

(*7) $T_{\varphi\wedge\psi}^* \subseteq (T_\varphi^*)_\psi^+$

(*8) If $\neg\psi \notin T_\varphi^*$ then $(T_\varphi^*)_\psi^+ \subseteq T_{\varphi\wedge\psi}^*$

The revision postulates also attempt to encapsulate the Principle of Minimal Change. According to (*1) revising a theory results in a theory. Postulate (*2) says that the information to be added by a revision is always successfully incorporated. Postulate (*3) tells us that revising a theory can never incorporate more information than an expansion operation. Postulate (*4), says if $\neg\varphi$ is not in T then the expansion of T with respect to φ is contained in the revision with respect to φ. This postulate is written in its weakest form, and the main point for our purposes is that the postulates (*3) and (*4) together say that if φ is consistent with T, then $T_\varphi^* = T_\varphi^+$. Postulate (*5) tells us that the only way to obtain an inconsistent theory is to revise with an inconsistent sentence φ. Postulate (*6) says that revision functions are syntax independent. Postulate (*7) says that the theory that results from revising with respect to $\varphi \wedge \psi$ should never contain more than the revision with respect to φ followed by the expansion with respect to ψ. According to (*8) if $\neg\psi$ is not contained in the revision with respect to φ then the revision with respect to φ followed by the expansion with respect to ψ should not contain more information than the theory that results from revising with respect to $\varphi \wedge \psi$. If the revision function * satisfies the first six postulates, then the postulates (*7) and (*8) considered together imply that $T_{\varphi\vee\psi}^*$ is equivalent to T_φ^*, T_ψ^* or $T_\varphi^* \cap T_\psi^*$.

14.5   Interrelationships

In this section we highlight several explicit relationships that exist between the various change functions. In the previous section we saw that if the new information is consistent with the knowledge base, then a revision becomes an expansion. In the theorems below Alchourron, Gärdenfors and Makinson demonstrated that contraction and revision functions are intimately related, indeed they are interdefinable. The proof of Theorem 14.1 is taken from their work.

Theorem 14.1 *If $^-$ is a contraction function and $^+$ the expansion function, then* * *defined by the* Levi Identity *below defines a revision function.*

$$T_\varphi^* = (T_{\neg\varphi}^-)_\varphi^+$$

Proof: Postulates (*1) and (*2) are immediate. $T^-_{\neg\varphi} \subseteq T$ by $(^-2)$, therefore $(T^-_{\neg\varphi})^+_\varphi \subseteq T^+_\varphi$, hence and postulate (*3) is satisfied. If $\neg\varphi \notin T$ then $T^-_{\neg\varphi} = T$ by $(^-3)$ and $(^-4)$, hence $T^+_\varphi = T^*_\varphi$ and (*4) is satisfied. If $T^*_\varphi = \perp$ then $(T^-_{\neg\varphi})^+_\varphi = \perp$ which implies that $\neg\varphi \in T^-_{\neg\varphi}$ hence $\vdash \neg\varphi$, and conversely. Hence (*5) is satisfied. Postulate (*6) follows immediately from $(^-6)$. For postulate (*7) suppose $\chi \in T^*_{\varphi\wedge\psi}$. Since $\neg\varphi$ is logically equivalent to $\neg(\varphi \wedge \psi) \wedge (\varphi \to \psi)$ by $(^-7)$ it suffices to show that $\chi \in (T^-_{\varphi\wedge\psi})^+_{\varphi\wedge\psi}$ and $\chi \in (T^-_{\varphi\to\psi})^+_{\varphi\wedge\psi}$. However, $\chi \in (T^-_{\varphi\wedge\psi})^+_{\varphi\wedge\psi}$ holds by supposition, hence we need to show that $\chi \in (T^-_{\varphi\to\psi})^+_{\varphi\wedge\psi}$ holds. Since $\chi \in T^*_{\varphi\to\psi}$ we have that $(\varphi\wedge\psi) \to \chi \in T$, consequently by $(^-5)$ $(\varphi \to \psi) \to ((\varphi\wedge\psi) \to \chi) \in T^-_{\varphi\to\psi}$. By propositional logic we have $(\varphi \wedge \psi) \to \chi \in T^-_{\varphi\to\psi}$, therefore $\chi \in (T^-_{\varphi\to\psi})^+_{\varphi\wedge\psi}$. For postulate (*8) suppose $\neg\psi \notin T^*_\varphi$. Hence $\neg\psi \notin (T^-_{\neg\varphi})^+_\varphi$. Since $\neg\varphi$ is logically equivalent to $(\neg\varphi \vee \neg\psi) \wedge \neg\varphi$ we have that $T^-_\varphi = T^-_{(\neg\varphi\vee\neg\psi)\wedge\neg\varphi}$. By supposition $\neg\psi \notin T^*_\varphi$, therefore $\neg\psi \notin (T^-_{\neg\varphi})^+_\varphi$, hence $\neg\varphi \vee \neg\psi \notin T^-_{\neg\varphi}$. By $(^-8)$ we have that $\neg\varphi \vee \neg\psi \notin T^-_\varphi$ hence $(T^*_\varphi)^+_\psi = ((T^-_{\neg\varphi})^+_\varphi)^+_\psi = (T^-_{\neg\varphi})^+_{\varphi\wedge\psi} \subseteq ((T^-_{\neg(\varphi\wedge\psi)})^+_\varphi)^+_{\varphi\wedge\psi} = T^*_{\varphi\wedge\psi}$. ∎

Theorem 14.2 *If* * *is a revision function, then* $^-$ *defined by the* Harper Identity *below defines a contraction function.*

$$T^-_\varphi = T \cap T^*_{\neg\varphi}$$

14.6   Epistemic entrenchment orderings

As noted earlier the rationality postulates for contraction and revision merely describe classes of functions; they do not provide a mechanism for defining a particular function. For any theory there might be a vast number of functions that satisfy the postulates for contraction and revision. So in order to single out a unique one, additional structure is necessary; this usually takes the form of a preference relation such as an epistemic entrenchment ordering.

According to Stalnaker, it is necessary "to impose additional structure on our notion of a belief state before we can say very much about the way beliefs change", and when it comes to deciding those beliefs to discard, "the choice will depend on assumptions about epistemic and causal dependence and independence of the reasons one has for one's beliefs as well as on the beliefs themselves".

Gärdenfors' epistemic entrenchment orderings are based on a relative ranking of information according to its importance in the face of change. This ordering can be used to uniquely determine a change function by providing a selection criteria that can be used to identify those sentences to be retracted, those to be retained, and those to be acquired during changes. Intuitively, when faced with a choice, sentences having the lowest degree of epistemic entrenchment are shed.

Definition *Given a theory T of $\mathcal{L}$, an epistemic entrenchment related to T is any binary relation $\leq$ on $\mathcal{L}$ satisfying the conditions below:*

(EE1) If $\varphi \leq \psi$ and $\psi \leq \chi$, then $\varphi \leq \chi$.

(EE2) For all φ, $\psi \in \mathcal{L}$, if $\varphi \vdash \psi$ then $\varphi \leq \psi$.

(EE3) For all φ, $\psi \in \mathcal{L}$, $\varphi \leq \varphi \wedge \psi$ or $\psi \leq \varphi \wedge \psi$.

(EE4) When $T \neq \perp$, $\varphi \notin T$ iff $\varphi \leq \psi$ for all $\psi \in \mathcal{L}$.

(EE5) If $\psi \leq \varphi$ for all $\psi \in \mathcal{L}$, then $\vdash \varphi$.

If $\varphi \leq \psi$, then we say ψ is at *least as entrenched as* φ. We define $\varphi < \psi$, as $\varphi \leq \psi$ and not $\psi \leq \varphi$. If $\varphi \leq \psi$ and $\psi \leq \varphi$, then we say φ and ψ are *equally entrenched*.

The condition (EE1) requires that an epistemic entrenchment ordering be transitive. (EE2) says that if φ is logically stronger than ψ, then ψ is at least as entrenched as φ. For example the sentence $\varphi \vee \psi$ is entailed by φ, and (EE2) tells us that $\varphi \vee \psi$ is at least as entrenched as φ, in other words we believe in $\varphi \vee \psi$ at least as much as φ. It certainly would not make any sense to believe in φ *more* strongly than $\varphi \vee \psi$; a rational agent could hardy be less certain of $\varphi \vee \psi$ than it is of φ. The condition (EE3) together with (EE1) and (EE2) implies that a conjunction is ranked at the same level as its least ranked conjunct. For example, if $\varphi \leq \psi$ then $\varphi \wedge \psi \leq \varphi$ and $\varphi \leq \varphi \wedge \psi$, so $\varphi \wedge \psi = \varphi$. The condition (EE4) tells us that sentences not in the theory T are minimal, and (EE5) says that the tautologies are maximal.

Definition *For an epistemic entrenchment ordering $\leq$ and a sentence φ, define $\mathrm{cut}_{\leq}(\varphi) = \{\psi : \varphi \leq \psi\}$.*

The set $\mathrm{cut}_{\leq}(\varphi)$ contains all those sentences that are at least as entrenched as φ. An important property of an epistemic entrenchment is that it is a total preorder of the sentences in $\mathcal{L}$ such that the following theorem holds.

Theorem 14.3 *If $\leq$ is an epistemic entrenchment, then for any sentence φ, $\mathrm{cut}_{\leq}(\varphi)$ is a theory.*

Since a subtheory of a finitely axiomatizable theory may not be finitely axiomatizable we give the following result concerning a *finite description* of an epistemic entrenchment ordering. In the next chapter we develop a computational model for change functions using a finite description of an epistemic entrenchment ordering, and the following theorem provides the theoretical basis for the one we adopt.

Theorem 14.4 *An epistemic entrenchment ordering $\leq$ is finitely representable if and only if it has a finite number of natural partitions, and for all $\varphi \in \mathcal{L}$, $\mathrm{cut}_{\leq}(\varphi)$ is finitely axiomatizable.*

The following results of Gärdenfors and Makinson provide us with a constructive method for building change functions from an epistemic entrenchment ordering. Theorem 14.5 gives a condition that can be used for constructing a contraction function, and Theorem 14.6 provides a similar one for constructing a revision function.

Theorem 14.5 *Let T be a theory of $\mathcal{L}$. For every contraction function $^-$ for T there exists an epistemic entrenchment $\leq$ related to T such that (E^-) is true for every $\varphi \in \mathcal{L}$. Conversely, for every epistemic entrenchment $\leq$ related to T, there exists a contraction function $^-$ such that (E^-) is true for every $\varphi \in \mathcal{L}$.*

$$(E^-) \qquad T_\varphi^- = \begin{cases} \{\psi \in T : \varphi < \varphi \vee \psi\} & \text{if } \nvdash \varphi \\ \\ T & \text{otherwise} \end{cases}$$

Proof*: Our aim is to give only a flavour of the second half of Gärdenfors and Makinson's proof. We show that if $\leq$ is an epistemic entrenchment related to T, then $(^-1) - (^-5)$ hold. Satisfaction of $(^-6) - (^-8)$ is left as an exercise.

To show that the postulate $(^-1)$ is satisfied. Suppose $T_\varphi^- \vdash \chi$ we show $\chi \in T_\varphi^-$. By compactness of $\vdash$ there exist $\psi_1, \psi_2, \ldots, \psi_n \in T_\varphi^-$ such that $\psi_1 \wedge \psi_2 \wedge \ldots \wedge \psi_n \vdash \chi$. To show $\chi \in T_\varphi^-$ we need to show that $\chi \in T$ and either $\varphi < \varphi \vee \chi$ or $\vdash \varphi$ by condition (E^-). Since $\psi_1, \psi_2, \ldots, \psi_n \in T_\varphi^-$ and T is a theory we have that $\chi \in T$. Let us now suppose $\nvdash \varphi$, we show that $\varphi < \varphi \vee \chi$. Since $\leq$ is a total ordering we only need show $\varphi \vee \chi \nleq \varphi$. For the principal case $n \geq 1$ we have that since $\psi_1, \psi_2, \ldots, \psi_n \in T_\varphi^-$ by condition (E^-) either $\vdash \varphi$ or for every ψ_i we have $\varphi < \varphi \vee \psi_i$. By supposition we have $\nvdash \varphi$ therefore $\varphi \vee \psi_i \nleq \varphi$ for every ψ_i. Hence by (EE2) and (EE3) we have $\varphi \vee (\psi_1 \wedge \psi_2 \wedge \ldots \wedge \psi_n) \nleq \varphi$. We have $\psi_1 \wedge \psi_2 \wedge \ldots \wedge \psi_n \vdash \chi$, therefore $\varphi \vee (\psi_1 \wedge \psi_2 \wedge \ldots \wedge \psi_n) \vdash \varphi \vee \chi$, hence by (EE2) $\varphi \vee (\psi_1 \wedge \psi_2 \wedge \ldots \wedge \psi_n) \leq \varphi \vee \chi$. By transitivity we obtain $\varphi \vee \chi \nleq \varphi$. For $n = 0$ we have that $\vdash \chi$, hence $\vdash \varphi \vee \chi$, and by (EE2), $\delta \leq \varphi \vee \delta$ for all δ. By supposition $\nvdash \varphi$, hence by (EE5) we have $\delta \leq \varphi$ for some δ. Therefore by transitivity we obtain $\varphi \vee \chi \nleq \varphi$. Thus we have shown that $(^-1)$ holds.

The postulate ($^-$2) follows immediately from the condition (E$^-$).

Suppose $\varphi \notin T$, to show ($^-$3) is satisfied we prove $T \subseteq T_\varphi^-$. Let $\psi \in T$, we need to show that $\varphi \vee \neg\varphi$. Since $\varphi \notin T$ we have $T \neq \perp$ and $\varphi \leq \delta$ for all δ by (EE4). Furthermore, since $\psi \in T$ we have $\psi \not\leq \delta$ for some δ. By transitivity we have $\psi \not\leq \varphi$, hence by (EE2) and transitivity we have $\varphi \vee \psi \leq \varphi$.

Suppose $\not\vdash \varphi$, to show ($^-$4) is satisfied we establish $\varphi \notin T_\varphi^-$. By (E^-) we need to show either $\varphi \notin T$, or both $\varphi \not< \varphi \vee \varphi$ and $\not\vdash \varphi$. Let us suppose that $\varphi \in T$, now since $\varphi \notin T_\varphi^-$ and T is a theory, we have that $\not\vdash \varphi$. Hence we show $\varphi \not< \varphi \vee \varphi$, since $\leq$ is total we need to show $\varphi \vee \varphi \leq \varphi$. Since $\varphi \vee \varphi \vdash \varphi$ we have $\varphi \vee \varphi \leq \varphi$ by (EE2).

Suppose $\psi \in T$, for ($^-$5) we show that $T_\varphi^- \cup \{\varphi\} \vdash \psi$. By the deduction theorem we need to show $\neg\varphi \vee \psi \in T_\varphi^-$, by the condition (E^-) that means $\neg\varphi \vee \psi \in T$ and either $\varphi < \varphi \vee (\neg\varphi \vee \psi)$ or $\vdash \varphi$. Since $\psi \in T$ and T is a theory we have that $\neg\varphi \vee \psi \in T$. Let us now suppose $\not\vdash \varphi$, and show $\varphi \vee (\neg\varphi \vee \psi) \not\leq \varphi$. Clearly $\varphi \vee (\neg\varphi \vee \psi)$ is a tautology, hence by (EE2), we have $\delta \leq \varphi \vee (\neg\varphi \vee \psi)$ for all δ, furthermore $\delta \not\leq \varphi$ for some δ by (EE5). Therefore by transitivity we have our desired result; $\varphi \vee (\neg\varphi \vee \psi) \not\leq \varphi$. ∎

Given an epistemic entrenchment related to T, the condition (E$^-$) explicitly determines the information to be retained, and retracted in a contraction operation. Furthermore, every contraction function can be constructed from some epistemic entrenchment ordering.

Returning to our example, if *Tweety can fly* $\vee$ *all birds fly* is strictly more entrenched than *Tweety can fly*, then *all birds fly* will remain after the contraction of *Tweety can fly*. Conversely, if *Tweety can fly* $\vee$ *all birds fly* and *Tweety can fly* are equally entrenched, then *all birds fly* will be retracted.

It is easy to show using (E$^-$) that if ψ is at least as entrenched as φ then under the contraction with respect to $\varphi \wedge \psi$, the conjunct φ is removed, and if φ and ψ are equally entrenched then both are retracted. This mirrors our intuition that sentences with the lowest epistemic entrenchment are given up.

An analogous result for revision is provided in the theorem below, the proof is left as an exercise for the reader.

Theorem 14.6 *Let T be a theory of $\mathcal{L}$. For every revision function * for T there exists an epistemic entrenchment $\leq$ related to T such that (E^*), below, is true for every $\varphi \in \mathcal{L}$. Conversely, for every epistemic entrenchment $\leq$ related to T, there exists a revision function * for T such that (E^*) is true for every $\varphi \in \mathcal{L}$.*

$$(E^*) \qquad T_\varphi^* = \begin{cases} \{\psi \in \mathcal{L} : \neg\varphi < \neg\varphi \vee \psi\} & \textit{if } \nvdash \neg\varphi \\ \\ \bot & \textit{otherwise} \end{cases}$$

14.7 Odds and ends*

Gärdenfors and Makinson showed that for a finite language, an epistemic entrenchment related to T is determined by the ordering of the dual atoms (maximal disjunctions) in T. They also showed that there is a one-to-one correspondence between epistemic entrenchment orderings and revision (and contraction) functions, consequently the number of revision (and contraction) functions for T is equal to the number of epistemic entrenchment orderings on the dual atoms[3] in T. Therefore, finding the number of possible revision (and contraction) functions for T amounts to calculating the number of ways we can place a total preorder on the dual atoms in T. But first note that if there are k atoms in the language, then there are 2^k dual atoms. For instance, if the only atoms are φ and ψ then the set of dual atoms is $\{\varphi \vee \psi, \varphi \vee \neg\psi, \neg\varphi \vee \psi, \neg\varphi \vee \neg\psi\}$.

Theorem 14.7 *For a theory T in a finite language, if n is the number of dual atoms in T, then the number of revisions (and contraction) functions is given by:*

$$p(n) = \Sigma_{m=1}^n m! S(m,n)$$

where $S(m,n)$, are Stirling numbers of the second kind, that is, the number of partitions of an $n-$element set into m parts.

The growth of $p(n)$ is more rapid than exponential; $p(1) = 1$, $p(2) = 3$, $p(3) = 13$, $p(4) = 75$, $p(5) = 541 \cdots$, hence the class of change functions described by the rationality postulates is colossal in n, the number of dual atoms!

Finally, an epistemic entrenchment ordering is a *total* preorder. It is possible to relax many of the definitions to allow *partial* orderings, discussing the ramifications of doing so is outside the scope of this book. Instead we'll mention some work in this direction. Katsuno and Mendelzon introduced a revision function based on a partial preordering of models and identified a weaker version of (^{*8}) that is satisfied by revision functions constructed from a partial preorder on models. Hans Rott explored the idea of generalising epistemic entrenchment to a partial ordering by weakening (EE3).

---

[3]If the language consists of the atoms $p_1, \ldots, p_n$, then a dual atom is a formula $L_1 \vee \ldots \vee L_n$, where for each i, L_i is either p_i or $\neg p_i$.

Problems

14-1. Show that $T^+_{\varphi \wedge \psi} = (T^+_\varphi)^+_\psi$.

14-2. Assume $^-$ is a contraction function. Show that either $T^-_{\varphi \wedge \psi} = T^-_\varphi$ or $T^-_{\varphi \wedge \psi} = T^-_\psi$ or $T^-_{\varphi \wedge \psi} = T^-_\varphi \cap T^-_\psi$.

14-3. If T is inconsistent what can you say about the consistency of T^*_φ? If φ is inconsistent, what can be said?

14-4. Prove Theorem 14.2.

14-5. Prove Theorem 14.3.

14-6. Show that an epistemic entrenchment ordering is a total preorder.

14-7. Show for an epistemic entrenchment $\leq$ that either $\varphi \wedge \psi = \varphi$ or $\varphi \wedge \psi = \psi$.

14-8. Complete the proof of Theorem 14.5 in the converse direction.

14-9. Prove that if $\psi > \varphi$ then $\psi \in T^-_\varphi$.

14-10. Assume $T = \mathrm{Th}(\{\varphi, \psi\})$, and the epistemic entrenchment ordering related to T is given by the following ordering of dual atoms: $\neg\varphi \vee \neg\psi < \neg\varphi \vee \psi < \varphi \vee \psi = \varphi \vee \neg\psi$. Determine whether the properties (i) – (vi) hold.
   (i) $\psi < \varphi$
   (ii) $\psi \in T^-_\varphi$
   (iii) $\varphi \in T^-_\psi$
   (iv) $\varphi \vee \psi \in T^-_\psi$
   (v) $\neg\varphi \vee \psi \in T^-_\psi$
   (vi) $T = (T^-_\psi)^+_\psi$ if (E^-) and $\leq$ are used to construct $^-$.

14-11. Show that there is a revision function * such that $(Th(\{p, q\}))^*_{\neg p} = Th(\{\neg p, \neg q\})$.

Chapter 15

Implementing Belief Revision

This chapter focuses on several problems that surface when one attempts to implement the process of belief revision. The major obstacles arise from the fact that a change function takes an epistemic entrenchment ordering together with a sentence, to be contracted or accepted, and produces a theory. An obvious difficulty arises because an epistemic entrenchment ordering typically ranks an infinite number of sentences and this presents a serious *representation* problem for a computer-based implementation.

Another difficulty is that the epistemic entrenchment ordering is lost in the process of change, and as a consequence the *iteration* of change functions is not naturally supported. In many applications information systems are relentlessly bombarded with new information, so from a practical perspective modeling the iteration of change is essential.

The computational model described in this chapter uses a *finite partial entrenchment ranking* defined in section 15.1 as a finite representation of a finitely representable epistemic entrenchment ordering. In section 15.2 we describe the computational model that adjusts this ranking using an *absolute measure of minimal change*. Any theorem prover can be used to realize it. The adjustment of a finite partial entrenchment ranking is a mechanical procedure that can be used to support the iteration of change functions; procedural pseudocode for implementing an adjustment is given in section 15.3. In section 15.4 we demonstrate the explicit relationships between change functions constructed from partial entrenchment rankings, and epistemic entrenchment orderings. Somewhat surprisingly it turns out that standard AGM revision and contraction functions can be constructed from partial entrenchment rankings.

It is important to realize from the onset that the iteration of change functions can also be studied at the the axiomatic level by developing postulates that describe desirable properties for iterated change functions. We pursue only the constructive approach here.

15.1 Finite partial entrenchment rankings

A *finite partial entrenchment ranking* grades the content of a finite knowledge base according to its epistemic importance, and as such it can be used to specify a finitely representable epistemic entrenchment ordering. Formally defined below, this ranking maps a finite set of sentences to rational numbers. Intuitively, the higher the value assigned to a sentence the more firmly held it is, or the more entrenched it is.

Definition *A* finite partial entrenchment ranking *is a function* $\mathbf{B}$ *from a finite subset of sentences into the interval* $[0, 1]$ *such that the following conditions are satisfied for all* $\varphi \in \mathrm{dom}(\mathbf{B})$:

(a) $\{\psi \in \mathrm{dom}(\mathbf{B}) : \mathbf{B}(\varphi) < \mathbf{B}(\psi)\} \nvdash \varphi$ *if* φ *is not a tautology.*   (PER1)

(b) *If* $\vdash \neg\varphi$, *then* $\mathbf{B}(\varphi) = 0$.   (PER2)

(c) $\mathbf{B}(\varphi) = 1$ *if and only if* $\vdash \varphi$.   (PER3)

(PER1) says sentences assigned a value higher than an arbitrary sentence φ, do not entail φ, (PER2) says inconsistent sentences are assigned zero, and (PER3) says that tautologies are assigned 1. An example of a finite partial entrenchment ranking is given below. Convince yourself that it satisfies the property (PER1).

Example Let $\mathbf{B}$ be given by

$\mathbf{B}(bird(tweety) \lor \neg bird(tweety)) = 1,$
$\mathbf{B}(\forall X(bird(X) \rightarrow feathers(X))) = 0.3,$
$\mathbf{B}(bird(tweety)) = 0.2,$
$\mathbf{B}(\forall X(bird(X) \rightarrow wings(X))) = 0.1,$
$\mathbf{B}(bird(tweety) \land \neg bird(tweety)) = 0.$

A finite partial entrenchment ranking can be used to represent a finitely representable epistemic entrenchment ordering. Of course, a finite ranking does *not* imply that the language is finite.

The numerical assignment can be viewed in two distinct ways: (i) *qualitatively*, where the relative ordering of sentences is used, or (ii) *quantitatively*, where the numerical value assigned to sentences possesses some extra meaning, such as probability, and a calculus based on their numerical value adopted.

We denote the family of all finite partial entrenchment rankings by $\mathcal{B}$. The intended interpretation of a finite partial entrenchment ranking is that sentences mapped to numbers greater than zero represent the *explicit* beliefs, and their logical closure represents its *implicit* beliefs.

Definition *Define the* explicit information content *represented by* $\mathbf{B} \in \mathcal{B}$ *to be* $\{\varphi \in \mathrm{dom}(\mathbf{B}) : \mathbf{B}(\varphi) > 0\}$, *and denote it by* $\exp(\mathbf{B})$. *Similarly, define the* implicit information content *represented by* $\mathbf{B} \in \mathcal{B}$ *to be* $\mathrm{Th}(\exp(\mathbf{B}))$, *and denote it by* content$(\mathbf{B})$.

A finite partial entrenchment ranking usually represents an *incomplete specification* of an agent's preferences from which an epistemic entrenchment ordering can be generated. Note there is no unique way of generating an epistemic entrenchment ordering from a partial specification in general. For example, if $\mathbf{B}(\varphi) = 0.2$ and $\mathbf{B}(\psi) = 0.4$ then all compatible epistemic entrenchment orderings will have $\varphi < \psi$, however one compatible epistemic entrenchment ordering will have $\psi < \varphi \vee \psi$, whilst another will have $\psi = \varphi \vee \psi$. The epistemic entrenchment ordering we generate for our computational model gives sentences the *minimum* possible degree of entrenchment. For the example above, the generated epistemic entrenchment ordering would have $\psi = \varphi \vee \psi$ because $\varphi \vee \psi$ must be at least as entrenched as ψ by (EE2) but need not be strictly more entrenched.

In order to describe epistemic entrenchment orderings generated from a ranking it will be necessary to rank implicit information. In the definition below we assign a minimal degree of acceptance to implicit information under the constraint of (PER1).

Definition *Let φ be a nontautological sentence. Let $\mathbf{B}$ be a finite partial entrenchment ranking. We define the* degree of acceptance *of φ to be*

$$
\mathrm{degree}(\mathbf{B}, \varphi) = \begin{cases} \textit{largest } j \textit{ such that } \{\psi \in \exp(\mathbf{B}) : \mathbf{B}(\psi) \geq j\} \vdash \varphi \\ \qquad\qquad\qquad\qquad\qquad\qquad \textit{if } \varphi \in \mathrm{content}(\mathbf{B}) \\ 0 \qquad\qquad\qquad\qquad\qquad\qquad \textit{otherwise} \end{cases}
$$

You should be able to see that we can design a simple procedural algorithm to calculate the degree of acceptance of a sentence φ given the information encoded in a finite partial entrenchment ranking. Tautologies have degree 1, and to determine the degree of a nontautological sentence φ we attempt to prove φ using the sentences assigned the largest value in the range of $\mathbf{B}$, say n, if we are successful then φ is assigned degree n, otherwise we try to prove it using sentences assigned the next largest degree, say m, and those assigned n, if φ is successfully proven then it is assigned degree m, etc. Try this procedure with the following example.

Example Let **B** be given by

$\mathbf{B}(bird(tweety) \vee \neg(bird(tweety))) = 1$,
$\mathbf{B}(\forall X(bird(X) \rightarrow feathers(X))) = 0.3$,
$\mathbf{B}(bird(tweety)) = 0.2$,
$\mathbf{B}(\forall X(bird(X) \rightarrow wings(X))) = 0.1$,
$\mathbf{B}(bird(tweety) \wedge \neg bird(tweety)) = 0$.

Using **B** we calculate the degree of acceptance of the following implicit information.

degree$(\mathbf{B}, feathers(tweety)) = 0.2$,
degree$(\mathbf{B}, (\forall X(bird(X) \rightarrow feathers(X))) \wedge bird(tweety)) = 0.2$,
degree$(\mathbf{B}, wings(tweety)) = 0.1$,
degree$(\mathbf{B}, feathers(tweety) \wedge wings(tweety)) = 0.1$,
degree$(\mathbf{B}, \neg bird(tweety)) = 0$,
degree$(\mathbf{B}, \neg feathers(tweety)) = 0$.
degree$(\mathbf{B}, feathers(tweety) \wedge \neg feathers(tweety)) = 0$.

Theorem 15.1, below, shows how a finite partial entrenchment ranking can generate an epistemic entrenchment ordering using degrees of acceptance.

Theorem 15.1 *Let* $\mathbf{B} \in \mathcal{B}$ *and* φ, ψ *be sentences. Define* $\leq_\mathbf{B}$ *by* $\varphi \leq_\mathbf{B} \psi$ *iff* $\vdash \psi$, *or* degree$(\mathbf{B}, \varphi) \leq$ degree$(\mathbf{B}, \psi)$. *Then* $\leq_\mathbf{B}$ *is an epistemic entrenchment ordering related to* content$(\mathbf{B})$.

We refer to $\leq_\mathbf{B}$ as *the minimal epistemic entrenchment ordering generated from* **B**. From Theorem 15.1 we see that the tautologies are maximal, and sentences not in content$(\mathbf{B})$ are minimal with respect to $\leq_\mathbf{B}$. Since dom$(\mathbf{B})$ is finite, the minimal epistemic entrenchment ordering generated is finite, that is, $\leq_\mathbf{B}$ possesses a finite number of natural partitions.

Back to our simple example, if $\mathbf{B}(\varphi) = 0.2$ and $\mathbf{B}(\psi) = 0.4$ then the minimal epistemic entrenchment ordering generated by **B** is given by the following ordering on dual atoms: $\neg\varphi \vee \neg\psi <_\mathbf{B} \varphi \vee \neg\psi <_\mathbf{B} \neg\varphi \vee \psi =_\mathbf{B} \varphi \vee \psi$. From this ordering we can derive $\varphi \wedge \psi =_\mathbf{B} \varphi <_\mathbf{B} \psi =_\mathbf{B} \varphi \vee \psi$

Recall from the previous chapter that an epistemic entrenchment ordering, $\leq$, is *finitely representable* if and only if every cut$_\leq(\varphi)$ is finitely axiomatizable. Consequently, $\leq$ is finitely representable if and only if there exists a finite partial entrenchment ranking **B** such that $\leq = \leq_\mathbf{B}$.

Intuitively, Theorem 15.2, below, says given a finitely representable epistemic entrenchment ordering there exists a finite partial entrenchment ranking that can generate it. Theorems 15.1 and 15.2 tell us that a partial entrenchment ranking can be considered to be a (possibly minimal) specification of a finite epistemic entrenchment ordering.

Theorem 15.2 *Let T be a theory, and $\Gamma \subseteq T$. Let $\leq$ be a finitely representable epistemic entrenchment related to T. Let $T_0, T_1, T_2, \ldots$ be the natural partitions of $\leq$ indexed so that $\varphi \in T_i$ and $\psi \in T_j$ whenever $i < j$ implies $\varphi < \psi$. For all $\varphi \in T$, if $\{\psi \in \Gamma : \varphi \leq \psi\} \vdash \varphi$, then the mapping of each sentence in Γ from the natural partition T_i to i for all i is a partial entrenchment ranking, $\mathbf{B}$, that generates $\leq$, that is, $\leq_\mathbf{B} = \leq$.*

The Γ referred to in the theorem above is the explicit information content of the finite partial entrenchment ranking that generates the epistemic entrenchment and while obviously not unique, it must contain enough sentences of *the right stuff* in each natural partition of the epistemic entrenchment ordering to enable its regeneration. In particular, it must satisfy the condition in the theorem; at least one such Γ exists since $\leq$ is finitely representable.

So going from a finitely representable epistemic entrenchment to a finite partial entrenchment ranking is a nonunique process. For example, consider the epistemic entrenchment ordering: $\neg\varphi \vee \neg\psi < \varphi \vee \neg\psi < \neg\varphi \vee \psi = \varphi \vee \psi$. Any of the following three finite partial entrenchment rankings could be used to generate it using the function degree, that is, $\leq = \leq_{\mathbf{B}_1} = \leq_{\mathbf{B}_2} = \leq_{\mathbf{B}_3}$.

(a) $\mathbf{B}_1(\neg\varphi \vee \neg\psi) = 0, \mathbf{B}_1(\varphi \vee \neg\psi) = 0.2, \mathbf{B}_1(\neg\varphi \vee \psi) = 0.4, \mathbf{B}_1(\varphi \vee \psi) = 0.4$.
(b) $\mathbf{B}_2(\neg\varphi \wedge \neg\psi) = 0, \mathbf{B}_2(\varphi \vee \neg\psi) = 0.2, \mathbf{B}_2(\psi) = 0.4$.
(c) $\mathbf{B}_3(\varphi) = 0.2, \mathbf{B}_3(\psi) = 0.4$.

We call finite partial entrenchment rankings *equivalent* if they generate the same minimal epistemic entrenchment ordering. In this sense the rankings $\mathbf{B}_1$, $\mathbf{B}_2$ and $\mathbf{B}_3$ above are equivalent.

15.2   A computational model

Recall that from a practical perspective the AGM paradigm does not provide a policy to support the iteration of its theory change functions. This property is attractive in a theoretical context because it allows the resultant theory to adopt any of many possible epistemic entrenchment orderings depending on the desired dynamic behaviour. In practice, however, a *policy for change* is necessary.

In this section we describe a procedure for *adjusting* a finite partial entrenchment ranking. This procedure governs the dynamic behaviour of the system.

For change functions described in the previous chapter the information input was a sentence. If our aim is to modify a ranking then not only do we need a sentence but we also need a degree of acceptance to assign it in the adjusted ranking. In other words, we need to know where in the new ranking the sentence should reside. We define the *adjustment of a partial entrenchment ranking*, below, the new information is a contingent sentence φ and a number $0 \le i < 1$ where φ is the information to be accepted, and i is the degree of acceptance φ is to be assigned in the adjusted ranking.

Adjustments use a *policy for change* based on an *absolute minimal measure*; they transmute a finite partial entrenchment ranking so as to incorporate the desired new information using an absolute minimal measure of change. The set of contingent sentences is denoted $\mathcal{L}^{\bowtie}$.

Definition *Let $\varphi \in \mathcal{L}^{\bowtie}$ and $0 \le i < 1$. We define the* adjustment of a finite partial entrenchment ranking $\mathbf{B}$ *to be an function $\star$ such that*

$$\mathbf{B}^{\star}(\varphi, i) = \begin{cases} (\mathbf{B}^{-}(\varphi, i)) & \text{if } i \le \text{degree}(\mathbf{B}, \varphi) \\ \\ (\mathbf{B}^{-}(\neg\varphi, 0))^{+}(\varphi, i) & \text{otherwise} \end{cases}$$

where

$$\mathbf{B}^{-}(\varphi, i)(\psi) = \begin{cases} i & \text{if degree}(\mathbf{B}, \varphi) = \text{degree}(\mathbf{B}, \varphi \vee \psi) \text{ and } \mathbf{B}(\psi) > i \\ \mathbf{B}(\psi) & \text{otherwise} \end{cases}$$

for all $\psi \in \text{dom}(\mathbf{B})$, and

$$\mathbf{B}^{+}(\varphi, i)(\psi) = \begin{cases} \mathbf{B}(\psi) & \text{if } \mathbf{B}(\psi) > i \\ i & \text{if } \varphi \leftrightarrow \psi \text{ or } \mathbf{B}(\psi) \le i < \text{degree}(\mathbf{B}, \varphi \rightarrow \psi) \\ \text{degree}(\mathbf{B}, \varphi \rightarrow \psi) & \text{otherwise} \end{cases}$$

for all $\psi \in \text{dom}(\mathbf{B}) \cup \{\varphi\}$.

Adjustments define change functions for *theory bases*, rather than logically closed sets of sentences as in the previous chapter. Note that an adjustment is not defined for inconsistent, or tautological sentences. Accepting inconsistent information will compromise the integrity of the system, and thus ought to be avoided, whilst tautologies must always be assigned 1. So the definition focuses on the principle case, and can easily be extended to include both tautological and inconsistent sentences, if desired. A procedural algorithm for adjustments is described in section 15.3.

Intuitively, an (φ, i)–adjustment of $\mathbf{B}$ involves minimal changes to $\mathbf{B}$ such that φ is accepted with degree i. In particular, each sentence $\psi \in \text{dom}(\mathbf{B})$ is reassigned a number closest to $\mathbf{B}(\psi)$ in the adjusted partial entrenchment ranking $\mathbf{B}^\star(\varphi, i)$ under the guiding principle that if we reduce the degree of an accepted sentence φ, to i, say, then we also reduce the degree of each sentence that would be retracted in φ's contraction to i as well.

There are essentially two processes at work in an adjustment; sentences migrate *up* or *down* the ranking. Migration downwards is related to contraction, whilst movement upwards is related to expansion; movement upwards must ensure that the new ranking satisfies (PER1).

Adjustments use the *relative ranking* of information encoded in a partial entrenchment ranking, and they *preserve finiteness*; adjusting a finite partial entrenchment ranking results in a finite ranking, and if $\exp(\mathbf{B})$ is finite then $\exp(\mathbf{B}^\star(\varphi, i))$ is finite. The following theorem illustrates the interrelationships between theory base revision and theory base contraction based on adjustments. In particular, Theorem 15.3(i) is analogous to the Harper Identity and it captures the dependence of contraction on the information content of the theory base, that is, $\exp(\mathbf{B})$. Similarly Theorem 15.3(ii) is analogous to the Levi Identity.

Theorem 15.3 *Let* $\mathbf{B} \in \mathcal{B}$, *let* * *be an adjustment, and let* $0 < i < 1$. *Then*

$\exp(\mathbf{B}^\star(\varphi, 0)) = \exp(\mathbf{B}^\star(\neg\varphi, i)) \cap \exp(\mathbf{B})$, *and*

$\exp(\mathbf{B}^\star(\varphi, i)) = \exp(\mathbf{B}^\star(\neg\varphi, 0)) \cup \{\varphi\}$.

We illustrate the adjustment of a theory base in the simple example below.

Example $\mathbf{B}(\varphi \vee \chi) = 0.4, \mathbf{B}(\varphi \rightarrow \psi) = 0.3,\ \mathbf{B}(\varphi) = 0.25,\ \mathbf{B}(\chi) = 0.1.$

(a) Consider the reorganization of $\mathbf{B}$ where more compelling evidence for φ is acquired, and we decide to increase the degree of acceptance of φ from 0.25 to 0.6. We obtain the following:

$\mathbf{B}^\star(\varphi, 0.6)(\varphi) = 0.6$,
$\mathbf{B}^\star(\varphi, 0.6)(\varphi \vee \chi) = 0.6$,
$\mathbf{B}^\star(\varphi, 0.6)(\varphi \rightarrow \psi) = 0.3$,
$\mathbf{B}^\star(\varphi, 0.6)(\chi) = 0.1$,
$\text{degree}(\mathbf{B}^\star(\varphi, 0.6), \varphi \vee \psi) = 0.6$,
$\text{degree}(\mathbf{B}^\star(\varphi, 0.6), \psi) = 0.3$

$\text{degree}(\mathbf{B}^\star(\varphi, 0.6), \varphi \to \chi) = 0.1,$

$\text{degree}(\mathbf{B}^\star(\varphi, 0.6), \neg\varphi) = 0,$

$\text{degree}(\mathbf{B}^\star(\varphi, 0.6), \neg\psi) = 0,$ and

$\text{degree}(\mathbf{B}^\star(\varphi, 0.6), \neg\chi) = 0.$

(b) Now let's consider the contraction of φ, that is, $\mathbf{B}^\star(\varphi, 0)$.

$\mathbf{B}^\star(\varphi, 0)(\varphi \lor \chi) = 0.4,$

$\mathbf{B}^\star(\varphi, 0)(\varphi \to \psi) = 0.3,$

$\mathbf{B}^\star(\varphi, 0)(\chi) = 0.1,$

$\mathbf{B}^\star(\varphi, 0)(\varphi) = 0,$

$\text{degree}(\mathbf{B}^\star(\varphi, 0), \varphi \to \chi) = 0.1,$

$\text{degree}(\mathbf{B}^\star(\varphi, 0), \varphi \lor \psi) = 0,$

$\text{degree}(\mathbf{B}^\star(\varphi, 0), \psi) = 0$

$\text{degree}(\mathbf{B}^\star(\varphi, 0), \neg\varphi) = 0,$

$\text{degree}(\mathbf{B}^\star(\varphi, 0), \neg\psi) = 0,$ and

$\text{degree}(\mathbf{B}^\star(\varphi, 0), \neg\chi) = 0.$

(c) Finally, we consider the acceptance of $\neg\varphi$ with degree 0.8, that is, $\mathbf{B}^\star(\neg\varphi, 0.8)$. Then we have

$\mathbf{B}^\star(\neg\varphi, 0.8)(\neg\varphi) = 0.8,$

$\mathbf{B}^\star(\neg\varphi, 0.8)(\varphi \to \psi) = 0.8,$

$\mathbf{B}^\star(\neg\varphi, 0.8)(\varphi \lor \chi) = 0.4,$

$\mathbf{B}^\star(\neg\varphi, 0.8)(\chi) = 0.4,$

$\mathbf{B}^\star(\neg\varphi, 0.8)(\varphi) = 0,$

$\text{degree}(\mathbf{B}^\star(\neg\varphi, 0.8), \varphi \to \chi) = 0.8,$

$\text{degree}(\mathbf{B}^\star(\neg\varphi, 0.8), \varphi \lor \psi) = 0,$

$\text{degree}(\mathbf{B}^\star(\neg\varphi, 0.8), \psi) = 0$

$\text{degree}(\mathbf{B}^\star(\neg\varphi, 0.8), \neg\psi) = 0,$

$\text{degree}(\mathbf{B}^\star(\neg\varphi, 0.8), \neg\chi) = 0.$

15.3   A procedural algorithm for adjustment*

This section can be skipped if the reader is not interested in implementing belief revision. In it we describe a procedural algorithm for implementing the adjustment of finite partial entrenchment rankings. It requires the support of your favourite theorem prover to implement the logical implication relation in the function **rank**. This function is used to determine the degree of a sentence. Loosely speaking the algorithm involves successive calls to **rank** for each sentence in the domain of a finite partial entrenchment ranking.

We represent a finite epistemic ranking as a *list* labeled **B**. The odd elements of **B** are lists, and the even elements are numbers in $(0, 1)$ which represent the degree to which elements of the previous odd element are assigned. The partial entrenchment ranking described in the example of section 15.2 would be represented as the list $[[\varphi \vee \chi], 0.4, [\varphi \rightarrow \psi], 0.3, [\varphi], 0.25, [\chi], 0.1]$. By convention, and without loss of generality, no sentences are assigned zero or one in the ranking, in other words we would not normally represent tautologies, nonbeliefs, or contradictions. After all they are redundant in the sense that they can always be derived from a ranking that does not explicitly represent them.

The data structure described above is not the optimum representation but one that is easily converted to other amenable representations, and the algorithm itself is not the most efficient but was chosen for its transparency. First we distinguish the notions of degree and rank. If **a** is in $\mathbf{B}_{i*2 - 1}$ then the degree of **a** is the value of $\mathbf{B}_{i*2}$, and the rank of **a** is **i**. The length of the list **B** is denoted by **len(B)**. In the example above the degree of φ is 0.25, the rank of φ is 3, and the length of **B** is 8.

The control procedure is **adjust**. It takes a ranking **B**, a contingent sentence **a**, and an $i \in [0, 1)$ as input and produces a new ranking **new_B** by adjusting **B**. It locates where in the list **a** should be placed, creating a new location if necessary, and finds the current degree of **a**. Then if the current degree of **a** is more than **i**, it moves **a** and all sentences which would be removed in the contraction of **a** down to **i**. Alternatively, if the current degree of **a** is less than **i**, then **a** is moved up to **i**, to ensure the satisfaction of (PER1) some other sentences may need to be moved up. Note sentences are move upwards and downwards in the ranking only as far as they need be.

```
PROCEDURE adjust(B,a,i)
{adjusts B so that a has degree i in new_B}
begin
  len := len(B)
  find_place(B,a,i,rank_i,len)
  rank_a := rank(B,a,len)
  degree_a := B_rank_a*2
  new_B:= B
  if degree_a ≥ i then movedown(B,a,rank_a,rank_i,len,new_B) end if
  if degree_a < i then moveup(B,a,rank_a,rank_i,len,new_B) end if
```

```
    crunch(new_B)
end


PROCEDURE movedown(B,a,rank_a,rank_i,len,new_B)
begin
   new_B_rank_a*2 - 1 := new_B_rank_a*2 - 1 − {a}
   new_B_rank_i*2 - 1 := new_B_rank_i*2 - 1 ∪ {a}
   for j = rank_a down to rank_i
   begin
      for all members b in B_j*2 - 1 do
      begin
         if rank_a = rank(B,a∨b,len) then
            new_B_j*2 - 1 := new_B_j*2 - 1 − { b }
            new_B_rank_i*2 - 1 := new_B_rank_i*2 - 1 ∪ { b }
         end if
      end
   end
end


PROCEDURE moveup(B,a,rank_a,rank_i,len,new_B)
begin
   rank_not_a := rank(B,¬a,len)
   if rank_not_a ≥ 1 then
      movedown(B,¬a,rank_not_a,1,len,new_B);
   end if
   new_B_rank_a*2 - 1 := new_B_rank_a*2 - 1 − {a}
   new_B_rank_i*2 - 1 := new_B_rank_i*2 - 1 ∪ {a}
   for all j = rank_i - 1 to 1 do
   begin
      for all members b in B_j*2 - 1 do
      begin
         rankb := rank(B,b,len)
         rank_a→b := rank(B,a→b,len)
         if rank_a→b > rank_i
         then
            new_B_rank_i*2 - 1 := new_B_rank_i*2 - 1 ∪ {b}
            new_B_rank_b*2 - 1 := new_B_rank_b*2 - 1 − {b}
```

```
            else
               new_B_{rank_a→b * 2 - 1} := new_B_{rank_a→b * 2 - 1} ∪ {b}
               new_B_{rank_b*2 - 1} := new_B_{rank_b*2 - 1} - {b}
            end if
         end
      end
end


PROCEDURE find_place(B,a,i,rank_i,len)
{finds the rank of sentences assigned i, and creates a new one if required}
begin
   rank_i := len/2
   while rank_i > 1 and B_{rank_i*2} >  i do
   begin
      rank_i := rank_i - 1;
   end
   if B_{(rank_i -1) * 2} < i then
   {there is no match, so insert a partition}
   begin
      for j = len to rank_i*2 do
      begin
         B_{j+2} := B_j
      end
      B_{rank_i*2} := i
      len := len + 2
      B_{rank_i*2 - 1} := [ ]
   end if
end


FUNCTION rank(B,a,len)
{calculates the rank of a in B}
begin
   rank := len/2 + 1
   if ⊬ a then
      do rank:= rank - 1
      until rank ≤ 1 or  ⋃_{i≥rank} B_{2i - 1} ⊢ a
   end if end
```

PROCEDURE crunch(**B**)
{removes empty partitions from **B**}

15.4 Connections with theory change

In this section we investigate the behaviour of adjustments by exploring their relationship with standard AGM theory change functions. In particular, the relationship between *theory base change* functions constructed by the adjustment of a finite partial entrenchment ranking, **B**, and *theory change* functions constructed by the minimal epistemic entrenchment ordering generated from **B** using the constructions of the previous chapter.

Theorem 15.4, below, is a delightful little result that demonstrates that if $i > 0$ then $\mathbf{B}^{\star}(\varphi, i)$ embodies a revision. In particular, content$(\mathbf{B}) \mapsto$ content$(\mathbf{B}^{\star}(\varphi, i))$ defines a revision function.

Theorem 15.4 *Let* $\mathbf{B} \in \mathcal{B}$, *let* * *be an adjustment, and let* $0 < i < 1$. *Let* * *be the revision function for* content$(\mathbf{B})$ *uniquely determined by* (E^{*}) *and* $\leq_{\mathbf{B}}$. *Then*

$$\exp(\mathbf{B}^{\star}(\varphi, i)) = (\text{content}(\mathbf{B}))^{*}_{\varphi} \cap \{\exp(\mathbf{B}) \cup \{\varphi\}\}, \text{ and}$$

$$(\text{content}(\mathbf{B}))^{*}_{\varphi} = \text{content}(\mathbf{B}^{\star}(\varphi, i)).$$

Theorem 15.5, below, shows that $\mathbf{B}^{\star}(\varphi, 0)$ represents a withdrawal function.

Theorem 15.5 *Let* $\mathbf{B} \in \mathcal{B}$, *let* * *be an adjustment. If* $^{-}$ *is defined by* $(\text{content}(\mathbf{B}))^{-}_{\varphi} = $ content$(\mathbf{B}^{\star}(\varphi, 0))$ *then* $^{-}$ *is a withdrawal function.*

The adjustment $\mathbf{B}^{\star}(\varphi, 0)$ does not describe a contraction because the recovery postulate, $(^{-}5)$, is not always satisfied. The underlying reason for this is that adjustments of **B** force $\exp(\mathbf{B}^{\star}(\varphi, 0))$ to be a subset of $\exp(\mathbf{B})$. The following example illustrates that recovery is not always satisfied. Consider **B** to be given by; $\mathbf{B}(\varphi) = 0.5$ and $\mathbf{B}(\psi) = 0.3$. According to the definition of an adjustment $\exp(\mathbf{B}^{\star}(\varphi, 0))$ is empty, hence $\psi \notin \text{Th}(\exp(\mathbf{B}^{\star}(\varphi, 0)) \cup \{\varphi\})$.

If it is desirable to satisfy recovery then we can adapt an idea of Bernhard Nebel's, which was independently observed by Norman Foo; namely assign $\mathbf{B}^{\star}(\varphi, 0)(\varphi \rightarrow \psi) = \mathbf{B}(\psi)$ for all $\psi \in \exp(\mathbf{B})$ reassigned zero in the adjustment (see exercise 15-9). This ensures the satisfaction of recovery because ψ will be reintroduced if φ is reassigned $i > 0$, that is, $\psi \in \text{content}(\mathbf{B}^{\star}(\varphi, i))$.

Consequently, the definitions and results in this chapter can be modified to capture recovery in a straightforward manner. We adopt the definition as given because it is more consistent with our interpretation of a finite partial entrenchment ranking being an *explicit* representation of an agent's information. Furthermore, it was shown in section 14.3 that satisfying recovery is not always appropriate.

Despite the result in Theorem 15.5, the next theorem shows that enough information is retained by adjustment to satisfy recovery if we expand with respect to $\neg\varphi$ and keep those sentences that were part of the original implicit information content. Therefore, somewhat surprisingly, $\exp(\mathbf{B}^\star(\varphi, 0))$ contains sufficient information to reconstruct a contraction function.

Theorem 15.6 *Let* $\mathbf{B} \in \mathcal{B}$, *let* $\star$ *be an adjustment. Let* $^-$ *be the contraction function for* content($\mathbf{B}$) *uniquely determined by* (E^-) *and* $\leq_\mathbf{B}$. *Then*

$$\exp(\mathbf{B}^\star(\varphi, 0) = (\text{content}(\mathbf{B}))_\varphi^- \cap \exp(\mathbf{B}),$$

$$(\text{content}(\mathbf{B}))_\varphi^- = \text{Th}(\exp(\mathbf{B}^\star(\varphi, 0)) \cup \{\neg\varphi\}) \cap \text{content}(\mathbf{B}), \text{ and}$$

if $\exp(\mathbf{B})$ *is a theory then* $(\text{content}(\mathbf{B}))_\varphi^- = \text{content}(\mathbf{B}^\star(\varphi, 0))$.

Theorems 15.4 (i) and 15.6 (i) highlight the syntax sensitivity of revision and contraction. It is generally conceded that the sensitivity to syntax should simply reflect a higher level of commitment to explicit information than the implicit information.

The problem of syntax dependence stems from the inherent property that, there may be a maximal subset of content($\mathbf{B}$), say X, which might be the result of an AGM contraction however there may not be a subset of $\exp(\mathbf{B})$, say Γ, such that $\text{Th}(\Gamma) = X$. As a consequence the syntactical description of $\exp(\mathbf{B})$ *constrains* the way a finite partial entrenchment ranking can be naturally modified. For instance, consider a ranking given by: $\mathbf{B}_1(\varphi \vee \psi) = 0.8$ and $\mathbf{B}_1(\varphi \wedge \psi) = 0.6$. Observe that $\psi \notin \text{content}(\mathbf{B}_1^\star(\varphi, 0))$ since ψ is lost in the contraction of φ. This happens because in order to contract φ the conjunction $\varphi \wedge \psi$ must be retracted, hence ψ is lost as a side-effect. However if the *equivalent* ranking $\mathbf{B}_2(\varphi \vee \psi) = 0.8$, $\mathbf{B}_2(\varphi) = 0.6$ and $\mathbf{B}_2(\psi) = 0.6$ had been used instead, then $\psi \in \text{content}(\mathbf{B}_2^\star(\varphi, 0))$.

Theorem 15.6(i) succinctly captures the dependence of a contraction on the explicit information content of the theory base, $\exp(\mathbf{B})$. In particular, a sentence is retained if and only if it is explicit information, and it would have been retained by corresponding contraction function on the theory content($\mathbf{B}$) using the construction based on $\leq_\mathbf{B}$. Theorem 15.4(i) establishes a similar result for revision. Hence, adjustments retain as much explicit information as possible.

Theorems 15.4(ii) and 15.6(ii) show that theory change functions can be formulated in terms of adjustments. Furthermore, Theorem 15.6 (iii) reassuringly tells us that if the explicit and implicit information content are identical then adjustment of the ranking corresponds to a contraction function for content$(\mathbf{B})$.

We conclude that the connections between the adjustment of partial entrenchment rankings and the standard AGM change functions established in this section provide strong support for the adjustment procedure. The main challenge then, is the design of the appropriate syntactical form of the partial entrenchment ranking, that is, determining the explicit information in a ranking that reflects the desired behaviour of the system. The results in this section tell us that important information should be explicit and the independence of information must also be explicit.

Problems

15-1. In the example of section 15.2 calculate degree$(\mathbf{B}, \psi)$, degree$(\mathbf{B}, \varphi \wedge \psi)$, and degree$(\mathbf{B}, \psi \to \chi)$.

15-2. Prove the following:
(i) degree$(\mathbf{B}, \varphi \wedge \psi) = \min(\text{degree}(\mathbf{B}, \varphi), \text{degree}(\mathbf{B}, \psi))$,
(ii) degree$(\mathbf{B}, \varphi \wedge \psi) = \text{degree}(\mathbf{B}, \{\varphi, \psi\})$,
(iii) degree$(\mathbf{B}, \varphi \vee \psi) \geq \min(\text{degree}(\mathbf{B}, \varphi), \text{degree}(\mathbf{B}, \psi))$,
(iv) degree$(\mathbf{B}, \varphi \wedge (\varphi \to \psi)) = \min(\text{degree}(\mathbf{B}, \varphi), \text{degree}(\mathbf{B}, \psi))$.

15-3. Determine if $\mathbf{B}_1$ and $\mathbf{B}_2$, below, are equivalent. $\mathbf{B}_1$ is given by $\mathbf{B}_1(\varphi \to \psi) = 2$, $\mathbf{B}_1(\varphi) = 2$, $\mathbf{B}_1(\chi) = 1$, and $\mathbf{B}_2$ is given by $\mathbf{B}_2(\psi) = 2$, $\mathbf{B}_2(\varphi) = 2$, $\mathbf{B}_2(\varphi \to \chi) = 1$.

15-4. If $\mathbf{B}_1$ and $\mathbf{B}_2$ are equivalent partial entrenchment rankings. Prove the following:
(i) $\text{Th}(\text{cut}_<(\mathbf{B}_1, \varphi)) = \text{Th}(\text{cut}_<(\mathbf{B}_2, \varphi))$.
(ii) content$(\mathbf{B}_1) = \text{content}(\mathbf{B}_2)$.
(iii) content$(\mathbf{B}_1^\star(\varphi, i)) = \text{content}(\mathbf{B}_2^\star(\varphi, i))$ where $i > 0$.

15-5. Prove Theorem 15-3.

15-6. Give an example of (i) an adjustment that does not satisfy recovery, and (ii) an adjustment that does satisfy recovery.

15-7.   Calculate degree$(\mathbf{B}^\star(\neg\varphi, 0.4), \psi)$ for parts (a), (b) and (c) in the example of section 15.2. How could you modify $\mathbf{B}$ so that $\psi \in$ content$(\mathbf{B}^\star(\varphi, 0))$ and $\psi \in$ content$(\mathbf{B}^\star(\neg\varphi, 0.4))$.

15-8.   Prove if $\mathbf{B}(\psi) \geq \max\{\mathbf{B}(\varphi), \mathbf{B}(\neg\varphi), i\}$ then $\mathbf{B}^\star(\varphi, i)(\psi) = \mathbf{B}(\psi)$.

15-9.   Modify the definition of an adjustment so that recovery is satisfied, that is, content$(\mathbf{B}) = $ Th$($content$(\mathbf{B}^\star(\varphi, 0) \cup \{\varphi\})$.

15-10.   Assume $\mathbf{B}(\varphi) = 0.4$, $\mathbf{B}(\psi) = 0.2$ defines a finite partial entrenchment ranking. Calculate the following:
  (i) degree$(\mathbf{B}, \varphi \vee \psi)$,
  (ii) $\mathbf{B}^\star(\varphi, 0)(\psi)$, and
  (iii) $\mathbf{B}^\star(\psi, 0)(\varphi)$.

15-11.* Using examples identify two potential problems with adjustments.

15-12.* Design your own **crunch** procedure and implement the **adjust** procedure.

Chapter 16

Interconnections*

Nonmonotonic reasoning and belief revision are closely related. This relationship stems from their common reliance on the property of *minimality*, a ubiquitous principle in modern science which manifests itself in energy transformations during chemical reactions, in the surface area of soap bubbles, in the geodesics associated with the theory of relativity, etc. Nonmonotonic inference and belief revision are bound to the notion of minimality principally through their semantics which can be described using a mechanism that *selects minimal models* in accordance with some underlying preference ordering. These minimal models, selected from the set of all possible models, can represent the most preferred, or most expected, situations that concord with the reasoning agent's understanding of its surroundings.

This chapter describes a formal relationship between nonmonotonic reasoning and belief revision at the axiomatic, the constructive and the dynamic levels. Section 16.1 describes how each rationality postulate for revision can be translated into an inference relation property, and vice versa. We shall see that the revision postulates can be translated into a set of properties which are satisfied precisely by the class of *rational consistency preserving nonmontonic inference relations*.

It should come as no surprise then, that this class of nonmonotonic inference relations can be constructed from the class of epistemic entrenchment orderings, and that as a consequence, partial entrenchment rankings induce rational consistency preserving nonmontonic inference relations. In section 16.2 a nonmonotonic inference relation is defined firstly using an epistemic entrenchment ordering, and then secondly using a partial entrenchment ranking. Furthermore it is shown that a partial entrenchment ranking and the epistemic entrenchment ordering it generates induce the *same* nonmonotonic inference relation.

In section 16.3 we use the computational model for belief revision described in chapter 15 to alter the behaviour of a nonmonotonic inference relation by modifying the ranking that induces it. This process provides support for the removal of old default assumptions and the incorporation of new default assumptions.

In section 16.4 we provide some examples which illustrate the main ideas.

16.1 Translations between revision and nonmonotonic inference

This section describes the work of Makinson and Gärdenfors who showed that a revision operation T_φ^* can be viewed as an inference operation, and conversely a certain inference relation can be defined using T_φ^*. If $\neg\varphi \notin T$ then the inference operation is *monotonic*, while if $\neg\varphi \in T$ then it is *nonmonotonic*.

We know from chapter 14 that an epistemic entrenchment ordering can be associated with a theory, T, and a revision function, $*$. Therefore the inference operation associated with them can be defined from the corresponding epistemic entrenchment ordering where T represents the background information from which default information is derived via $*$.

Conversely, we saw in chapter 13 that inference relations can be constructed from preferential model structures. In particular, $\{\varphi\} \mathrel{\vdash\!\!\!\!\sim} \psi$ if ψ holds in the *minimal models* containing φ. Epistemic entrenchment orderings can be used to build preferential model structures whose minimal models containing φ are precisely the models for T_φ^*. Therefore the inference, $\{\varphi\} \mathrel{\vdash\!\!\!\!\sim} \psi$, from φ to ψ can be described using a revision function.

The formal relationship between belief revision and nonmonotonic reasoning is based on their semantics which rely on the identification of minimal models according to some underlying preference ordering. For the purposes of this chapter we will suppose that our underlying preference relation is an epistemic entrenchment ordering; its specific role is highlighted in the next section.

We first explore the relationship between belief revision and nonmonotonic reasoning at the axiomatic level by describing the Makinson and Gärdenfors procedure which allows conditions concerning revision functions to be converted into conditions for inference relations, and vice versa. The translation procedure is straightforward, although it sometimes involves a little logical manipulation to facilitate its use. To translate conditions on revision functions to conditions on inference relations we convert statements of the form $\psi \in T_\varphi^*$ to $\{\varphi\} \mathrel{\vdash\!\!\!\!\sim} \psi$, or equivalently $\psi \in C(\{\varphi\})$. That is to say, if ψ is accepted after we incorporate φ into our background knowledge then ψ nonmonotonically follows from φ. This translation can be motivated by the fact that it can be shown, if $\psi \in T_\varphi^*$, then ψ is true in all the minimal models of φ given a special total preordering of models (see pointer to Grove's system of spheres constructions in References for Part IV). This special total preordering on models can be derived naturally from an epistemic entrenchment ordering.

Given this translation we generally restrict ourselves to singleton sets on the left-hand-side of the relation $\mathrel{\vdash\kern-0.6em\sim}$. Observe that according to the translation above we convert conditions of the form $\psi \in T$ to $\top \mathrel{\vdash\kern-0.6em\sim} \psi$ where $\top$ is the set of tautologies.

The outcome of translating all eight rationality postulates for revision into abstract properties for inference relations is provided in the Table 16.1

Revision Postulates	Inference Relation Properties
$(^*1)\ T_\varphi^* = \mathrm{Th}(T_\varphi^*)$	$C(\{\varphi\}) = \mathrm{Th}(C(\{\varphi\}))$
$(^*2)\ \varphi \in T_\varphi^*$	$\{\varphi\} \mathrel{\vdash\kern-0.6em\sim} \varphi$
$(^*3)\ T_\varphi^* \subseteq \mathrm{Th}(T \cup \{\varphi\})$	if $\{\varphi\} \mathrel{\vdash\kern-0.6em\sim} \psi$ then $\top \mathrel{\vdash\kern-0.6em\sim} (\varphi \to \psi)$
$(^*4)$ if $\neg\varphi \notin T$ then $\mathrm{Th}(T \cup \{\varphi\}) \subseteq T_\varphi^*$	if $\top \mathrel{\not\vdash\kern-0.6em\sim} \neg\varphi$ and $\top \mathrel{\vdash\kern-0.6em\sim} (\varphi \to \psi)$ then $\{\varphi\} \mathrel{\vdash\kern-0.6em\sim} \psi$
$(^*5)$ if $T_\varphi^* = \perp$ then $\top \vdash \neg\varphi$	$\mathrm{Th}(\{\varphi\}) = \perp$ then $C(\{\varphi\}) = \perp$
$(^*6)$ if $\mathrm{Th}(\{\varphi\}) = \mathrm{Th}(\{\psi\})$ then $T_\varphi^* = T_\psi^*$	if $\mathrm{Th}(\{\varphi\}) = \mathrm{Th}(\{\psi\})$ then $C(\{\varphi\}) = C(\{\psi\})$
$(^*7)\ T_{\varphi \wedge \psi}^* \subseteq \mathrm{Th}(T_\varphi^* \cup \{\psi\})$	if $\{\varphi \wedge \psi\} \mathrel{\vdash\kern-0.6em\sim} \chi$ then $\{\varphi\} \mathrel{\vdash\kern-0.6em\sim} (\psi \to \chi)$
$(^*8)$ if $\neg\psi \notin T_\varphi^*$	if $\{\varphi\} \mathrel{\not\vdash\kern-0.6em\sim} \neg\psi$ and $\{\varphi\} \mathrel{\vdash\kern-0.6em\sim} (\psi \to \chi)$
then $\mathrm{Th}(T_\varphi^* \cup \{\psi\}) \subseteq T_{\varphi \wedge \psi}^*$	then $\{\varphi \wedge \psi\} \mathrel{\vdash\kern-0.6em\sim} \chi$ (rational monotony)

Table 16.1
Translating Revision Postulates to Inference Relation Properties

Some of the inference relation properties obtained in Table 16.1 are familiar, such as rational monotony which corresponds to $(^*8)$, whilst others are derivable from those we saw in chapter 13.

The properties translated from postulates $(^*1) - (^*3)$ and $(^*5) - (^*7)$ are satisfied by classical and stoppered preferential model structures described in Theorem 13.13. Postulate $(^*4)$ translates to consistency preservation, and $(^*8)$ to rational monotony both of which require the underlying preferential model structure to satisfy properties that lie outside the scope of this text.

We can also translate properties on nonmonotonic inference relations to conditions concerning revision functions using the inverse translation where statements of the form $\{\varphi\} \mathrel{\vdash\kern-0.6em\sim} \psi$ are translated to $\psi \in T_\varphi^*$. Some examples are illustrated in Table 16.2.

The definition below identifies the particular class of inference relations that are related to revision functions.

Definition *An inference relation $\mathrel{\vdash\kern-0.6em\sim}$ is* rational and consistency preserving *if and only if it satisfies the following properties:*

If $\{\varphi\} \vdash \chi$, then $\{\varphi\} \mathrel{\vdash\kern-0.6em\sim} \chi$	(Supraclassicality)
If $\top \vdash (\varphi \leftrightarrow \psi)$ and $\{\varphi\} \mathrel{\vdash\kern-0.6em\sim} \chi$, then $\{\psi\} \mathrel{\vdash\kern-0.6em\sim} \chi$	(Left Logical Equivalence)
If $\{\psi\} \vdash \chi$ and $\{\varphi\} \mathrel{\vdash\kern-0.6em\sim} \psi$, then $\{\varphi\} \mathrel{\vdash\kern-0.6em\sim} \chi$	(Right Weakening)
If $\{\varphi\} \mathrel{\vdash\kern-0.6em\sim} \psi$ and $\{\varphi\} \mathrel{\vdash\kern-0.6em\sim} \chi$, then $\{\varphi\} \mathrel{\vdash\kern-0.6em\sim} \psi \wedge \chi$	(And)

Inference Relation Property	Conditions on Revision Functions
Supraclassicality	if $\varphi \vdash \psi$ then $\psi \in T_\varphi^*$
Cut	if $\psi \in T_\varphi^*$ and $\chi \in T_{\varphi \wedge \psi}^*$ then $\chi \in T_\varphi^*$
Cautious Monotony	if $\psi \in T_\varphi^*$ and $\chi \in T_\varphi^*$ then $\chi \in T_{\varphi \wedge \psi}^*$
Cumulativity	if $\psi \in T_\varphi^*$ then $T_\varphi^* = T_{\varphi \wedge \psi}^*$
Reciprocity	if $\psi \in T_\varphi^*$ and $\varphi \in T_\psi^*$ then $T_\varphi^* = T_\psi^*$
Distribution	if $\chi \in T_\varphi^*$ and $\chi \in T_\psi^*$ then $\chi \in T_{\varphi \vee \psi}^*$
Loop	if $\varphi_2 \in T_{\varphi_1}^*, \ldots, \varphi_n \in T_{\varphi_{n-1}}^*, \varphi_1 \in T_{\varphi_n}^*$ then $T_{\varphi_i}^* = T_{\varphi_j}^*$ for all $i, j \leq n$

Table 16.2
Translating Inference Relation Properties to Revision Properties

If $\{\varphi\} \mathrel{\vdash\mkern-7mu\sim} \psi$ and $\{\varphi\} \wedge \psi \mathrel{\vdash\mkern-7mu\sim} \chi$, then $\{\varphi\} \mathrel{\vdash\mkern-7mu\sim} \chi$	(Cut)
If $\{\varphi\} \mathrel{\vdash\mkern-7mu\sim} \bot$, then $\{\varphi\} \vdash \bot$	(Consistency Preservation)
If $\{\varphi\} \mathrel{\vdash\mkern-7mu\sim} \psi$ and $\{\psi\} \vdash \varphi$, then $\{\varphi\} \mathrel{\vdash\mkern-7mu\sim} \chi$ if and only if $\{\psi\} \mathrel{\vdash\mkern-7mu\sim} \chi$	(Cumulativity)
If $\{\varphi\} \mathrel{\vdash\mkern-7mu\sim} \chi$ and $\{\psi\} \mathrel{\vdash\mkern-7mu\sim} \chi$, then $\{\varphi \vee \psi\} \mathrel{\vdash\mkern-7mu\sim} \chi$	(Or)
If $\{\varphi\} \mathrel{\not\vdash\mkern-7mu\sim} \neg\psi$ and $\{\varphi\} \mathrel{\vdash\mkern-7mu\sim} \chi$, then $\{\varphi \wedge \psi\} \mathrel{\vdash\mkern-7mu\sim} \chi$	(Rational Monotony)

Theorem 16.1 *The inference relation $\mathrel{\vdash\mkern-7mu\sim}$ is rational and consistency preserving if and only if it satisfies the properties in Table 16.1*

Theorem 16.1 says an inference relation that satisfies the properties obtained by transforming the set of revision postulates, using the procedure described above, are rational and consistency preserving, and conversely every rational consistency preserving inference relation satisfies them.

16.2   Nonmonotonic reasoning using entrenchment

Epistemic entrenchment orderings attempt to characterise a reasoning agents information about the world. Not only do they describe information content but they encapsulate how the information should change upon the acquisition of new information. When they were first introduced they were understood to place an ordering on accepted information (a belief set), but from a technical point of view there is no reason not to extend the ordering to rank nonbeliefs as a means to capture default information. Default information is lower in the ordering than accepted information because a rational agent would view it as more defeasible. In other words, an epistemic entrenchment ranking can be used to rank not only an agent's accepted information but also the agent's expectations in the absence of complete information.

Gärdenfors and Makinson refer to an ordering that satisfies (EE1) – (EE3) as an *expectation ordering*. An epistemic entrenchment ordering is a special type of expectation ordering; one in which sentences other than the tautologies can be maximal, and one that is not explicitly related to a theory.

Gärdenfors and Makinson argue that the difference between accepted and default information is simply its degree of defeasibility, or firmness, and they showed how nonmonotonic inferences can be viewed in terms of expectation orderings and epistemic entrenchment orderings. They established a direct correspondence between rational consistency preserving inference relations and both orderings using the notion of a proper cut, defined below.

Definition *Let $\leq$ be a total preorder on $\mathcal{L}$. The φ proper cut of $\leq$ is defined by* $\text{cut}_<(\varphi) = \{\psi \in \mathcal{L} : \varphi < \psi\}$.

Observation 16.2 *If $\leq$ is an expectation ordering then the* largest consistent proper cut *of $\leq$ is* $\text{cut}_<(\varphi \wedge \neg\varphi)$ *which we denote by* $\text{content}(\leq)$.

Observation 16.3 *An epistemic entrenchment ordering $\leq$ is related to the theory* $\text{content}(\leq)$.

Given Observation 16.3 it can be seen that we are not compelled to explicitly specify the theory an epistemic entrenchment ordering is related to; it can be derived from the ordering itself.

For the remainder of the chapter we focus on epistemic entrenchment rather than the more general expectation orderings because our aim is to highlight connections between nonmonotonic reasoning and revision operators. In turns out that in a nomonotonic reasoning context there is little difference between inference relations generated from expectation orderings and epistemic entrenchment orderings (see Theorem 16.6 later).

In the light of Theorem 16.1 it is not surprising that a rational consistency preserving nonmonotonic inference relation can be constructed from an epistemic entrenchment ordering. In fact there is a one-to-one relationship between such inference relations and epistemic entrenchment orderings. In the same way that there is a one-to-one relationship between epistemic entrenchment orderings and revision functions.

In the theorem below Gärdenfors and Makinson showed that the class of inference relations based on epistemic entrenchment orderings is precisely the class of rational consistency preserving inference relations.

Theorem 16.4 *Given an epistemic entrenchment ordering $\leq$ the relation $\{\varphi\} \mathrel{\vdash_{\leq}} \psi$ defined by $\psi \in Th(cut_{<}(\neg\varphi) \cup \{\varphi\})$ is a consistency preserving and rational inference relation. Conversely, every consistency preserving and rational inference relation arises in this way.*

The following example, adapted from Gärdenfors and Makinson, illustrates how an epistemic entrenchment ordering induces a nonmonotonic inference relation. Let us suppose that $\mathcal{L}$ contains the following predicates:

$sicilian(X)$: X is a Sicilian,
$blonde(X)$: X is blonde,
$hot(X)$: X is hotheaded.

Using the default rules; *Sicilians are normally hotheaded* and *blonde persons are normally not hotheaded*. Let us assume our expectations are represented by the following fragment of an epistemic entrenchment ordering.

$sicilian(X) \rightarrow \neg hot(X) < sicilian(X) \rightarrow hot(X)$
$blonde(X) \rightarrow hot(X) < blonde(X) \rightarrow \neg hot(X)$
$sicilian(X) \wedge blonde(X) \rightarrow \neg hot(X) < (sicilian(X) \wedge blonde(X) \rightarrow hot(X))$.

Now consider a particular individual, $Fiora$, who we know to be a Sicilian. Is she hotheaded? In other words, does $\{sicilian(Fiora)\} \mathrel{\vdash} hot(Fiora)$? The answer is yes, since $cut_{<}(\neg sicilian(Fiora)) \cup \{sicilian(Fiora)\} \vdash hot(Fiora)$. What about the blonde German, Johanna. Is she hotheaded? According to our expectations she is not because $cut_{<}(\neg blonde(Johanna)) \cup \{blonde(Johanna)\} \vdash \neg hot(Johanna)$. Of course, we must not forget Rachel who we suspect is a blonde Sicilian. It turns out that we expect her to be hotheaded because $cut_{<}(\neg sicilian(Rachel) \vee \neg blonde(Rachel)) \cup \{sicilian(Rachel) \wedge blonde(Rachel)\} \vdash hot(Rachel)$.

The theorem, below, demonstrates the explicit relationship between an inference relation $\mathrel{\vdash_{\leq}}$, and the revision function constructed from $\leq$.

Theorem 16.5 $\{\varphi\} \mathrel{\vdash_{\leq}} \psi$ *if and only if* $\psi \in (content(\leq))_{\varphi}^{*}$ *where* * *is constructed using (E^{*}) and* $\leq$.

Theorem 16.6, below, was eluded to earlier, and demonstrates that an expectation ordering and an epistemic entrenchment ordering induce the *same* class of inference relations. Its converse trivially holds by Theorem 16.4.

Theorem 16.6 *Given an expectation ordering $\leq$ the relation $\{\varphi\} \mathrel{\vdash\!\!\sim}_{\leq} \psi$ defined by $\psi \in Th(\mathrm{cut}_{<}(\neg\varphi) \cup \{\varphi\})$ is a consistency preserving and rational inference relation.*

In other words, epistemic entrenchment orderings and expectation orderings are as expressive as one another when it comes to nonmonotonic reasoning. Given that (EE4) simply gives a name to the theory content($\leq$), it is not surprising that it is superfluous. However it is noteworthy that having the tautologies as the *only* maximal elements in the ordering is irrelevant for nonmonotonic reasoning. Hence, some contingent sentences can be maximal without effecting the behaviour of the induced inference relation.

Changing the relative ordering of information in an epistemic entrenchment ordering will allow different conclusions to be drawn since a different ordering gives rise to a different inference relation. A mechanism for changing the behaviour of an inference relation using finite partial entrenchment rankings and the computational model for belief revision is outlined in the following section. As a prelude we define an inference relation based on a partial entrenchment ranking in the following theorem which establishes that a partial entrenchment ranking and the minimal epistemic entrenchment ranking it generates induce the *same* nonmonotonic inference relation.

Theorem 16.7 *Let $\{\varphi\} \mathrel{\vdash\!\!\sim}_{\mathbf{B}} \psi$ be given by $\{\chi \in \mathrm{dom}(\mathbf{B}) : \mathrm{degree}(\mathbf{B}, \neg\varphi) < \mathbf{B}(\chi)\} \cup \{\varphi\} \vdash \psi$. Then $\{\varphi\} \mathrel{\vdash\!\!\sim}_{\mathbf{B}} \psi$ if and only if $\{\varphi\} \mathrel{\vdash\!\!\sim}_{\leq_{\mathbf{B}}} \psi$.*

Corollary 16.8 $\{\varphi\} \mathrel{\vdash\!\!\sim}_{\mathbf{B}} \psi$ *if and only if $\psi \in (\mathrm{content}(\leq_{\mathbf{B}}))_{\varphi}^{*}$ where $*$ is constructed using (E^{*}) and $\leq_{\mathbf{B}}$.*

16.3   Changing nonmonotonic inference relations

A problematical aspect of nonmonotonic reasoning methods is manifested in the difficulty of dealing with the acquisition of new information, in particular new facts and new defaults. For instance, what should happen to our expectations when we learn that Rachel is, in fact, chillingly rational, or we learn that she is not a natural blonde. An answer to this difficulty will require the services of a computational model for belief revision.

Default conclusions are by their very nature defeasible, and in this section we extend the techniques developed in chapter 15, for iterated belief change, to model changes to nonmonotonic inference relations. In particular, we use the adjustment procedure to revise a ranking, i.e. to raise and lower the rank of both accepted and default information.

Intuitively, defaults are more defeasible than beliefs. Sometimes we want to distinguish accepted and default information. In Default Logic, for example, accepted information and default information contained in an extension E of a default theory (W, D) can be distinguished using W and the consequents of E's generating defaults.

We adopt a simple convention that supports a similar distinction between information which is accepted and information that has been procured by default. In particular, we take the following interpretation of the numerical assignment: sentences with degree greater than 0.5 comprise *accepted information*, or *beliefs*, and sentences with degree less than or equal to 0.5 constitute *default information*.

Note that an adjustment, $\mathbf{B}^{\star}(\varphi, i)$, leaves all sentences assigned numbers greater than $\max(\{i, \mathbf{B}(\varphi), \mathbf{B}(\neg\varphi)\})$ in $\mathbf{B}$ unchanged. So lowering the rank of default information does not effect the rank of any beliefs. In fact the only way changing the rank of default information can effect the rank of accepted information is if the degree of the default information is increased such that it becomes accepted, that is, it acquires a rank greater than 0.5. On the other hand, changing the rank of accepted information may effect the rank of defaults.

The computational model developed to modify partial entrenchment rankings, provides a computational model for the modification of nonmonotonic inference relations. Changes to the ranking using this computational model are based on an absolute measure of minimal change, and we demonstrated in chapter 15 that the proposed model exhibits certain desirable behaviour. For instance: it preserves finiteness, and it maintains as much explicit information as the epistemic entrenchment ordering generated via the function degree.

The following theorem demonstrates that if $i > 0$ then precisely the same inference relation is obtained by adjusting a partial entrenchment ranking $\mathbf{B}$ as that obtained by adjusting the minimum epistemic entrenchment ordering generated by $\mathbf{B}$ (defined as $\mathbf{minB}$ below). The function $\mathbf{minB}$ is a ranking representation of an epistemic entrenchment ordering, that is, every sentence in the language, $\mathcal{L}$, is in its domain. In contrast the domain of $\mathbf{B}$ itself need only be a subset of $\mathcal{L}$. Recall that if $i > 0$ then adjustments perform a revision, and if $i = 0$ then they perform a withdrawal (from which a contraction can be defined).

Theorem 16.9 *Let* $\mathbf{B} \in \mathcal{B}$, *let* * *be an adjustment, let* χ *be a contingent sentence, and let* $\mathbf{minB}(\varphi) = \mathrm{degree}(\mathbf{B}, \varphi)$.

(i) If $i > 0$ *then* $\{\varphi\} \,\vdash_{\mathbf{B}^\star(\chi,i)} \psi$ *if and only if* $\{\varphi\} \,\vdash_{\mathbf{minB}^\star(\chi,i)} \psi$, *and*

(ii) If $\{\varphi\} \,\vdash_{\mathbf{B}^\star(\chi,0)} \psi$ *then* $\{\varphi\} \,\vdash_{\mathbf{minB}^\star(\chi,0)} \psi$.

The converse of Theorem 16.9 (ii) may not hold since there may be sentences lost in the $(\varphi, 0)$–adjustment of $\mathbf{B}$ that are entailed by $\exp(\mathbf{B})$ and retained in the $(\varphi, 0)$–adjustment of $\mathbf{minB}$.

16.4 Example

In the example, below, we illustrate how a nonmonotonic inference relation can be modified. But first we highlight some representational issues that immediately suggest themselves when one uses a partial entrenchment ranking to capture default information. It is standard practice in Default Logic to use open defaults not explicitly but rather as schemata for particular individuals. In this example we use entrenchment rankings in a similar way; if a default schema is used with respect to a given individual then we place the instantiated schema in $\mathbf{dom}(\mathbf{B})$. Using results from Gärdenfors and Makinson together with the observation that in the entrenchment setting normal defaults can be converted to supernormal defaults by way of, $\frac{\varphi : \psi}{\psi} \implies \frac{\top : \varphi \to \psi}{\varphi \to \psi}$, it can be seen that partial entrenchment rankings are as expressive as extensions constructed from normal defaults with linear priorities.

Recall that accepted information is assigned degree greater than 0.5, while default information is assigned degree greater than zero up to and at most 0.5. Contradictions and information we are agnostic about are assigned degree zero. The partial entrenchment ranking $\mathbf{B}$, below, uses the two defaults; *birds normally have feathers* and *birds normally fly* where Tweety is currently the only known bird.

$\mathbf{B}(\forall X penguin(X) \to bird(X)) = 0.9$,
$\mathbf{B}(animal(sylvester)) = 0.8$,
$\mathbf{B}(bird(tweety)) = 0.6$,
$\mathbf{B}(bird(tweety) \to feathers(tweety)) = 0.4$,
$\mathbf{B}(bird(tweety) \to fly(tweety)) = 0.2$.

Then

$\mathrm{degree}(\mathbf{B}, feathers(tweety)) = 0.4$, $\mathrm{degree}(\mathbf{B}, fly(tweety)) = 0.2$,
$\mathrm{degree}(\mathbf{B}, \neg feathers(tweety)) = 0$, $\mathrm{degree}(\mathbf{B}, \neg fly(tweety)) = 0$,

degree($\mathbf{B}, \neg bird(sylvester)$) = 0, degree($\mathbf{B}, \neg fly(sylvester)$) = 0,
degree($\mathbf{B}, penguin(tweety)$) = 0, and degree($\mathbf{B}, \neg penguin(tweety)$) = 0.

Therefore, we expect Tweety to have feathers and to possess the power of flight; our expectation that Tweety has feathers is higher than our expectation that Tweety can fly. However, our expectations do not assist us in deciding whether Tweety is a penguin or not, since both Tweety a penguin and Tweety not a penguin are equally (un)expected.

(a) Let us now add the new belief, *Tweety is a penguin* with degree 0.7:

$\mathbf{B}^\star(penguin(tweety), 0.7)(\forall X penguin(X) \to bird(X)) = 0.9$,
$\mathbf{B}^\star(penguin(tweety), 0.7)(animal(sylvester)) = 0.8$,
$\mathbf{B}^\star(penguin(tweety), 0.7)(penguin(tweety)) = 0.7$,
$\mathbf{B}^\star(penguin(tweety), 0.7)(bird(tweety)) = 0.7$,
$\mathbf{B}^\star(penguin(tweety), 0.7)(bird(tweety) \to feathers(tweety)) = 0.4$,
$\mathbf{B}^\star(penguin(tweety), 0.7)(bird(tweety) \to fly(tweety)) = 0.2$.
degree($\mathbf{B}^\star(penguin(tweety), 0.7), fly(tweety)$) = 0.2.
degree($\mathbf{B}^\star(penguin(tweety), 0.7), \neg fly(tweety)$) = 0.

Notice that when we acquire the information that Tweety is a penguin with degree 0.7, the plausibility that Tweety is a bird increases from 0.6 to 0.7. We are in a very naive state of mind because we are unaware that penguins normally cannot fly, therefore we still expect Tweety to fly.

(b) In this example we learn the default that *penguins normally cannot fly*. Let us assume that $\mathbf{B}_1 = \mathbf{B}^\star(penguin(tweety)), 0.7)$ from (a) above. We now add the new default, *penguins normally cannot fly* with degree 0.3 instantiated with *Tweety*, which suggests that we expect that a penguin cannot fly more than a bird can fly. We obtain:

$\mathbf{B}_1^\star(penguin(tweety) \to \neg fly(tweety)), 0.3)(\forall X penguin(X) \to bird(X)) = 0.9$,
$\mathbf{B}_1^\star(penguin(tweety) \to \neg fly(tweety)), 0.3)(animal(sylvester)) = 0.8$,
$\mathbf{B}_1^\star(penguin(tweety) \to \neg fly(tweety)), 0.3)(penguin(tweety)) = 0.7$,
$\mathbf{B}_1^\star(penguin(tweety) \to \neg fly(tweety)), 0.3)(bird(tweety)) = 0.7$,
$\mathbf{B}_1^\star(penguin(tweety) \to \neg fly(tweety)), 0.3)(bird(tweety) \to feathers(tweety)) = 0.4$,
$\mathbf{B}_1^\star(penguin(tweety) \to \neg fly(tweety)), 0.3)(penguin(tweety) \to \neg fly(tweety)) = 0.3$
$\mathbf{B}_1^\star(penguin(tweety) \to \neg fly(tweety)), 0.3)(bird(tweety) \to fly(tweety)) = 0$

Using our newly acquired information it is more likely that *Tweety* cannot fly than he can fly, given we believe him to be a penguin.

degree($\mathbf{B}_1^*(penguin(tweety) \rightarrow \neg fly(tweety), 0.3), \neg fly(tweety)) = 0.3$, and
degree($\mathbf{B}_1^*(penguin(tweety) \rightarrow \neg fly(tweety), 0.3), fly(tweety)) = 0$.

In Sylvester's case, however,

degree($\mathbf{B}_1^*(penguin(tweety) \rightarrow \neg fly(tweety), 0.3), \neg fly(sylvester)) = 0$, and
degree($\mathbf{B}_1^*(penguin(tweety) \rightarrow \neg fly(tweety), 0.3), fly(sylvester)) = 0$.

Therefore we do not have any purposeful expectations regarding Sylvester's power of flight.

(c) Contracting *Tweety is a bird* from the original partial entrenchment ranking, $\mathbf{B}$, is achieved by $\mathbf{B}^*(bird(tweety), 0)$, and results in the following:

$\mathbf{B}^*(bird(tweety)), 0)(\forall X penguin(X) \rightarrow bird(X)) = 0.9$,
$\mathbf{B}^*(bird(tweety), 0)(animal(sylvester)) = 0.8$,

and all other sentences in $\mathbf{dom}(\mathbf{B})$ are assigned 0.
In terms of inference relations:

$$\top \vdash_{\mathbf{B}} fly(tweety), \quad \top \not\vdash_{\mathbf{B}^*(bird(tweety), 0)} fly(tweety),$$
$$\top \vdash_{\mathbf{B}} feathers(tweety) \text{ and } \top \not\vdash_{\mathbf{B}^*(bird(tweety), 0)} feathers(tweety).$$

On the surface this may seem somewhat drastic, however the information encoded in $\mathbf{B}$ is interpreted to mean that removing *Tweety is a bird* requires that all other information concerning Tweety be disregarded. Alternative behaviour can be achieved using a different ranking.

(d) Contract the default *Tweety has feathers*.

$\mathbf{B}^*(feathers(tweety), 0)(\forall X penguin(X) \rightarrow bird(X)) = 0.9$,
$\mathbf{B}^*(feathers(tweety), 0)(animal(sylvester)) = 0.8$,
$\mathbf{B}^*(feathers(tweety), 0)(bird(tweety)) = 0.6$,
$\mathbf{B}^*(feathers(tweety), 0)(bird(tweety) \rightarrow feathers(tweety)) = 0$,
$\mathbf{B}^*(feathers(tweety), 0)(bird(tweety) \rightarrow fly(tweety)) = 0$.

In terms of inference relations we can say:

$\top \mathrel{\vdash_{\mathbf{B}}} fly(tweety)$ and
$\top \mathrel{\not\vdash_{\mathbf{B}^{\star}(feathers(tweety),0)}} fly(tweety)$.

Therefore, in this example we also lose the default information that *Tweety can fly*. The information encoded in **B** says: that if we lose faith in the fact that Tweety has feathers then he probably cannot fly either. If our intention is to keep the information that Tweety can fly even without feathers then we would need to specify the independence of Tweety's flight on his possession of feathers. This could be achieved by making the sentence $fly(tweety) \lor feathers(tweety)$ strictly more entrenched than $feathers(tweety)$. In particular, if $\mathbf{B}(\neg fly(tweety) \lor feathers(tweety)) = 0.8$, then we would obtain $\mathbf{B}^{\star}(feathers(tweety),0)(bird(tweety) \rightarrow fly(tweety)) = 0.4$. In other words, *tweety can fly* would remain default information and its degree of firmness would remain unchanged. Conceptually, contracting the general default rule *birds normally have feathers* would entail the contraction of all instantiations of it.

In parting we note that for simple database applications, system designers must identify the redundancy of information, the derivability of information, the semantic relationships among informational entities, and the functional dependencies between attributes during logical database design in order to develop a conceptual schema, and perform data normalization. Similarly, considerable effort must be expended in the design of partial entrenchment rankings for a particular application. The development of sophisticated systems that perform belief revision involves several difficult design decisions. For example, the systems designer must specify an appropriate ranking. This activity entails the determination of the explicit information to be ranked, and the identification of independencies with respect to change.

Problems

16-1. Why were we forced to consider singletons on the left-hand-side of our inference relation $\mathrel{\vdash}$ in this chapter? How can we translate a finite set of sentences on the left-hand-side of the inference relation $\mathrel{\vdash}$ to a condition on revision functions?

16-2. Translate idempotence, monotony, full absorption, right weakening, right and, left logical equivalence, left or, proof by cases, conditionalization into properties of revision. Indicate whether the resulting properties are satisfied by revision functions in general.

16-3. Convert the following into conditions on inference relations:

(i) If $\chi \in T_\varphi^*$ then $(T_\varphi^*)_\chi^* \subseteq T_{\varphi \wedge \chi}^*$, and

(ii) If $\varphi \in T_{\varphi \vee \psi}^*$ and $\psi \in T_{\psi \vee \chi}^*$ then $\varphi \in T_{\varphi \vee \chi}^*$.

16-4. Prove content$(\leq)$ is a theory.

16-5. Prove $T_\varphi^* = (\mathrm{cut}_<(\neg\varphi))_\varphi^+$.

16-6. Show that there are at most *two* epistemic entrenchment orderings that give rise to the same inference relation as an expectation ordering $\leq$.

16-7. Prove the following:

(a) $\{penguin(tweety)\} \;\vdash_{\mathbf{B}} \varphi$ if and only if $\top \;\nvdash_{\mathbf{B}^\star(penguin(tweety),0.7)} \varphi$.

(b) If $\{\varphi\} \;\vdash_{\mathbf{B}} \psi$ then $\top \;\nvdash_{\mathbf{B}^\star(\varphi,\min(\mathbf{B}))} \psi$.

16-8. Construct a counterexample to the converse of Theorem 16.9 (ii).

References for Part IV

Gabbay [25] was one of the first to bring some order into the field of nonmonotonic reasoning by studying the inference relation generated by a nonmonotonic system. A seminal paper in the area is the work of Kraus, Lehmann and Magidor [39]. Chapter 13 is based on a paper by Makinson [50], which provides much more detail.

Chapter 14 draws from the perspicacious work of Alchourón, Gärdenfors and Makinson [1]. Most of the material presented in the chapter comes from Gärdenfors and Makinson's paper [28] in which they showed the correspondence between epistemic entrenchment orderings and contraction functions. Throughout the chapter we refer to the work of Hansson [36], Rott [74], Niedereé [62], and Stalnaker [80]. Withdrawal functions were introduced by Makinson in [48] where an informative exploration of recovery can also be found. An epistemic entrenchment ordering is not the only preference relation from which change functions can be constructed. Some alternative constructions are based on: a systems of spheres [35], safe contractions [2], and selection functions [1]. Dubois and Prade have demonstrated that there are close connections between epistemic entrenchment orderings and certain orderings in possibilistic logic [21]. A discussion of the postulates can be found in [27], and Gärdenfors and Rott give a recent detailed survey of belief revision in [30]. In the final section the work of Katsuno and Mendelzon [37] and that of Rott [74] is briefly described. Another change function, called *update*, was identified by Winslett [88], and explored by Katsuno and Mendelzon [37]. Update functions are important in Reasoning about Action. Further work on update and its relationship to revision can be found in Peppas and Williams [64], and Boutilier [14].

Chapter 15 is based on the work of Williams and the material presented has been adapted from [84, 85, 87]. Nebel's solution to the problem of satisfying recovery is given in [61]. The study of change for theory bases has been conducted by authors such as Fuhrmann [24], Hansson [36], Makinson [48], Nebel [60, 61] Rott[73] and Williams [85]. Iterated change has been addressed from the constructive perspective by Spohn [79], Boutilier [13] and Nayak [59]. Lehmann [40] has proposed postulates for iterated revision.

Chapter 16 is based on Makinson and Gärdenfors' works in which they explore the relationship between nonmonotonic reasoning and belief revision. In particular, much of the content of section 16.1 is taken from [49], and section 16.2 contains material adapted from [29]. Section 16.3 which focuses on the dynamics of nonmonotonic inference is based Williams' work [86]. Problem 16-4 refers to properties introduced by Katsuno and Mendelzon [37].

Part V

Nonmonotonic Reasoning and Logic Programming

There exist close interconnections between logic programming and nonmonotonic reasoning. Firstly, logic programming offers a high–level implementation language with a declarative flavor. Therefore, it is not surprising that the first really successful system for nonmonotonic reasoning[1], Poole's system *Theorist*, was implemented in Prolog. Chapter 17 is dedicated to this system and its close relationship to Default Logic.

But the links between both fields go far beyond the use of logic programming as an implementation language. Actually, *negation as failure*, the interpretation of negation in logic programs as the failure to prove a ground atomic formula, is a prototypical example of nonmonotonic behaviour. Given the logic program

$$p \leftarrow not\ q,$$

p is derived if q is not known. But if we add the clause

$$q \leftarrow$$

to the logic program, p is no longer derived. So, by expanding the logic program we lose a consequence.

There are several ways of interpreting the negation operator in logic programming, and nonmonotonic logics have turned out to be very useful in the study of logic program semantics. In Chapters 18 and 19 we take a closer look at two different semantics. Chapter 18 introduces the *stable semantics* which is essentially the Default Logic interpretation of logic programs. Unfortunately, stable model

---

[1]Truth maintenance systems preceded *Theorist*, but it was unclear from the theoretical point of view what they were actually doing.

semantics inherits some shortcomings of Default Logic, among others the multiple extensions problem, and the possible nonexistence of any extensions.

The *well–founded semantics* (WFS), presented in Chapter 19, tries to overcome some of these shortcomings by determining a unique *partial* model of the logic program under consideration. A partial model assigns truth values to some atomic formulae only, while the validity of other formulae may remain undetermined[2].

Of the range of logic programming semantics we chose to present these two because, in a sense, they represent two extreme ways of assigning meaning to negation as failure: stable model semantics is two–valued, and most alternative three–valued semantics subsume WFS.

---

[2]Often we refer to *three–valued semantics* taking *undefined* to be a third truth value.

Chapter 17

The System *Theorist*

The system is based on a framework for default reasoning which looks quite different from Default Logic and its variants, but turns out to be strongly related to them. Section 17.1 introduces the basic concepts that underlie *Theorist*. In section 17.2 we show that the approach is equivalent to supernormal default theories in which all defaults are normal and have as prerequisite the formula *true*. The expressiveness of such default theories is severely restricted (we have seen in section 5.4 that even normal default theories are insufficient for many applications), therefore the approach has to be strengthened. Section 17.3 introduces naming of defaults and the use constraints to be able to express required interactions among defaults. In section 17.4 we describe the user interface of *Theorist*, and in section 17.5 we discuss the different treatment of defaults for explanation and prediction. *Theorist* has been compiled into Prolog; we refer the interested reader to the references at the end of Part V.

17.1 Basic concepts

Of the approaches for nonmonotonic reasoning that we introduced, Default and Autoepistemic Logic go beyond classical predicate logic, whereas Circumscription in its simple forms works within predicate logic, but changes the way reasoning is treated by adding new premises.

In the design of *Theorist*, Poole took the latter view (though his work is very different from Circumscription). He argued that there is nothing wrong with first–order logic, rather it is the way the logic is used that has to be modified to achieve default reasoning. According to his approach, the available knowledge is separated into two parts:

- A set of *facts*, knowledge that is accepted to be true in the intended interpretation. It represents knowledge we are not prepared to give up in the application at hand.

- A set of possible *hypotheses* that we are prepared to accept as part of an explanation.

Intuitively, an explanation of φ can be seen as a world view or as a possible scenario in which φ is true. Indirectly, the user describes what is acceptable in such scenarios by providing the facts and hypotheses. The formal definition of these ideas is straightforward.

- A *theory* consists of a set F of closed formulae (the *facts*), and a countable set Δ of (possibly open) formulae called *hypotheses*.

- A *scenario* of F, Δ is a consistent set $F \cup D$ where D is a set of ground instances of some elements from Δ. For convenience, we often refer to the members of D as hypotheses.

- A closed formula φ is *explainable from* F, Δ iff there is a scenario of F, Δ that logically implies φ; this scenario is called an *explanation* of φ.

- Let $F \cup D$ be a maximal scenario of F, Δ (w.r.t. set inclusion). $Th(F \cup D)$ is called an *extension of F, Δ*.

According to this definition, extensions are maximally consistent 'world views' sanctioned by the given knowledge, and scenarios are used for the explanation of formulae. In particular, φ is explainable from F, Δ if there is a set D of ground instances of elements of Δ such that

(a) $F \cup D \models \varphi$, and

(b) $F \cup D$ is consistent.

Let us look at an example. Consider the theory with $F = \{aussie(bob)\}$ and $\Delta = \{aussie(X) \rightarrow drinksBeer(X)\}$. Then $drinksBeer(bob)$ is explainable from F, Δ using the scenario

$F \cup \{aussie(bob) \rightarrow drinksBeer(bob)\}$.

Let F_1 be the set of facts

$\{aussie(bob), eatsPizza(bob), \forall X(eatsPizza(X) \rightarrow \neg drinksBeer(X))\}$.

Now $drinksBeer(bob)$ is not explainable from F_1, Δ since $\neg drinksBeer(bob)$ follows from the set of facts. But if we consider $F_2 = \{aussie(bob), eatsPizza(bob)\}$ and

$\Delta_2 = \{aussie(X) \rightarrow drinksBeer(X), eatsPizza(X) \rightarrow \neg drinksBeer(X)\}$

then both $drinksBeer(bob)$ and $\neg drinksBeer(bob)$ are explainable from F_2, Δ_2. In this case there are exactly two extensions.

It should be noted that the interpretation of hypotheses deviates from predicate logic: hypotheses are treated as *schemata* and not as (implicitly) universally quantified formulae which would be the standard predicate logic interpretation. This is essential for our purposes. To see the difference, consider the theory with $F = \{aussie(bob), aussie(lisa), \neg drinksBeer(lisa)\}$ and $\Delta = \{\forall X(aussie(X) \rightarrow drinksBeer(X))\}$. Now $drinksBeer(bob)$ is not explainable from F, Δ because the only scenario is F itself (there is only one hypothesis, which is a closed formula and therefore its only ground instance; the formula is inconsistent with F). Compare this result with the theory F and $D' = \{aussie(X) \rightarrow drinksBeer(X)\}$; obviously, $drinksBeer(bob)$ is explainable now.

17.2   Relationship to Default Logic

It is straightforward to consider hypotheses as special kinds of defaults. Both defaults and hypotheses are used to make plausible conjectures, and are defeasible in nature. In this section we show that indeed the formal framework described in the previous section is a special case of Default Logic.

For a formula φ we define $def(\varphi)$ to be $\frac{true:\varphi}{\varphi}$.[1] Such defaults are a special class of normal defaults, called *supernormal defaults*. Given a consistent set F of closed formulae and a countable set of possibly open formulae Δ, we define the default theory $def(F, \Delta)$ to be $(F, def(\Delta))$. Using this translation of F, Δ into Default Logic, the following result can be shown.

Theorem 17.1 (Equivalence to supernormal defaults) *Let F be a consistent set of closed formulae, and Δ a countable set of formulae. E is an extension of F, Δ (in the sense of section 17.1) iff E is an extension of $def(F, \Delta)$ (in the sense of Default Logic).*

Proof*:   Let E be an extension of F, Δ. Then $E = Th(F \cup D)$ for some maximal scenario $F \cup D$ of F, Δ. Let $\Pi = (\delta_0, \delta_1, \ldots)$ be an arbitrary permutation of $def(D)$. We show that Π is a closed and successful process of $def(F, \Delta)$.

First note that $def(D)$ is a subset of the default set of $def(F, \Delta)$ (according

---

[1]Note that in the case that φ is an open formula, $\frac{true:\varphi}{\varphi}$ is interpreted as a default schema, according to the usual convention in Default Logic. As we saw in the previous section, this convention is compatible with the interpretation of hypotheses.

to the interpretation of open defaults). Π is a process of $def(F, \Delta)$: for each k, the prerequisite of δ_k is trivially included in $In(\Pi[k])$, and its justification is consistent with $In(\Pi[k])$ because it is already consistent with $In(\Pi) = Th(F \cup D)$ (recall that every scenario is consistent by definition). Π is successful because all defaults are normal. Finally we show that Π is a closed process. Then we are finished, since $In(\Pi) = E$ by construction.

Suppose that a default $\frac{true:\varphi}{\varphi} \in def(\Delta)$ is applicable to $In(\Pi)$ but does not occur in Π. Then $\varphi \notin D$. Also, $In(\Pi) \cup \{\varphi\}$ is consistent, so $E \cup \{\varphi\}$ and $F \cup D \cup \{\varphi\}$ are consistent. This contradicts the assumption that $F \cup D$ is a maximal scenario of F, Δ.

In the opposite direction, let E be an extension of $def(F, \Delta)$. Then $E = In(\Pi)$ for a closed and successful process Π of $def(F, \Delta)$. The members of Π are ground instances of $def(\Delta)$. Let $D = \{\varphi \mid def(\varphi) \text{ occurs in } \Pi\}$. By definition, $E = Th(F \cup D)$. The proof is concluded by showing that $F \cup D$ is a maximal scenario of F, Δ. $F \cup D$ is a scenario of F, Δ because E and thus $F \cup D$ is consistent (F is consistent!). Suppose there is some ground instance ψ of a formula in Δ such that $\psi \notin D$ and $F \cup D \cup \{\psi\}$ is consistent. Then the default $def(\psi) = \frac{true:\psi}{\psi}$ is applicable to $E = In(\Pi)$ but does not occur in Π. Therefore Π is not closed which is a contradiction. So, $F \cup D$ is a maximal scenario of F, Δ. $\blacksquare$

This result has a positive aspect: It shows that the formal fundament of *Theorist* is something we already know – from now on we shall use the terms hypothesis and default interchangeably. On the other hand, it raises the question about the system's expressive power and its suitability for practical purposes. In Chapter 5 we saw that even normal default theories are often insufficient for practical purposes. This is even more true of *supernormal default theories* in which all defaults have the prerequisite *true*. The following section discusses some enhancements of the framework from section 17.1 that increase the expressive power of supernormal defaults significantly.

17.3   Names and constraints

In section 5.4 we discussed why normal default theories are insufficient for many problem domains. Let us repeat one example out of that section.

> Bill is a high school dropout.
> Typically, high school dropouts are adults.
> Typically, adults are employed.

These statements can be represented by the theory F, Δ with $F = \{dropout(bill)\}$, and $\Delta = \{dropout(X) \rightarrow adult(X), adult(X) \rightarrow employed(X)\}$. Both $adult(bill)$ and $employed(bill)$ are explainable from F, Δ, and this is problematic because we do not want to apply the second hypothesis for high school dropouts. In standard Default Logic this problem can be overcome by using semi–normal defaults or by introducing priorities among defaults.

Neither of these features is available in *Theorist* since they would go far beyond its simple formal background. Instead, the system allows for the introduction of *default names* and their use to explicitly block the application of hypotheses.

A *name* for a hypothesis φ with exactly the free variables $X_1, \ldots, X_n$ is a new n–ary predicate symbol p_φ not occurring in F or Δ. A named version F', Δ' of a theory F, Δ is defined by

$$F' = F \cup \{\forall(p_\varphi(X_1, \ldots, X_{n_\varphi}) \rightarrow \varphi) \mid \varphi \in \Delta, p_\varphi \text{ is a name for } \varphi\}$$

$$\Delta' = \{p_\varphi(X_1, \ldots, X_{n_\varphi}) \mid \varphi \in \Delta\}.$$

For notational convenience, $\forall X_1 \ldots \forall X_n (p_\varphi(X_1, \ldots, X_n) \rightarrow \varphi)$ is denoted by

$$p_\varphi(X_1, \ldots, X_n) : \varphi.$$

The elements of Δ' are called *named hypotheses*. Clearly if $p_\varphi(t_1, \ldots, t_n)$ is included in a scenario then the associated unnamed hypothesis $\varphi(t_1, \ldots, t_n)$ is also included in the scenario via the new rule in F'. Let us reconsider the previous example. The named theory consist of the facts

> $dropout(bill)$
> $adultIfDropout(X) : dropout(X) \rightarrow adult(X)$
> $employedIfAdult(X) : adult(X) \rightarrow employed(X)$

and the hypotheses

> $adultIfDropout(X)$
> $employedIfAdult(X)$.

As expected, we can still explain $adult(bill)$ and $employed(bill)$. In general, naming a theory in the form just described maintains the previous conclusions. The following result shows that a restricted form of the reverse is also true. Of course, the named theory can explain formulae that include occurrences of default names, in addition.

Theorem 17.2 (Conservativity of naming) *Let F', Δ' be a named version of F, Δ such that the used default names p_φ do not occur in F, Δ and the closed formula ψ. Then ψ is explainable from F, Δ iff ψ is explainable from F', Δ'.*

Proof*: Let ψ be explainable from F, Δ. Then there exists a scenario $F \cup D$ such that $F \cup D \models \psi$. Each member of D has the form $\varphi(t_1, \ldots, t_n)$, where $\varphi \in \Delta$, and $\varphi(t_1, \ldots, t_n)$ is a ground instance of φ.

Let $D' = \{p_\varphi(t_1, \ldots, t_n) \mid \varphi(t_1, \ldots, t_n) \in D\}$. Suppose $F' \cup D' \not\models \psi$. Then there must exist a model $\mathcal{A}$ of $F' \cup D' \cup \{\neg\psi\}$. By definition, we have $\mathcal{A} \models F \cup \{\neg\psi\}$. For each $\varphi(t_1, \ldots, t_n) \in D$ we know that both $p_\varphi(t_1, \ldots, t_n)$ and $\forall X_1 \ldots \forall X_n (p_\varphi(X_1, \ldots, X_n) \to \varphi)$ are true in $\mathcal{A}$, so $\mathcal{A} \models \varphi(t_1, \ldots, t_n)$. In summary, we have shown that $\mathcal{A}$ is a model of $F \cup D \cup \{\neg\psi\}$ which is a contradiction to $F \cup D \models \psi$.

As a scenario of F, Δ, $F \cup D$ is consistent. We show that $F' \cup D'$ is also consistent, and conclude that $F' \cup D'$ is a scenario of F', Δ' that explains ψ. Since $F \cup D$ is consistent, it has a model $\mathcal{A}$. Define an algebra $\mathcal{A}'$ over the expanded signature of F', Δ' to be identical to $\mathcal{A}$ except that p_φ is defined to be true of exactly those tuples of domain values for which φ is true (note that the arity of p_φ is the same as the number of free variables of φ). We conclude $\mathcal{A}' \models F$ (since no new predicate symbol p_φ occurs in F, and $\mathcal{A}$ is a model of F). Also $\mathcal{A}' \models D'$ because $\mathcal{A} \models D$ (by the interpretation of p_φ in $\mathcal{A}'$ and the definition of D'), and $p_\varphi(X_1, \ldots, X_n) \to \varphi$ is true in $\mathcal{A}'$, by definition. Altogether we obtain that $\mathcal{A}'$ is a model of $F' \cup D'$, so $F' \cup D'$ is consistent. The opposite direction is proven in an analogous way. ∎

Naming of defaults provides the possibility to *reason about hypotheses within the logical language*. Continuing our example above, if we want to prevent the application of the hypothesis that adults are typically employed for the case that the specific person is a high school dropout, we have the appropriate machinery now: simply add to the facts the formula

$$\forall X (dropout(X) \to \neg employedIfAdult(X)).$$

Now $employed(bill)$ is no longer explainable since the second hypothesis contradicts the set of facts.

If we compare the representation of the dropout–adult–employed problem with that given in section 5.4 we notice a difference in the form of the defaults used (if we interpret hypotheses as defaults). Whereas there we used defaults of the form $\frac{dropout(X):adult(X)}{adult(X)}$, here we use defaults of the form $\frac{true:dropout(X)\rightarrow adult(X)}{dropout(X)\rightarrow adult(X)}$ instead. They are very similar, of course, the main difference being the following: in the first case, the defaults do not 'fire' unless their prerequisite (in our example being adult) is included in the current knowledge. In the latter case, a 'plan' is prepared beforehand for the case that, say, information about being adult becomes available. For a formal comparison of the two approaches see problem 7-1.

There is one side effect of the preparation of plans beforehand: the defaults can be used in both directions. The reason is that in predicate logic, an implication $\varphi \rightarrow \psi$ can be used to infer ψ from φ, but also to infer $\neg\varphi$ from $\neg\psi$. The same is true of hypotheses, of course, since *Theorist* is based on first–order logic. In the example above, we can explain $employed(bill)$ from $adult(bill)$, but also $\neg adult(bill)$ from $\neg employed(bill)$.

This particular example does not seem to be counterintuitive. If we adopt the view that adults are typically employed, then there is nothing wrong with assuming an unemployed person to be non–adult (at least, this is how it should be, although in the times we are living ...). But there exist cases where the reversed interpretation of hypotheses leads to counterintuitive results. Consider the following example:

$righthandedIfPerson(X) : person(X) \rightarrow righthanded(X)$
$righthandedIfPerson(X).$

This hypothesis can be used to explain $righthanded(grigoris)$ from $person(grigoris)$ (which is reasonable), but also $\neg person(grigoris)$ from $\neg righthanded(grigoris)$ which is completely unintuitive. What we would like to do is guarantee that the hypothesis is only used in the desired direction. The problem can be solved by introducing the fact

$\neg righthanded(X) \rightarrow \neg righthandedIfPerson(X)$

which prevents the application of the hypothesis in the case of a person who is lefthanded. One undesirable aspect of this solution is that it mixes 'control information' with the declarative part of knowledge. The information about 'forbidden' cases for hypotheses should be kept apart from the facts and the hypotheses, otherwise it becomes part of the extensions. To do so, *Theorist* allows the introduction of so–called *constraints*, whose effect is to prune the set of scenarios without being part of scenarios or explanations themselves. The formal definition is straightforward.

- Apart from a set F of facts and a set Δ of hypotheses, a finite set C of closed formulae called *constraints* is given. A scenario of F, Δ, C is a scenario $F \cup D$ of F, Δ such that $F \cup D \cup C$ is consistent. An extension of F, Δ, C is $Th(F \cup D)$ for a maximal scenario $F \cup D$ of F, Δ, C.

This way, the set of scenarios is pruned without introducing new facts. Separation of domain and control knowledge is preserved. Note, though, that the control information is still low–level and error–prone in the face of changes in the set of hypotheses or facts. It lacks the flavor of more abstract forms of control such as reasoning about priorities as discussed in Chapter 8. Some examples are found in the next section and the *Problems* section at the end of the chapter.

We conclude this section by showing how *Theorist* with constraints relates to Constrained Default Logic. For $\varphi \in \Delta$ define

$$df(\varphi) = \frac{true : \varphi \wedge \bigwedge_{\psi \in C} \psi}{\varphi}.$$

Finally, $df(F, \Delta, C)$ is defined to be the default theory $(F, df(\Delta))^2$.

Theorem 17.3 *For a consistent F, E is an extension of F, Δ, C iff $(E, Th(E \cup C))$ is a constrained extension of $df(F, \Delta, C)$.*

Proof*:   Let E be an extension of F, Δ, C. Then there exists a scenario $F \cup D$ maximal with the property that $F \cup D \cup C$ is consistent, such that $E = Th(F \cup D)$. Let $\Pi = (\delta_0, \delta_1, \ldots)$ be any permutation of $df(D)$. By definition, $In(\Pi) = Th(F \cup D) = E$ and $Con(\Pi) = Th(F \cup D \cup C)$. We show that Π is a closed constrained process of $df(T)$.

We have $pre(\delta_i) = true \in In(\Pi[i])$. Also, $\{just(\delta_i)\} \cup Con(\Pi[i])$ is consistent because it is a subset of $Th(F \cup D \cup C)$. So δ_i is applicable to $(In(\Pi[i]), Con(\Pi[i]))$. Finally, suppose that Π is not closed; then there exists a default $\frac{true : \varphi \wedge \bigwedge_{\psi \in C} \psi}{\varphi}$ that is applicable to $(In(\Pi), Con(\Pi)) = (Th(F \cup D), Th(F \cup D \cup C))$ and does not occur in Π. By definition, φ is a ground instance of an element of Δ and $\varphi \notin D$. From the applicability of the default we know that $\varphi \wedge \bigwedge_{\psi \in C} \psi$ is consistent with $In(\Pi) = Th(F \cup D)$. Therefore $\{\varphi\} \cup F \cup D \cup C$ is consistent, and this gives us a contradiction to the maximality of the scenario $F \cup D$.

In the opposite direction let $(E, Th(E \cup C))$ be a constrained extension of

---

[2]As usual, if Δ contains open formulae, then Δ in *Theorist* and $df(\Delta)$ are treated as schemas.

$df(T)^3$, and Π a closed constrained process such that $(E, Th(E \cup C)) = (In(\Pi), Con(\Pi))$. Define $D = \{\varphi \mid df(\varphi) \text{ occurs in } \Pi\}$. Clearly, $E = Th(D \cup F)$ and $Th(F \cup D \cup C) = Con(\Pi)$, so $F \cup D \cup C$ is consistent (we assumed that F be consistent). So $F \cup D$ is a scenario of F, Δ, C. Maximality of $D \cup F$ follows easily from Π being a closed constrained process. $\blacksquare$

17.4   The programming language of *Theorist*

The user interface of the system is a language in which facts, hypotheses and queries can be expressed. The primitive constituents of the language are:

- **fact** φ, meaning that $\forall(\varphi)$ (the universal closure of φ) is included in the set F of facts.

- **default** $p_\varphi(X_1, \ldots, X_n)$, meaning that $p_\varphi(X_1, \ldots, X_n) \in \Delta$.

- **default** $p_\varphi(X_1, \ldots, X_n) : \varphi$, where $X_1, \ldots, X_n$ are all free variables of the formula φ, meaning that $p_\varphi(X_1, \ldots, X_n) \in \Delta$ and $\forall(p_\varphi(X_1, \ldots, X_n) \to \varphi) \in F$.

- **constraint** φ, meaning that $\forall(\varphi) \in C$.

- **explain** φ asks whether the formula $\exists(\varphi)$ can be explained from F, Δ, C. A consistent explanation is returned, if one exists.

The use and behaviour of the system is natural and consistent with the formal description given in the previous sections. For example, consider the information

> **default** *birdsFly(X) : flies(X) ← bird(X)*.
> **fact** ¬*flies(X) ← emu(X)*.
> **fact** *bird(X) ← emu(X)*.
> **fact** *bird(tweety)*.
> **fact** *emu(sam)*.

Now, the query

> **explain** *flies(tweety)*

---

[3]We note that by the specific form of $df(F, \Delta, C)$, all constrained extensions can be written as $(E, Th(E \cup C))$ (prove it!).

is answered with 'yes' and the explanation *birdsFly(tweety)*. That is, the system reports the hypothesis used to explain the query. The query

    explain *flies(sam)*

comes back with the answer 'no'. Now, if we add the fact

    fact ¬*flies(tom)*

and ask

    explain ¬*bird(tom)*

the answer will be positive. In order to prevent this, we have to add the constraint

    constraint ¬*birdsFly(X)* ← ¬*flies(X)*.

For another example, consider the theory

    default *quakersArePacifists(X)* : *pacifist(X)* ← *quaker(X)*.
    default *republicansNoPacifists(X)* : ¬*pacifist(X)* ← *republican(X)*.
    fact *republican(nixon)*.
    fact *quaker(nixon)*.
    fact *republican(dole)*.

Now, we can explain *pacifist(nixon)*, ¬*pacifist(nixon)*, and ¬*pacifist(dole)*. If we add the constraint

    constraint ¬*quakersArePacifists(X)* ← *republican(X)*

then *pacifist(nixon)* is no longer explainable, while ¬ *pacifist(nixon)* can still be explained. And if we add the constraint

    constraint ¬*republicansNoPacifists(X)* ← *quaker(X)*

as well, then nothing about Nixon's attitude towards pacifism can be explained. Of course, ¬*pacifist(dole)* is still explainable.

17.5 Explanation versus prediction

Up to now we have used *Theorist* only for the explanation of statements (e.g. observations). The system makes use of some hypotheses (defaults) that allow one to draw conclusions which entail the observation. But apart from explanation, *Theorist* can be used for *prediction* as well, which means that it can actively make some plausible assumptions. As Poole points out, it is important to distinguish between these two views of hypothetical (default) reasoning.

Consider, for example, the default 'Birds typically fly'. Using this information, we can *predict* that a bird flies unless we have information to the contrary. This is a typical example of a *normality default* which can, in general, we used both for explanation and prediction.

But there are other kinds of defaults as well. We know that brain tumors cause headaches. Now what about the hypothesis 'Somebody may have a brain tumor', perhaps expressed as a default

   default *brainTumor(X)*.

It is unreasonable to use this default to *predict* that a person has a brain tumor – after all, most people do not have one. What is intended by this default is to say that a person *may* have a brain tumor. It is reasonable to use this default to explain, say, that a person has strong headaches, if headaches have been observed. In a sense, we are faced with an *abnormality default* which is used for explanation only, but not for prediction.

In *Theorist*, normality defaults are called *defaults* as usual, and abnormality defaults are called *conjectures*. Let us look at a simple example illustrating the difference.

   default ¬*hasCold(X)*.
   conjecture *hasCold(X)*.
   default *hasHeadacheIfCold(X)* : *headache(X)* ← *hasCold(X)*.

Using this theory we can predict ¬*hasCold(peter)*, but not *hasCold(peter)*. On the other hand, *headache(mary)* can be explained using the conjecture *hasCold(mary)*.

The theoretical framework can be extended in a straightforward way to distinguish between explanation and prediction. The user has to provide:

- A set *F* of *facts*, which are true in the problem domain under consideration.

- A set Δ of *defaults*, possible hypotheses used both for explanation and prediction.

- A finite set C of *constraints*.

- A set K of *conjectures*, possible hypotheses that may be used for explanation only.

- A set O of *observations* that have been made about the actual world.

Facts, constraints and observations are closed formulae, defaults and conjectures are formulae that may be open. An observation o is explainable from F, Δ, C, K if there is a set D of ground instances of elements of Δ and a set H of ground instances of elements of K such that

- $F \cup D \cup H \models o$, and

- $F \cup D \cup H \cup C$ is consistent.

$F \cup D \cup H$ is called an *explanation* of o from F, Δ, C, K. This notion naturally generalizes to sets of observations.

A closed formula ψ is *predictable* from $F, \Delta, C, \mathrm{K}, O$ w.r.t. the explanation A of O from F, Δ, C, K if ψ is included in all extensions of A, Δ (extensions in the sense of section 17.1).

That means, given a set of observations O, we provide an explanation A. Then, using A and the normality defaults only we make predictions by sceptical reasoning (inclusion in all extensions). For example, after an explanation of a patient's symptoms is provided, this explanation is used to make some further predictions about her health.

In the example above, if $headache(mary)$ has been observed, then $hasCold(mary)$ is part of the explanation. In this case, $\neg hasCold(mary)$ cannot be predicted. Summarizing this section,

- *explanation* uses defaults and conjectures, and follows the credulous approach, whilst

- *prediction* uses defaults only, and follows the skeptical approach.

Problems

17-1. Show that the following claim is *wrong*: If φ is explainable from F, Δ, then it is explainable using a finite scenario of F, Δ. Propose a similar but correct property.

17-2. Show that φ is explainable from F, Δ iff φ is included in an extension of F, Δ.

17-3. Consider the following theory:

> **default** *mammalsDon'tFly(X)* : ¬*flies(X)* ← *mammal(X)*.
> **default** *batsFly(X)* : *flies(X)* ← *bat(X)*.
> **default** *deadCreaturesDon'tFly(X)* : ¬*flies(X)* ← *dead(X)*.
> **fact** *mammal(X)* ← *bat(X)*.
> **fact** *bat(dracula)*.
> **fact** *dead(dracula)*.

Give all possible explanations of *flies(dracula)* and ¬*flies(dracula)*. Modify the theory in such a way that only the third default is applicable to *dracula*.

17-4.* Complete the proof of theorem 17.2.

17-5. Poole motivates the introduction of constraints using the following example. *We want to assume that some person is suspect. But if we show that she is not guilty, then she should not be suspect. This can be expressed by the formula* ¬*guilty(X)* → ¬*suspect(X)*. *But this formula should not be a fact, otherwise we would conclude that somebody is guilty because she is suspect.*

(a) Formulate this example in *Theorist* with constraints.
(b) Give a formalization in *Theorist* without constraints.

17-6.* Theorem 17.3 relates *Theorist* with constraints to Constrained Default Logic. Can this be done with Default Logic?

17-7. Show that adding hypotheses can only increase the number of explainable formulae, adding constraints can only decrease the number of explainable formulae. Conclude that F, Δ, C has always an extension if $F \cup C$ is consistent.

17-8. A semi–normal default $\frac{\varphi : \psi \wedge \chi}{\chi}$ can be simulated in *Theorist* by creating a new name $p_{\psi,\chi}$ and using the theory

> **default** $p_{\psi,\chi} : \chi \leftarrow \varphi.$
> **constraint** $\neg p_{\psi,\chi} \leftarrow \neg \psi.$
> **constraint** $\neg p_{\psi,\chi} \leftarrow \neg \chi.$

The first constraint guarantees that the default is not applied when $\neg \psi$ is known. The second constraint prevents contrapositive uses of the default. This simulation is not equivalent to the original default theory. Compare the extensions of the original default theory and its translation into *Theorist* for the following two examples.

a) $T = (W, D)$ with $W = \{emu \vee ostrich\}$ and $D = \{\frac{emu:runs}{runs}, \frac{ostrich:runs}{runs}\}.$

b) $T = (W, D)$ with $W = \emptyset$ and $D = \{\frac{true:p \wedge \neg q}{p}, \frac{true:q \wedge \neg r}{q}, \frac{true:r \wedge \neg p}{r}\}.$

17-9. Show that the translation of a default theory according to the previous problem has always an extension (make use of problem 17-7).

17-10.* Give a simulation of general defaults in *Theorist*.

17-11.* Study the abstract properties of the nonmonotonic inference relation of *Theorist*. Determine at least one (central) property that is satisfied by *Theorist* but violated by Default Logic. If necessary, distinguish between theories without and theories with constraints.

Chapter 18

Stable Model Semantics of Logic Programs

In this chapter we introduce a semantics for logic programs using Default Logic. In section 18.1 we give some basic definitions and results from logic programming without going into details or presenting proofs. Section 18.2 discusses stable models as a way of interpreting negation in logic programming. Section 18.3 gives an alternative characterization of stable models, which historically was the first definition of stable models. Finally, in section 18.4 we investigate logic programs with two kinds of negation, *negation as failure* and *classical negation*.

18.1 Basic concepts of logic programming

In this section we define the syntax of logic programs, and discuss some semantic aspects that have nothing to do with negation or its interpretation using non-monotonic methods. We make extensive use of predicate logic concepts that were introduced in Chapter 2, so the reader may first wish to refresh their knowledge and recall the notation used. In the following, we lay down a fixed signature Σ.

A *logic program clause* is an expression of the form

$$A \leftarrow B_1, \ldots, B_n, not\ C_1, \ldots, not\ C_m,$$

where $A, B_1, \ldots, B_n, C_1, \ldots, C_m$ are atomic formulae, and $n, m \geq 0$. A is called the *head* of the clause, and $B_1, \ldots, B_n, not\ C_1, \ldots, not\ C_m$ form the *body*. If all formulae involved in the clause are ground then the clause is called *ground*. If $m = 0$ then the clause is called *definite*. If $n = m = 0$, then the clause is called a *fact*, otherwise a *rule*.

A *logic program* P is a set of program clauses. A *definite logic program* (or *Horn logic program*) is a logic program which consists of definite program clauses only.

In this section we give an interpretation of logic programs based on predicate logic; it is determined by considering the following representation of a program clause in first–order logic:

$$\forall(A \leftarrow B_1 \wedge \ldots \wedge B_n \wedge \neg C_1 \wedge \ldots \wedge \neg C_m).$$

The *predicate logic interpretation* of a logic program P is denoted by $pc(P)$, and is the first–order theory which consists of the predicate logic interpretation of all program clauses in P.

In the semantic considerations to follow, Herbrand models will play an important role. Recall that both the domain and the interpretation of function symbols is common in all Herbrand models (over the same signature), the only varying thing being the interpretation of predicates. Therefore, a Herbrand model can be represented as a set of ground atomic formulae $p(t_1, \ldots, t_k)$. Slightly abusing the notation, we use the same symbol to denote a subset of the *Herbrand base* (the set of all ground atomic formulae) and the corresponding Herbrand model.

Let P be a logic program. Every model of the first–order theory $pc(P)$ is called a *model of P*. Every Herbrand model of $pc(P)$ is called a *Herbrand model of P*. The following theorem holds.

Theorem 18.1 *Every logic program possesses at least one minimal (w.r.t. set inclusion) Herbrand model.*

In general, a logic program may possess several minimal Herbrand models. For example, the logic program consisting of the clause

$$p \leftarrow not\ q$$

(whose predicate logic interpretation is equivalent to the formula $p \vee q$) possesses two minimal Herbrand models, $\{p\}$ and $\{q\}$. But if we restrict attention to *definite* program clauses, then there is a uniquely determined *least* Herbrand model.

Theorem 18.2 *A definite logic program P has a unique least Herbrand model, denoted by $\mathcal{M}_P$.*

In the definition of stable models to follow we make use of the set of ground instances of a logic program P, resulting in a ground logic program which is denoted by $ground(P)$. In this program, every program clause

$$A \leftarrow B_1, \ldots, B_n, not\ C_1, \ldots, not\ C_m$$

is replaced by the set of ground program clauses

$$A\sigma \leftarrow B_1\sigma, \ldots, B_n\sigma, not\ C_1\sigma, \ldots, not\ C_m\sigma,$$

where σ is a substitution assigning ground terms to all variables in $A, B_1, \ldots, B_n,$ $C_1, \ldots, C_m$. It can be shown that for a logic program P, the (predicate logic) models of $pc(ground(P))$ are exactly the Herbrand models of P.

18.2   Stable models of logic programs

Given a program clause

$$A \leftarrow B_1, \ldots, B_n, not\ C_1, \ldots, not\ C_m,$$

the predicate logic interpretation treats the negation symbol *not* as classical negation: in order to conclude A, we have to know (or prove) that $\neg C_i$ is true, for all $i \in \{1, \ldots, m\}$.

What is 'wrong' with this interpretation? Well, in many cases we may wish to interpret *not* in a different way. For example, we may wish to interpret (or assume) *not connection(newcastle, sydney, 12pm)* to be 'true' if we look up the timetable and do not find this train connection (as opposed to actually *knowing* that there is no such connection). This type of negation is called *negation as failure*, and its nonmonotonic character is obvious: a change in the timetable may invalidate a previous conclusion which was based on the absence of some information. A first approximation of the meaning of a program clause is the following:

> If $B_1, \ldots, B_n$ are currently provable,
> and if none of $C_1, \ldots, C_n$ is currently provable,
> then conclude A.

Of course, this interpretation is still vague in that it does not specify what 'is currently known' actually means. Nevertheless, it resembles the intuitive interpretation of a default in Default Logic. The stable semantics uses this observation to assign meaning to logic programs. In particular, it uses the following translation of logic programs into default theories.

The Default Logic interpretation of a ground program clause Cl

$$A \leftarrow B_1, \ldots, B_n, not\ C_1, \ldots, not\ C_m$$

is given by the default

$$df(Cl) = \frac{B_1 \wedge \ldots \wedge B_n : \neg\ C_1, \ldots, \neg\ C_m}{A}\ ^1.$$

We define $df(P)$, the **default logic interpretation** of the logic program P, to be the default theory (W, D) with $W = \emptyset$ and $D = \{df(Cl) \mid Cl \in ground(P)\}$.

- Let M be a subset of the Herbrand base. M is a *stable model* of the logic program P iff $Th(M)$ is an extension of $df(P)$.

For example, the following program has only the stable model $\{p(1,2), q(1)\}$:

$p(1, 2)$
$q(X) \leftarrow p(X, Y), not\ q(Y).$

As another example, let P be the program

$p \leftarrow q, not\ r$
$q \leftarrow r, not\ p$
$r \leftarrow p, not\ q.$

Its only stable model is the empty set. Notice that both examples have a unique stable model. This is not necessarily the case, since default theories may have none, one, or several extensions. The reader is asked to give a logic program with more than one stable model.

Further note that in both cases above, the stable set is also a minimal Herbrand model of the logic program. This is not coincidental, as shown by the following result.

Theorem 18.3 *Let P be a logic program. A stable model of P is a minimal Herbrand model of P. In particular, if P is a definite logic program, then $\mathcal{M}_P$ is the unique stable model of P.*

---

[1]In case $n = 0$ or $m = 0$, the prerequisite resp. justification of $df(Cl)$ is the formula *true*.

Proof*:   Let M be a stable model of P. Then $Th(M)$ is an extension of $df(P)$. First we show that M is a Herbrand model of P, which means that M is a model of $pc(ground(P))$. Let

$$Cl = A \leftarrow B_1, \ldots, B_n, not\ C_1, \ldots, not\ C_m \in ground(P),$$

and suppose that $B_i \in M$ for all $i \in \{1, \ldots, n\}$, and $C_j \notin M$ for all $j \in \{1, \ldots, m\}$. Now consider

$$df(Cl) = \frac{B_1 \wedge \ldots \wedge B_n : \neg C_1, \ldots, \neg C_m}{A}.$$

We have that $df(Cl)$ is applicable to $Th(M)$. Since $Th(M)$ is an extension of $df(P)$, it follows $A \in Th(M)$. Then also $A \in M$, since A is a ground atomic formula. So, M is a model of the predicate logic interpretation of Cl.

Now we show that M is a *minimal* Herbrand model of P. Suppose, to the contrary, that there exists a Herbrand model M' of P such that $M' \subset M$. Then $Th(M') \subset Th(M)$. We show that $Th(M')$ is closed under the defaults in $df(P)$ w.r.t. $Th(M)$. To do so, consider a default

$$\frac{B_1 \wedge \ldots \wedge B_n : \neg C_1, \ldots, \neg C_m}{A},$$

and suppose that $\{B_1, \ldots, B_n\} \subseteq Th(M')$ and $\{C_1, \ldots, C_m\} \cap Th(M) = \emptyset$. Then also $\{B_1, \ldots, B_n\} \subseteq M'$ and $\{C_1, \ldots, C_m\} \cap M' = \emptyset$, since $B_1, \ldots, B_n$, $C_1, \ldots, C_m$ are ground atomic formulae and $M' \subset M$. Additionally, we know that

$$A \leftarrow B_1 \wedge \ldots \wedge B_n \wedge \neg C_1 \wedge \ldots \wedge \neg C_m \in pc(ground(P)).$$

Since M' is a Herbrand model of P, we conclude that $A \in M'$ and $A \in Th(M')$. In summary, $Th(M')$ is a set of formulae which is deductively closed, includes the facts of the default theory $df(P)$ (which is the empty set), and is closed under the set of defaults in $df(P)$ w.r.t. $Th(M)$. Since $Th(M')$ is a proper subset of $Th(M)$, we have a contradiction to the assumption that $Th(M)$ is an extension of $df(P)$ (recall that an extension $Th(M)$ is minimal with the three properties above).

If P is a definite logic program, then we note that the set of all justifications and consequents of $df(P)$ is consistent (since it contains only positive literals). Theorem 4.6 tells us that $df(P)$ has a unique extension. So P has a unique stable model which is $\mathcal{M}_P$ using what we just proved. ∎

But notice that the converse of this result is not true, which means that not every minimal Herbrand model of P is a stable model of P. To see this, consider the logic program consisting of the single clause $p \leftarrow not\ p$. P has the minimal Herbrand model $\{p\}$, but the corresponding default theory $(\emptyset, \{\frac{true:\neg p}{p}\})$ has no extension, so P has no stable model.

18.3   An alternative characterization

In this section we give the original definition of stable models of Gelfond and Lifschitz, and show that it is equivalent to that used in the previous section. Let M be a subset of the Herbrand base. We call a ground program clause

$$A \leftarrow B_1, \ldots, B_n, not\ C_1, \ldots, not\ C_m$$

irrelevant w.r.t. M if at least one C_i is included in M. Given a logic program P, we define the *reduct of P w.r.t.* M, denoted by P^M, to be the logic program obtained from $ground(P)$ by

1. removing all clauses that are irrelevant w.r.t. M, and

2. removing all premises $not\ C_i$ from all remaining program clauses.

Note that the reduct P^M is a definite logic program, and we are no longer faced with the problem of assigning semantics to negation, but can use the least Herbrand model instead. The (historically) original definition went along the lines that M is a stable model of P iff $M = \mathcal{M}_{P^M}$. The following result shows that this definition is equivalent to the one given in section 18.2.

Theorem 18.4 *Let P be a logic program, and M a subset of the Herbrand base. M is a stable model of P (in the sense of section 18.2) iff M is the least Herbrand model of P^M.*

    Proof*:   The theorem is shown by the equivalence of the following:

(a) M is a stable model of P.

(b) $Th(M)$ is an extension of $df(P)$.

(c) $Th(M)$ is an extension of $df(P^M)$.

(d) M is a stable model of P^M.

(e) M is the least Herbrand model of P^M.

The equivalence of (a) and (b), and of (c) and (d) is given by definition. (d) and (e) are equivalent by theorem 18.3, since P^M is a definite logic program. It remains to show the equivalence of (b) and (c).

Let $Th(M)$ be an extension of $df(P^M)$. Then there exists a closed and successful process $\Pi = (\delta_0, \delta_1, \ldots)$ of $df(P^M)$ such that $In(\Pi) = Th(M)$. All defaults in Π have the form

$$\frac{B_1 \wedge \ldots \wedge B_n : true}{A}.$$

By definition, for every such default δ_i there is a default δ_i' in the default theory $df(P)^2$ such that

(*) $\delta_i' = \frac{B_1 \wedge \ldots \wedge B_n : \neg C_1, \ldots, \neg C_m}{A}$, and

(**) $C_i \notin Th(M)$ for all $i \in \{1, \ldots, m\}$.

We show that $\Pi' = (\delta_0', \delta_1', \ldots)$ is a closed and successful process of $df(P)$. Then we have completed the proof that $Th(M)$ is an extension of $df(P)$, since $In(\Pi) = In(\Pi')$.

First we show that Π' is a process of $df(P)$. Let $\delta_i' = \frac{B_1 \wedge \ldots \wedge B_n : \neg C_1, \ldots, \neg C_m}{A}$. $\{B_1, \ldots, B_n\} \subseteq In(\Pi'[i]) = In(\Pi[i])$ since Π is a process of P^M. Also, $C_i \notin Th(M)$ for all $i \in \{1, \ldots, m\}$ (by the property (**)), and $In(\Pi'[i]) \subseteq In(\Pi') = In(\Pi) = Th(M)$. Therefore, δ_i' is applicable to $In(\Pi'[i])$. Using the property (**), it is easily seen that Π' is successful.

Finally we show that Π' is closed. Consider a default $\delta' = \frac{B_1 \wedge \ldots \wedge B_n : \neg C_1, \ldots, \neg C_m}{A}$ which is applicable to $In(\Pi') = Th(M)$. Then $B_i \in Th(M)$ for all $i = 1, \ldots, n$, and $C_j \notin Th(M)$, for all $j \in \{1, \ldots, m\}$. By definition,

$$\delta = \frac{B_1 \wedge \ldots \wedge B_n : true}{A}$$

is a default in $df(P^M)$, and δ is applicable to $In(\Pi) = Th(M)$. Since Π is a closed process, δ occurs in Π. Then δ' occurs in Π', and Π' is proven to be closed.

The opposite direction is shown in a similar way, and is left as an exercise to the reader. ∎

---

[2] For technical simplicity, we assume that δ_i' is uniquely determined. The reader is asked to work out what this property exactly means, where it is used below, and how the proof can be modified if this assumption is not true.

18.4   Logic programs with classical negation

One limitation of the discussion so far is that there is *only one* type of negation. Either we interpret *not A* in the sense of predicate logic ('We definitely know that *A* is false') or using negation as failure ('We cannot prove *A*, so assume that it is wrong'). But what if we wish to use both kinds of negation together? What if we want to be able to answer a query either with 'yes', or with 'no', or with 'not that I know of'? To achieve this we extend logic programs by including the classical negation operator ¬. An *extended program clause* is an expression of the form

$$L \leftarrow L_1, \ldots, L_n, not\ L^1, \ldots, not\ L^m,$$

where $L, L_1, \ldots, L_n, L^1, \ldots, L^m$ are literals, that is, atomic formulae or their negations. An *extended logic program* is a set of extended program clauses.

According to this definition, we are allowed to write the extended clause

$$cross \leftarrow \neg train$$

to express that a car should only cross the tracks if no train is approaching. Note that here we do want to use classical negation; the driver must be sure that no train is approaching before he decides to cross the tracks. The other possibility,

$$cross \leftarrow not\ train$$

is inappropriate, because a driver should not attempt to cross the tracks if, say, his vision is blocked (at least in case he is not prepared to die or is not a stuntman in an action movie).

Now we turn our attention to the interpretation of extended logic programs. Once again, our definition of the semantics uses Default Logic. The default interpretation of a ground extended clause

$$Cl = L \leftarrow L_1, \ldots, L_n, not\ L^1, \ldots, not\ L^m$$

is the default

$$df(Cl) = \frac{L_1 \wedge \ldots \wedge L_n : \sim L^1, \ldots, \sim L^m}{L}.$$

Recall that if a literal L is an atomic formula A, $\sim L$ is the formula $\neg A$, whereas if L has the form $\neg A$, $\sim L$ is the formula A. The default interpretation $df(P)$ of an extended logic program P is the default theory $(\emptyset, \{df(Cl) \mid Cl \in ground(P)\})$. Note

that this definition is a generalization of the default translation of logic programs
without classical negation.

- Let *Lit* be the set of ground literals in our language (recall that we are working
  with a fixed signature Σ). A subset M of *Lit* is a *stable answer set* for an
  extended logic program P iff $Th(M)$ is an extension of $df(P)$.

In the train example above, *cross* is not included in a stable answer set if classical
negation is used, whereas it is included in a stable model if negation as failure is
used. To see another example, consider the extended logic program P consisting of
the extended clause

$$\neg q \leftarrow \mathit{not}\ p$$

alone. The only answer set for P is $\{\neg q\}$.

Next we point out that stable answer sets, when restricted to logic programs
without classical negation, coincide with stable models. It is easy to see that if an
extended program P contains no occurrence of $\neg$, then the consequent of every default in $df(P)$ is an atomic ground formula. Then, stable models and stable answer
sets coincide by definition. Thus we have established the following:

Theorem 18.5 *Let P be a logic program (without classical negation). Then all
stable answer sets for P are subsets of the Herbrand base. Moreover, M is a stable
answer set for P iff M is a stable model of P.*

Finally, we show a way of translating extended logic programs into standard
logic programs. The technique used is to introduce new predicate symbols to represent negation, thus obtaining a new signature Σ' which is a superset of Σ; Σ'
includes a new predicate symbol p' for each predicate symbol p in Σ. The translation of an atomic formula is defined such that a literal $\neg p(t_1, \ldots, t_k)$ is translated
into an atomic formula $p'(t_1, \ldots, t_k)$. Formally:

- $tr(p(t_1, \ldots, t_k)) = p(t_1, \ldots, t_k)$
- $tr(\neg p(t_1, \ldots, t_k)) = p'(t_1, \ldots, t_k)$.

For an extended program clause

$$Cl = L \leftarrow L_1, \ldots, L_n, \mathit{not}\ L^1, \ldots, \mathit{not}\ L^m$$

we define

$$tr(Cl) = tr(L) \leftarrow tr(L_1), \ldots, tr(L_n), not\ tr(L^1), \ldots, not\ tr(L^m).$$

Finally, if P is an extended logic program, then $tr(P) = \{tr(Cl) \mid Cl \in P\}$.
For a default $\delta = \frac{L_1 \wedge \ldots \wedge L_n\ :\ \sim L^1, \ldots, \sim L^m}{L}$ in $df(P)$, we define $tr(\delta)$ to be

$$\frac{tr(L_1) \wedge \ldots \wedge tr(L_n)\ :\ \sim tr(L^1), \ldots, \sim tr(L^m)}{tr(L)}.$$

When comparing the stable answer sets for P with the stable models of $tr(P)$, we must note that the latter may contain a literal $p(t_1, \ldots, t_k)$ and $p'(t_1, \ldots, t_k)$. This is, of course, not a logical inconsistency because p and p' are different predicate symbols in Σ'. But still, we cannot expect that there is a matching stable answer set for P because that would indeed include an inconsistency ($p(t_1, \ldots, t_k)$ and $\neg p(t_1, \ldots, t_k)$). If we disregard these *pathological stable sets* of $tr(P)$, though, the following relationship can be established.

Theorem 18.6 *Let P be an extended logic program, and M a consistent set of ground literals over the signature Σ. Then M is a stable answer set for P iff $tr(M)$ is a stable model of $tr(P)$. Conversely, every non–pathological stable model M' of $tr(P)$ is of the form $tr(M)$ for some consistent stable answer set M for P.*

Proof*: First we make the following observation: If a ground literal L follows from a set of ground literals $\{L_1, \ldots, L_n\}$, then $tr(L)$ follows from $\{tr(L_1), \ldots, tr(L_n)\}$. The converse is also true, provided that the set $\{tr(L_1), \ldots, tr(L_n)\}$ is non–pathological that is, it does not contain literals $p(t_1, \ldots, t_k)$ and $p'(t_1, \ldots, t_k)$.

This observation can be easily proven using the well–known result that a set of ground literals is consistent iff it does not contain a complementary pair (that is, A and $\neg A$ for an atomic formula A). So, if $\{L_1, \ldots, L_n\} \models L$, then $\{L_1, \ldots, L_n, \sim L\}$ is consistent, which means that it does not contain a complementary pair. Then, $\{tr(L_1), \ldots, tr(L_n), \sim tr(L)\}$ does not contain a complementary pair, so $\{tr(L_1), \ldots, tr(L_n), \sim tr(L)\}$ is consistent, and $\{tr(L_1), \ldots, tr(L_n)\} \models tr(L)$. The opposite direction is shown in the same way; when we consider $\{tr(L_1), \ldots, tr(L_n), \sim tr(L)\}$, we need additionally the condition that is non–pathological to be able to conclude that $\{L_1, \ldots, L_n, \sim L\}$ does not contain a complementary pair.

Using this lemma, the theorem is shown easily by taking a closed and successful process $\Pi = (\delta_0, \delta_1, \ldots)$ of $df(P)$ and showing that $\Pi' = (tr(\delta_0), tr(\delta_1), \ldots)$ is a closed and successful process of $df(tr(P))$, and conversely. ■

Problems

18-1. Give a logic program with more than one stable set.

18-2. Show the following: If the body of every rule in a logic program P contains a positive literal (i.e. $n \neq 0$), then $\emptyset$ is the only stable set of P.

18-3.* Complete the proof of theorem 18.4. Also, carry out the exercise outlined in the footnote associated with the part of the proof given in section 18.3.

18-4. Determine the stable answer sets of the extended logic program which consists of the extended clauses $\neg p \leftarrow$ and $p \leftarrow \neg q$. Compare your result with the stable answer sets of the extended program consisting of $\neg p \leftarrow$ and $q \leftarrow \neg p$. Conclude that rules are not interpreted to be contrapositive. Does this surprise you?

18-5. An extended logic program P is *contradictory* if it has an inconsistent stable answer set. Show that in this case, P has exactly one stable answer set, the set of all ground literals *Lit*.

18-6. Show that an extended logic program cannot have two stable answer sets such that one is a proper subset of the other.

18-7. Express the 'closed world assumption' using an extended logic program.

18-8. Express the following rules, used by an imaginary college to determine the eligibility of students for scholarships, in an extended logic program:

- Every student with high marks is eligible.
- Every minority student with fair marks is eligible.
- No student whose marks are not (at least) fair is eligible.
- The students whose eligibility is not determined by these rules are invited for an interview.

What is the stable answer set for a student with fair, but not high marks, if nothing concerning his minority status is known?

18-9. In previous chapters we saw that Default Logic is not cumulative. Give an appropriate definition of cumulativity for the stable model semantics of logic programs, and give a counterexample.

18-10.* Complete the proof of theorem 18.6.

18-11. Determine the stable models of the logic program

$a \leftarrow not\ b.$
$b \leftarrow not\ a.$

18-12. Determine the stable models of the logic program

$a \leftarrow not\ b.$
$b \leftarrow not\ a.$
$p \leftarrow not\ p.$

18-13. Determine the stable models of the logic program

$a \leftarrow not\ b.$
$b \leftarrow not\ a.$
$p \leftarrow not\ p.$
$p \leftarrow a.$

Chapter 19

Well-Founded Semantics

This chapter presents the well–founded semantics of logic programs, which seeks to overcome some problems of the stable model semantics, for example, the multiple extension problem and the possibility of a program without any stable models. In section 19.1 we motivate the basic idea which is the use of partial models. Section 19.2 describes partial models formally, whilst section 19.3 defines the well–founded semantics and describes its relationship with the stable model semantics. In section 19.4 we give some pragmatic guidelines for determining the well–founded model of a logic program, and apply them to examples.

19.1 Motivation

Why is the stable model semantics not always satisfactory? One reason is that a program may have more than one stable model. Which is the 'correct' one? Or should we look at the intersection of all stable models? The problem is that in logic programming, as usual in programming, it is common to associate with every program an *intended meaning* (in the case of definite logic programs, it is the least Herbrand model), whereas knowledge representation is more flexible in admitting alternative, competing views of the knowledge. Therefore, it is easier to tolerate multiple extensions of a default theory (often, it is even required to have an overview of all alternatives that are supported by the knowledge given), whereas it is desirable to assign a unique meaning to each logic program.

Another critical problem of the stable model semantics is that a logic program P may not have any stable models; in that case, no meaning is assigned to P, which is undesirable, of course. Even worse, the phenomenon of nonexisting extensions is very irregular. To see what we mean, consider the following logic program P_1:

$a \leftarrow not\ b$
$b \leftarrow not\ a.$

P_1 has two stable models, $\{a\}$ and $\{b\}$. If we add the clause

$$p \leftarrow not\ p,$$

the resulting program P_2 does not possess any stable models. But after adding the rule

$$p \leftarrow a$$

to P_2, the resulting program P_3 has the unique stable model $\{a, p\}$. To overcome these and other difficulties with stable models, an alternative approach was introduced which is based on the following design decisions:

- Exactly *one model*, called the well–founded model, is associated with each logic program. Therefore, both problems outlined above are prevented.
- That model is *partial*, meaning that it assigns truth values to *some* (ground) atomic formulae only, while the rest remains uninterpreted.

Here is a motivating example in support of the use of partial models:

$$work \leftarrow not\ tired$$
$$sleep \leftarrow not\ work$$
$$tired \leftarrow not\ sleep$$
$$angry \leftarrow work, not\ paid$$
$$paid \leftarrow$$

The first three rules describe general interconnections among the predicates *work*, *tired* and *sleep*, but provide no information about which of them is true. On the other hand, *paid* must always be true, and therefore *angry* must be false. The well–founded model of this program is $\{paid, \neg angry\}$; it provides no information regarding *work*, *tired* and *sleep*, meaning that their interpretation is open because we do not have enough information to decide.

19.2 Partial models

Let Σ be a fixed signature which contains in its alphabet the propositional symbols **t**, **u** and **f**, denoting the properties of being true, undefined and false respectively.

In what is to follow, we define partial Herbrand interpretations that can assign one of *three* possible truth values to every formula, namely *true*, *false* or *undefined*. Intuitively, undefined means that no classical truth value can be assigned to the formula.

A *partial Herbrand interpretation* M is a set of ground literals. We assume that every partial interpretation contains $\mathbf{t}$ and $\neg\mathbf{f}$, but neither $\mathbf{u}$ nor $\neg\mathbf{u}$. We can represent M as the union $Pos(M) \cup Neg(M)$, where $Pos(M)$ is the set of positive ground literals in M, and $Neg(M)$ the set of negative ground literals in M. M is *total* if for all ground atomic formulae A except for $\mathbf{u}$, either A or $\neg A$ is a member of M.

Next we define when a partial Herbrand interpretation M is a model of a ground logic program P.

- A ground atomic formula A is true in M if it belongs to M, and false if $\neg A$ belongs to M.

- *not* A is true (respectively, false) in M iff A is false (respectively, true) in M.

- A program clause $A \leftarrow B_1, \ldots, B_n, not\ C_1, \ldots, not\ C_m$ is true in M if the following two conditions hold:

    - If all B_i and all *not* C_j are true in M, then A is true in M.

    - If A is false in M, then at least one B_i or *not* C_j is false in M.

- M is a *model* of the logic program P iff all program clauses in P are true in M.

There are two natural orderings between partial interpretations. One of them uses the usual set–theoretic inclusion:

$$M \preceq M' \text{ iff } Pos(M) \subseteq Pos(M') \text{ and } Neg(M) \subseteq Neg(M').$$

The other inclusion is defined as follows: For two partial interpretations M and M'

$$M \leq M' \text{ iff } Pos(M) \subseteq Pos(M') \text{ and } Neg(M') \subseteq Neg(M).$$

The *smallest* interpretation within a collection of interpretations $\mathcal{M}$ is the least with respect to $\preceq$ (of course, $\mathcal{M}$ may not have a smallest interpretation). A smallest interpretation assigns definite truth values to as few ground atomic formulae as possible.

The *least* interpretation within a collection of interpretations $\mathcal{M}$ is one which is least with respect to the ordering $\leq$ (of course, $\mathcal{M}$ may not have a least interpretation). This concept minimizes the degree of truth of atomic formulae by minimizing $Pos(M)$ and maximizing $Neg(M)$.

We call a logic program P *non–negative* if no program clause in P contains an occurrence of *not* or $\mathbf{f}$ in a rule body[1]. The following result is central in the definition of well–founded models.

Definition and Theorem 19.1 (Least partial model) *Every non–negative ground logic program P has a unique least partial model $LPM(P)$. If P is not ground, $LPM(P)$ is defined to be $LPM(ground(P))$.*

So, to construct the least partial model of a given logic program P, we build $ground(P)$ first. Further, notice that this result is a generalization of theorem 18.1. Consider the non–negative logic program

$$
\begin{aligned}
&a \leftarrow \\
&b \leftarrow a, \mathbf{u} \\
&c \leftarrow c, \mathbf{u}.
\end{aligned}
$$

a has to be true by the first rule, and b cannot be false because no literal in the body of the second rule can be false. Therefore b will be undefined (if we would make it true the resulting model would not be least). But c can be chosen to be false. In summary, the least partial model of the program is $\{a, \neg c\}$.

19.3   Definition of the well–founded model

The following presentation of WFS is due to Przymusinski. We begin by defining a *quotient operator* $\frac{P}{M}$ where P is a logic program and M a partial interpretation. $\frac{P}{M}$ is obtained from P by replacing in every clause of P all *not* A which are true (respectively false; respectively undefined) in M by $\mathbf{t}$ (resp. $\mathbf{f}$; resp. $\mathbf{u}$).

It is easy to see that if $\mathbf{t}$ appears in the premises of a rule, then it can be omitted, and if $\mathbf{f}$ appears in the premises of a rule, the whole rule can be deleted

---

[1] Actually, such a logic program is definite in the signature Σ. But remember that $\mathbf{u}$ may well occur in the body of a rule, and we have made the assumption that neither $\mathbf{u}$ nor its negation is allowed to be included in any partial Herbrand model. In this sense, non–negative programs should be distinguished from definite programs. The latter forbid the occurrence of $\mathbf{u}$ as well, and are called *positive* in the logical framework of this chapter.

without changing the partial models of the program. If we do so, $\frac{P}{M}$ is guaranteed to be non–negative, therefore it has a unique least partial model.

Theorem 19.2 *For every logic program P and every partial interpretation M, there exists a unique least partial model $LPM(\frac{P}{M})$ of $\frac{P}{M}$.*

For example, consider the logic program P

$$a \leftarrow$$
$$b \leftarrow not\ a$$
$$p \leftarrow not\ p$$

and the partial interpretation $M = \{a, \neg b\}$. Then, $\frac{P}{M}$ is the program

$$a \leftarrow$$
$$b \leftarrow \mathbf{f}$$
$$p \leftarrow \mathbf{u}$$

The second rule can be deleted because $\mathbf{f}$ occurs in its body, so we consider the non–negative logic program P':

$$a \leftarrow$$
$$p \leftarrow \mathbf{u}$$

The least partial model of $\frac{P'}{M}$ is $\{a, \neg b\}$ ($\neg b$ because b can be arbitrarily interpreted, and the Neg–part has to be maximized).

The intuition behind the quotient is very natural: The partial interpretation M can be thought of as our current, perhaps partial knowledge about the atomic formulae that occur in $ground(P)$. What the quotient operator does is incorporate this knowledge into the logic program itself by replacing all expressions $not\ A$ by their truth value according to the partial interpretation M (Clearly, only negated atomic formulae should be affected since they represent the 'default' part of the information we are trying to capture).

After building the quotient, we use the least partial model to assign meaning to $\frac{P}{M}$; this way, we may get more information about the validity of atomic formulae occurring in $ground(P)$, thus enhancing our previous knowledge M. In fact, the idea of the well–founded semantics is to iterate this process as long as new information can be obtained. When the end (technically: the fixed–point) is reached, we have the well–founded model we were seeking to determine. Before we proceed with the formal definition, here is a simple example. Let P be the logic program

$$b \leftarrow not\ a$$
$$c \leftarrow not\ b, p$$
$$p \leftarrow not\ p.$$

Initially we have no information about the program whatsoever, therefore we start with the empty interpretation $M_0 = \emptyset$. Now we build the quotient $\frac{P}{M_0}$ and obtain the non–negative program

$$b \leftarrow \mathbf{u}$$
$$c \leftarrow \mathbf{u}, p$$
$$p \leftarrow \mathbf{u}.$$

It should be clear that $LPM(\frac{P}{M_0}) = \{\neg a\}$, that is, a is false and the rest undefined. Next, we take this interpretation $M_1 = \{\neg a\}$ and use it to build the quotient $\frac{P}{M_1}$:

$$b \leftarrow \mathbf{t}$$
$$c \leftarrow \mathbf{u}, p$$
$$p \leftarrow \mathbf{u}.$$

Its least partial model is $M_2 = \{\neg a, b\}$. Our knowledge about P has already increased. We repeat the process again, build $\frac{P}{M_2}$

$$b \leftarrow \mathbf{t}$$
$$c \leftarrow \mathbf{f}, p$$
$$p \leftarrow \mathbf{u},$$

delete the second rule and obtain $M_3 = LPM(\frac{P}{M_2}) = \{\neg a, b, \neg c\}$. If we repeat the process once again, it is easily seen that we obtain exactly the same result. Therefore M_3 represents *the maximum information* we can extract from the program P, and it is nothing other than the well–founded model of P. Next we present the formal definition.

Define M_0 to be the empty partial interpretation (all ground atomic formulae have the truth value *undefined*). Suppose that M_n has been defined for all $n < k$. If $k = n + 1$ then we define

$$M_{n+1} = LPM(\frac{P}{M_n}).$$

Otherwise, that is if k is a limit ordinal, we define

$$M_k = \bigcup_{n<k} M_n.$$

The definition should be clear for finite steps. For so–called 'limit steps'[2] we put together all the information we gathered up to k.

Theorem[3] and Definition 19.3 (The well–founded model) *The sequence of interpretations M_n defined above is always increasing (in the sense of set–theoretic inclusion) and has a uniquely determined fixed–point M with the property $M = LPM(\frac{P}{M})$. M is called the* well–founded model *of P, denoted by $WFM(P)$.*

Theorem 19.4 *Let P be a logic program.*

(a) *$WFM(P)$ is a model of P.*

(b) *Any stable model of P extends $WFM(P)$ in the sense that it assigns definite truth values to more ground atoms than $WFM(P)$ does.*

(c) *If $WFM(P)$ is total then it is the unique stable model of P.*

The converse of (c) is not true. The logic program

$$p \leftarrow not\ p$$
$$p \leftarrow not\ q$$
$$q \leftarrow not\ p$$

has the unique stable model $\{p\}$, but its well–founded model is $\emptyset$.

19.4   Some pragmatic guidelines

In this section we give some pragmatic hints about how to determine the well–founded model without having to use the formal definition; the presentation is based on [65]. The following hints can be applied in any order, and often simplify

---

[2]which are necessary in cases where $ground(P)$ is infinite

[3]In this chapter we do not give any proofs because the technical preparations would have been too etxensive. The interested reader can find good references at the end of this chapter.

the task of determining the well–founded model. We point out once again that to determine the well–founded model of P, we must first build $ground(P)$; the guidelines below apply to this instantiated program.

Guidelines for determining the well–founded model

G1 Divide the program P into disjoint partitions $P_1, \ldots, P_n$ (that is, for $i \neq j$, P_i and P_j do not share any predicate). Then determine the well–founded model of each partition separately, and build the union of them to get the well–founded model of the entire program.

G2 Let A be a positive ground atomic formula.

G2.1 If $A \leftarrow$ is a fact of the program, then its truth value is *true*.

G2.2 If there is no clause with head A, then its truth value is *false*.

G2.3 If there is only one rule for A, and if the truth value of all members of the rule's body has already been determined, then the truth value of A is the smallest of them (according to the ordering $false < undefined < true$).

G2.4 In case there are more than one rule defining A, proceed as follows: For each defining rule, delete the other rules defining A, and determine the truth value of A in the remaining program. After this has been done for all defining rules of A, take the greatest of the truth values obtained for A.

Consider the logic program consisting of the following rules:

$$p \leftarrow not\ q$$
$$p \leftarrow q, p$$
$$r \leftarrow not\ t$$
$$t \leftarrow not\ r$$
$$a \leftarrow not\ b$$
$$b \leftarrow e$$
$$e \leftarrow not\ d.$$

The logic program can be divided into three disjoint parts; the first two rules constitute the first part P_1, the next two rules the second partition P_2, and the remaining rules the third partition P_3. According to the guideline $G1$, we may determine the well–founded models of the three partitions, and then put them together.

In the *first partition* there is no defining rule for q, so, by $G2.2$, q is false. Then, using the first rule we see that p must be true (using guidelines $G2.3$ and $G2.4$, and recalling that *true* is the greatest truth value). So, the well–founded model of P_1 is $\{p, \neg q\}$.

The *second partition* P_2 is the logic program

$$r \leftarrow not\ t$$
$$t \leftarrow not\ r$$

$M_0 = \emptyset$, $\frac{P_2}{M_0}$ is the program

$$r \leftarrow \mathbf{u}$$
$$t \leftarrow \mathbf{u}$$

$M_1 = \emptyset = M_0$, so the well–founded model of P_2 is $\emptyset$. P_3 consists of the clauses

$$a \leftarrow not\ b$$
$$b \leftarrow e$$
$$e \leftarrow not\ d$$

$M_0 = \emptyset$, and $\frac{P_3}{M_0}$ is the program

$$a \leftarrow \mathbf{u}$$
$$b \leftarrow e$$
$$e \leftarrow \mathbf{u}$$

$M_1 = \{\neg d\}$. $\frac{P_3}{M_1}$ is the program

$$a \leftarrow \mathbf{u}$$
$$b \leftarrow e$$
$$e \leftarrow \mathbf{t}.$$

$M_2 = \{\neg d, e, b\}$. The program $\frac{P_3}{M_2}$ contains the rule $a \leftarrow \mathbf{f}$, so $M_3 = M_4 = \{\neg d, \neg a, e, b\}$ which is the well–founded model of P_3.

Putting all the information together, we conclude that the well–founded model of the entire program is $\{p, b, e, \neg q, \neg a, \neg d\}$.

Next we see what happens with a case where the stable model semantics does not work properly. Consider the following program from section 19.1:

$a \leftarrow not\ b$

$b \leftarrow not\ a$

$p \leftarrow not\ p.$

This program has no stable model. To determine its well–founded model, we consider the two partitions (the first two rules constitute one, and the third rule the other). We saw in the previous example that the well–founded model of the first partition is $\emptyset$. In the second partition we have the clause

$p \leftarrow not\ p$

Starting with $M_0 = \emptyset$ we assign to p the value *undefined*, so M_1 gives us no additional information and we conclude that the WFM of this partition is the empty set. So, the well–founded model of the whole program is $\emptyset$. For another example consider the following program P:

$wins(X) \leftarrow move(X, Y), not\ wins(Y)$

$move(a, b)$

$move(b, a)$

$move(b, c)$

$move(c, d).$

The well–founded model of P is constructed by considering $ground(P)$, which means the ground instances of the first rule. In $ground(P)$ there is no rule for $wins(d)$, therefore it is false. Then, by G2.3, $wins(c)$ is true. For $wins(b)$ there are two defining rules[4], and we consider them separately. The first possibility is to use the rule

$wins(b) \leftarrow move(b, c), not\ wins(c).$

Since $wins(c)$ is true, $wins(b)$ gets the truth value *false*; but note that this is according to the first defining rule for $wins(b)$. We can use the other one instead, and combine it with the only rule for $wins(a)$:

---

[4]Actually, there are many more, but they always fail because the predicate *move* does not support them.

$$wins(b) \leftarrow move(b,a), not\ wins(a)$$
$$wins(a) \leftarrow move(a,b), not\ wins(b).$$

We know that in this case, both $wins(a)$ and $wins(b)$ are undefined. To summarize: There are two rules for $wins(b)$. Following the first one we get the truth value *false*, following the second we obtain the truth value *undefined*. By the guideline $G2.4$, $wins(b)$ is undefined. Therefore $wins(a)$ is undefined as well. All in all, the well–founded model of P is $\{wins(c), \neg wins(d)\}$.

It is interesting to notice that P has two stable models, $\{wins(a), wins(c)\}$ and $\{wins(b), wins(c)\}$. That means, the stable model semantics gives the alternative truth values, whereas the well–founded semantics is cautious in case it cannot decide the truth value of some atomic formulae and leaves them undefined. Actually, in this example the *Pos*–part of the well–founded model coincides with the intersection of the stable models of the logic program. But this is not always the case. Consider the logic program:

$$a \leftarrow not\ b$$
$$b \leftarrow not\ a$$
$$p \leftarrow a$$
$$p \leftarrow b.$$

It has two stable models, one containing a and the other b, so $a \lor b$ and p are included in the intersection of the stable models. But the well–founded model is empty because it cannot decide the validity of a and b.

Problems

19-1. Check all unproven statements in this chapter regarding the well–founded and stable models of examples.

19-2. Determine the well–founded model of the following program which uses Tweety for the last time in this book; farewell, dear friend! In this example, classical negation is represented by the use of new predicate symbols; for example, $\overline{flies}$ should be read as $\neg flies$.

$$flies(X) \leftarrow bird(X), not\ \overline{flies}(X)$$

$$\overline{flies}(X) \leftarrow penguin(X), not\ flies(X)$$
$$bird(X) \leftarrow penguin(X)$$
$$bird(rupert)$$
$$penguin(tweety).$$

19-3. Compute the well–founded model of the following program.

$$p \leftarrow not\ q$$
$$p \leftarrow a$$
$$r \leftarrow p, r$$
$$a \leftarrow not\ b$$
$$b \leftarrow not\ a$$
$$c \leftarrow e$$
$$e \leftarrow$$
$$d \leftarrow not\ d.$$

References for Part V

Poole introduced the logical framework of *Theorist* in [66]; this paper presented the basic ideas of the system, and it forms the basis for our presentation in Chapter 17, including some examples. *Theorist* attracted much attention because it was the first operational and successful system for default reasoning. It was implemented in Prolog, as described in [69]. The use of *Theorist* for explanation and prediction has been described in [67] and [68].

The classical paper on logic programming is [9], and the classical textbook on the field is [45]. The study of the meaning of negation in logic programming using nonmonotonic semantics has exploded since the late 80s. Stable model semantics was introduced by Gelfond and Lifschitz in [31]. The relationship between stable models and Default Logic was discovered by Bidoit and Froidevaux [12], and Marek and Truszczynski [53]. Logic programs with classical negation were introduced and studied by Gelfond and Lifschitz [32]. An in–depth comparison between stable model semantics and Default Logic can be found in Marek and Truszczynski's book [54], from which theorem 18.5 was taken.

The well–founded semantics was introduced by van Gelder, Ross and Schlipf in [82]. There is a procedural mechanism for WFS called *SLS–resolution* [76], and an implementation in Prolog, the so–called *OLDT–algorithm* [81, 83]. Our presentation of the well–founded semantics in Chapter 19 is based on papers by Przymusinski [70] (sections 19.2 and 19.3) and Pereira *et al.* [65] (section 19.4). For good overviews of different semantics for logic programs and their properties, see [10, 19]. For a recent book on reasoning with logic programming see [3].

Part VI

Finale

Chapter 20

Future Directions of Nonmonotonic Reasoning Research

This chapter contains a few comments about the state of the art and collects some promising research directions. The following discussion gives my personal view, and does not raise any claim of completeness or accuracy.

20.1 Theory versus practice

Up to recently, a typical scientific paper in the field could be summarized as follows:

- Here is an example that cannot be treated properly by the existing formalisms. I propose logic X which works well with this example. It has properties $P_1, \ldots, P_k$ and is related to the known formalisms $Y_1, \ldots, Y_n$ according to the theorems $Z_1, \ldots, Z_m$.

This led to the situation where at every major AI conference new logics were proposed, only to be rejected the next year because yet another example was discovered which could not be treated properly. I am not suggesting that all the theory that has been developed was a waste of time and resources. On the contrary, it was the pioneer work of Reiter, McCarthy, Moore, Makinson and others that helped us develop a better understanding of nonmonotonicity based on sound theory. Their motivation often stemmed from self–observation, but I think we have reached a point where significant advance seems unlikely to be achieved if we continue to rely on the trial–and–error approach.

In fact, the argument that a logic is deficient if it does not work properly with a specific example is flawed, because it assumes that we must develop a universal theory of nonmonotonic reasoning. I argue that the situation will turn out to be as in other disciplines such as engineering or physics, where different methods are used for different kinds of problems. Newtonian mechanics works perfectly well for building bridges, but nobody would seriously consider using it to study the behaviour of subatomic particles.

There are two conceivable alternatives to the introspective trial–and–error approach. One way, taken for example by Sandewall, is to define *classes of problems* against which specific reasoning methods can be tested; it is a valid and ambitious approach worth pursuing.

The other approach is to develop real–world applications using NMR and learn some lessons. Currently we are trying to model intelligence using methods that we do not know how to use. Let me draw an analogy between Default Logic on one side, and programming and chess playing on the other side: Currently we are making progress in understanding how a small number of defaults interact, similar to writing three lines of code in a conventional programming language without unexpected effects. Obviously our aim is to be able to 'program in Default Logic'. A comparison with chess playing may help illustrate where we are and where we should be heading for. The current state of the art in NMR is similar to mastering the rules of chess. Important as this is, it is only a first step towards developing an understanding of the fundamental principles of chess playing (strategy and tactics). We still have to work on the understanding of how to use nonmonotonic reasoning methods on a larger scale.

I expect work on real problems to be of great benefit to this task. Moreover I expect valuable feedback to theoreticians as to the *real* problems they should address. It is unthinkable that theoretical physics would have reached its current stage without feedback from experimental physics; equally I believe that the field of nonmonotonic reasoning will reach a mature level only after some of us have left the ivory towers of theory and dirtied our hands working on applications.

As a prerequisite for applications we need operational systems. In recent years several such systems have been developed; even though work on improving the performance is still under way, today's systems are already capable of reasoning with, say, hundreds of default rules.

What I think is necessary is a *toolkit of nonmonotonic reasoning methods*, offering the user a variety of different techniques he may experiment with. This is a direct implication of what I said before (and several times throughout the book), that there does not exist *the* correct NMR method, but rather the most appropriate for the problem at hand. The following sections collect some features that I consider essential to include in such a toolkit.

20.2   Dynamics of nonmonotonic reasoning

The working title of this book was 'Nonmonotonic reasoning with incomplete and changing information'[1], so the notion of *change* is central in our considerations; when faced with a changing environment we have to withdraw some previous conclusions.

If we look at most NMR methods presented in the previous chapters we can make an observation that is both surprising and disturbing: Actually most NMR methods neglect aspects of change. Look at Default Logic; it provides methods for computing extensions based on default rules. If the set of facts W is modified then the default rules still draw correct conclusions with respect to the modified W. But this approach is *static* in that we have to abandon all previous conclusions (extensions) and recompute everything from scratch! This is necessary even if the modification is small.

This agnostic approach with respect to change is completely inappropriate, of course. Nonmonotonic reasoning is computationally more expensive than classical reasoning; therefore every effort should be made to preserve as many previous conclusions as possible when faced with new information. That means, in cases where a change has a limited effect on the conclusions, we should try to preserve as much 'old' information as possible. And again, this must be done on the conceptual level based on sound theory, rather than in the form of implementation 'shortcuts'. Belief revision can reason with changing information, but *only* in classical logic; at present it cannot be applied to, say, default theories. The following figure illustrates the 'missing link' for preserving nonmonotonic conclusions.

These observations suggest that combination of NMR and belief revision techniques is an interesting research topic which has the potential to advance the state of the art significantly.

20.3   Pragmatics of nonmonotonic reasoning

If we are serious about putting nonmonotonic reasoning to work we have to look at its methods as we would look at software engineering or more well–established forms of knowledge representation. Here are some *engineering aspects* that should be addressed.

---

[1]which was perceived too long as a book title

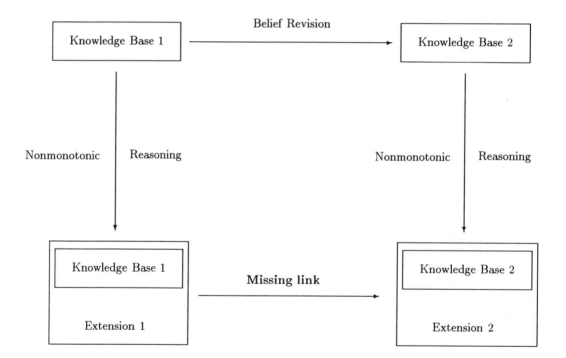

Figure 20.1
Combination of nonmonotonic reasoning and belief revision

- *Modularity*. Modular design was one of the most principal answers software engineering offered to the software crisis. It enhances comprehensibility and thus maintainability of any complex system. In NMR we would have additional efficiency benefits; in fact, one of the greatest hopes of applying NMR successfully is to be able to split a knowledge base into small parts and perform nonmonotonic reasoning *in a local, thus manageable setting*.

- *Integration with object–orientation*. In classical software engineering object–oriented methodologies emerged from modularity as the next natural step. We can hope that NMR would benefit from the use of object–oriented techniques, in particular from the use of taxonomies and inheritance.

- *Refinement*. We will have to develop a better understanding and sound theory for the stepwise refinement of knowledge bases which use a nonmonotonic machinery. For real–world applications we cannot possibly expect to write down the whole knowledge base at once, but must work on different levels of abstraction, as is the case in the development of any complex system.

- *Correctness and verification*. In classical computer science the need for formal methods to check the correctness of systems has been recognized, particularly for safety–critical applications. There is no reason to assume that correctness will not be an essential issue once real applications of NMR emerge. In fact, the more complex the adopted knowledge representation formalism is and the less understood its behaviour (to the non–expert), the more significant are the potential benefits we can expect from the use of formal methods.

Bibliography

[1] C. Alchourrón, P. Gärdenfors and D. Makinson. On the Logic of Theory Change: Partial Meet Functions for Contraction and Revision, *Journal of Symbolic Logic*, 50(1985): 510-530.

[2] C. Alchourrón and D. Makinson. On the logic of theory change: Contraction functions and their associated revision functions. *Theoria* 48 (1982): 14 – 37.

[3] J. Alferes and L.M. Pereira. *Reasoning with Logic Programming*, LNAI, Springer 1996.

[4] G. Antoniou and V. Sperschneider. Computing extensions of nonmonotonic logics. In *Proc. 4th Scandinavian Conference on AI*, IOS Press 1993, 20–29.

[5] G. Antoniou and V. Sperschneider. Operational Concepts of Nonmonotonic Logics. Part 1: Default Logic. *Artificial Intelligence Review* 8(1994): 3–16.

[6] G. Antoniou, E. Langetepe and V. Sperschneider. New proofs in default logic theory. *Annals of Mathematics and Artificial Intelligence* 12(1994): 215–229.

[7] G. Antoniou. An operational interpretation of justified default logic. In *Proc. 8th Australian Joint Conference on Artificial Intelligence*, World Scientific 1995, 67–74.

[8] G. Antoniou. Operational characterization of extensions in some logics for default reasoning. *Information Sciences* 1996 (forthcoming).

[9] K.R. Apt and M.H. van Emden. Contributions to the theory of logic programming. *Journal of the ACM* 29(1982): 841–862.

[10] K.R. Apt and R.N. Bol. Logic Programming and Negation: A Survey. *Journal of Logic Programming* 19,20(1994): 9–71.

[11] P. Besnard. *An Introduction to Default Logic.* Springer 1989.

[12] N. Bidoit and C. Froidevaux. General logic databases and programs: default logic semantics and stratification. *Information and Computation* 91(1991): 85–112.

[13] C. Boutilier. Revision Sequences and Nested Conditionals. In the *Proceedings of the Thirteenth International Joint Conference on Artificial Intelligence*, Morgan Kaufmann, 519 – 525, 1993.

[14] C. Boutilier. Generalized Uppdate: Belief Change in Dynamic Settings. In the *Proceedings of the em Fourteenth International Joint Conference on Artificial Intelligence*, 1550 – 1556, 1995.

[15] G. Brewka. *Nonmonotonic reasoning: logical foundations of commonsense.* Cambridge University Press 1991.

[16] G. Brewka. Reasoning about Priorities in Default Logic. In the *Proceedings of the 12th National Conference on Artificial Intelligence (AAAI-94)*, 940–945. AAAI/MIT Press 1994.

[17] P. Cholewinski, W. Marek, A. Mikitiuk and M. Truszczynski. Experimenting with default logic. In *Proc. International Conference on Logic Programming*, MIT Press 1995.

[18] J.P. Delgrande, T. Schaub and W.K. Jackson. Alternative approaches to default logic. *Artificial Intelligence* 70(1994): 167–237.

[19] J. Dix. Semantics of Logic Programs: Their Intuitions and Formal Properties. An Overview.

[20] P. Doherty, W. Lukaszewicz, A. Szalas. Computing Circumscription Revisited: Preliminary Report. In the *Proceedings of the 14th International Joint Conference on Artificial Intelligence*, 1502–1508. Morgan Kaufmann 1995. See also *http://www.ida.liu.se/labs/kplab/projects/dls*.

[21] D. Dubois and H. Prade. Possibilistic Logic. *Handbook of Logic in Artificial Intelligence and Logic Programming*, Volume3, Nonmonotonic Reasoning and uncertain Reasoning, Gabbay, D., Hogger, C., and Robinson, J. (eds), Claredon Press, Oxford, 1994.

[22] D.W. Etherington, R. Mercer and R. Reiter. On the Adequacy of Predicate Circumscription for Closed–World Reasoning. *Computational Intelligence* 1 (1985): 11–15.

[23] D. Etherington. Formalizing Nonmonotonic Reasoning Systems. *Artificial Intelligence* 31(1987): 41–85.

[24] A. Fuhrmann. Theory Contraction through Base Contraction. *Journal of Philosophical Logic*, 20(1991): 175 – 203.

[25] D. Gabbay. Theoretical foundations for nonmonotonic reasoning in expert systems. In K. Apt (ed.), *Logic and Models of Concurrent Systems*, Springer 1985.

[26] D. Gabbay and H.J. Ohlbach. Quantifier elimination in second–order predicate logic. In the *Proceedings of the 3rd International Conference on the Principles of Knowledge Representation and Reasoning*, 425–435. Morgan Kaufmann 1992. See also *http://www.mpi-sb.mpg.de/guide/staff/ohlbach/scan/scan.html*.

[27] P. Gärdenfors. *Knowledge in Flux: Modeling the Dynamics of Epistemic States*, Bradford Books, The MIT Press, Cambridge Massachusetts, 1988.

[28] P. Gärdenfors and D. Makinson. Revisions of Knowledge Systems using Epistemic Entrenchment. In the *Proceedings of the Second Conference on Theoretical Aspects of Reasoning about Knowledge*, 83 – 96, 1988.

[29] P. Gärdenfors and D. Makinson. Nonmonotonic Inference Based on Expectations. *Artificial Intelligence Journal*, 65(1994): 197 – 245.

[30] P. Gärdenfors and H. Rott. Belief Revision. *Handbook of Logic in Artificial Intelligence and Logic Programming Volume IV: Epistemic and Temporal Reasoning*, Chapter 4.2, Gabbay, D., Hogger, C., and Robinson, J. (eds), Claredon Press, (in press).

[31] M. Gelfond and V. Lifschitz. The stable semantics for logic programs. In *Proceedings of the 5th International Symposium on Logic Programming*. MIT Press 1988.

[32] M. Gelfond and V. Lifschitz. Logic programs with classical negation. In *Proceedings 7th International Conference on Logic Programming*. MIT Press 1990.

[33] M. Gelfond and H. Przymusinska. On Consistency and Completeness of Autoepistemic Theories. *Fundamenta Informaticae* 16 (1992): 59–92.

[34] G. Gottlob. Complexity results for nonmonotonic logics. *Journal of Logic and Computation* 2(1992): 397–425.

[35] A. Grove. Two Modellings for Theory Change. *Journal of Philosophical Logic*, 17(1988): 157 – 170.

[36] S.O. Hansson. New Operators for Theory Change. *Theoria*, 55(1989): 115 – 132.

[37] H. Katsuno and A.O. Mendelzon. On the Difference between Updating a Knowledge Database and Revising it. In Belief Revision, Gärdenfors, P. (ed), Cambridge Press, Cambridge, 1992.

[38] K. Konolige. On the relation between default and autoepistemic logic. *Artificial Intelligence* 35 (1988): 343–382; see also *Artificial Intelligence* 41 (1989): 115.

[39] S. Kraus, D. Lehmann and M. Magidor. Nonmonotonic reasoning, preferential models and cumulative logics. *Artificial Intelligence* 44 (1990): 167–207.

[40] D. Lehmann. Belief Revision, Revised. In the *Proceedings of the Fourteenth International Joint Conference on Artificial Intelligence*, 1995.

[41] V. Lifschitz. Computing Circumscription. In *Proc. 10th International Joint Conference on Artificial Intelligence*, MIT Press 1985, 121–127.

[42] V. Lifschitz. Circumscriptive Theories: A Logic–Based Framework For Knowledge Representation. *Journal of Philosophical Logic* 17 (1988): 391–441.

[43] V. Lifschitz. Circumscription. In Gabbay, Hogger, Robinson (eds): *The Handbook of Logic in Artificial Intelligence and Logic Programming* Vol. 3, 297–352, Oxford University Press 1993.

[44] T. Linke and T. Schaub. Lemma Handling in Default Logic Theorem Proving. In *Proc. Symbolic and Quantitative Approaches to Reasoning and Uncertainty*, Springer 1995, LNAI 946, 285–292.

[45] J. Lloyd. *Foundations of logic programming*, 2nd ed. Springer 1987.

[46] W. Lukaszewicz. Considerations on Default Logic. *Computational Intelligence* 4(1988): 1–16.

[47] W. Lukaszewicz. *Non-Monotonic Reasoning – Formalization of commonsense reasoning.* Ellis Horwood 1990.

[48] D. Makinson. On the Status of the Postulate of Recovery in the Logic of Theory Change. *Journal of Philosophical Logic*, 16(1987): 383 – 394.

[49] D. Makinson and P. Gärdenfors. Relations between the logic of theory change and non-monotonic logic. In *The Logic of Theory Change*, Fuhrmann, A. and Morreau, M. (eds), Lecture Note Series in Artificial Intelligence, Springer-Verlag, Berlin, 1991.

[50] D. Makinson. General Patterns in Nonmonotonic Reasoning. In: D. Gabbay (ed.), *Handbook of Logic in Artificial Intelligence and Logic Programming, Vol. II: Non-Monotonic and Uncertain Reasoning*, Oxford University Press 1994, 35–110.

[51] W. Marek. Stable Theories in Autoepistemic Logic. *Fundamenta Informaticae* 12 (1989): 243–254.

[52] W. Marek and M. Truszczynski. Relating Autoepistemic Logic and Default Logic. In *Proc. 1st International Conference on Knowledge Representation and Reasoning*, Morgan Kaufmann 1991.

[53] W. Marek and M. Truszczynski. Stable semantics for logic programs and default theories. In *Proceedings of the North American Conference on Logic Programming*, 243–256. MIT Press 1989.

[54] W. Marek and M. Truszczynski. *Nonmonotonic Logic.* Springer 1993.

[55] J. McCarthy. Circumscription – A Form of Non-Monotonic Reasoning. *Artificial Intelligence* 13 (1980): 27–39.

[56] J. McCarthy. Applications of Circumscription to Formalize Commonsense Knowledge. *Artificial Intelligence* 28 (1986): 89–116.

[57] R.C. Moore. Possible-world semantics for autoepistemic logic. In R. Reiter (ed.): *Proc. of the workshop on non-monotonic reasonig*, 344–354, 1984. Reprinted in: M. Ginsberg (ed.): *Readings on nonmonotonic reasoning*, Morgan Kaufmann 1990, 137–142.

[58] R.C. Moore. Semantical considerations on non-monotonic logic. *Artificial Intelligence* 25 (1985): 75–94.

[59] A. Nayak. Iterated Belief Change Based on Epistemic Entrenchment. *Erkenntnis* 4 (1994): 353 – 390.

[60] B. Nebel. A Knowledge Level Analysis of Belief Revision. In *Principles of Knowledge Representation and Reasoning: Proceedings of the First International Conference*, Morgan Kaufmann, San Mateo, CA, 301 – 311, 1989.

[61] B. Nebel. *Representation and Reasoning in Hybrid Representation Systems*, Springer-Verlag, Berlin, 1990.

[62] R. Niederee. Multiple contraction: A further case against Gärdenfors' principle of recovery. In *The Logic of Theory Change*, Fuhrmann, A. and Morreau, M. (eds), Lecture Note Series in Artificial Intelligence, Springer-Verlag, Berlin, 1991.

[63] I. Niemela and P. Simmons. Evaluating an algorithm for default reasoning. In R. Ben–Eliyahu and I. Liemela (Eds.) *Applications and Implementations of Nonmonotonic Reasoning Systems - Proceedings of the IJCAI'95 Workshop*, 66–72.

[64] P. Peppas and M.A. Williams. Constructive Modelings for Theory Change. *Notre Dame Journal of Formal Logic*, Vol 36, No. 1, 120 – 133, 1995.

[65] L.M. Pereira, J. Alferes and J.N. Aparicio. A Practical Introduction to Well–Founded Semantics. In *Proceedings of the Third Scandinavian Conference on Artificial Intelligence*. IOS Press 1991.

[66] D. Poole. A Logical Framework for Default Reasoning. *Artificial Intelligence* 36(1988): 27–47.

[67] D. Poole. Explanation and prediction: an architecture for default and abductive reasoning. *Computational Intelligence* 5(1989): 97–110.

[68] D. Poole. A Methodology for Using a Default and Abductive Reasoning System. *International Journal of Intelligent Systems* 5(1990): 521–548.

[69] D. Poole. Compiling a Default Reasoning System into Prolog. *New Generation Computing* 9(1991): 3–38.

[70] T.C. Przymusinski. Well-Founded and Stationary Models of Logic Programs. *Annals of Mathematics and Artificial Intelligence* 12(1994): 141–187.

[71] R. Reiter. A Logic for Default Reasoning. *Artificial Intelligence* 13(1980): 81–132.

[72] H. Rott. Two Methods of Constructing Contractions and Revisions of Knowledge Systems. *Journal of Philosphical Logic*, 20(1991): 149 – 173.

[73] H. Rott. A Nonmonotonic Conditional Logic for Belief Revision I. In A. Fuhrmann and M. Morreau (eds), *The Logic of Theory Change*, Springer-Verlag, LNAI 465, Berlin, 135 – 183, 1991.

[74] H. Rott. Preferential belief change using generalized epistemic entrenchment. *Journal of Logic, Language and Information*, 1(1992): 45 – 78.

[75] V. Risch and C. Schwind. Tableau–Based Characterization and Theorem Proving for Default Logic. *Journal of Automated Reasoning* 13(1994): 223–242.

[76] K. Ross. A procedural semantics for well–founded negationin logic programs. *Journal of Logic Programming* 13(1992): 1–22.

[77] T. Schaub. On Constrained Default Theories. In *Proc. 10th European Conference on Artificial Intelligence*, Wiley 1992, 304–308.

[78] V. Sperschneider. *Lecture Notes on a course on nonmonotonic logic*. University of Osnabruck 1992.

[79] W. Spohn. Ordinal Conditional Functions: A Dynamic Theory of Epistemic States. In Harper, W.L., and Skyrms, B. (eds), *Causation in decision, belief change, and statistics, II*, Kluwer Academic Publishers, p105 – 134, 1988.

[80] R. Stalnaker. A theory of conditionals. in Recher, N. (ed), *Studies in Logical Theory*, Blackwell, Oxford, 98 – 112, 1968.

[81] H. Tamaki and T. Sato. OLD Resolution and Tabulation. In *Proceedings of the Third International Conference on Logic Progrmming*. Springer 1986.

[82] A. van Gelder, K.A. Ross and J.S. Schlipf. The Well–Founded Semantics for General Logic Programs. *Journal of the ACM* 38,3(1991): 620–650.

[83] D.S. Warren. Computing the Well–Founded Semantics of Logic Programs. *Technical Report 91/12*, Computer Science Department, SUNY at Stony Brook 1991.

[84] M.A. Williams. Transmutations of Knowledge Systems. In J. Doyle, E. Sandewall, and P. Torasso (eds), *Principles of Knowledge Representation and Reasoning: Proceedings of the Fourth International Conference*, Morgan Kaufmann, San Mateo, CA, 619 – 629, 1994.

[85] M.A. Williams. On the Logic of Theory Base Change. In Logics in Artificial Intelligence, C. MacNish, D. Pearce and L.M. Pereira (eds), LNCS No 835, 86 – 105, Springer Verlag, 1994.

[86] M.A. Williams. Changing Nonmonotonic Inference Relations. In the *Proceedings of the Second World Conference on the Foundations of Artificial Intelligence*, Paris, 1995.

[87] M.A. Williams. Theory Base Change: A Computational Model. In the *Proceedings of the Fourteenth International Joint Conference on Artificial Intelligence*, 1541 - 1547, 1995.

[88] M. Winslett. Reasoning about action using possible models approach. In the *Proceedings of the National Conference on Artificial Intelligence (AAAI)*, 89 – 93, 1988.

Index

absorption 168
    left 168
    right 168
adjustment 202
AGM paradigm 186
algebra 14
    Herbrand algebra 16
    with belief set 113
applicable 27,40,79
atom 12
autoepistemic logic 109
autoepistemic theory 111

belief revision 183

cautious monotony 166
closure 181
circumscription 143,146
    predicate 144
    prioritized 157
    variable 154
closed set of formulae 28
closed world assumption 148
Coincidence Lemma 127
Compactness Theorem 16
complexity 87
computability 87
conditionalization 171
consequent 25

consistency 15
    preservation 43,178
constant 12
constraint 236,237
contraction 187
cumulativity 74,166
cut 166,192
    proper 217

deductive closure 15
default 21,25
    default theory 25
    named default theory 95
    normal 49
    open default 25
    ordered default theory 60
    semi-normal 59
    supernormal 231
default logic 19,25
    constrained 78
    justified 75
    prioritized 92
degree 112
    of acceptance 199
distribution 169

epistemic entrenchment (ordering) 192
expansion (in AEL) 114
    minimal 133
    moderately grounded 134
    SS-minimal 134
    strongly grounded 136

expansion (in BR) 186

expectation ordering 217

explanable 230

explanation 230,240

extension 27,33,230
    constrained 79
    DL–extension 95
    modified 76
    PDL–extension 93
    priority 97

fact 25,229,239

formula 12
    atomic 12
    autoepistemic 110
    closed 12
    ground 12

function (symbol) 11

Harper identity 191

Herbrand's Theorem 16

hypothesis 230

idempotence 166

inclusion 166

inference relation 163,165
    rational and consistency preserving
    215

information
    changing 4
    incomplete 3

information content
    explicit 199
    implicit 199

interpretation 14
    autoepistemic 112

joint consistency 73

justification 25

kernel 112

least Herbrand model 244

left logical equivalence 168

left or 170

lemma 81

Levi identity 190

literal 13

logic program 243
    definite 243
    with classical negation 250
    extended 250

loop 171

model
    least partial 258
    minimal 150,175
    partial 256,257
    preferential 175
    P–minimal 150
    stable 246
    well–founded 261

model structure
    classical 177
    preferential 175
    stoppered 176
    modular 180

monotony 166

name 233

nonmonotonic reasoning 4
    dynamics of 273

normal forms 15,112

orthogonality 52,118

PRDL 94

partial entrenchment ranking 199

predicate logic 11

predicate (symbol) 11

prediction 239

prerequisite 25

Preservation Lemma 126

priorities among defaults 91

process 32
    closed 32
    constrained 79
    failed 32
    maximal 75
    successful 32

process tree 34,97

proof by cases 170

proof theory 53

propositional logic 13

quantifier 11

rationality
    disjunctive 178
    negation 178

rational monotony 178

reciprocity 167

recovery 187

resolution 17

revision 189

right and 168

right weakening 168

scenario 230

semi–monotonicity 50

sentence 12

signature 11

stable set 110,115

stable answer set 251

substitution 13
    admissible 13

supraclassicality 168

T–sound 114

T–complete 114

tautology 15

term 12

Theorist 229

theory 15

unifier 13

variable 11
    free 12

Wang's algorithm 17

weaving technique 51

withdrawal function 189